BERLITZ

C000076033

BUSINESS
Travel Guide
EUROPE

Printed by Rotatie Boekendruk, Holland

17th Edition (1995/1996)

BUSINESS
Travel Guide
EUROPE

Preface

In this age of rapid decision-making across national frontiers, businessmen and women have contacts in a wide range of countries around the world. Even for the seasoned traveller across the continent, the confusing variations in currency, local transportation facilities, office hours and many other matters from one country to another (and sometimes within one nation) can cause the loss of valuable time – and money.

Berlitz has sifted through a wealth of practical information on 37 European countries for its Business Travel Guide. From Reykjavík to Athens, from Lisbon to Moscow, a network of business and travel specialists has researched and vetted data on the spot. The result: thousands of useful facts packed into one pocket-size volume. A selection of helpful phrases in local languages completes relevant country chapters, and a quick-reference section can be found at the back of the book.

Whether you're an on-the-go executive or a relative newcomer to the world of international commercial and diplomatic relations, this comprehensive compendium of facts at your fingertips will productively smooth your path throughout Europe.

Contents

How to Use This Guide

The 37 countries covered in this guide are arranged alphabetically.
The overall structure adopted for each country is as follows:

1 Basic facts	3 Business briefing	5 After hours
2 Planning your trip	4 On the spot	6 Cities and sights

To avoid undue repetition, information of general validity is grouped below. Cross-references are made to this information for data which may be of cardinal importance in planning your trip (visa and vaccination requirements, duty-free allowances and currency restrictions).

1 Basic Facts

Member of: The organizations listed for each country concern trade and commerce. Purely political or military alignments are not mentioned. (For explanation of abbreviations see p.12.)

Population: All figures are approximate; where two figures are given, the first indicates the population of the municipal area, the second, the greater urban area (GUA).

2 Planning your Trip

Visa requirements: Details given apply to holders of ordinary passports, in normal circumstances, who are nationals and residents of the following countries:

Australia	Iceland	Norway
Austria	Ireland	Portugal
Belgium	Italy	South Africa
Canada	Liechtenstein	Spain
Denmark	Luxembourg	Sweden
Finland	Malta	Switzerland
France	Monaco	Turkey
Germany	The Netherlands	United Kingdom
Greece	New Zealand	United States

Those holding special travel documents (stateless persons, United Nations officials etc.), citizens of countries not in the above list or who are at all in doubt **should check on possible visa requirements with the consulates of the countries they intend to visit**.

Vaccination requirements: In normal circumstances, European countries impose no particular health requirements. However, visitors arriving within a certain number of days after leaving or transiting through areas in the world infected by certain serious diseases (in particular smallpox, yellow fever and cholera) may need vaccinations. These must be officially recorded in an International Certificates of Vaccinations booklet, available from travel agencies or airline companies – who are able to furnish up-to-date details of vaccination requirements and other specific health recommendations.

Import allowances: Though major changes are rare, minor adjustments are sometimes made to import allowances. Some countries content themselves with the rather vague formulation 'reasonable quantities allowed'. In such cases, prudence is advised.

In addition to the categories of general interest mentioned for each country in this book (tobacco, alcohol, perfume and gifts), some countries impose restrictions on a variety of other items ranging from tea to cigarette paper. If in doubt, check with the consulate of the country to be visited before leaving home. Be particularly careful when travelling to those countries of eastern Europe which are in the throes of political change, where regulations are likely to be in a state of flux.

Currency restrictions: Though the details presented in this book were meticulously checked, it is always wise to inquire about the latest situation with your travel agent. The data given does not necessarily apply to returning nationals.

Hotels: Whenever possible, book ahead – especially during holiday and trade fair periods, and in eastern Europe. Some major hotel chains offer frequent guests a 'fidelity card' which guarantees preferential treatment and a number of additional benefits, sometimes including discounts, at their establishments worldwide.

3 Business Briefing

GNP: Figures given are the latest available as we go to press. The term 'billion' is used in the American sense of one thousand million.

Inflation rate: Figures given are the latest available as we go to press. For countries with particularly erratic inflation rates (eg some eastern European countries) a figure has not been quoted.

Trade fairs: Foreign chambers of commerce or commercial attachés can supply detailed information on trade fairs in their countries.

Selected background reading: More detailed information is available through your home and foreign chambers of commerce, government organizations for the promotion of foreign trade, employers' associations in the target countries, and banks.

Chambers of commerce abroad: If no chamber of commerce is listed for your country, apply to the commercial department of the nearest embassy or consulate for business information.

4 On the Spot

Public holidays: In some countries local public holidays, in addition to the general ones shown, are too numerous to list. It is always advisable to confirm in advance that your foreign business contact will indeed be at work on the day you plan to visit.

Banks and currency exchange: In many cases procedures for the transfer of money into, and especially out of, the country are tightly bound up in red tape. It is advisable in such situations to secure the services of a local agent to expedite formalities for you. Make sure you keep all documentary evidence (exchange slips, etc.) of currency transactions for presentation to customs officials when you leave.

Credit cards and traveller's cheques: The top international credit cards are widely accepted in shops and banks throughout Europe, particularly in the major tourist and business centres. In some countries in eastern Europe credit cards may still only be accepted in the larger establishments, although the situation is improving.

Post and telecommunications: In many countries, area codes have an initial digit or digits (often 0) which must be dropped when making calls from outside the country.

For a list of international access and country codes, see pp.380-381.

Medical care and health: Reciprocal agreements exist between a number of countries in Europe for partial or even full payment of medical charges. Social security offices in the United Kingdom and equivalent institutions in other European countries can supply details. Whether or not you benefit from such an arrangement, it is wise to take out private travel insurance which will cover the cost of all eventualities. Your regular insurance or travel agency will be able to advise you.

Services: Where difficulty is encountered in obtaining secretarial or other help, the commercial department of your embassy or consulate will be able to direct you to reliable addresses. Diplomatic representations cannot usually furnish these services themselves.

Transport

Air: The complexity of air passenger tariffs and regulations worldwide that govern travel in all categories, from supersonic Concorde to the humble standby, can test even highly experienced travel agents. The most important step is to find a really well-informed agent – preferably one who specializes in business travel.

In principle, the more precisely you can determine your exact itinerary in advance, the more convenient and economical your travel arrangements will be. Bear in mind that, particularly on long-haul routes, rates vary substantially according to 'season'. On the North Atlantic, for example, May-September (roughly) is the high season, and if your departure date falls before the start of the high-fare period you'll save money. Reduced excursion and midweek tickets, widely available for flights within Europe as well as on intercontinental routes, mean important savings if the restrictions on the length of stay and days of travel are acceptable. APEX (advance purchase excursion) and charter arrangements offer rock-bottom rates, but their inflexibility (little or no possibility of changing flight dates or **9** carrier, no stopovers) often eliminate them from the options available for business travel. Even on no-restriction tickets, some airlines make a small charge if you fail to appear for the flight you have booked, so it is worthwhile establishing the cancellation and 'no-show' procedures and charges.

Rail: First-class rail travel can be widely recommended for business purposes. The fastest trains are France's TGVs, which cruise at about 300km per hour (186mph). Some 200 cities are served by the Euro-City network. Rapid, comfortable and silent, these trains feature good dining facilities and sometimes offer secretarial services.

Most western European countries offer special 'tourist' tickets which may also be suitable for business travel. These may be flat-rate passes for unlimited use of the domestic rail network, or circular tickets for a fixed itinerary which must be decided in advance.

Visitors residing outside Europe and North Africa can take advantage of the Eurailpass, for sale at travel agencies outside Europe only. Residents of Europe aged under 26 can take advantage of the Inter-rail card, a flat-rate pass valid in most European countries, also available for specific 'zones', for 2 weeks or one month. An inter-rail card is available to European residents over 26, but is valid only for travel in Britain, Ireland, Denmark, Norway, Sweden and Finland. The Freedom Pass is available to travellers of all ages, for unlimited travel over a specified period in the countries of your choice.

Taxis: In southern Europe, taxi drivers are often willing to be hired out for the day, at reasonable rates. This may work out the most convenient means of getting around.

Car rental: Rental arrangements should preferably be made in advance – especially during holiday periods and in eastern Europe. A number of airlines offer a fly-drive formula which combines a special air fare with a rental arrangement at the destination. These packages may offer substantial savings on the usual rates.

Driving: Except where otherwise stated, your home driving licence is recognized throughout Europe, though if you intend to visit countries which do not use our alphabet (Greece, Russia, Federal

10

Republic of Yugoslavia), it would be advisable to take along a translation of this document or an international driving licence, obtainable through your own motoring association.

In Europe all countries drive on the right except for the United Kingdom, Ireland and Malta. Those unused to this mode of driving are advised to exercise special care. Confusion arises particularly when first taking the wheel, at crossroads and when approaching roundabouts (traffic circles).

Some European countries used to insist on the use of special vouchers for fuel purchases. Although a lot of red tape has now been lifted, political uncertainties can still lead to shortages. Inquire the moment you hire your vehicle, or through your motoring association before leaving home.

5 After Hours

TV and radio: On an ordinary portable transistor radio in almost any part of Europe – particularly after dark – you will have little difficulty tuning in to an English-speaking station. The BBC World Service, Voice of America and similar programmes generally come in clearest after nightfall or early in the morning.

6 Cities and Sights

Tourist information offices: These provide useful services for the business visitor, as well as the tourist, as a source of free street plans and general background information. They sometimes handle conference arrangements and other business matters.

Chambers of commerce: These, along with other business-oriented organizations, are listed for individual cities.

Sightseeing, museums, excursions: Many business travellers acquire an intimate knowledge of an airport, a hotel, a conference room – and little else. Yet, if time allows, a sightseeing tour or a visit to a museum can provide a pleasurable and useful insight into the cultural background of the area you are visiting. Our suggestions cover the salient points of interest in the major cities.

11

Acknowledgements

We wish to thank the many national chambers of commerce, tourist offices and embassy commercial departments for their help in the preparation of this guide. We are also grateful to the following individual contributors: Robert Avery, David Ballard, Jill Biskin, Bill Bond, Charles Bremner, Tim Brown, Christiane Campia, Wes Christner, Venezeslav Dimitrov, Petar Hadji-Ristic, Justine Hamilton, Jozsef Hollos, Bryan Jeeves, Jill Jolliffe, Ruth R Keene, Arnold Keilberth, Angela Kelly, Marketta Kopinski, Wilford J Kramer, Mik Magnusson, Claude Marbaix, Aglika Markova, Constance Moes, Jade Neergaard, Suzanne Patterson, Ivana Pivková, Bodo Reinhardt, Norman Scott, Margaret Studer, Roda Tinis, Hilary Louise Turner, Kaarina Turtia, J G Vassallo and Patrick Worsnip. We are particularly grateful for the research and editorial assistance of Julian Blake in compiling this updated volume.

While every effort has been made to ensure the accuracy of the information contained in this book immediately prior to going to press, no responsibility can be accepted for any errors or omissions.

Abbreviations

This list gives the less familiar abbreviations used in this book.

abbr.	abbreviated	IFC	International Finance Corporation
AC	alternating current		
AG	Aktiengesellschaft (c. Limited Company – German)	IMF	International Monetary Fund
		int.	international
BC	British Commonwealth	kHz	kilohertz
C	centigrade	km	kilometres
c.	circa, approximately	kph	kilometres per hour
DST	Daylight Saving Time	l	litres
EU	European Union (formerly EC)	m	million or metres
		mg	milligrams
EFTA	European Free Trade Association	ml	millilitres
		mph	miles per hour
esq	esquina (street corner – Portuguese)	nám	náméstí (square – Czech)
		OECD	Organization for Economic Cooperation and Development
EST	Eastern Standard Time		
g	grams		
GATT	General Agreement on Tariffs and Trade	P	Piazza (square – Italian)
		Pl	Place (square – French)
GMT	Greenwich Mean Time	SA	Société Anonyme (c. Limited Company – French)
GNP	Gross National Product		
GUA	greater urban area		
Hz	Hertz (cycles per second)	sq km	square kilometres
IBRD	International Bank for Reconstruction and Development	sq miles	square miles
		ul	ulitsa (street – Slav)
		ut	utca (street – Hungarian)
IDA	International Development Association	VAT	value-added tax

Albania

Type of government:	Embryonic liberal democracy, following decades of state socialism
Population:	3.4 million
Area:	28,748sq km (11,100sq miles)
Capital:	Tirana (*Tiranë*, 400,000)
Other major cities:	Durrës (85,000)
	Elbasan (80,000)
	Shkodër (78,000)
	Vlorë (69,000)
	Korçë (63,000)
Language:	Albanian; English, French or Italian (the most widely known foreign language among the older generation) are spoken in business circles.
Religion:	Muslim (70%), Eastern Orthodox (20%), Catholic (10%)
Time zone:	GMT+1, EST+6; DST (Apr-Sep)
Currency:	Lek (abbr. L) = 100 qintars or quindarka Coins: 5, 10, 20, 50 qintars; 1, 2 leks Notes: 1, 3, 5, 10, 25, 50, 100, 500, 1000 leks
Electricity:	220V, 50Hz, AC

Planning your Trip

Visa requirements: For nationals of Australia, Liechtenstein, Malta, Monaco, New Zealand and South Africa. (See also p.6.) Citizens of other countries currently pay an entry fee at the border point.

Vaccination requirements: None, but it is advisable to have a Hepatitis A injection before visiting Albania. (See also p.7.)

Import allowances: A 'reasonable quantity' of tobacco products, alcoholic beverages and perfume for personal use. To facilitate re-export, any articles of value (dictaphones, portable computers etc.) should be declared upon entry. (See also p.7.)

Currency restrictions: None, but all amounts must be declared on arrival. It is virtually impossible to exchange Albanian currency outside Albania. (See also p.7.)

Other restrictions: Strange restrictions on general appearance, such as long hair, and on religious and political literature, have been lifted since 1990.

Climate: Mediterranean along the coast, but continental in the mountains where winters are much cooler and precipitation heavier (though summers are generally rather dry). The temperature has been known to reach -26°C (-15°F) in winter and 44°C (111°F) in summer.

Some average temperatures in Tirana:

Spring	Summer	Autumn	Winter
15°C (59°F)	26°C (79°F)	10°C (50°F)	9°C (48°F)

Clothing: Lightweight clothing is adequate in summer, but a warm coat is advisable in winter. Rainwear may be needed at any time of year. Dark, conservative suits and ties are worn in business circles. On a very hot summer's day a lighter-coloured suit is also acceptable.

Hotels: Hotel reservations are normally made by Albanian travel officials and communicated to the visitor's travel agency abroad. There are only two main hotels in Tirana, and most other towns only have one tourist hotel.

Tourist offices: There are no official Albanian tourist offices abroad; contact a specialist travel agency.

15

Business Briefing

Economic Background

Main industries: Metallurgy, foodstuffs, mineral processing, oil by-products, textiles, chemicals, electric power, engineering.

Main agricultural products: Grains, tobacco, olives, citrus fruit.

Main imports: Machinery, man-made textiles, chemicals, paper.

Main exports: Chromium, nickel, copper, petroleum, bitumens, electricity, foodstuffs, tobacco.

GNP: $1.93 billion; per capita: $603.

Principal trading partners: Italy, Germany, Czech Republic, Slovakia, Romania, Bulgaria, Greece.

Trade fairs: None in Albania, but the country is represented in fairs at Bari (Italy), Salonica (Greece), Izmir (Turkey), Malmö (Sweden), Bucharest (Romania), Munich (Germany) and Barcelona (Spain).

Selected background reading: *Albanian Business News* is published monthly in English by the Albanian Chamber of Commerce. *Economic Tribune*, published in Tirana, monthly. The Albanian Commercial Office in the UK publishes a *Quarterly Update*.

On the Spot

Office hours: 7am-3pm Monday-Friday and 5-8pm on Mondays and Tuesdays (summer); 7.30am-2.30pm Monday-Saturday and 4-7pm on Mondays and Tuesdays (winter).

Public holidays

Jan 1	New Year's Day	Nov 28	Proclamation of
Jan 11	Proclamation of the		Independence
	Republic	Nov 29	Liberation Day
May 1	Labour Day		

Banks and currency exchange: Hours: 8.30am-1pm Monday-Friday. Outside banking hours, currency can be changed at Rinas Airport near Tirana, border crossing points and the major hotels. US dollars and western European currencies are readily accepted. As long as a money transfer results from officially approved trade transactions there are no difficulties. Main banking institution: Drejtkursig.

Credit cards and traveller's cheques: Credit cards and traveller's cheques are still relatively unfamiliar items and, generally, will only be accepted at the Hotel Dajti in Tirana.

Post and telecommunications: It is probably better not to arrange to receive mail while you are in Albania although sending mail out is not a problem. The post offices have public telephones but they are in great demand. Opening hours are 7am-noon Monday-Friday. International calls can also be made from either of Tirana's main hotels.

Embassies and consulates: Countries with embassies in Tirana are Algeria, Bulgaria, China, Czech Republic, Egypt, France, Germany, Greece, Hungary, Italy, Korea, Poland, Romania, Turkey and Vietnam. Other countries have their representatives in Italy, Greece or Romania. Citizens of countries not listed above should ask, before leaving home, which diplomatic representation they can turn to in case of emergency. Embassies are listed under *Ambasad* in the telephone book.

Medical care and health: Medical facilites in Albania are appalling. Insurance is almost impossible to get. If you fall ill you will be taken to a hospital but you can expect only the most basic treatment in unhygienic conditions. The tap water is safe to drink but it is essential to have a Hepatitis A injection before going to Albania, which will last for two months. There is no bottled water available in the country. There are no drugs available from the hospitals and there are no pharmacies. Visitors must take all medicines and sanitary equipment (which is unheard of) with them. There is no baby food or anything like disposable diapers to be found. There are dentists, should you require one urgently, but they have few anaesthetics and conditions are primitive.

17

Services: Translation and secretarial services are no longer provided by the state. Enquire at the tourist office or chamber of commerce.

Newspapers: The main national dailies are *Zeri i Popullitt*, *Bashki-mi* and *Rilindja Demokratike*. Foreign newspapers are all available in Tirana within two days of publication. Two monthly magazines, *New Albania* and *Albania Today*, published in several languages including English, French and Spanish, give the official view of the country's economic, cultural and social life.

Transport

Air: Tirana possesses the nation's sole commercial airport. There are few international flights per week, so travel to and from Albania requires careful planning. There are no regular domestic services.

Local public transport: Buses are generally very cheap but do not operate to a fixed timetable. They often become dangerously overcrowded due to the fact that they only depart when they are full. In cities, businessmen generally take taxis.

Taxis: A visiting businessman can usually arrange for a taxi through his hotel reception desk. Taxis are very expensive, with a typical fare from Tirana to Girokaster costing $65-$70.

Car rental: Car rental is not available in Albania.

Social customs: Albanians are known for their hospitality, which is sincere and generous – sometimes overwhelmingly so. Although Albanians are not formal people, a toast is usually drunk at the beginning of a meal. Don't be surprised if your host offers you a bracing *rraki* (distilled from grape pulp) to start off your early-morning discussions. Refusal could be considered an offence. Invitations to a house are rare unless you have been acquainted for some while, in which case a small gift will suffice. A hint to help communication: in Albania, a nod means 'No' and a shake of the head 'Yes' – although, with the influx of Westerners, people have started to do the opposite.

Hints for business: Don't go unless you have made prior contact with an Albanian counterpart, or with the Albanian Commercial

Office (in several British cities and in New York). There is no replacement for the state-run commercial process, and it is virtually impossible for business to be effective on an unplanned visit.

Crime and theft: Although the crime rate has decreased from its peak during the winter of 1991/92 it is still inadvisable for tourists to walk around after dark or to stray too far from the main town and city centres.

After Hours

Food and drink: Albanian food has a very poor reputation and many foodstuffs are in short supply. The situation improves in the south where there is a greater Greek influence, but it is still basic, and in general the country is still very dependent on the Italian food convoys which distribute EU food parcels. Food is rationed and milk and cheese are extremely hard to find, although eggs are becoming increasingly available. Meat is virtually impossible to buy. Basic meals are served in the hotels but it is advisable to bring as much food as possible into the country, especially if you are vegetarian or planning to travel outside Tirana.

Drinks are often in short supply. There is no problem buying good whisky, brandy or wine from the tourist stores in the major hotels in Tirana, but hotels in other towns may not have such goods available. It is worth bringing any drink you may need into the country with you. Albanian beer and white wine is of poor quality, but red wine from the region is excellent, if it can be found.

There are a few restaurants in Tirana but they are rare elsewhere.

Mealtimes: lunch noon-2pm, dinner 7-9pm.

Entertainment: The new government of Albania has abolished the festivals and events connected to the old regime, but theatre productions and concerts continue to take place in most cities, and you can obtain details of current productions from your hotel.

Taxes, service charges and tipping: Tipping is up to the individual but it is important to remember that Albania is a very poor country and giving too much money could be seen as arrogant.

19

Sports and recreation: Soccer is the most popular sport. As in other Balkan countries the most popular leisure activity is enjoying the company of friends in the evenings, when families promenade up and down the streets, talking and greeting each other until about 8pm.

TV and radio: Albanian television shows mainly American and Italian films, many of low quality. Voice of America and the BBC World Service can be picked up on the radio.

What to buy: Due to the extreme poverty of the country it is only possible to buy a few handicrafts from the main hotels. Some kiosks sell items crudely painted with Albanian designs or with the symbol of the black eagle. It is sometimes possible to buy hand-woven rugs from local people by the roadside, but only rarely. Albanians make very good quality briar pipes which are very cheap and sold in the Hotel Tirana.

Cities and Sights

TIRANA

Airport: Rinas (23km/14 miles from city centre), international; duty-free shop. Bus service coincides with flight arrivals and departures, though this is unreliable.

Tourist information office: Albturist, 8 Bulevard Deshmoret e Kombit; tel/fax: 34359.

Chamber of commerce: Rruga Konferenca e Pezes 6; tel/fax: 27997.

Sightseeing: National museums of art and history (some of the exhibitions have been closed because of extensive looting); Palace of Culture, with theatre and restaurants; Tirana University; Qemal Stafa stadium, regularly hosting football matches.

Excursions: Durrës (Roman baths, medieval fortress, archaeological **20** museum, beach); Elbasan (old town bazaar, mosques).

Some Useful Expressions in Albanian

good morning/afternoon	**mirëmengjez/mirëdita**
good evening/night	**mirëmbrema/natën e mirë**
good-bye	**mirë u pafshim**
yes/no	**po/jo**
please/thank you	**ju lutem/ju falem nderit**
excuse me	**më falni**
you're welcome	**mirë se erdhët**
where/when/how	**ku/kur/si**
how long/how far	**sa gjatë/sa larg**
yesterday/today/tomorrow	**dje/sot/nesër**
day/week/month/year	**dita/java/muaji/viti**
left/right	**majtas/djathtas**
up/down	**lartë/poshtë**
good/bad	**mirë/keq**
big/small	**i madh/i vogël**
cheap/expensive	**lirë/shtrenjtë**
hot/cold	**nxehtë/ftohtë**
old/new	**i vjetër/i ri**
open/closed	**hapur/mbyllur**
early/late	**herët/vonë**
easy/difficult	**lehtë/vështirë**
Does anyone here speak English/French/German?	**A flet ndokush këtu anglisht/ frëngjisht/gjermanisht?**
I don't understand.	**Unë nuk po kuptoj.**
Do you take credit cards/ traveller's cheques?	**A pranoni karta kreditore/ çeke të udhëtarëve?**
Waiter!/Waitress!	**Kamarier!/Kamariere!**
Where are the toilets?	**Ku është toaleti?**
I'd like…	**Kisha dashtë…**
How much is that?	**Sa kushton kjo?**
What time is it?	**Sa është ora?**
Help me please.	**Ju lutem më ndihmoni.**

Austria

Type of government:	Federal republic, multi-party, largely centralized
Member of:	EU, GATT, IBRD, IDA, IFC, IMF, OECD
Population:	8 million
Area:	83,851sq km (32,375sq miles)
Capital:	Vienna (*Wien*, 1.5m)
Other major cities:	Graz (232,150)
	Linz (203,000)
	Salzburg (144,000)
	Innsbruck (115,000)
Language:	German; English, and occasionally French, spoken in business circles.
Religion:	Catholic (89%), Protestant (6%)
Time zone:	GMT+1, EST+6; DST (Apr-Sep)
Currency:	Schilling (abbr. S) = 100 Groschen
	Coins: 10, 50 Groschen; 1, 5, 10, 20, 50, 100S
	Notes: 20, 50, 100, 500, 1,000, 5000S
Electricity:	220V, 50Hz, AC

Planning your Trip

Visa requirements: For South African and Turkish nationals. (See also p.6.)

Vaccination requirements: None. (See also p.7.)

Import allowances (see also p.7):

(see also p.7)

	Cigarettes		Cigars		Tobacco	Spirits		Wine
1)	200	or	50	or	250g	1l	and	2l
2)	200	and	50	or	250g	1l	and	2l
3)	(800)	or	(200)	or	(1kg)	(10l)	and	(90l)
1) Passengers from countries outside Europe.								
2) Duty-free goods bought in EU countries by European residents.								
3) Non-duty-free goods bought within the EU.								

Perfume: 1) 75g; 2) 50g; *Toilet water*: 1) ⅜; 2) 250ml.

There are no official restrictions on goods bought non-duty-free within the EU, provided they are for personal use only. The above figures are guidelines to the quantities customs officials will generally find acceptable, so if you are carrying larger quantities you should be prepared to provide proof that the goods are for your personal use.

Currency restrictions: There are no restrictions on importing Austrian currency, but not more than 100,000S may be taken out of the country. Any amount of foreign currency may be imported or exported. Banks must report transactions of 100,000S or more, in line with laws aimed at preventing money-laundering. (See also p.7.)

(See also p.7.)

Climate: Austria has a continental climate with cold winters, warm summers and moderate rain- and snowfall. Snow falls in Vienna from December to early March, although it usually melts within a few days and hardly hinders traffic. Average temperatures in Vienna are:

Jan	Apr	July	Oct
-1°C (30°F)	9°C (49°F)	19°C (67°F)	10°C (50°F)

Clothing: In summer, most of your clothing ought to be light, with something warmer for chilly evenings. Rainwear is advisable at any time. A warm overcoat is necessary in wintertime. In business circles conservative dress is usual; for men, dark suits are still most acceptable, though in summer lighter colours may also be worn. A tie is **23**

always essential. Visitors planning to go to the opera or concerts are well advised to take some formal dress with them.

Hotels: The Austria Information Centre publishes an annual booklet listing full details of all hotels. It's advisable to book rooms in advance, especially during the summer season (May-Sep) as well as at Christmas and Easter. In Vienna, tourist offices at the airport, main railway stations (Westbahnhof and Südbahnhof), at the west (all year) and south (March-Oct) motorway (expressway) exits and in Opernpassage can help visitors to find a room.

Austrian tourist offices abroad: Amsterdam, Berlin, Brussels, Cologne, Copenhagen, Dublin, Frankfurt, Hamburg, Houston, Johannesburg, London, Los Angeles, Madrid, Milan, Munich, New York, Paris, Rome, Stockholm, Tokyo, Toronto, Zurich.

Business Briefing

Economic Background

Main industries: Iron and steel, engineering, wood and paper products, electrical engineering, food processing, chemical industry, vehicles, tourism.

Main agricultural products: Wheat, barley, sugar beet, maize.

Main imports: Foodstuffs, machinery, motor vehicles, oil, chemicals, raw materials, finished consumer goods.

Main exports: Machinery and transport equipment, semi-finished and finished products, chemical products, wood and paper products.

GNP: $118 billion; per capita: $16,470.

Inflation rate: 4% (1994).

Principal trading partners: Germany, Switzerland, Italy, Belgium, Japan, Hungary, UK, USA.

Trade fairs: Most trade exhibitions are held in Vienna. They include the International Spring Fair (March), Aqua-Term International (heating, air-conditioning, sanitary engineering) (mid-April), IFABO (office equipment) (May), International Autumn Fair (September) and International Furniture and Interior Decoration Fair (March).

Selected background reading: *Austria, Facts and Figures* (in English) (Austrian Press Agency). *Österreichischer Wirtschaftsdienst,* published monthly by the Austrian Federal Chamber of Economy (Bundeswirtschaftskammer), Wiedner Hauptstrasse 63, 1045 Vienna, is available in English, French, German, Italian and Spanish. It may also be ordered directly from Austrian embassies or consulates abroad. The Vienna Institute for Comparative Economic Studies and the Austrian Press Agency also have several publications concerning the Austrian economy, most of them in German only, but some also available in other languages.

Austrian chambers of commerce abroad: Boston, Buenos Aires, Dallas, Milan, New York, São Paulo, Zurich.

On the Spot

Office hours: 8am-5.30pm Monday-Friday, with a lunch break between noon and 1pm, or 1 and 2pm. Government offices are open 8am-4pm.

Public holidays

Jan 1	New Year's Day	Dec 25	Christmas Day
Jan 6	Epiphany	Dec 26	St Stephen's Day
May 1	Labour Day		
Aug 15	Assumption	**Movable dates**:	Easter Monday
Oct 26	National Day		Ascension
Nov 1	All Saints' Day		Whit Monday
Dec 8	Immaculate Conception		Corpus Christi

Banks and currency exchange: Banking hours vary, but are generally 8am-12.30pm and 1.30-3.30pm Monday-Friday, with late closing at 5.30pm on Thursdays. All major Austrian banks handle international transactions.

Outside banking hours, exchange bureaux operate at the Vienna airport, both main railway stations (Westbahnhof and Südbahnhof), at **25**

Stephansplatz and at the tourist office in Opernpassage. Money-changing machines (under the sign CHANGE) are to be found in Kärntnerstrasse, at the side of the Opera, and near the cathedral, Stephansdom, in Vienna.

Major banks: Creditanstalt-Bankverein, Österreichische Länderbank AG, Österreichisches Credit-Institut AG, Bank für Arbeit und Wirtschaft AG (BAWAG) and Zentralsparkasse und Kommerzialbank (Z).

Credit cards and traveller's cheques: Both are widely accepted in major hotels, restaurants and shops. Among credit cards, American Express, Diner's Club and Visa are the best known.

Post and telecommunications: Postal and telecommunications services are very good. Hours are generally 8am-6pm Monday-Friday, with an hour's lunchtime break. In Vienna, 24-hour counters are open every day of the week at the main post office (Fleischmarkt 19), the main telegraph office (Börseplatz 1) and the principal railway stations (Westbahnhof, Südbahnhof and Franz Josefs-Bahnhof).

The Austrian telephone network is largely automatic, and you can dial direct to many foreign countries, even from telephone booths.

Most of Vienna's major hotels have telex and fax facilities. All the major post offices have public fax facilities and there is a public telex in the main telegraph office (Börseplatz 1).

Some useful numbers in Vienna:

Ambulance	144	Doctor	141
Fire	122	Inquiries (Europe)	1613
Inquiries (inland)	1611	Inquiries (International)	1614
Operator (English)	09	Police/emergency	133

Principal area codes: Graz 0316; Innsbruck 0512; Linz 070; Salzburg 0662; Vienna 01

Embassies and consulates: Consult the listings in the telephone directory under *Botschaften* for embassies and *Konsulate* for **26** consulates.

Medical care and health: The standard of medical treatment is generally high. The largest and best-known hospital in the country is the Allgemeine Krankenhaus (Währinger Gurtel 18-20, 1090 Vienna). Popular among foreigners is the Wilhelminenspital (Montleartstrasse 37, 1160 Vienna) where most of the staff speak some English. Most medical supplies are easily available. Internationale Apotheke (Kärntner Ring 17, 1010 Vienna) is particularly patronized by foreigners. After hours, all pharmacies have a sign on their door stating the address of the nearest duty-pharmacy (or tel. 1550).

Medical fees are rather high compared to other western European and North American countries. British nationals should inquire with their local Social Security offices about reciprocal arrangements with Austria for the payment of medical costs.

The Viennese tap water is not only safe for drinking but also tastes good as it comes directly from the Styrian Alps.

Services: Various secretarial agencies have offices in Vienna and other major cities. Interpreters can be found under the yellow pages heading *Dolmetscher* and translators under *Übersetzer*.

Photocopying machines are found in large department stores, print-shops, etc., and such services are listed under *Photokopieranstalten* in the yellow pages.

Newspapers: Leading Austrian dailies are *Kurier, Neue Kronen-Zeitung* and *Die Presse*. Most major European newspapers, and the English-language *International Herald Tribune,* can be bought at airports and large news-stands. The monthly publication *Falter* (available in German only) provides listings of events in the city.

Transport

Air – international: Vienna's Schwechat airport, 18km (11 miles) from the centre of town, has direct connections with major cities in Europe. Travellers coming from further afield usually have to change planes en route, although some international flights go to Salzburg.

Air – domestic: There are daily flights on weekdays between Vienna and Graz, Innsbruck, Linz, Klagenfurt and Salzburg.

Rail: Trains are usually punctual, and the faster ones are also very comfortable, with two classes of seating available. Dining and sleeping cars are attached on longer runs. Inter-city trains *(Städteschnellzüge)* connect all major cities in the shortest possible time at frequent intervals, and are a favourite means of business travel. The Austrian Railcard allows discount rail travel throughout the country. At less than half the price, the regional 'Netzkarte' offers the same conditions but is limited to one of the 18 regions of Austria.

Postal buses: Outlying places not covered by the rail network are served by the postal bus system. Buses are punctual and reasonably comfortable, though you are unlikely to get much work done on them.

Local public transport: The city transport system in Vienna is very efficient, consisting of trams *(Strassenbahn)*, buses and underground/subway *(U-Bahn)*. Rapid-transit trains *(Schnellbahn)* serve certain outlying districts. In Vienna, the underground, currently with four lines in operation, constitutes the quickest means of getting around. Other cities have trams and buses.

In Vienna, the same tickets are valid for all means of transport. Tickets can be purchased individually from bus and tram conductors or in booklets of 5 at tobacco shops *(Tabak-Trafik)* at a reduced rate. The tickets are also valid for transfers; they must be punched in machines in buses and trams or at the entrance to underground stations. Also available are 1-, 3- and 8-day tickets for unlimited travel anywhere in Vienna.

Taxis: Cabs can be hailed, ordered by phone (tel. 31 300, 40 100, 60 160 or 91 011) or taken at taxi ranks. They are metered.

Car rental: International and local firms operate, some of which have desks at Vienna's Schwechat airport. Chauffeur-driven cars are also available.

Driving in Austria: Vehicles must be equipped with a red warning triangle and a first-aid kit. Seat belts must be worn. Blood alcohol limit is 80mg/100ml. Fuel (petrol/gas) available is normal (87-92 octane), super (96-99 octane), lead-free (91 octane) and diesel. At crossings, vehicles coming from the right have priority if not otherwise indicated. Trams always have precedence, and may not be passed on the right if serving a stop. Never overtake when less than 80 metres from a railway crossing. Speed limits are 130kph (81mph) or 100kph (62mph) on motorways, 100kph or 80kph (50mph) on other roads and generally 50kph (31mph) in towns. Roads are usually well maintained. No tolls are charged on the *West-* and *Süd-* (South) *autobahnen,* but on the Salzburg–Villach motorway you pay at tunnels.

For breakdown assistance, phone 120 *(ÖAMTC –* Austrian Automobile, Motorcycling and Touring Association) or 123 *(ARBÖ –* Austrian Automobile, Motorcycling and Cycling Association).

Some distances from Vienna: Graz 200km (125 miles), Salzburg 300km (180 miles), Innsbruck 470km (290 miles).

Social customs: Great importance is attached to academic and professional titles, which should be used if you know them and are speaking German. Shaking hands is customary when meeting and taking your leave from a person. The Austrians like to take their time before going onto a first-name basis, and seldom invite business acquaintances to their homes.

Hints for business: Austrians approach business in a rather indirect fashion – it is customary to spend a few minutes talking about generalities such as the weather or other neutral matters before getting down to the actual object of the meeting. Courtesy is always an asset; a few compliments about what has especially pleased you in Austria should not be neglected.

The month of August, the Christmas–New Year period and the weeks before and after Easter are best avoided for business, when most Austrians take their holidays.

Foreign chambers of commerce in Austria: American, Dutch, Mexican, Israeli, Italian, Swiss, German.

Crime and theft: Usual precautions are in order. Although the crime and theft rate is quite low, it is advisable not to leave valuable objects in your car.

After Hours

Food and drink: Among Austrian specialities are soups, like *Leber-knödelsuppe* (liver dumpling soup) or *Gulaschsuppe* (goulash soup). Main dishes comprise *Wiener Schnitzel* (breaded veal cutlet), *Wiener Backhendl* (breaded fried chicken), *Tafelspitz* (boiled beef with chive sauce or horseradish), various kinds of dumplings *(Knödel)*, and game in season. A wide selection of Hungarian, Czech and Balkan dishes also feature on restaurant menus. Delicious Viennese desserts include numerous pastries, especially *Sachertorte* (chocolate cake with jam), *Apfelstrudel* (apple pastry) and *Topfenstrudel* (type of cheese cake). Hot desserts: *Palatschinken* (thin pancakes filled with cottage cheese, jam or nuts and chocolate), *Kaiserschmarrn* (diced pancake with raisins and sugar) and *Salzburger Nockerl* (sweet omelette soufflée).

Local white wines are dry, often slightly sparkling and very refreshing. A speciality is the new wine, called *Heuriger,* drunk in rustic wine taverns or open-air restaurants on the outskirts of Vienna. Austrian red wines tend to be rather flat, and it's better to stick to reds imported from South Tyrol (Italy), Hungary or Bulgaria, some of which can be excellent.

Most internationally known spirits are available in bars and restaurants. Among the fruit brandies much appreciated locally, try the Hungarian *Barack* (apricot), Yugoslavian *slivovitz* (plum), or the Austrian *Obstler* which may be distilled from whatever fruit is available.

The most popular drink in Vienna, however, is coffee, served in all strengths and sizes of cup, from a *kleinen Mokka* (a tiny cup of strong black coffee) to a *Melange* (half milk, half coffee).

Mealtimes: lunch noon to 2.30 or 3pm, dinner 6 to 9 or 10pm. Major restaurants serve warm meals until midnight.

Entertainment: The Vienna Opera is world-famous. Those who have at least a smattering of German will find the plays staged at the Burgtheater worthwhile. English and French theatres offer foreign-language plays. The two famous orchestras, the Wiener Philharmoniker and the Wiener Symphoniker, perform throughout the winter season. In summer, classical concerts are given in old palaces and gardens, and the Vienna Festival (*Wiener Festwochen*) in May and June, with concerts and theatre performances from all over the world, is a seasonal highlight.

Several nightclubs and discotheques exist, and there are two casinos in the Vienna area, one in the capital itself and the other 20km (12 miles) away in Baden. Most foreign films are dubbed into German. One cinema, the Burg-Kino, shows foreign films regularly in the original language.

Taxes, service charges and tipping: A service charge is included in hotel and restaurant bills but a 5% tip is customary. Taxi drivers, round off fare; cloakroom attendants and porters 10S per piece; hairdressers and barbers 10%.

Sports and recreation: Sports facilities are available throughout the country, with hiking and mountain-climbing obvious favourites. In Vienna, swimming is popular at several big indoor and (in summer) outdoor pools. The Alt-Donau (Old Danube) also offers sailing, rowing and canoeing. Dozens of tennis courts are scattered all over the city, and the Prater amusement park has a bowling alley and stables. Ice-skating can be enjoyed all year round in the Wiener Stadthalle, and in winter an open-air rink operates next to the Intercontinental Hotel. Ski slopes begin only a few miles from the city in the Vienna Woods, though most skiers prefer to go to the Alps further south or west. Top spectator sports are soccer in summer and ice-hockey in winter.

TV and radio: Programmes are in German. News in English is broadcast every day on Programme One at 8.05am and in French at 8.10am. Blue Danube Radio gives information in English.

What to buy: Petit-point embroidery, Augarten porcelain and Loden coats and suits are the most popular buys to take home. Vienna is also a good hunting-ground for all kinds of souvenirs and antiques, especially old coins and stamps.

Shopping hours: generally 8am-6pm Monday-Friday, Saturdays until noon or 1pm. Smaller shops close for lunch somewhere between 12.30 and 3pm.

Cities and Sights

VIENNA (*Telephone area code 01*)

Airport: Schwechat (18km/11 miles from city centre), international; duty-free shop, bank and cafés. Frequent bus and rail connections.

Tourist information office: Obere Augartensstrasse 40; phone service seven days a week, tel. 21 11 40. Kärtnerstrasse 38; tel. 513 88 92. Offices also in the Opernpassage (pedestrian underpass near the Opera), in the Westbahnhof and Sudbahnhof railway stations and at the airport.

Chamber of commerce: Stubenring 8-10; tel. 51450, fax 513778.

Sightseeing: Inner city (St Stephen's Cathedral, Hofburg, Ringstrasse), Spanish Riding School, Schönbrunn, Grinzing (wine taverns), Prater, Vienna International Centre (United Nations).

Museums: Kunsthistorisches Museum, Albertina, Schatzkammer (Imperial Treasury), Belvedere Palace (art galleries).

Excursions: Wachau, Wienerwald (Vienna Woods), Burgenland.

LINZ (*Telephone area code 070*)

Airport: Hörsching (15km/10 miles from city centre), international; duty-free shop. Bus services to and from main railway station connect with incoming and outgoing flights.

Tourist information office: Schillerstrasse 50, 4010 Linz; tel. 60 02 2110, fax 600 220.

Chamber of commerce: Hessenplatz 3, 4020 Linz; tel. 7800 0, fax 7800 444 or 7800 395.

Sightseeing: Hauptplatz (main square), 16th-century Landhaus (seat of provincial government), Church of the Minorite Brothers, St Martin's Church (15th-century frescoes), castle, Provincial Museum of Upper Austria.

Excursions: Mühlviertel, Freistadt.

For some useful expressions in German, see page 135.

Baltic States

ESTONIA

Type of government:	Democratic parliamentary republic
Population:	1.5 million
Area:	47,549sq km (18,370sq miles)
Capital:	Tallinn (484,000)
Other major towns:	Tartu (113,400)
Languages:	Estonian (official language); Russian; English and German widely spoken in business circles.
Religion:	Lutheran (78%), Greek Orthodox (19%)
Time zone:	GMT+2, EST+7; DST (Apr-Oct)
Currency:	Kroon (abbr. EEK) = 100 sents Coins: 5, 10, 20, 50 sents; 1, 5 kroon Bills: 1, 2, 5, 10, 25, 100, 500 kroon
Electricity:	220V, 50Hz, AC

LATVIA

Type of government:	Democratic parliamentary republic
Population:	2.7 million
Area:	65,786sq km (25,400sq miles)
Capital:	Riga (916,078)
Other major cities:	Daugavpils (127,280) Liepaja (113,815) Jelgava (72,300)
Languages:	Latvian (official language); Russian

LATVIA (cont'd)

Religion:	Lutheran, Catholic, Russian Orthodox
Time zone:	GMT+2, EST+7; DST (Apr-Oct)
Currency:	Lat (abbr. Ls) = 100 santimi
	Coins: 1, 2, 5, 10, 20, 50 santimi; 1, 2Ls
	Bills: 5, 10, 20, 50, 100Ls
Electricity:	127/220V, 50Hz, AC

LITHUANIA

Type of government:	Democratic parliamentary republic
Population:	3.7 million
Area:	64,445sq km (25,174sq miles)
Capital:	Vilnius (590,100)
Other major cities:	Kaunas (429,000)
Language:	Lithuanian
Religion:	Predominantly Catholic, some Russian Orthodox
Time zone:	GMT+2, EST+7; DST (Apr-Sep)
Currency:	Litas (abbr. Lt) = 100 kopeks
	Coins: 1, 2, 5 kopeks; 1, 2, 5Lt
	Bills: 10, 20, 50, 100Lt
Electricity:	127/220V, 50Hz, AC

Planning your Trip

Visa requirements: **Estonia**: required, except for nationals of Australia, Denmark, New Zealand, United States and the UK. Visas can be obtained on arrival. **Latvia**: required, except for UK nationals. Obtainable on arrival. **Lithuania**: required, except for nationals of Denmark, Norway and the UK. Obtainable on arrival. Estonia accepts visas for

Latvia and Lithuania; Latvia accepts Lithuanian but not Estonian visas; Lithuania requires a separate visa before entry. (See also p.6.)

Vaccination requirements: None. (See also p.7.)

Import allowances: (see also p.7). The amounts given below are for personal use only:

	Cigarettes		Tobacco	Spirits or Wine
Estonia/ Lithuania	250	or	225g of other tobacco products	3-4 bottles
Latvia	200	or	200g of other tobacco products	1l

Currency restrictions: **Latvia**: no restrictions. **Estonia**: currency of up to US$1,000 in value can be imported or exported duty-free. **Lithuania**: check before departure. (See also p.7.)

Climate: All three Baltic States are located on the eastern banks of the Baltic Sea, ensuring a changeable climate. Winter temperatures in each country can drop way below zero, although in summer the republics enjoy a temperate north European climate, with fine, sunny weather quite common on the coast.

	Jan	Apr	July	Oct
Riga	-5°C (22°F)	4°C (39°F)	17°C (63°F)	3°C (37°F)
Tallinn	-1°C (30°F)	5°C (41°F)	21°C (60°F)	5°C (41°F)
Vilnius	-2C (28°F)	7.2°C (25°F)	19°C (56°F)	3.5°C (38°F)

Clothing: In summer, lightweight clothing is adequate, although it is a good idea to bring a raincoat and umbrella at any time of the year, and some warm clothing for cool evenings. Heavy suits and an overcoat, hat, scarf and gloves are needed for a winter trip. Business dress is formal, though less so than in some areas of eastern Europe. Smart dress is often worn to go out in the evenings, and jeans may be frowned upon at certain establishments.

Hotels: All three Baltic States have a shortage of quality hotels – the best are generally confined to the capital cities, although some good ones can be found in the resorts. It is easier to find a reasonable hotel now than it was under Soviet rule, as new establishments are opened to cater for the influx from the west. Book before departure.

Baltic States tourist offices abroad: As the state tourist boards have only recently been established you should contact embassies or consulates for further information.

Business Briefing

Economic Background

Main industries: **Estonia**: metals, textiles, transport vehicles, wood products, minerals. **Latvia**: mechanical engineering, textiles, chemicals, wood processing, electronics. **Lithuania**: mechanical engineering, metals, cement, textiles, clothing and leather, food processing.

Main agricultural products: **Estonia**: livestock, dairy products, fish, rye, wheat. **Latvia**: dairy products, livestock, fish, cereals, grain, potatoes. **Lithuania**: livestock, livestock fodder, fish, grain.

Main imports: **Estonia**: minerals, machinery, transport vehicles, textiles, food and drinks. **Latvia**: fuel, energy, farm machinery, cars, new technology. **Lithuania**: oil, energy, raw materials, chemicals.

Main exports: **Estonia**: agricultural products, metals, textiles, transport vehicles. **Latvia**: wood products, agricultural products, cement, textiles, small electronic goods, furniture. **Lithuania**: textiles and clothing, chemical products, fertiliser, rubber, electrical appliances.

Principal trading partners: **Estonia**: Finland, Russia, Sweden, Germany. **Latvia**: CIS, Germany, USA, Sweden, Finland. **Lithuania**: CIS, Poland, Germany, UK, USA.

GNP: **Estonia**: not available. **Latvia**: $13 billion; per capita: $ 4,861. **Lithuania**: $19.3 billion; per capita: $5,210.

Inflation rate: **Estonia**: 25% (1993) **Latvia**: 2% (1st qtr 1993); **Lithuania**: 49% (1993).

Trade fairs: Tallinn hosts an international travel exhibition in September, catering for the growing tourist trade. Vilnius hosts a number of trade fairs thoughout the year, catering for (among others) agriculture, transport, shoes and textiles.

Selected background reading: *Estonia: Guidelines for Foreign Investors*, published by the Estonian Ministry of Economy in Tallinn, provides essential data for potential investors in Estonia. *Tallinn This Week*, published by Revalia in Tallinn, offers comprehensive local information. The monthly *Europe-Latvia*, published by Izdevnieciba Baltika in Riga, provides Latvian economic and business information in English. *Vilnius in your Pocket* is a two-monthly city guide to the Lithuanian capital, published by UAB in Vilnius. The Lithuanian Information Institute in Vilnius publishes an annual *Guide for Foreign Investors*.

Baltic States chambers of commerce abroad: contact embassies or consulates.

On the Spot

Office hours: 8.30 or 9am to 5 or 5.30pm Monday-Friday, with lunch between 2 and 3pm. Closed on Saturdays. Government offices generally keep to the same hours.

Public holidays

Estonia:			
Jan 1	New Year's Day	**Moveable dates**:	Good Friday
Feb 24	Independence Day		Easter Sunday
May 1	May Day		Whitsun
June 23	Victory Day		Mother's Day
June 24	Midsummer (St John's) Day		
Dec 25	Christmas Day		
Dec 26	Boxing Day		
Dec 31	New Year's Eve		

Latvia:

Jan 1	New Year's Day	Dec 25	Christmas Day
May 1	May Day	Dec 26	Boxing Day
June 24	Midsummer Day	Dec 31	New Year's Eve
Nov 18	National Day	**Moveable dates**:	Good Friday

Lithuania:

Jan. 1	New Year's Day	Dec 25	Christmas Day
Feb 16	Restoration of the	Dec 26	Boxing Day
	Lithuanian State	**Moveable dates**:	Easter Monday
July 6	Day of Statehood		Mother's Day
Nov 1	All Saints Day		(1st Sunday in May)

Banks and currency exchange: Money can be changed at banks and the exchange offices in airports, railway stations and hotels. A few exchange offices are open beyond normal banking hours and on Sundays. Banking hours are: **Estonia**: 9am-6pm Monday-Saturday. **Latvia**: 9am-5pm Monday-Friday. **Lithuania**: 9am-5pm Monday-Friday. The main Baltic banks are: **Estonia**: Hansabank, Evea Bank and the Bank of Tallinn; **Latvia**: Riga Commercial Bank and Baltija Bank; **Lithuania**: Litimpex Bankas, Balticbank and Hermis Bankas.

Credit cards and traveller's cheques: Both are increasingly used in all three states – but still only at larger establishments. It is important to carry plenty of local currency for smaller establishments and for trips outside urban areas.

Post and telecommunications: To avoid loss or delay, post should be sent from main post offices. **Estonia**'s main office is in Tallinn at 1 Narva Maantee, which opens 8am-8pm Monday-Friday and until 5pm on Saturdays. *Post restante* and private courier services are also available here. In **Latvia**, Riga's main post office is at Brivibas Bulvari 21, Riga PDP, LV 1000, open 8am-5pm Monday-Friday. In **Lithuania**, the central post office is in Vilnius at 7 Gedimino; open 8am-8pm Monday-Friday, 11am-7pm Saturday and Sunday.

One of the legacies of the Soviet system is the inefficient telephone system in the Baltics. Long distance and fax calls cause the most delays. To avoid problems, use telephones at the main post offices. In Vilnius, use the 24-hour telegraph office at 33/2 Vilniaus. The Estonian telephone system is in the process of being overhauled. Local public pay phones (if they are not out of order!) are used free of charge. Long distance calls can be made direct from special telephones, found in hotel lobbies or at main post offices. Lithuania's service has been overhauled and you can now dial direct. You can also use cellular and satellite phones in Lithuania and in parts of Estonia. To call home from the Baltics, dial 8 and wait for a long constant tone. Then dial 10 followed by the country code and the number.

Some useful numbers:

Ambulance	03	Fire	01
Inquiries	09	Police	02
Operator	8 194/5	Time	004

Country codes: Estonia 372; Latvia 371; Lithuania 370.

Embassies and consulates: These are listed in the main telephone directories and in local tourist guides.

Medical care and health: Medical provision in all three Baltic States is adequate and emergency health care is provided free of charge. For any other treatment you will have to pay, but medical fees are quite low. In Tallinn, there is an emergency medical service hospital at 19 Sutistetee. Medical and dental facilities can be fairly basic. Medicines are on sale from pharmacies, which are generally open 9am-8pm Monday-Friday and 9am-4pm on Saturday. More medicines are available now than under Soviet rule, but visitors are still strongly recommended to bring any special medicines with them. Tap water is safe to drink, if not particularly pleasant in the cities. Hot water is sometimes in short supply in Vilnius.

Services: Interpreters, guides and translation services are available through local travel agents. Conference facilities and meeting rooms can be hired at some of the larger hotels in the capitals and resorts. In Estonia, business services can be obtained through Frens Ltd in Tallinn; tel. (372 2) 446 987.

Newspapers: The weekly *Baltic Observer* and the *Baltic Independent* provide news and business updates in English in all three states. Most of the main western and Russian newspapers are also available the day after publication. *Tallinn This Week* provides essential information for visitors to the Estonian capital, while *Vilnius in your Pocket* offers the same every two months for Lithuania's capital. *Lithuania in the World* contains business and tourist features. All are widely available locally.

Transport

Air – international: Estonia's Tallinn airport has connections with major Scandinavian, east European and German cities. Riga airport is Latvia's gateway, with the national airline Latvijas Aviolinijas providing services to London and centres in Germany, Scandinavia and Russia. Vilnius airport in Lithuania serves 16 European cities.

Air – domestic: Regular flights are available between each of the republics' main airports. Few other internal connections exist.

Boats, waterways: Tallinn has sea connections from Helsinki (1½-4 hours, depending on the type of boat) and from Stockholm (overnight). The Lithuanian port of Klaipeda has weekly connections to Germany – but you must book well in advance.

Rail: In the absence of internal flights inside each Baltic state, train is probably the best way to travel longer distances. Services operate between all the main Baltic cities, with first and tourist classes available. Tickets can be purchased from main stations and from local travel agents. The *Balti jaam* (Baltic station) near central Tallinn has connections to Riga and Vilnius as well as Minsk, St Petersburg and Moscow. The Baltic Express, connecting Tallinn and Warsaw, opened in 1993.

Local public transport: All three capital cities have reasonable, if crowded, bus services. In Tallinn and Vilnius there are also trolleybus systems. Bus tickets can be bought at the main bus stations, at news stands or on buses.

Taxis: Taxis can be hired from ranks or from your hotel. While taxis are metered, it is still a good idea to agree a fare before you set off.

You cannot hire a taxi on the street. To call a cab in Tallinn, telephone 603 044. Tallinn also has 'route taxis', operating on fixed routes and stopping when passengers ask. Buy a ticket on board. In Vilnius, you can arrange shared rides as far as Berlin or Paris. Contact Tranzito Centras on 353 710.

Car rental: Many of the major international car-rental firms now operate in the Baltics. Rental can be arranged in advance or from your hotels. Chauffeur-driven cars are also available.

Driving in the Baltic States: All three states have well-developed road networks. The *Via Baltica* motorway network is under construction; it will connect the three Baltic capitals with Helsinki and Warsaw, and should dramatically improve long-distance links.

An international driving licence is required in the Baltic States. Drive on the right, pass on the left. Drivers and front-seat passengers must wear seat belts. The alcohol limit is a strictly enforced zero. To drive in old Tallinn and old Vilnius you must pay a toll. Parking meters are rare.

Speed limits: 50kph (31mph) in built-up areas, 90kph (56mph) on highways.

Breakdown problems: In Estonia, call the police (02) or Tallinna Liikluspolitsei (44 54 50). In Lithuania, call the Vilnius breakdown service on 64 08 54.

Fuel (petrol/gas) is available at fuel stations in unleaded, normal (92 and 93 octane), super (95 and 99 octane) and diesel. Some fuel stations are open 24 hours, particularly those near airports and ports.

Some distances: Tallinn-Riga 307km (192 miles), Tallinn-Vilnius 605km (378 miles), Riga-Vilnius 390km (244 miles).

Social customs: Residents of the Baltic States are, understandably, proud of their national traditions and heritage, so make an effort to share this enthusiasm. Environmentalism is a major concern in all three states, so avoid leaving litter or polluting the atmosphere. Smoking is banned in almost all public places in Lithuania. Invitations to a colleague's home are rare. Soviet traditions die hard, so treat officialdom with respect and patience. Tolerance may also be **41**

needed when eating out or checking in and out of hotels. Religious tradition is strong, particularly in Catholic-dominated Lithuania.

Hints for business: Government economic policy in each state is aimed primarily at encouraging foreign investment, so business opportunities are generally very good. But, while the states are moving enthusiastically towards the free market, state enterprises still dominate. It is important to use the formal (often state) channels to gain access to local businesses. Rules are changing all the time, so obtain as much up-to-date information as possible before departure. Business protocol is fairly relaxed, although it is important to be punctual and to keep to agreements made.

Foreign trade organisations in the Baltic States: Canada, Finland, France, Germany, Norway, Sweden, United States.

Crime and theft: Black market currency dealers should be avoided. Otherwise, normal precautions apply.

After Hours

Food and drink: The Baltic diet is heavily influenced by both Germany and Russia. Grilled pork is a speciality in the Baltics, and beef and chicken are also available. Fish, a staple food, is widely available in all three republics, especially on the coastlines. Soups are also worth trying. Lithuanian cuisine includes *cepelinai* (potato dumplings), *kugelis* (potato pudding) and mushroom dishes. Fresh cakes and pastries, made to traditional recipes, are very popular.

As there is no local wine, most is imported from Germany. *Bauska*, a local Latvian beer, is very popular and very good. Black balsam (*melnais balsams*), an alcoholic (and medicinal!) drink prepared from 45 herbs, is a particular speciality in Latvia. An Estonian speciality is the liqueur *vana toomas*. In Lithuania the best beer is *utenos alus*, and the best vodka is *kvietine*. Schnapps is also available.

The three capitals offer an increasing choice of restaurants and cafés, although many less friendly establishments, operating under the old Soviet ethos, still exist. Many restaurants operate informal daily menus: ask what's available. Smarter restaurants and hotels operate a full menu. It's best to reserve tables in advance at the most popular restaurants.

Mealtimes: lunch 12-2pm, dinner 7-9pm.

Entertainment: Folk dancing is an important part of life in all three states. Huge song and dance festivals are held annually in Riga and Vilnius and once every five years in Tallinn. Tallinn also hosts the annual 'Rock Summer' music festival, and all three capitals offer live rock and jazz music. The Estonian theatre season (from October to April) features the Estonian opera and ballet theatre. Several theatre companies exist in Latvia, performing mainly at the capital's three big concert halls. Nightclubs and cabaret venues also operate.

Taxes, service charges and tipping: Service is not generally included in hotel or restaurant bills in the Baltic States, · e 5-10% extra for tips – if you think it appropriate. Taxi d · hould be given about the same.

Sports and recreation: The most popular sports in the Baltic States are running, swimming, ice hockey, cycling, fishing, rowing, basketball and volleyball. For those who want to keep fit, tennis, squash and swimming facilities are available, if scarce, in the cities.

TV and radio: Estonia has no English-language television, but radio broadcasts in English go out on Eesti Raadio from 6.20 to 6.30pm Monday-Friday and on Mondays and Thursdays from 11.30pm to midnight. Estonian radio also broadcasts in Esperanto! In Latvia, the Riga-based NTV-5 provides nightly news summaries in English. TV broadcasts from CNN, the BBC and the German Deutsche Welle are also available. Latvia's national radio station SWH provides 4 hours of English programming every day. Radio 2A also has English and Russian news broadcasts. Lithuanian State Television broadcasts BBC News on weekdays from 7pm. Radio Vilnius External Service offers a daily 30-minute round-up in English at 10pm and 12.30am. Voice of America and the BBC World Service are also available across the Baltic region.

What to buy: Handicrafts, including local leatherwork, hand-made sweaters and Russian nestling dolls (*matryoshkas*) are popular in all **43**

three states. Antiques, porcelain, crystals and other jewellery can also be picked up quite cheaply. Amber is a speciality in Lithuania.

Shopping hours: from 9 or 10am to 2pm and 3-6pm Monday-Friday; some shops are open until 8pm on Saturday; early closing at around 1pm. Many shops close for two days – either Saturday or Sunday or Sunday and Monday.

Cities and Sights

ESTONIA: Tallinn (*Telephone area code: 372-2*)

Airport: Tallinna Lennujam (5km/3 miles from city centre), international. Bus service (number 22) to main railway station every 20-30 minutes; journey time 10 minutes.

Tourist information offices: Kinga 6; tel. 666 959, 448 886, fax 441 221. Pikk 71; tel. 601 700, fax 602 743.

Chamber of commerce: Toom-Kooli 17; tel. 444 929, fax 443 656.

Ministry of economy: Harju 11; tel. 440 577, fax 446 860.

Sightseeing: Old town, 13th- and 14th-century churches and town hall, guild houses and merchant dwellings.

Museums: Music museum, medieval art museum, maritime museum.

Excursions: Tartu (Dome cathedral, 17th-century university), Haanjamaa (Suur Munamagi mountain and observatory), Parnu (beaches, health spas), Lahemaa National Park.

LATVIA: Riga (*Telephone area code: 371*)

Airport: Riga International (16km/10 miles from city centre). Bus connection to centre.

Tourist information office: 22-24 Grecinieku Street; tel/fax 8 820 020, telex 161 195 SU.

Chamber of commerce: Brividas Boulevard 21; tel. 332 202, fax 332 276.

Sightseeing: Monument to Freedom; old Riga, including 12th-century castle, churches and other buildings from Hanseatic League days; central park.

Museums: Ethnographic museum, museum of Latvian history, museum of Riga and navigation, automobile museum, national gallery.

Excursions: Sigulda (13th-century castles and ruins), Jurmala (beach town).

LITHUANIA: Vilnius *(Telephone area code: 370-2)*

Airport: Vilnius International (10km/6 miles from city centre), international; duty-free shop. Bus connection (number 2) to city.

Tourist information office: 18 Seimyniskiu Street; tel. 353 931, fax 351 815, telex: 261009 SU.

Chamber of commerce: Algirdo 31, 2600 Vilnius; tel. 661 550, fax 661 542, telex 261114 LCO SU.

Sightseeing: Ruins of Gediminas Castle overlooking old town, gate of dawn, gothic and baroque churches, onion-domed synagogue, Vilnius university (16th-century).

Museums: History and ethnography; applied art; art and modern art.

Excursions: Trakai (ancient Lithuanian capital, fortress), Kaunas (museums, 16th-century churches and town houses).

Some Useful Expressions in Lithuanian

good morning/afternoon	**labas rytas/laba dięna**
good evening/night	**labas vakarąs/labąnakt**
good-bye	**viso gero**
yes/no	**taip/ne**
please/thank you/excuse me	**prašom/aciū/atsiprašau**
Does anyone here speak English/French/German?	**Ar čia kas nors kalba anliškai prancūziškai/vokiškai?**
I don't understand.	**Aš nesuprantu.**
Where are the toilets?	**Kur yra tualetas?**

Latvian

good morning/afternoon	**labrīt/labdien**
good evening/night	**labvakar/ar labu nakti**
good-bye	**sveiki, ardievu**
yes/no	**jā/nē**
please/thank you/excuse me	**lūdzu/paldies/atvainojiet**
Does anyone here speak English/French/German?	**Vai kāds te runā angliski/franciski/vāciski?**
I don't understand.	**Es nesaprotu.**
Where are the toilets?	**Kur ir tualetes/atejas?**

Estonian

good morning/afternoon	**tere hommikust/päevast**
good evening/night	**head õhtut/ööd**
good-bye	**head aega**
yes/no	**jaa/ei**
please/thank you/excuse me	**palun/tänan/vabandage**
Does anyone here speak English/French/German?	**Kas keegi siin räägih inglise keelt/prantsuse keelt/ saksa keelt?**
I don't understand.	**Ma ei saa aru.**
Where are the toilets?	**Kus asub WC?**

Belgium

Type of government:	Constitutional monarchy, multi-party, largely centralized
Member of:	Benelux, EU, GATT, IBRD, IDA, IFC, IMF, OECD
Population:	10.1 million
Area:	30,513sq km (11,781sq miles)
Capital:	Brussels (*Bruxelles/Brussel,* 150,000/GUA 1m)
Other major cities:	Antwerp (*Antwerpen/Anvers* 467,785) Ghent (*Gent/Gand,* 230,246) Charleroi (206,928) Liège (*Luik,* 195,201)
Languages:	Flemish (Dutch) (56%), French (32%); Flemish is spoken in the north of the country, French in the south, and German in a small area in the east. Brussels is officially bilingual. English is widely used in business circles.
Religion:	Predominantly Catholic
Time zone:	GMT+1, EST+6; DST (Apr-Sep)
Currency:	Belgian franc (abbreviated BF or FB) = 100 centimes Coins: 50 centimes (rare); 1, 5, 20, 50BF Notes: 100, 500, 1,000, 5,000BF
Electricity:	220V, 50Hz, AC

Planning your Trip

Visa requirements: For nationals of Turkey (except permanent residents of an EU country) and South Africa. (See also p.6.)

Vaccination requirements: None. (See also p.7.)

Import allowances (see also p.7):

	Cigarettes		Cigars		Tobacco	Spirits		Wine
1)	200	or	50	or	250g	1l	and	2l
2)	200	and	50	or	250g	1l	and	2l
3)	(800)	or	(200)	or	(1kg)	(10l)	and	(90l)

1) Passengers from countries outside Europe.
2) Duty-free goods bought in EU countries by European residents.
3) Non-duty-free goods bought within the EU.

Perfume: 1) 75g; 2) 50g; *Toilet water*: 1) ⅜; 2) 250ml;
Gifts: 1) 25,500BF max. value; 2) 2,600BF max. value

There are no official restrictions on goods bought non-duty-free within the EU, provided they are for personal use only. The above figures are guidelines to the quantities customs officials will generally find acceptable, so if you are carrying larger quantities you should be prepared to provide proof that the goods are for your personal use.

Currency restrictions: None. (See also p.7.)

Climate: From the coast inland to about Brussels, the climate is temperate maritime, similar to that in southeast England; in the Ardennes conditions become more continental, with colder winters and warmer summers.

Some average temperatures in Brussels:

Spring	Summer	Autumn	Winter
12°C (55°F)	22°C (72°F)	11°C (52°F)	5°C (41°F)

Clothing Some warm clothing is necessary at all times except possibly in high summer. An umbrella is as essential as a briefcase for the business visitor to Belgium. Dark, conservative suits and ties are worn in business circles.

Hotels: A wide range of good hotels exists at all levels, and bookings are rarely difficult to make upon arrival. Rooms may be booked anywhere in Belgium through a free service offered by Belgian Tourist Reservations, BTR, Boulevard Anspach, 111 Bte 4; tel. (02) 513 74 84, fax 513 92 77.

Belgian tourist offices abroad: Amsterdam, Basle, Copenhagen, Düsseldorf, Lille, Lisbon, London, Luxembourg, Madrid, New York, Oslo, Paris, Rome, Stockholm, Strasbourg, Tokyo, Vienna.

Business Briefing

Economic Background

Main industries: Iron, steel, non-ferrous metals, machinery, coal, engineering, shipbuilding, fabricated metal products, linens, textiles, synthetic fibres, diamond cutting.

Main agricultural products: Wheat, barley, flax, oats, rye, fodder and sugar beet, fruit, potatoes, dairy farming.

Main imports: Raw materials, capital equipment, motor vehicles, consumer goods, diamonds, petroleum.

Main exports: Motor vehicles, foodstuffs, machinery, iron, steel, metal products, textile yarns and fabrics, chemicals, precious stones.

Major trading partners: Germany, Netherlands, France, Italy, Japan, UK, USA.

GNP: $144 billion: per capita: $14,555.

Inflation rate: 2.6% (1994).

Trade fairs: Some major trade fairs held in Brussels are: BATI-BOUW (International Building Trade Exhibition) (February), Interior

Decoration Exhibition (March), and International Spring Fair (food, household goods and jewellery).

Selected background reading: Economic statistics are published regularly in Dutch and French by the Ministry of Economic Affairs. Price Waterhouse and Co issues a regularly updated guide called *Doing Business in Belgium* which gives a comprehensive background on current economic developments and fiscal regulations.

Belgian chambers of commerce abroad: Barcelona, Bryanston (South Africa), Buenos Aires, Casablanca, Cologne, The Hague, Istanbul, Lille, Lisbon, London, Madrid, Marseilles, Mexico City, Milan, Montevideo, Montreal, New York, Paris, Sao Paulo, Sydney, Teheran, Tel Aviv, Tokyo, Zurich.

On the Spot

Office hours: 8.30am-noon and 1-5pm, Monday-Friday.

Public holidays

Jan 1	New Year's Day	Nov 11	Armistice Day
May 1	Labour Day	Dec 25	Christmas Day
July 21	National Day	**Movable dates**:	Easter Monday
Aug 15	Assumption		Ascension
Nov 1	All Saints' Day		Whit Monday

If one of the above holidays falls on a Sunday, the following Monday is taken off instead.

Banks and currency exchange: Banking hours are generally 9am-3.30 or 4pm Monday-Friday. Some banks are open Saturday morning. In Brussels and Antwerp, currency-exchange offices operate in the city centre, at the airport and in railway stations, usually until 9 or 10pm every day of the week. There are currency-exchange machines at the airport which make transactions in four currencies.

Principal banks are Générale de Banque SA, Banque Bruxelles-Lambert and Kredietbank. Payments and transfers of capital are executed without delay. Most of the large international banking institutions have public-relations and legal departments that provide valuable service to international businessmen.

Credit cards and traveller's cheques: Most credit cards and traveller's cheques are readily accepted.

Post and telecommunications: All services are highly reliable. Post offices are separate from telegraph and telephone offices.

In Brussels, the all-night post office is at 48A, avenue Fonsny (right by the Gare du Midi), while the city's main office is at 1, place de la Monnaie.

In Brussels, the Belgacom telegraph and telephone office at 17, boulevard de l'Imperatrice is open 8am-10pm, every day of the week. Away from your hotel, the Belgacom office is the place to go to make intercontinental calls or to send telegrams and faxes or telexes. Direct-dialling facilities exist to virtually all subscribers in Belgium as well as to a large number of other countries. Public payphones take 5- or 20-franc coins or electronic 'Telecards' (available at post offices and news-stands).

Some useful numbers:

Fire brigade	100	Inquiries (Europe)	1304
Ambulance	649 1122	Operator (Int.)	1324
Red Cross	105	Police	101
24h Doctor (Brussels)	479 1818	Time	1300
Inquiries (Belgium)	1307	Weather	1703

Principal area codes: Antwerp 03, Bruges 050, Brussels 02, Charleroi 071, Ghent 091, Liège 041.

Embassies and consulates: Consult the telephone directory listings under *Ambassades* or *Consulats* in the Brussels telephone book. In Dutch-speaking areas, consulates are given under *Consulaten*.

Medical care and health: Health care is of the highest standard but expensive. Clinics and hospitals are plentiful, and it's said that in case of emergency one is never more than a 20-minute ride away from a medical centre anywhere in Belgium.

Medical and pharmaceutical supplies are readily available. A few pharmacies always stay open in each neighbourhood after hours. The weekly list is posted outside every pharmacy and published in the weekend editions of the local newspapers. Many doctors speak some English. In Brussels, phone 479 18 18 for a 24h doctor service, and 648 4014 for round-the-clock information in English. Emergency answering service for dentists: tel. 426 10 26. Tap water is drinkable.

Services: The yellow pages of the telephone directory list the principal business services. Indexes in the front of the volume are compiled in English and German as well as Dutch and French.

Newspapers: Main dailies are *Le Soir* and *La Libre Belgique* (French); *De Standard* and *Het Laatste Nieuws* (Dutch). Foreign newspapers, including the Paris-edited *International Herald Tribune* and Brussels-edited *Wall Street Journal/Europe*, are on sale at most centrally located news-stands and in some hotel lobbies. *The Bulletin*, Brussels' English-language weekly, lists entertainment and other news.

Transport

Air – international: Though some direct flights also operate into Antwerp, Liège, Charleroi and Ostend from European points, Brussels has the only truly international airport, situated at Zaventem, 15km (9 miles) from the city centre. There are no domestic flights.

Rail: Belgium's rail network provides good coverage of the country, and international links are good. Some trains have dining facilities.

The Benelux Tourrail ticket is valid for 5 days of unlimited rail travel within a one-month period, in Belgium, the Netherlands and Luxembourg. Inquire at a local travel agency or railway station.

Cross-Channel ferries: Ostend is linked to Dover and Folkstone by half-hourly ferries in summer, with a reduced service operating in winter. Overnight crossings operate between Zeebrugge and Hull.

Local public transport: Most Belgian cities are served by buses, and three of them – Brussels, Antwerp and Ghent – operate trams and a metro (underground, subway) system. In Brussels and Antwerp, bus or tram tickets can be bought on board or, in case of the metro, at the station. If you plan to use trams and metros extensively, a reduced-rate ten-ride ticket will be a worthwhile investment.

Taxis: Cabs may be hailed or picked up at taxi ranks near large intersections. A telephone call to a local taxi company (see yellow pages) will usually bring prompt service at almost any time of day or night. Taxi fares are among the highest in Europe but are all-inclusive: no further gratuity is called for or expected.

Car rental: International and local firms operate throughout the country, some with agencies at Brussels airport. Credit cards are the preferred means of payment. Chauffeur-driven cars are also available.

Driving in Belgium: In style of driving, Belgians may be considered to lie somewhere between the phlegmatic British and the sometimes reckless French. In Brussels, the tempo can be somewhat disconcerting to begin with. Note that many roads do not have marked traffic lanes, though they are generally well surfaced. Motorways (expressways) are fully lighted right across the country. Yield right of way to traffic coming from the right unless otherwise indicated. Trams have priority at all times. A red reflector warning triangle, a first-aid kit and a fire-extinguisher must be carried, and seat belts are obligatory. Blood alcohol limit is 80mg/100ml. Fuel (petrol/gas) available is normal (90-94 octane), super (98-100 octane), lead-free and diesel. Speed limits are 50kph (31mph) in built-up areas, 120kph (75mph) on motorways (expressways), and otherwise as signposted.

In case of breakdown, use the emergency phones along motorways, or telephone (02) 287 09 00 (Royal Automobile Club de Belgique, Brussels), (02) 233 22 11 (Touring Club de Belgique, Brussels) or (03) 252 62 70 (Vlaamse Automobilistenbond in Antwerp), for instructions. English will be spoken to a sufficient extent.

Some distances from Brussels: Antwerp 46km (29 miles), Liège 70km (43 miles), Ostend 118km (73 miles).

Social customs: Not particularly extroverted people, the Belgians have great respect for social formalities, and personal privacy is important. Belgians take some time to get onto first-name terms. At **53**

social and business gatherings, it's customary to greet and say good-bye to each person individually with a handshake. It's also considered polite to address a person by name or title when arriving or leaving.

Hints for business: Belgians are rather formal in business situations, and appointments are preferred. Holiday periods to be avoided are Christmas, New Year, Holy Week, July and August.

Foreign chambers of commerce in Belgium: American, Arab, Argentinian, Brazilian, British, Canadian, Chilean, Danish, Dutch, French, German, Greek, Indian, Irish, Israeli, Italian, Luxembourg, Norwegian, Polish, Portuguese, South African, Spanish, Swedish, Swiss, Turkish, Uruguayan, Zaïre.

Crime and theft: Normal precautions are in order.

After Hours

Food and drink: Often caricatured as mere eaters of *pommes frites* (chips, French fries), the Belgians can in fact boast an excellent cuisine which has little to fear in comparison with the French. Some local specialities you'll want to sample: *anguilles au vert* (eel in a herb sauce), *moules* (mussels and French fries), *waterzooi* (stewed chicken made with a creamy white broth), *carbonnade flamande* (beef stewed in beer), *civet de lièvre* (rabbit stew), *jambon d'Ardenne* (cured ham) and the famous *boudin noir* or *blanc* (blood sausage).

Beer, the national drink, wine and liquors are all readily available in bars. Besides the normal lager-type beer, you might like to try the unusual cherry beer *(kriek lambiek)* and malt beer *(trappistenbier)*.

Mealtimes: lunch noon-3pm, dinner 7-10pm.

Entertainment: Musical offerings are particularly good in Brussels and Antwerp, and opera houses in both cities stage some excellent productions. Brussels is also the place for nightclubs and discos. Cinemas usually show films in their original version.

Taxes, service charges and tipping: Value-added tax (Dutch abbreviation BTW, French abbreviation TVA) and service are almost always included in hotel and restaurant bills. Anything extra for the waiter is optional. Airport porters, if you are lucky enough to find them, have fixed, posted rates. Taxi fares are all-inclusive. Tipping recommendations: hotel porters, bell-boys or cloakroom attendants 30BF per bag or errand, barbers 20% and cinema or theatre ushers 10BF per person.

Sports and recreation: Cycling, tennis, squash, horseriding and water sports are favourite recreational pastimes. Golf is not widely played.

Spectator sports: soccer and bicycle races are very popular spectator sports.

TV and radio: Programming is in Flemish and French. On the Flemish-language TV channels, foreign films and interviews are generally shown in the original language.

What to buy: Good buys include lace, crystal, porcelain, cigars (Antwerp), *trappistenbier, kriek lambiek* beer.

Shopping hours: generally 9.15 or 9.30am to 6.30pm Monday-Saturday; most department stores stay open at midday, but smaller shops close for an hour or two.

Cities and Sights

BRUSSELS (*Telephone area code 02*)

Airport: National (15km/9 miles from city centre), international; duty-free shop. Direct rail connection to the Gare Centrale and the Gare du Nord in Brussels, from 6am-midnight. Sabena buses connect the airport with Liège, Ghent, Antwerp and Hasselt/Maastricht.

Tourist information office: National Tourist Office, 61, rue du Marché aux Herbes; tel. 504 0390. Tourist and Information Office of Brussels (TIB), Grand-Place (town hall); tel. 513 89 40.

Chamber of commerce: avenue Louise 500, 1050 Brussels; tel. 648 50 02, fax 640 92 28.

Sightseeing: Grand-Place, town hall, Manneken Pis, Church of Notre-Dame-de-la-Chapelle, Sablon area (market), Egmont Palace, **55**

Law Courts, Royal Palace and Brussels Park area, St. Michael's Cathedral, Atomium, Autoworld.

Museums: Museum of Modern Art, Museum of Fine Art (both in Musées Royaux des Beaux Arts), Horta Museum, Belgian Comic Strip Centre.

Excursions: Waterloo, Ghent, Antwerp, Namur, Bruges.

ANTWERP (Telephone area code 03)

Airport: Deurne (7km/4.5 miles from city centre). Bus service to central station. Antwerp is also served by Brussels-National airport; regular bus service to National.

Tourist information office: Grote Markt 15; tel. 232 01 03, fax 231 19 37.

Chamber of commerce: Markgravestraat 12; tel. 232 22 19, fax 233 64 42.

Sightseeing: Hovenierstraat (diamond-cutting and museum), Middelheim Park, town hall, Rubens House, Sterckshof, Cathedral of Our Lady.

Museums: Royal Museum of Fine Arts, Mayer Van Den Bergh Museum, Plantin-Moretus Museum.

Excursions: Bruges, Brussels, Ghent, Goes and Middelburg (Netherlands).

For some useful expressions in Dutch, see page 235.

For some useful expressions in French, see page 116.

Bulgaria

Type of government:	Presidential republic
Population:	8.4 million
Area:	110,912sq km (42,823sq miles)
Capital:	Sofia (1,140,800)
Other major cities:	Plovdiv (340,810)
	Varna (307,915)
	Bourgas (190,054)
	Russe (169,658)
	Stara Zagora (150,482)
	Pleven (130,515)
Language:	Bulgarian; English, German, French, Russian and Spanish are often spoken in business circles.
Religion:	Predominantly Bulgarian Orthodox (90%)
Time zone:	GMT+2, EST+7; DST (Apr-Sep)
Currency:	Lev (plural leva) = 100 stotinki
	Coins: 1, 2, 5, 10, 20, 50 stotinki; Notes: 1, 2, 5, 10, 20, 50, 120, 200, 500, 2,000 leva
Electricity:	220V, 50Hz, AC

Planning your Trip

Visa requirements: except for nationals of the USA staying less than a month; nationals of Austria, Czech Republic, Poland, Hungary, former Yugoslavia, South Korea and Tunis; nationals of EU countries, Canada, Australia, New Zealand, South Africa or Singapore, travelling on package holidays with more than 3-day stay in Bulgaria. (See also p.6.) **57**

Vaccination requirements: None. (See also p.7.)

Import allowances (see also p.7):

Cigarettes		Cigars	Tobacco	Spirits		Wine	
200	or	250g of other tobacco products.		1l	and	2l	

Perfume: 100g; *Gifts*: Up to a max. amount of $US 300.

Currency restrictions: Up to 10,000 leva can be imported into the country. There is no restriction on the amount of foreign currency that may be imported, provided it is declared upon arrival. The same amount, minus what has been changed into leva during your stay, may subsequently be exported. (See also p.7.)

Climate: Bulgaria's climate is in general temperate continental, with hot summers and cold winters, though much milder conditions predominate on the coast and in sheltered valleys. Winter in Sofia can be harsh, with temperatures well below freezing. In summer 20-25°C (68-77°F) is normal, with peaks of up to 32-33°C (c. 90°F).

Clothing: Light clothing is adequate in the summer. Warm clothes including a heavy overcoat and winter shoes are necessary in most parts of the country in winter. Conservative dress such as a dark suit is usual in business circles.

Hotels: You are advised to make reservations well in advance. Most of the best hotels are in Sofia or the resorts around the Black Sea. Reservations may be made through the Bulgarian National Tourist Organisation, 1, Boulevard Vitosa; tel. 88 37 39, telex 22583, or through branches of the Bulgarian National Tourist Office abroad.

Bulgarian tourist ofices abroad: Amsterdam, Athens, Belgrade, Berlin, Bratislava, Brussels, Bucharest, Budapest, Copenhagen, Frankfurt, Helsinki, Istanbul, Kiev, London, Madrid, Moscow, New York, Odessa, Paris, Prague, Rome, Stockholm, Vienna, **58** Warsaw, Zurich.

Business Briefing

Economic Background

Main industries: Power/electricity, chemicals, coal, machinery, metals, building materials, printing, paper, textiles, leather, goods, oil.

Main agricultural products: Cereals, sugar beet, tobacco, sunflowers (for seed), grapes, apples, tomatoes.

Main imports: Industrial goods, fuel, livestock, machinery, minerals, metals, pharmaceutical products.

Main exports: Dairy products, tobacco, machinery, wine, vegetables, chemicals, rose oil.

Principal trading partners: CIS, Germany, Czech Republic, Slovakia, Poland, Middle East.

GNP: $22 billion; per capita: $2.455.

Inflation rate: 120% (1994).

Trade fairs: The major exhibition is the international trade fair in Plovdiv, split up into spring fair for consumer goods and an autumn exhibition of technical products (September), including various specialized exhibitions.

Selected background reading: *Area Handbook for Bulgaria* (US-Government Printing Office), *Bulgarian Foreign Trade* and *Economic News from Bulgaria* (both monthly, published by the Bulgarian Chamber of Commerce), *The Insider* (monthly, published by Insider Agency, Sofia), *Doing Business with Bulgaria* (Kogan Page Publishers), *Bulgarian Business News* (168 Hours Press Group), *Bulgarian Economic Review* (published daily by Pari) . Sofia Press produces a series of booklets on various aspects of the national economy.

Bulgarian chambers of commerce abroad: Apply to the commercial departments of Bulgarian embassies or consulates.

On the Spot

Office hours: 8.30 or 9am to noon or 12.30pm, and 1 or 1.30 to 5.30 or 6pm, Monday-Friday.

Public holidays:

Jan 1	New Year's Day	24 Dec	Christmas Eve
March 3	National Day	25 Dec	Christmas Day
May 1, 2	Labour Days	**Movable dates:**	
May 24	SS Cyril and Methodius; Day of Bulgarian culture	Easter Sunday (usually one week later than in western Europe)	

Banks and currency exchange: Banking hours are generally 8am-12.30pm and 1-3pm Monday-Friday, and until 11am on Saturdays. Currency may only be changed at official exchange offices at the airport, banks, major hotels, national tourist offices and department stores. Outside banking hours, money can also be changed at a limited number of other points. Some of the main banks are the Bulgarian National Bank, Balkan Bank, Bulgarian Post Bank and First Private Bank. Many other new banks are being established.

Credit Cards and traveller's cheques: Internationally recognized credit cards and traveller's cheques are accepted at major hotels, restaurants and currency-exchange offices and all tourist outlets.

Post and telecommunications: In Sofia, the main post office at 6, ul Gourko has a telegram counter operating 24 hours a day. The telephone and fax headquarters at 4, ul Gourko are open round the clock. Major hotels will handle long-distance calls (expect some waiting time), cables and telex communications.

Some useful numbers:

Operator (domestic)	121	Ambulance	150
Operator (international)	123	Fire	160
Telegrams	140	Police	166

Embassies and consulates: Hotels maintain lists of diplomatic representations.

Medical care and health: Medical services are well organized throughout the country. Free emergency attention is provided for all foreigners, and in non-vital cases treatment is reasonably priced at set prices. Though not many doctors are likely to speak your language, basic communication will be assured. Take along with you a supply of any pharmaceutical products you need on a regular basis. A clinic for foreigners is situated at 1, ul Evgeni Pavlovski, Sofia; tel. 75361.

Services: Your Bulgarian business contacts should be able to recommend secretarial, language or photocopying assistance. Interpreters can be hired through tourist offices at reasonable charges, and there are numerous translation agencies. Try Komos; tel. 891 816, or Dialogue; tel. 89 00 61, both in Sofia.

Newspapers: Principal daily newspapers are *Duma*, *Demokratsiya*, *24 Hours*, *Trud* and *Dialog*. Some of the western dailies are on sale, but German newspapers are most common. *Sofia News* is published once a week in English, French, German, Spanish, Russian and Bulgarian and can be purchased at news-stands. *Business Club* is a trade magazine published in English and Bulgarian.

Transport

Air – international: A limited number of flights link Sofia directly with a handful of European cities; same-day connections are available from most main centres.

Air – domestic: Balkan Airlines runs frequent services to Russe, Sofia and Varna; Balkan Holidays run charted flights to Bourgas and Varna. Some services may be suspended, or less frequent, in winter.

Rail: Frequent daily services operate between major towns. Seating is comfortable: dining facilities are provided. Express trains require advance seat reservations (through Balkantourist agencies).

Local public transport: City transport is highly organised. Tickets must be purchased in advance at any tobacconist's or news-stand.

Taxis: Taxis are available in the main cities, and can be rented by the day.

Car rental: Cars can be rented through major international agencies at Sofia airport and from tourist agencies, but if possible it is wise to make your reservations early.

Driving in Bulgaria: An international driving licence is required. Speed limits: 50 or 60kph (31 or 37mph) in towns, 120kph (75mph) on motorways (expressways) and 80kph (50mph) on other roads. Use of seat belts is compulsory, and a red reflector warning triangle must be carried. Blood alcohol limit is a strictly enforced zero. Most roads are quite well maintained and clearly signposted. A particularly good new motorway (expressway) system runs between Sofia, Plovdiv, Bourgas, Varna and back to Sofia, forming part of a European route.

Service stations are located only at considerable intervals (about every 30-50km/20-30 miles), and are generally open 6am-9pm; some operate round the clock, mainly those on main roads or near Sofia. Fuel (petrol/gas) is in very short supply, so a long wait can sometimes be expected. Fuel available is normal (86 octane), medium (93 octane), super (96 octane) and diesel.

Breakdown patrol vehicles on principal highways can undertake many repairs on the spot; tel. 146. In the case of an accident you can call the traffic police on 166.

Some distances from Sofia: Plovdiv 155km (96 miles), Bourgas 400km (250 miles), Varna 500km (310 miles).

Social customs: Remember in this country a nod means 'no' and a shake of the head means 'yes'.

Hints for business: Foreign-trade organisations prefer advance appointments. There is usually quite an exchange of hospitality with contacts in Bulgarian companies. The country is opening up rapidly to trade from the west, and companies dealing with foreign trade and tourism are proliferating rapidly.

62 **Foreign chambers of commerce in Bulgaria**: German, Swiss.

Crime and theft: Avoid any illegal currency transactions which could still lead to serious trouble. Normal precautions are in order to guard against petty theft.

After Hours

Food and drink: All hotels serve both local and international dishes. Typical Bulgarian food can be found in *mehana* restaurants. Some popular national dishes are *tarator* (chilled cucumber-and-yoghurt soup), *ovneshko vareno* (boiled mutton), *moussaka* (potato and minced pork and veal casserole), *sarmi* (cabbage or grape leaves stuffed with rice and minced pork and veal). Salads are popular and grilled meats are also great favourites. Examples include *kebap* (skewered and grilled meat served with a spicy sauce), *kebapcheta* (spiced, minced pork and veal), *kewfteta* (spiced, minced pork and veal with raw onions), *shishcheta* (spit-roasted pork), *parjola* (grilled pork tenderloin) and *meshana skara* (mixed grill).

Bulgarian wines can be very good and are rapidly aquiring an international reputation. Try Misket (white) or Kaberné (red). The local plum brandy, *slivova*, aniseed-flavoured *mastika* and vodka are quite strong. Besides local beer, Czech, German and Polish brands are available.

Mealtimes: lunch noon-2.30pm, dinner 7 to 10 or 11pm.

Entertainment: Sofia has a dozen theatres, an opera house, music hall and concert halls. A few nightclubs can be found. Most restaurants have their own dance bands. Foreign films are shown in their original language.

Taxes, service charges and tipping: Hotel and restaurant bills are all inclusive. While tipping has been officially discouraged in the past, gratuities are nevertheless welcomed; they should be given discreetly.

Sports and recreation: Tennis, swimming and bowling facilities exist in main centres and resorts, and skiing is popular in the Vitosha mountains, just a few miles outside Sofia.

Soccer, boxing, basketball, volleyball, wrestling and cycling are popular spectator sports.

TV and radio: Aside from the regular Bulgarian scheduling, in summer Varna radio and TV and (between 10.30 and 11.15am) Sofia TV put out short tourist-oriented programmes in English, French, German and Russian.

What to buy: Good buys include embroidered dresses, tablecloths, icons, woodcarvings, wrought iron and copper, leather goods, rose essence, ceramics and costumed dolls.

Shopping hours: generally 9am-1pm and 2-7pm Monday-Saturday.

Cities and Sights

SOFIA (*Telephone area code 02*)

Airport: Vrajdebna (11km/7 miles from city centre), international; duty-free shops offer a wide choice of goods. Special bus service every few minutes to town terminal.

Tourist information office: 1, Boulevard Vitosa, Sofia; tel. 88 37 39. 3 Stara Planina Street; tel.80 91 81, fax 88 30 72.

Chamber of commerce and industry: 42 Parchevich Street, Sofia; tel. 80 08 21, fax 87 11 24. Information Services also provide information on companies in Bulgaria; 2 Panayot Volov Street, 1504 Sofia; tel. 44 22 35, ext. 217

Sightseeing: Old town, Serdica-Sredetz Fortress, St Sofia Basilica, St Petka Samarcjiiska medieval church, Alexander Nevsky cathedral, St Nicholas Russian Church, National Art Gallery, Ethnography museum.

Excursions: Plovdiv (old town), Russe (Renaissance city centre), Kazanlak valley, Black Sea coast.

Some Useful Expressions in Bulgarian

good morning/afternoon	**dobro outro/dobur den**
good evening/night	**dobur vecher/leka nosht**
good-bye	**dovizhdane**
yes/no	**da/ne**
please/thank you	**molya/blagodarya**
excuse me	**izvinyavaïte**
you're welcome	**molya**
where/when/how	**kude/koga/kak**
how long/how far	**kolko vreme/kolko daleche**
yesterday/today/tomorrow	**vchera/dnes/outre**
day/week/month/year	**den/sedmitza/mesetz/godina**
left/right	**lyavo/dyasno**
up/down	**gore/dolou**
good/bad	**dobre/losho**
big/small	**golyam/maluk**
cheap/expensive	**eftino/skupo**
hot/cold	**goreshto/stoudeno**
old/new	**star/nov**
open/closed	**otvoreno/zatvoreno**
early/late	**rano/kusno**
easy/difficult	**lesno/troudno**
Does anyone here speak English/French/German?	**Govori li nyakoi angliiski/frenski/nemski?**
What does this mean?	**Kakvo znachi tova?**
I don't understand.	**Ne razbiram.**
Do you take credit cards/traveller's cheques?	**Vzemate li kreditni karti/travel check?**
Waiter!/Waitress!	**Kelner!/Kelnerka!**
Where are the toilets?	**Kade e toaletnata?**
I'd like ...	**Az bih iskal ...**
How much is that?	**Kolko strouva tova?**
Help me please.	**Pomognete mi, molya.**

Czech Republic and Slovakia

CZECH REPUBLIC

Type of government:	Democratic republic, emerging after four decades of communism
Population:	10.3 million
Area:	78,902sq km (30,464sq miles)
Capital:	Prague (*Praha*, 1.2m)
Other major cities:	Brno (387,986)
	Ostrava (327,553)
	Pilsen (*Plzeň*, 173,129)
Languages:	Czech
Religion:	Catholic (75%) with a significant Protestant minority
Time zone:	GMT+1, EST+6; DST (Apr-Sep)
Currency:	Czech crown (koruna, abbr. Kčs) = 100 halers
	Coins: 10, 20, 50 halers; 1, 2, 5, 10, 20, 50Kčs
	Bills: 10, 20, 50, 100, 500, 1,000, 2,000, 5,000Kčs
Electricity:	220V, 50Hz, AC

SLOVAKIA

Type of government:	Liberal democratic republic
Population:	5.3 million
Area:	48,995sq km (18,917sq miles)
Capital:	Bratislava (443,000)
Other major cities:	Košice (234,840)
	Zilina (95,000)
Languages:	Slovak
Religion:	Catholic (75%) with a Protestant minority
Time zone:	GMT+1, EST+6; DST (Apr-Sep)
Currency:	Slovak crown (koruna, abbr. Sk) = 100 halers
	Coins: 10, 20, 50 halers; 1, 2, 5, 10, 20, 50Sk
	Bills: 10, 20, 50, 100, 500, 1,000Sk
Electricity:	220V, 50Hz, AC

Planning your Trip

Visa requirements: For nationals of Australia, Canada, New Zealand, and Turkey. (See also p.6.) Most other nationals need only a full passport, valid for at least 8 months, but are limited to stays of either 30 days or three months. German nationals need only an ID card for entry to Slovakia.

Vaccination requirements: None. (See also p.7.)

Import allowances (see also p.7):

Cigarettes		Cigars		Tobacco	Spirits		Wine
200	or	50	or	250g	1l	and	2l

Perfume: 500ml; *Toilet water*: 2,550ml; *Gifts*: Up to a max. amount of 3,000kčs/Sk.

Upon arrival, it's advisable to present a list of all personal articles of value (portable computer, camera etc.) to the customs official, who will confirm that these items have been imported for personal use.

Currency restrictions: Czech and Slovak currency may not be brought into or taken out of the country. There is no limit on foreign currencies. (See also p.8.)

Climate: Continental climate, quite hot summers, often very cold winters. Rain throughout the year. In winter, city streets are rapidly cleared of snow.

Some average temperatures in Prague and Bratislava:

Prague	Jan	Apr	July	Oct
	-1°C (30°F)	9°C (48°F)	19°C (66°F)	9°C (48°F)
Bratislava	Jan	Apr	July	Oct
	-3°C (28°F)	13°C (55°F)	21°C (69°F)	10°C (50°F)

Clothing: Light clothing, with something warmer for cool days, is adequate in summer; a warm overcoat and heavy shoes are needed in winter. Rainwear will come in handy throughout the year. Colour-coordinated attire is quite frequent in business circles, though a conservative suit is called for on formal occasions and in the evening.

Hotels: In view of the shortage of hotel rooms, reservations should be made well in advance. Be sure you have a confirmation before your departure. Bills must be settled in hard currency.

Czech and Slovak tourist offices abroad: Amsterdam, Belgrade, Berlin, Brussels, Bucharest, Budapest, Frankfurt, London, Moscow, New York, Paris, Rome, Sofia, Stockholm, Vienna, Warsaw, Zurich.

Business Briefing

Economic Background

Main industries: Coal, iron, steel, glass, porcelain, pottery, paper, cellulose, textiles, shoes.

Main agricultural products: Sugar beet, sweet corn, barley, wheat, hops, rye, oats, fruit, potatoes, vegetables, meat and dairy products.

Main imports: Raw materials, manufactured goods, foodstuffs, machinery, oil.

Main exports: Machinery, iron, steel, textiles and garments, motor vehicles, hops, malt, shoes, chemicals, glass, porcelain, nuclear-power equipment, sugar, beer, sugar-processing factories, breweries.

Principal trading partners: CIS, Germany, Poland, Hungary.

Inflation rate: Slovakia 8.7%, Czech Republic 12.5% (1994)

Trade fairs: Principal international fairs are devoted to consumer goods. Other themes: Incheba (chemical products), Bratislava, June; engineering, Brno, September.

Czech and Slovak chambers of commerce abroad: Amman, Athens, Belgrade, Berlin, Brussels, Bucharest, Budapest, Cologne, The Hague, Helsinki, Istanbul, London, Madrid, Milan, Moscow, Paris, Sofia, Stockholm, Teheran, Tokyo, Vienna, Warsaw, Zurich.

On the Spot

Office hours: Variable between 7.30am and 5pm Monday-Friday.

Public holidays:

Jan 1	New Year's Day	Sep 1	Constitution Day [2]
Jan 6	Epiphany[2]	Oct 28	Republic Day [1]
May 1	May Day	Dec 24	Christmas Eve
May 8	Victory over Fascism [1]	Dec 25	Christmas Day
July 5	St Cyril and	Dec 26	Boxing Day
	St Methodius	**Movable dates:** Easter Monday	
July 6	Jan Hus Day [1]	(1) Czech Republic only	
Aug 29	National Uprising	(2) Slovakia only	

Banks and currency exchange: Banking hours are 8am-noon and 1-5pm Monday-Friday.

Foreign currency and traveller's cheques can be changed at Čedok branches, and hotel reception desks also have currency exchange services open on Sundays and holidays. Principal banks are: Česká národní banka, Česká banka, Československá Obchodni Banka, Živnostenská Banka Všeobecná úverová banka.

Credit cards and traveller's cheques: The major internationally recognized credit cards, as well as major traveller's cheques, are widely accepted in tourist-oriented establishments.

Post and telecommunications: Postal and telecommunications facilities are generally reliable.

Telephone and fax services are available at major hotels and at the main post offices listed below. Long-distance calls are best placed from the hotel. Direct dialling exists to most European countries.

The main post offices in Prague (Jindřišská 14, Prague 1) and Bratislava (Nám SNP 35) are open 24 hours a day. Brno's central post office (Poštovská 3/5) offers round-the-clock service during spring and autumn fairs.

Some useful numbers:

Ambulance	155	Fire	150
Police	158	Car breakdown	154
Telegrams	127	Directory Inquiries (int)	0149

Principal area codes: Bratislava 7, Brno 5, Ostrava 69, Pilsen 19, Prague 2.

Embassies and consulates: Embassies and consulates are listed in the telephone directory under *Zastupitelské úřady*.

Medical care and health: Medical care is very good. Emergency treatment for foreign visitors is provided free; other treatment must be paid for where no reciprocal agreements exist with the traveller's country. Medical fees are moderate. A 24-hour clinic for foreigners is located at Roentgenova 2, Prague 5, where English and German are spoken. Treatment here must be paid for.

Drugs other than the simplest analgesics require a doctor's prescription. Every town has pharmacies with night service. Tap water is safe to drink.

Services: Pražská informační služba, located at Letenská 2, Prague 1; tel. 53 98 71/53 98 73, specializes in providing interpreters and guides. In Bratislava contact BIS, Nedbalova ul 12, 814 28 Bratislava; tel. 5334059, fax 5332708. For photocopying facilities, see the listings under *Fotografie* in the telephone directory; service may be slow.

Newspapers: Principal Czech Republic dailies are *Lidove noviny*, *Mlada fronta Dnes*, *Ceský deník*. In Slovakia: *Národná obroda*, *Práca Smena and Pravda*. Most foreign newspapers (eg *Le Monde* and the *Financial Times*) are available at hotels.

Transport

Air – international: Prague is the major gateway to the Czech Republic and Slovakia. Some direct international flights operate to Košice, while Austria's Vienna airport is only 50km from Bratislava.

Air – domestic: ČSA and Tatra Air operate regular flights all year between Prague, Bratislava and a number of towns. Air-taxi service is available but reservations should be made a week in advance.

Rail: An extensive rail network with first- and second-class service covers both countries. Trains tend to be crowded, and it's advisable to book in advance. Sleeping accommodation can be booked through Čedok or SATUR or at a railway station. Long-distance expresses have dining-cars. Trains are comfortable but not always punctual.

Long-distance buses: An extensive long-distance bus system covers both countries, with three or four runs daily between main towns. Suburban services are well developed. Vehicles are comfortable and run on time. Tickets may be bought at the terminus or directly from the driver.

Local public transport: All trams and buses have automatic ticket punchers which means tickets must be bought in advance, either at hotel desks or any tobacconist's, or from coin-operated machines at bus or tram stops. Prague has three underground (subway) lines.

Taxis: Have your hotel reception desk call a cab. Meters start from the moment the call is received. Taxis can be scarce after 9pm.

Car rental: Car-rental agencies have booths at airports and major cities. Insurance extras are added to the rental rates. Chauffeur-driven cars can be rented in both countries through Pragocar or Čedok.

Driving in the Czech Republic and Slovakia: Motorists must have a valid driving licence. Roads, though often rather narrow, are well maintained and mostly asphalted. A motorway (expressway) connects Prague, Brno and Bratislava. Speed limits are 110kph (68mph) on motorways and 90kph (56mph) on main roads outside towns. A 60kph (37mph) speed limit is in force in built-up areas except between 11pm and 5am. The alcohol limit is a strictly enforced zero; fines are high for drinking and driving or for speeding. Fuel available is special (90 octane), super (96 octane), lead-free and diesel.

Cars parked in a no-parking zone may be towed away. Seat belts must be worn outside towns, and a red reflector warning triangle must be carried. Foreigners bringing their own cars to the republics are advised to contact Autoturist Road Service which operates throughout both countries and will provide a list of its patrol points; any service station can also direct you to the nearest patrol point. Motorists hiring a car will receive all information and emergency phone numbers from the car rental agency. Heavy commercial traffic on weekdays slows down motoring on principal arteries. In the case of an accident call 154 for assistance.

Some distances to main towns from Prague: Pilsen 90km (56 miles), Brno 200km (125 miles), Bratislava 330km (205 miles), Košice 680km (425 miles).

Social customs: Handshakes all around upon arrival and departure mark any meeting, business or private. If you're invited into a colleague's home, a gift of flowers or a bottle of good wine will be appreciated. A certain amount of central European charm tends to mark social occasions.

Hints for business: Punctuality is appreciated, and prior appointments are essential (but avoid Friday afternoons when the pace of work slows). Foreign visitors are usually accorded a warm welcome, and discussions are likely to take place in a relaxed atmosphere.

Access for foreign trade has opened up since the velvet revolution, and there is no longer any requirement to go through the state foreign-trade bodies. Negotiations may be long and tedious, but once a firm business relationship has been established it's likely to endure. Women play an increasing role in business life in both the Czech Republic and Slovakia. Always address letters to the firm, as your business contact is likely to change. Business cards are appreciated. Negotiations are often conducted over drinks and coffee. Toasts are frequently raised and should be returned. Business luncheons or dinners are customary. Avoid the end of July or August for business visits as key officials are likely to be on holiday.

Foreign chambers of commerce in the Czech Republic and Slovakia: Austrian, Belgian, British, Bulgarian, Dutch, French, German, Greek, Hungarian, Iranian, Italian, Japanese, Jordanian, Moroccan, Polish, Romanian, Russian, Swedish, Swiss, Turkish.

Crime and theft: Changing money on the black market continues to be an offence in both the Czech and Slovak republics. Otherwise, normal precautions apply. Remove any valuables from parked cars.

After Hours

Food and drink: Popular local dishes in the Czech Republic include *vepřová* (roast pork) or *husa* (goose) with *zelí* (sauerkraut). In Slovakia food is based on Austro-Hungarian dishes and the national dish is *bryndzove halusky* (potato pasta with ewe cheese and pieces of fried bacon). Pork, roast mutton and goose are popular. Dumplings are the usual accompaniment in both countries.

Wines: imported Bulgarian, French or Hungarian wines are common, as are domestic wines from Czech regions (Ludmila – both red and white), Moravia (Vavřinecké, Frankovka, Rulandské – red; Veltlinské zelené, Vlašský Ryzling, Burgundské – white) or Slovakia (Košický poklad, Nitrianská perla, Bratislavské Hrozno, Rynsky – **73** white; Kláštorné, Frankovka – red). Wine cellars serve from the cask. Both republics are noted for their fine beers, both light and dark. Pilsner Urquell, Budweiser and Staropramen – all light beers – are particularly good. Those who prefer a dark brew will enjoy Braník. Go for a drink at the beer halls of U Fleků or Sv. Tomáš, both former monasteries.

Mealtimes: lunch noon-2.30pm, dinner 6.30-10pm.

Entertainment: Plays, opera and ballet are staged in major cities. The Prague Spring Music Festival in May offers a wide programme of classical music. In summer, concerts are held daily in Prague's parks. In Bratislava the Slovak National Theatre puts on regular performances of ballet and opera. The main cities have nightclubs and discos, and hotels tend to have their own entertainment.

Taxes, service charges and tipping: Service charges are generally included in hotel and restaurant bills. Tips are appreciated. Tipping recommendations: waiters 10%; taxi drivers 10%; hotel porters 5 crowns per piece; hairdressers 10%.

Sports and recreation: Skiing, skating, soccer, volleyball and tennis are popular, as are hunting, fishing, mountain hiking and climbing (particularly in Tatra Mountains). Golf is played mainly near Prague and in Karlovy Vary (Karlsbad) and Mariánské Lázné (Marienbad).

Soccer is by far the most popular spectator sport, but skiing, skating, volleyball and tennis competitions are held in season.

TV and radio: Radio and TV programmes are in Czech in the Czech Republic and in Slovak in Slovakia. In Bratislava and southern Moravia, Austrian television can be received. On the radio, tourist information is broadcast daily in summer in English, French and German.

What to buy: Crystalware, china, porcelain, costume jewellery, antiques and old books can be bought at Tuzex shops. In Prague, UVA and Úluv are good for handicrafts; Bijoux de Bohême for jewellery; České Sklo a Keramika for glass and ceramics; and Moser for crystalware. Department stores in large towns have a wide choice of goods.

Hours: Monday-Friday 8.30am-6pm; Saturdays until 2pm. Food **74** shops open 6am-6pm, Saturdays 6-11am.

Cities and Sights

PRAGUE (*Telephone area code 2*)
Airport: Ruzyně (17km/11 miles from city centre), international; duty-free shop. Airport bus service, also city bus.

Tourist information office: Čedok, Na Příkopě 18, Prague 1; tel. 241 971 11. Czech Tourist Authority, Staroměstké nám. 6; tel. 24 89 71 11

Czech chamber of commerce: Argentinská 38, Prague 7; tel. 8736.

Sightseeing: Hradčany castle, National Museum, Týn Church, St Mikuláš Church, Dvořák Museum, Smetana Museum, town hall.

Excursions: Castle Karlštejn, Slapy Dam, Mělník.

BRATISLAVA (*Telephone area code 7*)
Airport: Ivanka (11km/7 miles from city centre), international; duty-free shop. Airport bus service, also city bus.

Tourist information office: Bratislava; tel. 33 40 59.

Chamber of commerce: Gorkého 9: tel. 31 64 02, fax 33 07 54.

Sightseeing: Primate's Palace, the Devín Castle, Michael's Gate, old town hall, cathedral, Slavín, Slovakian National Museum, Slovakian National Gallery.

Excursions: Modra, Červený Kameň (castle), Trnava, Piešťany (spa), Trenčin (castle).

BRNO (*Telephone area code 5*)
Airport: Turany (7km/4 miles from city centre), mainly domestic; international flights only during fairs. Airport bus service.

Tourist information office: Čedok, Nádražni 10/12; tel. 42 21 20 11.

Sightseeing: Špilberk Castle and Museum, Capucin Monastery, Dietrichstein Palace, town hall.

Excursions: Slavkov (Austerlitz), Telč, Brno Dam.

Some Useful Expressions in Czech

Although Slovak and Czech are two distinct languages they share many basic words and expressions. The Czech phrases supplied below will also be understood in Slovak speaking areas.

good morning/afternoon	**dobré ráno/dobré odpoledne**
good evening/night	**dobrý večer/dobrou noc**
good-bye	**na shledanou**
yes/no	**ano/ne**
please/thank you	**prosím/děkuji**
excuse me	**promiňte**
you're welcome	**rádo se stalo**
where/when/how	**kde/kdy/jak**
how long/how far	**jak dlouho/jak daleko**
yesterday/today/tomorrow	**včera/dnes/zítra**
day/week/month/year	**den/týden/měsíc/rok**
left/right	**vlevo/vpravo**
up/down	**nahoře/dole**
good/bad	**dobrý/špatný**
big/small	**velký/malý**
early/late	**brzy/pozdě**
easy/difficult	**snadný/obtížný**
Does anyone here speak English/French/ German?	**Mluví zde někdo anglicky/francouzsky/ německy?**
What does this mean?	**Co to znamená?**
I don't understand.	**Nerozumím.**
Do you take credit cards/ traveller's cheques?	**Přijímáte úvěrové legitimace/cestovní šeky?**
Waiter!/Waitress!	**Pane vrchní!/Paní vrchní!**
Where are the toilets?	**Kde jsou toalety?**
I'd like…	**Rád bych…**
How much is that?	**Kolik to stojí?**
Help me please.	**Pomozte mi, prosím.**

Denmark

Type of government:	Constitutional monarchy, multi-party centralized
Member of:	EU, GATT, IBRD, IDA, IFC, IMF, OECD
Population:	5.2 million
Area:	43,075sq km (16,631sq miles)
Capital:	Copenhagen (*København*, 478,000/GUA 1.4m)
Other major cities:	Aarhus (*Ørhus*, 261,000) Odense (176,000) Aalborg (155,000)
Language:	Danish; English and German widely spoken in business circles; occasionally French.
Religion:	Predominantly Protestant
Time zone:	GMT+1, EST+6; DST (Apr-Sep)
Currency:	Danish krone, abbr. kr = 100 øre Coins: 25, 50 øre; kr 1, 2, 5, 10, 20 Notes: kr50, 100, 500, 1,000
Electricity:	220V, 50Hz, AC

Planning your Trip

Visa requirements: For nationals of Turkey and South Africa. (See also p.6.)

Vaccination requirements: None. (See also p.7.)

Import allowances (see also p.7):

	Cigarettes		Cigars		Tobacco	Spirits		Wine
1)	200	or	50	or	250g	1l	and	2l
2)	(800)	or	(200)	or	(1kg)	(10l)	and	(90l)

1) Passengers from countries outside Europe, or duty-free goods bought in EU countries by European residents.
2) Non-duty-free goods bought within the EU.

There are no official restrictions on goods bought non-duty-free within the EU, provided they are for personal use only. The above figures are guidelines to the quantities customs officials will generally find acceptable, so if you are carrying larger quantities you should be prepared to provide proof that the goods are for your personal use.

Perfume: 1) 50g; *Toilet water*: 1) 250ml; *Gifts*: 1) kr350 max. value

Currency restrictions: Any amount of Danish or foreign currencies may be brought into or taken out of the country by non-residents. However, any amount in local currency in excess of kr50,000 can only be exported if it can be proved that these were imported or obtained by conversion of foreign currencies imported.

Climate: The Danish coastal climate is temperate, usually damp and windy. No locality is further than 53km (32 miles) from the sea. Mean temperatures are around 0°C (32°F) in winter and 16-18°C (61-65°F) in mid-summer, with very short days in winter and long days in summer. Snowfall is seldom heavy, and city streets are usually clear (though often wet).

Clothing: A light raincoat is useful between May and October, and a heavy coat the rest of the year. Business dress is conservative, and a dark suit is appropriate for anything other than a very informal dinner.

Hotels: Denmark does not practise a star system of rating, but tourist office hotel lists give an indication of various facilities.

During major trade fairs and conventions, rooms can be most difficult to obtain in Copenhagen. Book through a travel agent or airline in advance. The Accommodation Bureau ('Kiosk P') at the Central Railway Station is open 9am-midnight daily in summer.

Danish tourist offices abroad: Brussels, The Hague, Hamburg, Helsinki, London, Melbourne, Milan, New York, Oslo, Paris, Stockholm, Tokyo, Toronto, Vienna, Zurich.

Business Briefing

Economic Background

Main industries: Clothing, textiles, food processing, iron-ore mining (Greenland), iron and steel products, chemicals, pharmaceuticals, wood and paper machinery, beverages, leather, tourism.

Main agricultural and fishery products: Wheat, barley, oats, rye, potatoes, sugar beet, tobacco, fishing.

Main imports: Minerals, oil, iron, steel, machinery, vehicles.

Main exports: Machinery, meat, dairy produce, furniture, chemicals, ships.

Principal trading partners: Sweden, Germany, UK, Belgium, Finland, Japan, US, Norway.

GNP: $94.8 billion; per capita: $18,470.

Inflation rate: 2.0% (1994).

Trade fairs: Annual trade exhibitions held in Copenhagen include the Future Fashions Scandinavia (February/March and August/September), the Building Trade Fair every two years (September) and the Scandinavian Furniture Fair (April and May). An important trade fair held in Herning Hallen, Jutland, is the International Furniture Fair (August).

Selected background reading. *The Scandinavian Economies* (Barnes) is a monthly business-economic report on Scandinavia; *The Economist* Intelligence Unit Ltd publishes a quarterly report in English on Denmark; *Doing Business in Denmark* (Midsnell).

Literature is also available from the Federation of Danish Industries, the Agricultural Council and the Ministry of Foreign Affairs, while Kjøbenhavns Handelsbank issues an English-language quarterly review, *Danish Economy in Brief*.

On the Spot

Office hours: From 8, 8.30 or 9am to 4, 4.30 or 5pm, Monday-Friday. Private industry usually keeps the earlier hours, while government offices open later. Some offices advance their working hours in summer.

Public holidays:

Jan 1	New Year's Day	Dec 25	Christmas Day
June 5	Constitution Day	Dec 26	Boxing Day (afternoon)
Dec 24	Christmas Eve	Dec 31	New Year's Eve
Movable days:			
Maundy Thursday		Good Friday	
Easter Monday		General Prayer Day	
Ascension Day		(4th Friday after Easter)	
Whit Monday			

Banks and currency exchange: Copenhagen's banks are open 9.30am-4pm Monday-Friday, except on Thursday when they stay open until 6pm. In the provinces, hours vary.

Outside banking hours, exchange bureaux in Copenhagen operate at the Central Railway Station 7am-9pm daily; at Den Danske Bank branch on Østergade (Strøget) 9am-5.30pm Monday-Wednesday, 9am-6pm Thursday and Friday, and 9am-2pm Saturday; and (from May 1 to mid-September) at the entrance to Tivoli (H.C. Andersens Boulevard 22) noon-11pm daily.

Major banks: Den Danske Bank and Arbejdernes Landsbank A/S.

Credit cards and traveller's cheques: Both forms of payment are widely accepted.

Post and telecommunications: Postal and telecommunications services are excellent.

The main post office in Tietgensgade 37 (just behind Tivoli) is open 10am-7pm Monday-Friday, and 9am-1pm on Saturday. The Telecom Center at the Central Station is open 8am-10pm Monday-Friday, 9am-4pm on Saturdays and 10am-5pm Sundays and holidays. News-stands and souvenir stores also sell stamps.

Public telephone boxes take 1- or 5- krone coins for long-distance connections. Some telephone booths require the use of a card (a *Telet*), obtained from kiosks all over town.

Telegrams, faxes and telexes can be sent from the Telecom Center.

Some useful numbers:

Fire, police, ambulance	112	Operator assistance	140
Directory inquiries	118		

For long-distance calls within Denmark, there are no area codes, just dial the 8-digit number of the person you want to call.

Recorded reports on time, weather, news, etc. are only in Danish, and details are to be found, also in Danish, on page 1 of the blue tele-phone book (*Navnebog A-K*).

Embassies and consulates: Consult the telephone directory under *Ambassader og konsulater*.

Medical care and health: Medical services are excellent. In the event of serious illness, foreign patients will be treated or hospitalized without charge at any hospital. For less urgent cases an appointment can be made with a general practitioner.

Visitors from some EU countries (including the United Kingdom) and the rest of Scandinavia are covered by reciprocal agreements and payment won't be required if the necessary documents are produced (British nationals should obtain the appropriate forms and instructions from their Social Security offices). Most medical personnel speak good or passable English and/or German.

Medical and pharmaceutical supplies are readily available. However, Danish legislation requires a doctor's prescription for almost all drugs stronger than aspirin. In Copenhagen, the Steno Apotek (pharmacy) at Vesterbrogade 6C opposite the Central Station (tel. 33 14 82 66) is open 24 hours a day.

Emergency dental service (Oslo Plads 14, near Østerport Station) is open 8-9.30pm daily; on Saturdays, Sundays and public holidays from 10am to noon.

Tap water is safe to drink.

Services: Secretarial services can be obtained under *Vikarbureauer* in the yellow pages.

Interpreters and translators can be found under *Oversættelse* in the yellow pages. Small print shops, department stores and larger hotels have photocopying services.

Newspapers: Leading Copenhagen dailies are *Berlingske Tidende* and *Politiken*. Major British and Continental newspapers and US news weeklies are on sale at news-stands, shops and hotels throughout central Copenhagen, as is the *International Herald Tribune*, edited in Paris. A free English-language brochure, *Copenhagen This Week*, lists information for visitors.

Transport

Air – international: Copenhagen Airport, about 10km (6 miles) from the city centre, is one of Europe's busiest, a major gateway to Europe for overseas travellers. Connections within Europe are excellent.

Air – domestic: Danish cities and towns are very extensively covered by 11 airports, none of which is more than a 30-minute flight from Copenhagen. Because boat connections between the many islands of the Danish archipelago are necessarily somewhat time-consuming, local air travel is very popular among businessmen. Domestic flights can sometimes be included in overseas tickets at no extra charge. Air-taxi service is available, see *Luft trafik 11* in the yellow pages.

Keep in mind that if you have to travel 40km (25 miles) or so to a provincial airport a rental car may work out cheaper than a taxi, in the absence of a bus service.

Rail: Modern express trains (Lyntog) equipped with buffet bars and public phones serve the Jutland route, as do ordinary inter-city trains Most rail travel in Denmark requires taking a ferry, on which dining and/or cafeteria facilities are always provided. The Scanrail Pass permits unlimited rail travel in Denmark, Finland, Norway and Sweden, over a specified number of days. For Eurailpass, see p.10.

Waterways: Regular ferry services link most islands and the mainland. On summer weekends particularly, ferry space should be booked in advance. Telephone 33 14 88 80 (Copenhagen) for information and reservations.

Other ferries have good connections with English, Norwegian, Swedish and German ports. A hydrofoil makes the Copenhagen-Malmö (Sweden) run hourly and every 30 minutes during rush hours. Scandinavian Seaways passenger lines operate an overnight Copenhagen-Oslo (Norway) run (15 hours) and an Esbjerg–Harwich (England) passage (19 hours). Vessels are comfortable.

Local public transport: All major cities have excellent bus transport, and the Greater Copenhagen area has a rapid-transit train. On the bus, buy your ticket from the driver, and when using the rapid-transit train be sure your ticket has a time stamp on it or stamp it at the entrance to the platform.

Taxis: Cabs can be hailed in the street or ordered by phone. Most drivers speak English.

Car rental: International and local firms operate, some of which have desks at Copenhagen Airport. They are listed in the trade telephone directory under *Autoudlejning*.

Driving in Denmark: You should have a red warning triangle for use in case of breakdown, and a parking disk (*parkeringsskive*) which you can obtain free from police stations, garages, post offices and many banks. Seat belts are compulsory for front-seat passengers. Police require blood tests from all drivers involved in accidents in which personal injury is incurred. With more than 50mg/100ml blood alcohol level you face stiff fines, loss of your licence for a year and possible imprisonment.

The Danes are generally well-disciplined drivers. Speed limits are 110kph (70mph) on motorways (expressways), 80kph (50mph) on other roads and 50kph (31mph) in built-up areas. All vehicles must have dipped headlights switched on at all times, even in broad **83** daylight. Fuel (petrol/gas) available is normal (92 octane), super (96 and 98 octane), lead-free and diesel.

For mechanical or towing services, call Falck, the road assistance organization, on 33 14 22 22 in Copenhagen and ask for the number of the nearest Falck service station.

Some distances from Copenhagen: Aarhus 100km (62 miles) plus ferry Kalundborg-Aarhus, c. 3 hours; Esbjerg 170km (105 miles) plus ferry Korsør-Nyborg, c. 1½ hours.

Social customs: Should you receive an invitation to lunch or dinner at a private home, you should arrive within a quarter of an hour of the time specified. It's customary to offer flowers, chocolates, wine or liquor to the hostess. At the table, you shouldn't drink until the host has bid a welcome *skål*.

Hints for business: Punctuality is a must in Denmark, and should you be unable to keep an appointment, cancel or postpone it by phone. Most office workers take a half-hour break for lunch. Note that Danes regard their weekends with their families as sacred, and business not concluded on Friday will usually have to wait till the following Monday for resumption. Beware the potency of *akvavit*. Business travel should be avoided between mid-June and the beginning of August as well as at national holiday periods.

Crime and theft: Avoid walking alone late at night in the Christiania area and areas behind Copenhagen Central Railway Station.

After Hours

Food and drink: Lunch usually consists of two or three open sandwiches (*smørrebrød*) and a beer. A hot dinner is reserved for the evening. Denmark's outstanding culinary speciality is the cold buffet, which is generally very lavish and not so cheap. Fish is fresh and good; the variety of pickled herring is another national speciality.

The national drinks are beer and *akvavit*, the fiery local schnapps. The latter is served only with food and is potent. Scotch, vodka and gin are readily available but very expensive both in bars and retail shops. The same applies to good wine; house wine is usually acceptable and more reasonably priced.

Mealtimes: lunch noon-2pm, dinner 6-10pm.

Entertainment: Many cinemas in central Copenhagen show English-and French-language films with Danish subtitles. Opera and ballet are offered at the Royal Theatre during the season (September-May). Details of films, theatres, concerts, discotheques, night clubs and other entertainment can be found in *Copenhagen This Week*.

Taxes, service charges and tipping: VAT (in Danish, *moms*) is always included in the bill. Tipping is a non-existent problem, since basically you don't give tips. Only in a very few cases is there an exception to this rule as, for example, when you leave the odd krone tip for use of the facilities in toilets or if the taxi driver at the airport helps you with your luggage (kr5 per bag).

Sports and recreation: Visitors can find possibilities for practising most sports from archery to water-skiing in or around the capital, depending on the season.

Top spectator sport is soccer, with high-quality if mainly amateur matches played every weekend almost all the year round. Trotting, horse and cycle races also draw large crowds.

TV and radio: While most programming is in Danish, foreign TV shows produced in English, German or French are telecast in the original language.

On Radio 3, news is broadcast in English at 8.15am, Monday-Saturday.

What to buy: Particularly appreciated Danish products are glassware, household items, porcelain and silver jewellery. Two specialities in the jewellery line are Danish amber and Flora Danica (flowers and leaves dipped in silver and gold).

In some cases VAT is deducted if goods are shipped directly from the shop to a foreign address.

Shopping hours: Generally 9am to 5.30pm, Monday-Thursday, with late closing (7 or 8pm) on Fridays and early closing (noon or 2pm) on Saturdays, some stores close on Monday or Tuesday.

Cities and Sights

COPENHAGEN

Airport: Copenhagen Airport, 10km (6 miles) from the city centre, is Denmark's international airport. Usual amenities include duty-free shops. Airport buses run directly from the terminal building to the central railway station in Copenhagen, 30 minutes away. Others connect with the port of Dragør, south of the airport, for the ferry connection to Limhamn in southern Sweden, and with the downtown hydrofoil crossing to Malmö (Sweden).

Tourist information office: 1 Bernstorffsgade (next to Tivoli Gardens and opposite the railway station); tel. 33 11 13 25.

Chamber of commerce: Børsen (Stock Exchange), 1217 Copenhagen K; tel. 33 95 05 00, fax 33 32 52 16.

Federation of Danish Industries: H.C. Andersens Boulevard 18, 1596 Copenhagen V; tel. 33 77 33 77, fax 33 77 33 00.

Copenhagen Card: Similar to a plastic credit card, this discount tourist card offers unlimited travel on buses and trains in metropolitan Copenhagen, free entrance to many museums and sights and up to 50 per cent discount on ferry routes connecting Sealand with Sweden and on hydrofoils between Copenhagen and Malmö. The card is valid for one, two or three days and is on sale at travel agencies and main railway stations in Denmark and at certain Copenhagen hotels.

Sightseeing: Strøget (mall), Christiansborg, parliament, Børsen (old stock exchange), Amalienborg Palace, Little Mermaid (harbour at Langelinie), Rosenborg Castle, Nyhavn, Round Tower, Tivoli pleasure park (summer only).

Museums: Exhibitions in most of the palaces, David's Art Collection, Copenhagen City Museum and Kierkegaard Collection, Ny Carlsberg Glyptotek Museum, Royal Museum of Fine Arts, Thorvaldsen Museum.

Excursions: Castles tour of North Zealand, open-air folk museum at Sorgenfri, Roskilde.

Some Useful Expressions in Danish

good morning/afternoon	**godmorgen/goddag**
good evening/night	**godaften/godnat**
good-bye	**farvel**
yes/no	**ja/nej**
please/thank you	**vaer så venlig/tak**
excuse me	**undskyld**
you're welcome	**åh, jeg be'r**
where/when/how	**hvor/hvornår/hvordan**
how long/how far	**hvor laenge/hvor langt**
yesterday/today/tomorrow	**i går/i dag/i morgen**
day/week/month/year	**dag/uge/måned/år**
left/right	**venstre/højre**
up/down	**op/ned**
good/bad	**god/dårlig**
big/small	**stor/lille**
cheap/expensive	**billig/dyr**
hot/cold	**varm/kold**
old/new	**gammel/ny**
open/closed	**åben/lukket**
early/late	**tidlig/sen**
easy/difficult	**let/svaer**
Does anyone here speak English/French/German?	**Er der nogen her, der taler engelsk/fransk/tysk?**
What does this mean?	**Hvad betyder dette?**
I don't understand.	**Jeg forstår ikke.**
Do you take credit cards/ traveller's cheques?	**Tager De kreditkort/ rejsechecks?**
Waiter!/Waitress!	**Tjener!/Frøken!**
Where are the toilets?	**Hvor er toilettet?**
I'd like…	**Jeg vil gerne have…**
How much is that?	**Hvor meget koster det?**
Help me please.	**Vaer venlig at hjaelpe mig.**

Finland

Type of government:	Republic, multi-party centralized
Member of:	EU, GATT, IDA, IDB, IFC, IMF, OECD
Population:	5.1 million
Area:	337,009sq km (130,119sq miles)
Capital:	Helsinki (501,740/GUA 785,000)
Other major cities:	Tampere (175,200/GUA 240,000)
	Turku (160,320/GUA 240,000)
	Espoo (178,900)
	Vantaa (145,000)
	Oulu (95,000)
Language:	Finnish-speaking 93%, Swedish-speaking 6%. English is overwhelmingly the most commonly known foreign language, especially among the younger generation. Many older people speak German.
Religion:	Lutheran (88%); Orthodox (1%)
Time zone:	GMT+2, EST+7; DST (Apr-Sep)
Currency:	Finnish mark (markka, abbr. mk) = 100 penni
	Coins: 10, 20, 50 penni; 1, 5, 10mk
	Notes: 10, 50, 100, 500, 1,000mk
Electricity:	220V, 50Hz, AC

Planning your Trip

Visa requirements: For nationals of Turkey and South Africa. (See also p.6.)

Vaccination requirements: None. (See also p.7.)

Import allowances (see also p.7):

	Cigarettes		Cigars		Tobacco	Spirits		Wine
1)	200	or	50	or	250g	1l	and	2l
2)	300	or	75	or	400g	1.5l	and	3l
3)	(800)	or	(200)	or	(1kg)	(10l)	and	(90l)

1) Passengers from countries outside Europe.
2) Duty-free goods bought in EU countries by European residents.
3) Non-duty-free goods bought within the EU.

Currency restrictions: No limits on the import of local or foreign currencies. (See also p.7.)

Climate: Weather is sometimes surprisingly hot in the short summer and predictably cold in winter with temperatures in the north plunging to a frigid -20°C (-4°F). Most rain falls between September and December. Winter lasts from December to April. Average temperatures in Helsinki:

Jan	Apr	July	Oct
-3°C (27°F)	6°C (43°F)	22°C (72°F)	8°C (46°F)

Efforts are made to keep city streets open, but snow can impede traffic in early winter and spring. In coastal areas around Helsinki snow often turns to slush. Daylight time in Helsinki extends to 20 hours in summer, while in December and January there are only about six hours of sunlight. In the north the midnight sun shines June-July.

Clothing: In summer, light clothing, with something warm for the evenings, is adequate. Spring and autumn can be quite cold. A raincoat **89**

is always advisable. In winter, warm clothing, including a heavy over-coat, a cap or hat and possibly fur-lined boots, is essential. In business circles a conservative dark suit is customary for men, with similarly conservative dress for women.

Evening dress is required only for special social functions. Better restaurants often require a jacket and tie.

Hotels: Advance booking is necessary, particularly in Helsinki be-tween May and September. Bookings for Helsinki and surroundings can be handled by the Hotel Reservation Centre next to the railway station at Asema-aukio 3, tel. 17 11 33, fax 17 55 24. Open summer: Monday-Friday 9am-9pm, Saturdays 9am-7pm, Sundays noon-7pm; winter: Monday-Friday 9am-6pm, Saturdays and Sundays closed. For accommodation elsewhere contact Hotel Reservations in Fin-land, Nervanderinkatu 5D 40, Helsinki, tel. 49 91 55, fax 44 03 83. The Finnish Tourist Board publish details of hotels, available free.

Most Finnish hotels are modern and comfortable, and new luxury hotels and conference centres abound even in the countryside. Most hotels have a sauna.

To encourage visitors to come by car, the government sponsors a special discount programme offering books of *Finn Cheques*, valid from May 1 to September 31 in some 250 hotels throughout the coun-try. These cheques can only be purchased outside the country. Further information is available from Finnish Tourist Board offices and travel agencies for Scandanavia abroad.

Finnish tourist offices abroad: Amsterdam, Copenhagen, Frankfurt, Hamburg, London, Los Angeles, Madrid, Milan, New York, Oslo, Paris, Stockholm, Tallin, Tokyo, Zurich.

Town names: Since Finland has two official languages, Finnish and Swedish, many towns have two totally different names. The former capital of Turku, for example, is known to Swedish speakers as Åbo, Helsinki as Helsingfors. Other Finnish towns with Swedish names are Tampere/Tammerfors, Oulu/Uleåborg, Pori/Björneborg, Espoo/Esbo, Vantaa/Vanda, Lappeenranta/Villmanstrand and Hämeenlinna/Tavastehus.

Business Briefing

Economic Background

Main industries: Wood-processing, cement, cellulose, food, machinery, metals and engineering, chemicals, textiles and garments, mineral mining.

Main agricultural products: Barley, oats, wheat, rye, potatoes, sugar beet.

Main imports: Oil, fuels, minerals, vehicles, machinery, foodstuffs, consumer goods.

Main exports: Wood products, pulp, paper and timber, machinery and transport equipment (especially ships), engineering products, chemicals and garments.

Principal trading partners: Sweden, UK, CIS, Germany, USA, Belgium, France.

GNP: $92 billion; per capita: $18,600.

Inflation rate: 1.6% (1993).

Trade fairs: The main fairs in Helsinki cover a variety of fields, and include the International Boat Show (February), the Nordic Fashion Fair (January and August) and an Office Equipment Exhibition every two years (September). Agricultural fairs are held periodically in provincial towns.

Selected background reading: *Finland as a Trading Partner* (in English, French, German, Swedish) (Finnish Foreign Trade Association), *Finnish Paper and Timber Calendar* (Finnish Paper and Timber Publishing Co) (every 2 years), *Bank of Finland* (monthly bulletin), quarterly *Economic Review* (Kansallis-Osake-Pankki), annual *Economic Review* (Ministry of Finance), *Unitas,* Economic Review (quarterly) (Union Bank of Finland, Ltd) *Finnish Trade Review* (8 issues annually) (Finnish Foreign Trade Association), *Finnfacts Bulletin* (6-8 issues annually, free) (Finnfacts Institute), *Foreign Exchange Regulations* (Bank of Finland), annual *Import System of Finland* (Ministry for

Foreign Affairs), *Statistical Yearbook of Finland* (Central Statistical Office), annual *Industrial Statistics* (Central Statistical Office), *Foreign Trade Monthly Bulletin and Foreign Trade Annual Statistics* (Board of Customs), *Finland, Facts and Figures* (in English and German) (Otava), *Finland, an Introduction* (George Allen & Unwin), *Facts about Finland* (Otava), *The Finns and the Lapps: How They Live and Work* (David & Charles), *Finland* (B.T. Batsford), *La Finlande au miroir* (Seghers). The Board of Customs publishes monthly and annual trade statistics in English, Finnish and partially in Swedish.

Finnish chambers of commerce abroad: Moscow, Stockholm, Zurich.

On the Spot

Office hours: Industry and commerce: from 8 or 8.30am to 4 or 4.30pm Monday-Thursday; 8.30am-8pm Friday. Lunch break is usually 30 minutes to one hour between 11.30am and 1pm. Government offices: 8am-4.15pm in winter, 8am-3.15pm in summer, Monday-Friday.

Public holidays

Jan 1	New Year's Day	Dec 6	Independence Day
Jan 6	Epiphany	Dec 25	Christmas
April 30/May 1	Labour Day	Dec 26	Boxing Day
Movable dates:	Good Friday	Midsummer Eve and Day
	Easter Monday	(Thurs/Fri nearest June 24)
	Ascension Saturday	All Saints' Day
	Whitsun Eve	(Fri nearest Nov 1)

On the eve of a public holiday most shops, banks and post offices close as much as half a day earlier.

Banks and currency exchange: Banking hours: 9.15am-4.15pm Monday-Friday, closed Saturdays, Sundays and public holidays. Outside of these hours money can be changed at hotel desks or at currency-exchange offices at the following locations: Helsinki railway station (from 11 or 11.30am to 6pm daily); the Olympia boat terminal in Helsinki's South Harbour (daily, 9am-noon, 3-6pm and during arrival and departure of ships); Katajanokka Harbour in Helsinki and harbours in Turku and Naantali, open during arrival and departure of ships; Helsinki airport (7am-11pm daily).

Main banking institutions are: Kansallis-Osake-Pankki (KOP) and Union Bank of Finland Ltd. (SYP, or Suomen Yhdyspankki).

Credit cards and traveller's cheques: Internationally recognized credit cards and traveller's cheques are quite widely accepted.

Post and telecommunications: Post offices can be identified by the words *Posti/Post,* and are generally open Monday-Friday 9am-5pm. The main post office in Helsinki, at Mannerheimintie 11, is open for poste restante (general delivery) services 8am-9pm weekdays and 11am-9pm Sundays. Mail boxes are yellow, with a black post-horn.

Stamps can be bought from post offices, bookshops, stationers', railway stations, some news-stands and hotels, and from yellow stamp machines.

Telegrams and telexes: 7am-11pm daily at Helsinki General Post Office, entrance B, or from your hotel. Telegraph counters are also located in most post offices.

Finland has automatic telephone service within the country and direct dialling to many countries abroad; see the telephone directory for codes and rates. Public telephones everywhere can be used for long-distance calls. The prefix 9 should always be used with the area code.

Some useful numbers:

Police/fire/ambulance	112	Inquiries (other inland)	118
Medical emergency	10 023	Inquiries (int.)	92020
Hospital (for foreigners)	4711	News (in English)	10 040
Inquiries (local)	118	Telegrams	021

Principal area codes: Helsinki 0, Oulu 81, Tampere 31, Turku 21.

Embassies and consulates: Embassies are listed in the telephone book under their names in each respective language (in English: American Embassy, British Embassy; in French: Ambassade de France, Ambassade de Belgique). For a complete listing of consulates **93**

and embassies, you have to refer to the *Corps Diplomatique et Consulaire*, obtainable in bookshops.

Medical care and health: The quality of medical service is very high, and so are fees (though reciprocal payment agreements exist with certain other countries). Pharmacies (*apteeki*) are strictly for medicine, much of which is on prescription. After hours, at least one pharmacy remains open in every larger locality; a notice indicating the addresses of the on-duty pharmacies is posted in the window. British, Swiss and German pharmaceutical supplies are plentiful. Most doctors speak some English. Tap water is safe to drink. 24-hour emergency treatment for foreigners is available at Helsinki University Central Hospital, Töölö Hospital, Topeliuksenkatu 5, tel. 4711. For 24-hour medical information and doctor services call 10 023.

Services: For translators and interpreters look in the yellow pages of the telephone book under *Käännöstoimistoja ja kielenkääntäjiä* (translators) and *Tulkkeja* (interpreters). Many bookshops, stationers' and department stores offer photocopying services.

Newspapers: Principal dailies: *Helsingin Sanomat* and *Urusi Suomi* (Finnish), *Hufvudstadsbladet* (Swedish). Leading European dailies, including the Paris-edited *International Herald Tribune*, are found at major bookshops, usually the day after publication. The Helsinki railway station news-stands also sell foreign periodicals. Some Finnish dailies include short English-language news summaries during summer. *Helsinki This Week* provides tourist information.

Transport

Air – international: While airports at Maarianhamina. Turku and Vaasa have flights to Sweden, Helsinki has the only true international airport.

Air – domestic: Some 20 domestic airports are linked by an efficient air system. The Finnair Holiday Ticket entitles the traveller to up to 10 flights within the country for 15 days at a flat rate. This pass is available only to permanent residents of countries outside Scandinavia. Reduced-fare tourist tickets for some short air routes can be combined with train, coach or boat tickets during the summer season. Fare reductions are possible by taking weekend flights.

Boats, **waterways**: There are regular boat services to the Tourist Islands. Åland ferries leave from Turku and Naantali. Old-fashioned steamers ply many lakes in Finland's lake district, but only from May to September. In winter the sea and Finland's lakes are frozen. Ice-breakers keep major ports in southern Finland open.

Rail: First- and second-class rail travel is relatively inexpensive. Diesel trains are fast, punctual, sleek and safe. Excellent accommodation and dining-cars are available. The Finnrail Pass allows unlimited travel throughout the country on 3, 5 or 10 days within a 1-month period. The Scanrail Pass permits unlimited rail travel in Finland, Denmark, Norway and Sweden on a specified number of days.

Long distance buses: Finland is the promised land of coach services: the bus network is very dense with frequent services (over 300 departures and arrivals daily at Helsinki) and connections to all parts of the country. Buses are modern, comfortable and punctual – a recommended means of transport all over the country.

Local public transport: Buses and trams serve Helsinki and other major centres. Helsinki also has an underground-railway system. Public transport is quite good. For some tram and many bus lines, marked on the front with a big black E on a yellow background, the fare is paid to the driver. Otherwise, buses and trams have machines inside the vehicle, at the back or at the front, for validating tickets bought beforehand. Books of multi-trip tickets for unlimited travel on buses and trams are available, as are 24-hour tourist tickets.

Taxis: Taxis can be ordered by telephone or hailed in the street. All taxis have an orange border around the licence plate and a yellow *taksi* sign; if this sign is lit, the cab is available. All taxis have meters, which go on as soon as they receive a call; a supplement is added at night and on Sundays and holidays. Special fares exist for long journeys.

Car rental: Major international car-rental firms operate throughout Finland and have offices at Helsinki airport and in town. Look under **95**

Autovuokraamoja or *Biluthyrning* in the yellow pages of the telephone directory. Rates usually include oil, maintenance and liability insurance. Chauffeur-driven cars aren't easily obtainable; taxis are recommended even for long distances.

Driving in Finland: Main roads are good throughout the country but many secondary roads are unsurfaced. In winter, principal roads are kept clear of snow even in northernmost parts of the country, but winter tires or studded tires are highly recommended in the cold season. The few motorways (expressways) which exist are limited to some stretches around the major towns. Watch out for elk and reindeer wandering in the road, especially at dusk – these heavy animals can cause very serious accidents, and if you collide with one you must report it to the police. Speed limits: 50kph (31mph) in town, 60-120kph (37-75mph) on the open road, as marked, 120kph (75mph) on motorways. Where no indication is given, a speed limit of 80kph (50mph) is in force. Wearing seat belts for front-seat passengers is required in both town and country. Traffic coming from the right has right of way. The horn may only be sounded in cases of impending danger. Use of dipped headlights at all times of day is obligatory on the open road, even in broad daylight. Driving under the influence of alcohol (limit 50mg/100ml) or drugs is strictly forbidden. Infringement of this law means imprisonment or fines. A red warning triangle is obligatory.

The Automobile and Touring Association of Finland operates a 24-hour service telephone number in Helsinki (tel. 77 47 61) which refers motorists to garages and service stations that can help in case of a breakdown. See also the yellow pages of the telephone book under *hinausautoja*. Service stations are frequent in the south but less so in the north. Fuel (petrol/gas) available is lead-free, normal (92 octane), super (96 and 99 octane) and diesel.

Some distances from Helsinki: Lahti 90km (56 miles), Tampere 175km (110 miles), Turku 165km (100 miles), Vasa 415km (260 miles).

Social customs: Although Finns aren't formal people, a toast is generally drunk at the beginning of a meal. Guests shouldn't touch their drink before the host has offered a toast. No further toasts or speeches are generally expected except perhaps, depending on the occasion, a small response to the host's toast by the guest of honour towards the end of the meal. If invited to a Finnish home for dinner (which is fairly likely) take some flowers for the hostess. If you issue an invitation to lunch or dinner, you're the one to pay – bills are never split.

Hints for business: Punctuality is strictly observed on all occasions, business or otherwise. Appointments should always be made. Finns easily come onto first-name terms, often over a drink, and certainly in the sauna. Every foreign business contact is taken to a sauna session by his hosts sooner or later; no unnecessary shyness should be felt as this is a perfectly normal custom in Finland. Don't let your eager Finnish host overdo the sauna for you if you are a first-timer.

Alcohol is often drunk in great quantities and varieties at dinners so be wary if unaccustomed to heavy drinking.

Periods to be avoided for business travel are from Christmas to January 6 and from mid-June to the end of August.

Foreign chambers of commerce in Finland: American.

Crime and theft: The underground shopping centre at Helsinki Railway Station should be avoided late at night. Otherwise, normal precautions are in order.

After Hours

Food and drink: Fish dishes are the real Finnish specialities, particularly salmon (smoked, slightly salted or grilled), whitefish, Baltic herring or *muikku* (vendace), roe of whitefish, or burbot or *kalakukko* (fish baked in a crust). Late July to early September is crayfish season and crayfish parties abound. Other favourites include reindeer meat and tongue, venison (elk) and *blinit* (small pancakes with roe and sour cream). Common in many restaurants at lunchtime is the *voileipäpöytä*, buffet lunch. Most restaurants serve international cuisine and Finnish specialities. Reservations are advisable in better restaurants.

Finnish vodka is excellent. Many liqueurs made from exotic berries are worth sampling. Foreign or domestic alcoholic beverages are readily available in licensed bars (note that *baari* also means a snack-bar or **97** a milk-bar). Only licensed restaurants and bars are entitled to serve alcoholic drinks. (Some more modest 'B-licensed' restaurants serve only wine and/or beer.) Restaurants sell beer from 9am and spirits from noon. Alcohol is served until half an hour before closing time.

Mealtimes: breakfast 7.30am-9am, lunch 11.30am-1.30pm, dinner from 7 to 10 or 12pm

Entertainment: Several late-night dinner-and-dance restaurants – some with floor shows or even striptease – are found in the capital. Discotheques have a young crowd. The concert, theatre, opera and ballet season runs from the end of September to mid-May. Cinemas show recent films, mostly American, British, French, Italian and Swedish, in the original language.

Taxes, service charges and tipping: Not widespread in Finland. At hotels and restaurants the service charge is included, but it is customary to leave some small change for the waiter. Tipping recommendations: porters 5mk per bag; taxi drivers, round up to the next mark; cloakroom attendants 3-5mk per person. Barbers and hairdressers don't expect tips.

Sports and recreation: The visitor has a wealth of recreational possibilities at his disposal, depending on the time of year: swimming (indoor and outdoor in most towns), boating and sailing (coasts and lakes; boats can be hired at some hotels), golf (in Helsinki and Hämeenlinna), tennis, squash, bowling, cycling (bicycle rental through some tourist offices), skiing (ski rental at ski resorts and hotels), fishing and hunting (seasonal, permit needed, information from tourist offices).

From May to October, soccer matches and athletics competitions abound. From January to March, cross-country skiing and ice-hockey are the popular spectator sports.

TV and radio: Programming is in Finnish and Swedish. All foreign films are telecast in the original language with subtitles.

What to buy: Glass and ceramics, kitchenware, textiles, handicrafts, sports and leisure wear, boots, furs, children's wear, wooden items
(especially toys), jewellery.

Shopping hours vary, but are normally 9am-5pm (sometimes 8pm) Monday-Friday, till 2pm (also 3 or 4pm) on Saturday. Helsinki railway station has an underground shopping centre with closing hours as late as 10pm. Some shops here are open on Sunday from noon to 10pm.

Cities and Sights

HELSINKI (*Telephone area code 0*)

Airport: Helsinki-Vantaa (19km/12 miles from city centre), international; duty-free shop. Bus service every 20-30 minutes.

Tourist information office: Pohjoisesplanadi 19; tel. 169 37 57, fax 169 38 39. Telephone 058 for recorded information in English on what's happening in Helsinki today.

Chamber of commerce: Fabianinkatu 14, Helsinki; tel. 650 133, fax 650 303.

Finnish Foreign Trade Association: Arkadiankatu 4-6B, Helsinki; tel. 695 91.

Helsinki Card: The Helsinki Tourist Association offers Helsinki Cards that grant free entrance to museums, free travel on city buses, trams, underground (subway) and boats, tour reductions, hotel-rate discounts, etc. The card is valid for periods of one, two or three days and can be purchased at the Helsinki City Tourist Office (see above).

Sightseeing: Market Square, Senate Square (cathedral), Government Building and University, Finlandia Hall, Olympic Stadium, Parliament Building, Suomenlinna fortress island, Sibelius Monument, Temppeliaukio Church, Seurasaari open-air museum, Dipoli student centre, Tapiola Garden City.

Museums: National and City museums.

Excursions: Archipelago cruise, Porvoo, composer Jean Sibelius' and architect Eliel Saarinen's homes.

Some Useful Expressions in Finnish

good morning/afternoon	**hyvää huomenta'/päivää**
good evening/night	**hyvää iltaa/yötä**
good-bye	**hyvästi**
yes/no	**kyllä/ei**
please/thank you	**olkaa hyvä/kiitos**
excuse me	**anteeksi**
you're welcome	**ei kestä**
where/when/how	**missä/milloin/kuinka**
how long/how far	**miten kauan/miten kaukana**
yesterday/today/tomorrow	**eilen/tänään/huomenna**
day/week/month/year	**päivä/viikko/kuukausi/vuosi**
left/right	**vasen/oikea**
up/down	**ylös/alas**
good/bad	**hyvä/huono**
big/small	**suuri/pieni**
cheap/expensive	**halpa/kallis**
hot/cold	**kuuma/kylmä**
old/new	**vanha/uusi**
open/closed	**avoin/suljettu**
early/late	**aikainen/myöhäinen**
easy/difficult	**helppo/vaikea**
Does anyone here speak English/French/German?	**Puhuuko kukaan englantia/ranskaa/saksaa?**
What does this mean?	**Mitä tämä tarkoittaa?**
I don't understand.	**En ymmärrä.**
Please write it down.	**Olkaa hyvä ja kirjoittakaa se.**
Do you take credit cards/ traveller's cheques?	**Voinko maksaa luottokortilla/ matkašekillä?**
Where are the toilets?	**Missä on wc?**
I'd like…	**Haluaisin…**
How much is that?	**Mitä se maksaa?**
Help me please.	**Auttaisitteko minua.**

France

Type of government:	Republic, multi-party centralized
Member of:	EU, GATT, IBRD, IDA, IFC, IMF, OECD
Population:	58 million
Area:	547,026sq km (212,918sq miles)
Capital:	Paris (2.15m/GUA 10.6m)
Other major cities:	Lyons (*Lyon*, 415,000/GUA 1.2m)
	Marseilles (*Marseille*, 810,000/GUA 1.2m)
	Lille (172,000/GUA 960,000)
	Bordeaux (201,000/GUA 700,000)
	Toulouse (359,000/GUA 650,000)
	Nantes (245,000/GUA 495,000)
	Nice (342,000/GUA 515,000)
	Strasbourg (252,000/GUA 430,000)
Language:	French; English spoken in business circles.
Religion:	Catholic (81%), Protestant (1.7%), Muslim (5%), Jewish (1.2%)
Time zone:	GMT+1, EST+6; DST (Apr-Sep)
Currency:	French franc (abbr. F or FF) = 100 centimes
	Coins: 5, 10, 20, 50 centimes; 1, 2, 5, 10, 20F
	Notes: 20, 50, 100, 200, 500F
Electricity:	220V, 50Hz, AC, 110V in some areas

Planning your Trip

Visa requirements: For nationals of Turkey and South Africa. (See also p.6.)

Vaccination requirements: None (see also p.7).

Import allowances (see also p.7):

	Cigarettes		Cigars		Tobacco	Spirits		Wine
1)	200	or	50	or	250g	1l	and	2l
2)	300	or	75	or	400g	1.5l	and	3l
3)	(800)	or	(200)	or	(1kg)	(10l)	and	(90l)

1) Passengers from countries outside Europe.
2) Duty-free goods bought in EU countries by European residents.
3) Non-duty-free goods bought within the EU.

Perfume: 1) 50g; 2) 75g; *Toilet water*: 1) 0.25l; 2) 0.375l;
Gifts: 1) 300F max. value; 2) 4,200F max. value

There are no official restrictions on goods bought non-duty-free within the EU, provided they are for personal use only. The above figures are guidelines to the quantities customs officials will generally find acceptable, so if you are carrying larger quantities you should be prepared to provide proof that the goods are for your personal use.

Currency restrictions (see also p.7): There's no limit on the importation or exportation of local or foreign currencies or traveller's cheques, but amounts exceeding 50,000 French francs or equivalent must be declared on arrival.

Climate: France enjoys a mainly maritime temperate climate in northern and western areas (including Paris). To the east and in the interior Massif Central the regime tends to be more continental, with warmer summers and colder winters. The Mediterranean coastal area is marked by hot, dry summers and mild, showery winters. With the exception of this part of the country, rainfall is sporadic all year round with most precipitation between January and April and least in August and September. Snow is only rarely a problem in winter city streets.

Some average temperatures:

	Jan	Apr	July	Oct
Paris	3°C (37°F)	10°C (50°F)	19°C (66°F)	11°C (52°F)
Nice	9°C (48°F)	13°C (55°F)	23°C (73°F)	17°C (63°F)

Clothing: Except in winter, when warm clothing is a necessity in virtually all parts of the country – particularly in mountainous regions and in the sometimes damp northeast – medium-weight dress is usually adequate. However, even in the southern summer, when light clothing is all you'll need during the day, something warmer for a cool evening is advisable. You are likely to need rainwear at any time of the year. Conservative dress is standard for business, with suits for men, though this rule is relaxed considerably in the south, where more casual jackets are commonly worn.

Hotels: Hotels throughout France are officially classified into five categories, from one-star to four-star luxury. Room prices, fixed according to amenities, size and the hotel's star rating, must be posted at reception desks and inside rooms. French National Tourist offices abroad have this information on file. Individual city or regional tourist offices supply local hotel lists, and hotel guide books are commercially available.

The Accueil de France service in municipal tourist offices will make room reservations for you for a small fee. Major airports and railway stations have hotel reservation services. Advance bookings are essential during holiday periods and when trade fairs are on.

French tourist offices abroad: Amsterdam, Athens, Brussels, Copenhagen, Frankfurt, Geneva, Lisbon, London, Madrid, Milan, Montreal, New York, Oslo, São Paulo, Stockholm, Sydney, Tokyo, Vienna, Zurich. **103**

Business Briefing

Economic Background

Main industries: Iron, steel, chemicals, motor vehicles, machinery, aerospace, shipbuilding, instruments, plastics and electrical equipment, textiles, clothing, wine-making, processed foods, tourism.

Main agricultural products: Wheat and other grains, sugar beet, potatoes, meat and dairy products, vegetables and fruit, grapes.

Main imports: Machinery, petroleum and by-products, iron and steel, livestock, miscellaneous manufactured goods.

Main exports: Transport equipment, iron and steel, cereals and preparations, chemical elements and compounds, miscellaneous manufactured goods.

Principal trading partners: Germany, Benelux, Spain, Italy, USA, Switzerland, UK, Netherlands, Japan.

GNP: $1001 billion; per capita: $17,030.

Inflation rate: 2.1% (1994).

Trade fairs: Most large towns have at least one trade fair per year, with most international ones held in Paris. The main ones are: agricultural and household-appliance shows in spring, ready-to-wear clothes in spring and autumn, Foire Internationale in April-May, International Motor Show every two years (even years) in October, SICOB (International Office Equipment Show) in September, International Air Show every two years (odd years) in June.

Selected background reading: *French Law on Commercial Companies* (Commerce Clearing House, USA), *Doing Business in France* (Price Waterhouse, USA), *Business in France* (Lloyds and Bolsa International Bank Ltd, London), *Guide Statistique de France* (Francis Lefèvre, Paris), *Le Guide de Vos Droits et Démarches* (Service Gouvernemental d'Information et de Diffusion, Paris, annually).

The French Industrial Development Agency, 610 5th Ave, New York, NY 10020, publishes some useful booklets on various aspects of industry and trading in France.

French chambers of commerce abroad: Algiers, Antwerp, Athens, Bangkok, Barcelona, Bogotá, Bombay, Brussels, Buenos Aires, Caracas, Casablanca, Geneva, Ho Chi Minh City, Istanbul, Lima, Lisbon, London, Madrid, Mexico City, Milan, Montevideo, Montreal, New York, Rio de Janeiro, Saarbrücken, Santiago, Stockholm, Sydney, Tokyo, Tunis, Valencia.

On the Spot

Office hours: Generally 9am-12pm and 2-6pm Monday-Friday.

Public holidays:

Jan 1	New Year's Day	Aug 15	Assumption
May 1	Labour Day	Nov 1	All Saints' Day
May 8	Victory Day	Nov 11	Armistice Day
July 14	Bastille Day	Dec 25	Christmas Day
Movable dates: Easter Monday, Ascension, Whit Monday			

Banks and currency exchange: Most banks open Monday-Friday only, but hours vary. Paris hours are 9am-5pm, and many banks may close over lunchtime and all day either on Saturday or Monday.

Outside of banking hours, money can be changed at *bureaux de change,* at international airports and at major railway stations. Most airport currency-exchange offices are open from 6.30am to 11pm. Those at train stations open between 6.30 and 7.30am and close around 8pm as a rule. Some currency-exchange offices, even at airports, close on weekends.

Principal banks: Banque Nationale de Paris, Crédit Agricole, Crédit Lyonnais, Société Générale.

Credit cards and traveller's cheques: Leading credit cards are accepted at most hotels, restaurants and shops. Traveller's cheques are **105**

also widely accepted, though exchange rates in stores will be less favourable than rates in a bank or *bureau de change*.

Post and telecommunications: Postal services are generally reliable. Post offices handle mail, telegrams and telephone calls.

Post office hours are generally 8am-7pm Monday-Friday (branch offices in small towns open 9am-noon and 2-5pm), and 8am-noon on Saturdays. Paris has a round-the-clock service at 52 rue du Louvre, 75001 Paris. Main post offices in provincial cities are generally also open on Sunday mornings.

Long distance and international calls can be made from any phone box, but if you need assistance in placing the call, go to the post office or ask your hotel to do it. Phone boxes (*cabine téléphonique* or *taxi-phone*) are scattered round the towns and countryside, and most of them now accept only *télécartes*. Telecards are sold at post offices, railway ticket counters and shops recognized by a 'Télécarte' sign. If you make a call from your hotel, a café or a restaurant, you are likely to be charged a little extra.

Some useful numbers:

Fire	18	Weather (Paris)	36 65 00 00
Police and ambulance	17	Weather (over rest	
Emergency doctors	47 07 77 77	of France)	36 65 01 01
(Paris area)		Directory Inquiries	12

For long-distance calls within France, there are no area codes (just dial the 8-digit number), *except* when telephoning from the Paris region to the provinces (dial 16 and wait for the dialling tone, then dial the 8-digit number of the subscriber), and from the provinces to Paris or the Paris region (dial 16, wait for the dialling tone, then dial 1 followed by the 8-digit number). For information, dial 12.

To ring abroad from France, dial 19, followed, after the change of tone, by the country's number (listed in all boxes and phone books). If direct dialling is not available to that country, dial 19 and wait for the tone, then dial 33 followed by the code number of the country in **106** question (see p.383) to reach the operator. If you don't know the telephone number of the subscriber, dial 19 33 12, followed by the code number of the country in question.

The Minitel has invaded most French homes and public buildings. It's used for everything from looking up phone numbers to booking theatre tickets.

Embassies and consulates: Consult the *ambassades* or *consulats* entries in the phone book.

Medical care and health: The standard of medical treatment is generally very high. Fees for medical treatment vary widely, and doctors who are *non-conventionnés,* i.e. who practise outside the framework of the French national health system, are more expensive. Visitors from EU countries such as Britain which have reciprocal agreements with France for government payment of medical costs should obtain the requisite forms and information for free treatment from their local Social Security offices or equivalent before leaving home.

Many physicians speak English; the visitor's consulate or embassy will have a list of local doctors and dentists who speak his language. The American Hospital in Neuilly outside Paris is often preferred by English-speakers of whatever nationality.

Medicine and pharmaceutical supplies are readily available in all cities. Duty pharmacies are open after hours, on Sundays and public holidays, and details are listed in local newspapers, including 'What's On' guides, and in other pharmacy windows.

Tap water is safe to drink, unless it is labelled 'non potable' (unsafe to drink).

Services: Temporary French-speaking or bilingual secretaries can be found under *secrétariat* in phone books and in the yellow pages. Interpreting and translation services are listed under *interprètes* or *interprétation* and *traducteurs* or *traductions*, respectively. Tourist offices and leading hotels also provide this kind of information. Good-quality photocopies can be made at printshops and some stationers', public libraries, large stores and post offices.

Newspapers: France's leading business-oriented daily is *Le Monde*; others include *Le Figaro*, and, in English, The *International Herald* **107**

Tribune. A selection of foreign newspapers, particularly British, German and Italian, is generally available at larger news-stands in the main cities on the day of publication.

Transport

Air – international: Paris Roissy-Charles-de-Gaulle is far and away the major gateway to France, though a number of international flights operate to Lyons and Nice and to certain other cities.

Air – domestic: France's principal domestic airline, Air Inter, and other minor carriers connect Paris with airports in various parts of the country and link some provincial cities directly with each other.

Rail: French trains generally run on time. First-class seating is recommended for business travel. Dining-cars and sleepers are of good quality. Excellent high-speed services (TGV – *train à grande vitesse*) operate on selected routes.

The SNCF (French railways) offers various reductions on rail travel, available to all European as well as French citizens. These include the *Carte Kiwi* (under-16), the *Carte Carissimo* (16-25) and the *Carte Vermeil* (over-60). The BritFrance rail pass allows free travel on French and British railways to residents of North America only. For Eurailpass, Inter-rail and Freedom Pass see page 10.

Local public transport: All major cities have good bus services. Paris has the underground *metro* (for inner-city travel) and the RER (for districts). For information on Paris, call 43 46 14 14. Lyons, Marseilles and Lille operate clean, efficient and speedy *métro* systems. Reduced-rate booklets *(carnets)* of tickets are available, often offering unlimited travel.

Taxis: You can hail a cab on the street, phone for one or go to a taxi rank. In main cities taxis are metered. Tip the driver about 10% of the fare.

Car rental: International and local car-rental agencies operate throughout France, with offices at major airports as well as in town.

Driving in France: A red-reflector warning triangle for use in case of breakdown and a set of spare bulbs are compulsory. A blue-zone parking disc is useful and can be obtained from police stations. Seat belts are compulsory. Children under 10 years old may not travel in the front. Speed limits: 130kph (81mph) on motorways (expressways), 110kph (63mph) on dual carriageways (divided highways), 90kph (56mph) on other roads and 45kph (28mph) or 50kph (31mph) in residential areas. In case of rainfall or snow, all limits are reduced by 10kph (6mph). Except where otherwise indicated, traffic coming from the right has priority. French drivers tend to be impatient and somewhat unpredictable, so drive cautiously until you are used to driving conditions. Blood alcohol limit is 70mg/100ml. Fuel (petrol/gas) available is super (98 octane), lead-free (*sans plomb*) and diesel (called *gas-oil*). Road conditions are good and motorways (with high tolls) excellent. In the case of a serious accident dial 15 for SAMU emergency medical services or 17 for police.

Some distances from Paris: Calais 300km (185 miles), Lyons 465km (290 miles), Bordeaux 585km (365 miles), Marseilles 780km (485 miles).

Social customs: Don't forget to shake hands when meeting someone or taking your leave. Being invited to somebody's home, even after a long acquaintance, is rare. But for that occasion a small gift of flowers or chocolates for the hostess will be appreciated. If it's you who are doing the entertaining, remember that the French are discerning diners, so seek advice on a good restaurant (which will be expensive).

Foreign chambers of commerce in France: American, Argentine, Austrian, Belgian, British, Canadian, Chilean, Cypriot, Czech, Dutch, Greek, Indonesian, Irish, Israeli, Italian, Japanese, Lebanese, Libyan, Luxembourg, Portuguese, Russian, Slovak, Spanish, Swedish, Swiss, German, Yugoslav.

Crime and theft: Paris, Nice, Lyons and Marseilles are cities to be wary in, more so than, for example, Strasbourg and Bordeaux. But it's always wise to keep to well-lit streets at night and to watch your wallet. Never leave any belongings in your car overnight.

Hints for business: The French tend to be rather formal and conservative in business. Prior appointments are the rule. Except for some **109**

younger international executives, French businessmen and women do not feel at ease on first-name terms. Certainly initially, it's advisable to address your partner in French as simply *monsieur* or *madame*, without surname. Leisurely examination (the French like to talk) of all aspects and details of a deal is to be expected. Snap executive decisions are rare. Subtle tactics and presentation are very important. Rational arguments larded with facts and figures are most likely to lead to success. Avoid the period from mid-July to mid-September for your trip, when the French business world virtually closes down for the summer.

After Hours

Food and drink: French food and wine hardly need any introduction, and wherever you go there's a wealth of wonderful food and local specialities waiting. Lyons specialities include *poulet de Bresse* (farm-raised chicken), incomparable in taste, sometimes truffled; and *gras double lyonnais* (tripe simmered in wine sauce). Provence and the south generally excel in fish, fish soup and vegetable preparations; a famous speciality is *ratatouille,* a concoction of peppers, aubergines, courgettes, onions and tomatoes, served hot or cold. Food here tends to be highly spiced with herbs and garlic. Alsace is known for its *tarte aux oignons* (onion tart) and *choucroute* (sauerkraut), and Lorraine is known for its *quiche lorraine* (a tart of eggs, cream and bacon).

French wines merit a visit in themselves. Burgundy reds tend to be full-bodied, while the great burgundy whites include Meursault and Puligny-Montrachet. Bordeaux wines have four main regional divisions: Médoc, an aromatic mellow red; Graves, a soft, easy-to-drink, dry red; Saint-Emilion, dark, strong and full-bodied; and the pale golden Sauternes, a sweet and fragrant desert wine. The Loire Valley produces fine dry white wines, such as Vouvray and Sancerre, and robust reds; the Rhone Valley produces rosé wines and hearty reds, of which the best known are Châteauneuf-du-Pape and Gigondas.

Both Michelin and Gault & Millau publish excellent guides to restaurants. Mealtimes: Lunch noon-2pm, dinner 7 to 9 or 10pm.

Entertainment: Paris boasts a plethora of nightclubs and discos, and there's no lack of concerts, plays, opera, ballet and cinemas. Films are often shown in their original language, especially around the Champs-Elysées and the Latin Quarter. Nightlife also flourishes in the provinces – particularly on the Riviera.

Taxes, service charges and tipping: Value-added tax (in French abbreviated TVA) and a 10-15% service charge will generally be included in hotel or restaurant bills, but it is usual to round off the amount. Other tips: porter 5F per bag; taxi driver 10-12%; cloakroom attendant 2F; hairdresser/barber 10-15%; hotel maids 50-100F per week.

Sports and recreation: Tennis courts abound, though advance booking is often necessary. There are golf links with reasonable fees in the Paris, Riviera (Nice), Bordeaux, Lille, Lyons, Strasbourg and Toulouse areas. Hunting and fishing are popular seasonally in all parts of the country. Water-sports facilities are outstanding, with sailing, swimming and snorkelling in all coastal areas. Stables with mounts for hire are found throughout the country. There are excellent hiking possibilities to suit all levels. France's web of little-travelled country lanes facilitates that other very popular national sport, cycling. All winter sports are available within striking distance of Nice and Lyons.

Soccer is the most popular spectator sport, followed by rugby and cycling. Paris holds open tennis championships at the end of May. Several horse-race courses (including Auteuil and Longchamps) are located around Paris. The Tour de France cycle race takes place in July.

TV and radio: There are several TV channels. All programmes are in French (except for a few late-night foreign films). The news is broadcast at 1pm, 8pm and at around 11pm; films usually start at 8.30pm.

What to buy: Good buys include perfume, silk scarves, antiques, crystal and porcelain, luxury foods such as *foie gras*, wine, spirits, cheese and other foodstuffs. High-quality women's ready-to-wear and haute couture are widely available, but prices are high.

As a rule, large department stores are open between 10am and 6pm, six days a week. Smaller shops outside Paris generally close for 2 hours around noon: the rule in Nice and Marseilles, for instance, is 8 or 9am to noon, and 2-7pm. Small boutiques are usually open all day Saturday and close on Monday.

Cities and Sights

PARIS (*Telephone area code 161, see p.106*)

Airports: Charles-de-Gaulle-Roissy (25km/16 miles northeast of city centre) and Orly (16km/10 miles south of city centre) are both international. Both airports have currency-exchange offices, restaurants and duty-free shops. Regular bus service from Paris. Town terminal for Charles-de-Gaulle: Porte Maillot; for Orly: Invalides. Trains from Gare du Nord to Charles-de-Gaulle. From Quai d'Orsay, St Michel or Austerlitz métro stations to Orly. Bus and helicopter services between the airports.

Tourist information office: 127 avenue des Champs-Elysées, 75008 Paris; tel. 49 52 53 54. For a selection of the principal weekly events in English, call 49 52 53 55.

Chambers of commerce and other business organizations: Paris Chamber of Commerce (Chambre de Commerce de Paris), avenue de Friedland,75008; tel. 42 89 70 00, fax 42 89 78 68. International Chamber of Commerce: 38 Cours Albert 1er; tel. 49 53 28 28.

Sightseeing: Etoile, Champs-Elysées, place de la Concorde, Palais Royal, Place Vendôme, Opéra, Faubourg St-Honoré, Madeleine, Montmartre and Sacré Coeur, Le Marais, Ile de la Cité (Notre-Dame), Ile St-Louis, Latin Quarter and place St-Michel, Sorbonne, St-Germain-des-Prés, Panthéon, Luxembourg gardens, Montparnasse, Invalides, Eiffel Tower, Trocadéro.

Museums: Louvre, Orangerie, Centre Pompidou (Beaubourg), Cluny, Arts Décoratifs.

MARSEILLES

Airport: Provence (international) (28km/17 miles from city centre). Duty-free shop. Bus service to Gare Saint-Charles.

Tourist information office: 4 la Canebière, 13001 Marseille; tel. 91 54 91 11, and in railway station (summer only).

Chamber of commerce: Palais de la Bourse, 13001 Marseille cedex 1; tel. 91 39 33 33, fax 91 91 91 51.

Sightseeing: Notre-Dame-de-la-Garde basilica, La Canebière, old port, Corniche Président-Kennedy, new harbour, St-Victor basilica, Parc du Pharo, Belvédère St-Laurent (lookout point).

Museums: Grobet-Labadie, Cantini (Faïence), Beaux-Arts, Archéologie, Vieux Marseille.

Excursions: Château d'If, Massif de Ste-Baume, boat trip round bay and surrounding cliffs *(calanques)*.

LYONS

Airport: Satolas (international) (27km/17 miles from city centre). Duty-free shop. Bus service to Gare de Perrache.

Tourist information office: place Bellecour, 69002 Lyon; tel. 78 42 25 75.

Chamber of commerce: 20 rue de la Bourse, Lyon; tel. 72 40 58 58.

Sightseeing: Le Vieux Lyon (old town), Notre-Dame-de-Fourviére basilica, parc de la Tête d'Or.

Museums: Musée des Tissus (fabric museum), Beaux-Arts (fine arts), Arts Décoratifs.

Excursions: Pérouges (medieval town), Signal de St-André, Musée de l'Automobile, Couvent d'Eveux, Arches de Chaponost.

TOULOUSE

Airport: Blagnac (international) (7km/4 miles from city centre). Duty-free shop. Bus services to Gare Matabiau.

Tourist information office: Donjon du Capitole, 31000 Toulouse; tel. 61 11 02 02

Chamber of commerce: Palais consulaire, 2 rue d'Alsace Lorraine, BP 606, 31002 Toulouse cedex; tel. 61 33 65 00, fax 61 55 41 26.

Sightseeing: St-Sernin basilica, Les Jacobins church, Capitol, Hôtel d'Azzézat, cathedral.

Museums: Augustins, Histoire Naturelle, St-Raymond.

Excursions: Foix, Carcassonne, Albi, Gorges of the Tarn.

NICE

Airport: Nice-Côte d'Azur (international) (7km/4 miles from Nice). Duty-free shop. Bus service to Nice. Bus and helicopter services to Monaco.

Tourist information office: 2, rue Massenet, 06000 Nice; tel. 93 87 60 60; at airport (parking Ferber); in railway station.

Chamber of commerce: 20 Boulevard Carabacel, 06005 Nice; tel. 93 13 73 00, fax 93 13 73 99.

Sightseeing: Promenade des Anglais, old town, Opéra, Cours Saleya, rue Droite and Palais Lascaris, castle and harbour.

Museums: Cimiez, Chagall, Matisse, Terra Amata (prehistoric), Beaux-Arts (fine arts), Masséna, Vieux-Logis.

Excursions: Corniche roads, Villefranche, Beaulieu, Eze, Monaco (Monte-Carlo), Gorges du Cians, Vésubie valley, Antibes, Cannes, the Esterel, Vence and St-Paul-de-Vence, Haut-de-Cagnes.

Other museums: Fondation Maeght (St-Paul-de-Vence), Picasso (Antibes), Fernand-Léger (Biot), Greek Villa Kerylos (Beaulieu), Matisse Chapel (Vence), Ephrussi-Rothschild (St-Jean-Cap-Ferrat).

STRASBOURG

Airport: Entzheim (international) (12km/8 miles from city centre). Duty-free shop. Bus service to Place Kléber, Passage de l'Aubette and Grand Hotel/Place de la Gare.

Tourist information office: 17 Place de la Cathedrale, 67000 Strasbourg; tel. 88 52 28 28.

Chamber of commerce: 10 Place Gutenberg, 67000 Strasbourg cedex; tel. 88 75 25 25, fax 88 22 31 20.

Sightseeing: Cathedral (astronomical clock), old town, La Petite France, rue du Bain-aux-Plantes, Maison Kamerzel, Château des Rohan, Barrage Vauban, St Thomas church and mausoleum, boat rides on Ill river and visit to port.

Museums: Œuvre Notre-Dame, collections in Rohan château.

Excursions: Route du Vin to Colmar; Bruche valley, Massif du Donon, Dabo-Wangenbourg region.

BORDEAUX

Airport: Mérignac (international) (11km/7 miles from city centre). Duty-free shop. Bus service to Cours du 30 Juillet and Gare St-Jean.

Tourist information office: 12 cours du 30 Juillet, 33000 Bordeaux; tel. 56 44 28 41.

Chamber of commerce: 12 Place de la Bourse, 33076 Bordeaux; tel. 56 79 50 00, fax 56 81 80 45.

Sightseeing: Cathedral, Grand Théâtre, Place de la Bourse (tower and basilica).

Museum: Beaux-Arts (fine arts).

Excursions: Bordeaux vineyards (Saint-Emilion, Margaux, Château Latour, Château d'Yquem), Périgord, Arcachon, Royan, Cognac, St-Jean d'Angely, La Rochelle.

LILLE

Airport: Lesquin (international) (8km/5 miles from city centre). Duty-free shop. Bus service to Nouvelle Gare Routière.

Tourist information office: Palais Rihour, 59000 Lille; tel. 20 30 81 00.

Chamber of commerce: 2 Palais de la Bourse, 59800, Lille; tel. 20 63 79 79, fax 20 13 02 00.

Sightseeing: Ancienne Bourse (old stock exchange), old town, Hospice Comtesse, Palais de Justice, Citadelle, Porte de Paris, belfry.

Museum: Beaux-Arts (fine arts).

Excursions: Dunkirk; Bruges and Ostend in Belgium.

Some Useful Expressions in French

good morning/afternoon	**bonjour**
good evening/night	**bonsoir/bonne nuit**
good-bye	**au revoir**
yes/no	**oui/non**
please/thank you	**s'il vous plaît/merci**
excuse me	**excusez-moi**
you're welcome	**je vous en prie**
where/when/how	**où/quand/comment**
how long/how far	**combien de temps/à quelle distance**
yesterday/today/tomorrow	**hier/aujourd'hui/demain**
day/week/month/year	**jour/semaine/mois/année**
left/right	**gauche/droite**
up/down	**en haut/en bas**
big/small	**grand/petit**
cheap/expensive	**bon marché/cher**
hot/cold	**chaud/froid**
old/new	**vieux/neuf**
open/closed	**ouvert/fermé**
early/late	**tôt/tard**
easy/difficult	**facile/difficile**
Does anyone here speak English/German?	**Y a-t-il quelqu'un ici qui parle anglais/allemand?**
What does this mean?	**Que signifie ceci?**
I don't understand.	**Je ne comprends pas.**
Do you take credit cards/traveller's cheques?	**Acceptez-vous les cartes de crédit/les chèques de voyage?**
Waiter!/Waitress, please!	**S'il vous plaît!**
Where are the toilets?	**Où sont les toilettes?**
I'd like…	**Je voudrais…**
How much is that?	**Combien est-ce?**
Help me please.	**Aidez-moi, s'il vous plaît.**

Germany

Type of government:	Federal republic, multi-party decentralized
Member of:	EU, GATT, IBRD, IDA, IFC, IMF, OECD
Population:	81.2 million
Area:	357,000sq km (137.838sq miles)
Capital:	Berlin (3.4 million)
Other major cities:	Bonn (310,000)
	Hamburg (1.6 million)
	Munich (*München*, 1.2 million)
	Cologne (*Köln*, 955,000)
	Essen (626,100)
	Frankfurt (*Frankfurt am Main*, 647,200)
	Dortmund (599,900)
	Düsseldorf (576,700)
	Stuttgart (583,700)
	Leipzig (507,800)
	Dresden (530,000)
	Hanover (*Hannover*, 514,000)
Language:	German; English widely spoken.
Religion:	Protestant (26.1%), Catholic (61.1%)
Time zone:	GMT+1, EST+6; DST (Apr-Sep)
Currency:	Deutsche Mark (abbr. DM) = 100 Pfennige (Pf)
	Coins: 1, 2, 5, 10, 50Pf; 1, 2, 5, 10DM
	Notes: 5, 10, 20, 50, 100, 200, 500, 1,000DM
Electricity:	220V, 50Hz, AC

Planning your Trip

Visa requirements: For nationals of South Africa and Turkey. (See also p.6.)

Vaccination requirements: None. (See also p.7.)

Import allowances (see also p.7):

	Cigarettes		Cigars		Tobacco		Spirits		Wine
1)	200	or	50	or	250g		1l	and	2l
2)	(800)	or	(200)	or	(1kg)		(10l)	and	(90l)

1) Passengers from countries outside Europe; passengers arriving from an EU country with duty-free goods.
2) Non-duty-free goods bought within the EU.

Perfume: 1) 50g; *Toilet water*: 1) 250ml; *Gifts*: 1) DM115, max. value

There are no official restrictions on goods bought non-duty-free within the EU, provided they are for personal use only. The above figures are guidelines to the quantities customs officials will generally find acceptable, so if you are carrying larger quantities you should be prepared to provide proof that the goods are for your personal use.

Currency restrictions: None. (See also p.7.)

Climate: Germany's climate is mainly continental with quite warm summers and cold winters. Precipitation is moderate and distributed quite evenly throughout the year though the Leipzig vicinity is particularly rainy. In winter, city streets and main roads are generally kept clear of snow, but ice can be a menace. In August, temperatures hover around 20°C (68°F), with heatwave peaks above 30°C (86°F); in January they descend to between 1°C and -10°C (32-14°F), with harsh spells likely.

Clothing: Attire in business circles should err on the side of conservatism in colours and patterns. Warm overwear is essential in the cooler months, and an umbrella will come in useful at any time of year. A dinner jacket (tuxedo) or dark-blue suit is appropriate for formal occasions. Women's wear is similar to French or Italian fashion.

Hotels: Bookings can be very difficult at any time of year, depending on trade fairs, conventions and other events, and should be made well in advance. Telephones with connection to the local tourist office are located in airports. Accommodation is more limited in areas of former East Germany, where the best service is provided by the Interhotel chain, although the service is expanding rapidly.

German tourist offices abroad: Amsterdam, Brussels, Copenhagen, Johannesburg, Ljubljana, London, Los Angeles, Madrid, Mexico City, Milan, Montreal, New Dehli, New York, Oslo, Paris, Stockholm, Sydney, Tel Aviv, Tokyo, Toronto, Vienna, Zurich.

Business Briefing

Economic Background

Main industries: Iron and steel, motor vehicles, chemicals, electrical engineering and electronics, machinery, plastics, textiles, paper and pulp, ceramics (particularly optical glass).

Main agricultural products: Rye, wheat, oats, barley, potatoes, sugar beet, forestry products, grapes.

Main imports: Oil, non-ferrous metals, foodstuffs, meat, raw materials.

Main exports: Machinery, transport equipment, iron and steel, chemical products, electrical and electronics equipment, textiles, clothing.

GNP: $1,480 billion; per capita: $16,575.

Inflation rate: 3% (1994).

Principal trading partners: Austria, Switzerland, CIS, Czech Republic, Slovakia, Hungary, Poland, Bulgaria, US, France, Netherlands, Japan.

Trade fairs: Berlin, Hanover, Hamburg, Frankfurt and Leipzig are the major trade-fair cities, with Stuttgart, Munich, Cologne, Düsseldorf and others increasing their activities. The vast range of subjects covered runs from confectionery to computer systems. For full details apply to the nearest German chamber of commerce.

Selected background reading: *Doing Business in Germany* (International Publications), *After the Economic Miracle* (Halsted), *A Study of the Evolution of German Business Economics* (Strathclyde), *Facts about Germany* (Federal Press and Information Office, Bonn, or Franz Steiner Verlag GmbH, Wiesbaden) for economic statistics.

German chambers of commerce abroad: Asunciòn, Athens, Bangalore, Bangkok, Barcelona, Bogota, Bombay, Brussels, Buenos Aires, Cairo, Calcutta, Caracas, Chicago, Edmonton, Guatemala City, The Hague, Helsinki, Houston, Jakarta, Johannesburg, La Paz, Lima, Lisbon, London, Los Angeles, Madras, Madrid, Melbourne, Mexico City, Milan, Montevideo, Montreal, New Delhi, New York, Oslo, Paris, Porto, Porto Alegre, Quito, Rio de Janeiro, Rome, Salzburg, San Francisco, Santiago, São Paulo, Stockholm, Sydney, Teheran, Tokyo, Toronto, Tunis, Vienna, Washington DC, Zurich.

On the Spot

Office hours: Very variable, sometimes starting as early as 7.30am. Make business phone calls between 9am and noon or 2.30 and 4pm.

Public holidays

Jan 1	New Year's Day	**Movable dates**:	Good Friday
Jan 6	Epiphany[1, 2]		Easter Monday
May 1	Labour Day		Ascension
Aug 15	Assumption[2, 3]		Whit Monday
Oct 3	National Day		Corpus Christi
Nov 1	All Saints' Day		[1, 2, 3, 4, 5, 6, 7]
	[1, 2, 4, 5, 6, 7]		Day of Penitence
Dec 25	Christmas Day		
Dec 26	Boxing Day		

Notes 1 = Baden-Würtemberg; 2 = Bavaria; 3 = Hesse; 4 = North Rhine-Westphalia; 5 = Rhineland-Palatinate; (6) = Saar; 7 = Thuringia

Banks and currency exchange: Banking hours are generally 8.30am-1pm and 2.30-4pm Monday-Friday (often till 5.30pm on Thursdays).

After hours, money can be changed at airports and railway stations at slightly less advantageous rates than those offered by banks.

Major banks are Deutsche Bank, Dresdner Bank and Commerzbank.

Credit cards and traveller's cheques: Credit cards are increasingly used. Traveller's cheques find wide acceptance, but Eurocheques are the most popular form of non-cash payment.

Post and telecommunications: Postal and telecommunications services are highly reliable for both domestic and international use.

Post offices handle mail, long-distance telephone calls and telegrams, and sometimes have a public telex available. Opening hours are generally 8am-6pm Monday-Friday, and 8am-noon Saturdays. Late-night and weekend service can be obtained at airports and railway stations. In most cities, a night counter *(Nachtschalter)* can be found in a central location for telephone or telegraph purposes.

The telephone network in most areas of Germany is fully automatic, and you can dial direct to many foreign countries. In case of difficulty or emergency a call to the information *(Auskunft)* number given in the front of the telephone directory will put you in touch with an English-speaking operator.

Some useful numbers: (Valid in most large towns)

Fire/First-aid (nationwide)	112	Police (emergencies)	110
Information (inland)	01188	Telegrams	1131
Information (int.)	00118	Time	119
Operator (inland)	010	Weather	1164
Operator (int.)	0010	Pharmacies	1141

Principal area codes: Berlin 030, Bonn 0228, Cologne 0221, Dortmund 0231, Dresden 0351, Düsseldorf 0211, Frankfurt 069, Hamburg 040, Hanover 0511, Leipzig 0341, Munich 089, Nuremberg 0911, Stuttgart 0711.

Embassies and consulates: Embassies are listed under *Botschaften* and consulates under *Konsulate* in telephone directories.

Medical care and health: The standard of medical treatment is generally excellent but expensive. Visitors from the United Kingdom and other EU countries are advised to consult their local social security offices as to the extent of medical coverage they may expect in Germany. Note that, while doctors' fees are generally comparable to those in other west European countries and the US, dental treatment is relatively expensive.

Medicine and pharmaceutical supplies are available everywhere. For service after hours, duty pharmacists, *(Apotheke)* are listed in local daily newspapers, and hotel receptionists, police and tourist offices will also have details. Call 11 41 in an emergency.

In the event of an accident or serious illness, call the Red Cross (*Rotes Kreuz*) or the medical emergency service (*Ärztlicher Notdienst*) listed in the local directory (31 00 31 in Berlin), or call 115 for an ambulance.

English is generally spoken by doctors and medical personnel.

Tap water is safe to drink, though it is customary for bottled mineral water to be ordered in restaurants.

Services: In the yellow pages, interpreters and translators are listed under *Dolmetscher* and *Übersetzer* respectively. International temporary work agencies exist in all larger centres. Photocopying facilities abound in supermarkets, small printshops and public libraries.

Newspapers: Principal dailies are *Die Zeit*, *Die Welt* (Bonn), *Frankfurter Allgemeine* (Frankfurt), *Süddeutsche Zeitung* (Munich), *Leipziger Volkszeitung* (Leipzig) and *Stuttgarter Zeitung* (Stuttgart). The daily *Handelsblatt* and the weekly *Capital* magazine are popular in business circles.

Major British and continental newspapers and US news-magazines are on sale at large railway stations, airports, news-stands and leading hotels throughout the country, as is the *International Herald Tribune*, edited in Paris. The larger cities publish English-language entertainment guides of the type *This Week in…*

Transport

Air – International: Frankfurt is the major gateway to Germany for flights from overseas, with good onward connections. Hamburg, Munich, Cologne, Berlin and other points are linked either directly or with connecting flights to most major cities within Europe and the Middle East.

Air – domestic: Early-morning flights provide direct links between many German cities, but later in the day a change of plane may be required. Except for long-distance flights such as Munich-Hamburg, business people prefer rail travel within the country itself. An express train for passengers with valid flight tickets runs between Frankfurt's airport and Düsseldorf (2½ hours), calling in at Bonn and Cologne. There is also a service to Stuttgart. Book rail tickets with your flight.

Rail: The German rail network is undergoing fundamental change as the original networks, Deutsche Bundesbahn in the west and Deutsche Reichsbahn in the east, are integrated into one commercial network, the Deutsche Bahn AG. The process will take some time but rail travel is still an efficient means of transport throughout Germany, although the quality of some of the rolling stock does vary. Trains in western Germany are comfortable, fast and punctual; in the east, a few express trains are modern, others older but in satisfactory condition, and services are in the process or being upgraded to match the standards of the Bundesbahn.

Intercity (IC) trains are best, with special facilities for business travel. D and FD are intermediate to long-distance trains. Dining service is often available and can be rated from adequate to excellent. Sleeping-car accommodation is provided on certain long runs.

Tickets for distances of up to 100km (60 miles) are valid for one day. In the case of longer distances a single ticket is valid for four days and a return ticket for one month. Tickets for single and return journeys for distances of over 50km (30 miles) are valid, without any extra charge, for travel on long-distance express trains and fast trains. There are special supplements for travel in the rapid and luxurious Euro-city and Intercity trains. A number of special reduced-price offers and bargain tickets are available. Regional passes, which are available only to residents of the UK and Ireland, allow unlimited travel within one of the fifteen German rail regions for five or ten days. For Eurailpass, see p10.

Local public transport: Buses and trams operate in larger towns. Cities like Bonn, Dusseldorf, Frankfurt and Munich are also served by efficient subway (*U-Bahn*) and rapid train (*S-Bahn*) systems. Maps showing the various lines and stations are displayed at every station. The trains usually run from 5am to 1am. Tickets are dispensed from machines, ticket booths at bus/tram stops or from conductors and/or drivers. Be sure to validate tickets in the cancelling machines located at platform entrances and in buses and streetcars.

Taxis: In the villages or the big cities taxis abound, either cruising the streets or waiting at stands (usually right beside the rail station). You can also phone for a taxi wherever you are; numbers are listed on a separate page in the front of the phone directories. All cabs are equipped with meters; drivers charge a supplement for luggage carried in the boot. Tip the driver 10-15% of the fare.

Car rental: International and local firms operate, some of which have desks at airports. You can find the addresses of leading firms in the yellow pages of the telephone directory, under *Autovermietung*. Chauffeur-driven vehicles are widely available.

Driving in Germany: Seat belts must be worn by both front- and back-seat passengers if your car is fitted with them. If you don't wear one, insurance compensation in the event of an accident could be reduced. High fines and other penalties (temporary loss of licence, etc.) are imposed on drivers with more than 80mg/100ml blood alcohol content. Traffic police may confiscate the car keys of people they consider unfit to drive.

On the toll-free Autobahnen (motorways, freeways) a suggested maximum speed is 130kph (81mph), but many drivers habitually exceed 160kph (100mph) and will flash their lights if you don't make way quickly. On secondary roads the limit is 100kph (62mph) and in cities generally 50kph (31mph). Germans drive more conservatively on secondary roads and seldom exceed limits in built-up areas.

Telephones at frequent intervals on the motorways can be used to summon help from ADAC (automobile association) or from the nearest service station. ADAC patrol cars are often in evidence. Fuel (petrol/gas) available is normal (91-92 octane), super (97-99 octane), lead-free (91 octane) and diesel.

Some distances from Frankfurt: Cologne 190km (120 miles), Munich 370km (230 miles), Hamburg 500km (310 miles); from Berlin: Dresden 195km (120 miles), Leipzig 205km (130 miles), Bonn 603km (374 miles), Munich 584km (362 miles).

Social customs: Invitations into German homes are a special privilege. Wine and beer are served with evening meals, which are topped off with coffee and brandy, or German champagne *(Sekt)*. One should not smoke between courses, and should wait until all others have finished eating before lighting up. Be particularly careful about smoking cigars and pipes until after dinner, and then ask the hostess if she minds. Toasts are reduced to a few words of welcome by the host, at which all present raise their glasses, and a brief 'thank you' from the guests after the meal. A man should bring flowers (but not red roses), to be unwrapped discreetly in the entrance-hall and presented to the hostess upon greeting her. When introduced, greet women first, but don't reach for their hand unless it is extended. A thank you note should be sent within a few days for any hospitality.

Hints for business: Punctuality is essential in Germany, and should you be unable to keep an appointment, cancel or postpone it by phone. Germans are increasingly fond of a certain degree of informality and openness, but it's advisable to let your business partners set the pace on this score. Introductions and references are important, and once confidence is won it will pay off with future dividends. It's as well not to practise hard-sell tactics. Business lunches usually include some light drinking. Holiday periods to avoid are the month of August and the weeks of December 15-January 6.

Foreign chambers of commerce in Germany: American, Belgian, British, Dutch, French, Indian, Iranian, Irish, Italian, Luxembourg, Spanish, Swedish, Tunisian.

125

Crime and theft: The crime rate is relatively low in Germany, though you might feel a bit uneasy walking round the red-light districts in the cities. Take normal, common-sense precautions – keep an eye on your baggage, watch out for pickpockets in crowded places, and put your wallet in an inside pocket. Leave money and valuables in your hotel safe, not in your car or hotel room, and avoid carrying large sums of money. Always lock your car – you can be fined otherwise. If you are robbed, report the incident to the hotel and the nearest police station. The police will provide you with a certificate to present to your insurance company, or to your consulate if your passport has been stolen.

It is a good idea to keep photocopies of the important pages of your passport. If ever it gets lost, embassies will accept photocopies as proof that you do possess a passport, and within a few days they will issue a replacement document. Also keep a list of all your credit card numbers, separate from your cards, and photocopies of your plane tickets.

After Hours

Food and drink: French cuisine, or a derivative thereof, is usually found in better hotels and restaurants, alongside German regional specialities.

Breakfast is richer than the traditional continental breakfast and includes cold meats, such as *Schinken* (ham), various salami-like sliced sausages and maybe *Leberwurst* (liver-sausage) in addition to *Käse* (cheese), both hard and soft. Selection of bread is also varied, covering the entire range from white to the dark *Pumpernickel*.

Lunch is usually served from 11.30am to 2pm and dinner between 6.30 and 8.30. In big cities hot meals are available in the evening until 10 or 10.30. Most Germans prefer to have their main meal at noon and eat lighter fare in the evening – cold meats, cheeses and a salad.

Suppe (soup) is always prominent on German menus. *Tagessuppe* simply means today's soup. *Bohnensuppe* is made of beans and *Linsensuppe* of lentils, often served with pieces of sausage. *Kartoffelsuppe* contains potatoes, celery, leeks and parsnips in it. More interesting is *Leberknödlsuppe* in which spicy dumplings of flour, bread crumbs, beef liver, onions, marjoram and garlic take a swim.

Pork is the cornerstone of German cooking. *Schinken* (ham) comes in many different preparations as does *Wurst* (sausage). It takes a solid appetite to finish the Rheingau speciality *Sulperknochen*, made of the ears, the snout, the tail and the feet, especially as it is served on a bed of *Sauerkraut* with a puree of peas. It also requires gallons of beer. More refined is *Spanferkel* (a roasted suckling pig from Bavaria).

From the Rhineland come specialities like *Himmel und Erde*, literally heaven and earth, which is a delicious mixture of apples, blood-sausage and leeks. While on the subject of blood-sausage you should know that *Kölsche Kaviar* on a menu in Cologne means blood-sausage with slices of raw onions. Another Rhinelander trick is *Halve Hahn*, which ought to be half a chicken. Instead it turns out to be a rye-bread roll stuffed with hot mustard and Dutch cheese.

Germany offers many fine fish dishes of *Lachs* (salmon) and *Hecht* (pike). A genuine delicacy is *Moselaal in Riesling* (a Mosel eel simmered in Riesling wine).

In and around the deep forests in Germany are the hunting grounds for a wide variety of game – venison, hare, partridge and, with luck, woodcock. *Hunsrücker Rehkeule* is a leg of venison served with red currant sauce and chestnut puree.

The king of vegetables is the potato. *Bratkartoffeln* (sauteed potatoes) might be boring after a while but *Reibekuchen* (potato pancakes) and *Kartoffelsalat* (potato salad) is spiced with different ingredients in different regions. *Sauerkraut* is that lovely prepared cabbage in white wine with juniper berries, caraway seeds and cloves, served in Berlin with a puree of peas and pig's knuckle. *Rotkraut* is sweet-and-sour red cabbage, and is done with apples, raisins and white vinegar.

Desserts are not only linked with the main meals; there is also a *Konditorei*, coffee and pastry shop, on virtually every street corner. Among the favourites is *Schwarzwälder Kirschtorte*, the world-famous cherry cake from the Black Forest. And *Apfelstrudel* (the delicate apple pie) is eaten as often in Munich and Berlin as in Vienna. Dresden is famous for its *Pflaumenkuchen* – plum cake.

The Germans like to say that there is good beer and better beer but no bad beer in Germany. Beer *vom Fass* (on tap) can be had in half-litre glasses in restaurants, but in a Bavarian *Bierkeller* (beer cellar) **127** the standard size is a full-litre tankard called *Masskrug* or simply *Mass*. *Dunkles* means dark, slightly sweet, malt-flavoured beer. *Helles* is light and is served cooler.

German wines are worth an entire chapter. *Rotwein* (red wines) are few so the *Weisswein* (white wines) dominate. The Rhine and Mosel valleys produce the most prominent wines. From Rhine come Rüdesheimer, Hattenheimer, Niersteiner, Liebfraumilch and Oppenheimer, just to mention a few. Famous names from Mosel include Bernkasteler, Piesporter and Zeltinger. Mosel wines are bottled in green glass, Rhine wines in brown. Prime qualities are designated *Spätlese, Auslese, Beerenauslese*, and, for the rarest and most expensive, *Trockenbeerenauslese*. Germany also produces Sekt, a champagne-like wine.

Entertainment: Nightclubs, discotheques and cinemas are found in all but the smallest towns in western Germany. Foreign films are almost invariably dubbed into German. Casinos are located in several cities. Germany is noted for its numerous and excellent state-subsidized theatres, operas and concert halls. The Stuttgart ballet is among the best in the world, and the Bayreuth Wagner festival each summer is an outstanding musical highlight.

In the major cities, see the weekly or monthly tourist-oriented publications in English for what's on.

Taxes, service charges and tipping: Hotel and restaurants bills are all inclusive, but an additional 5-10% tip for staff is customary. Porters should be tipped DM2 per bag, taxi drivers 10-15%, cloakroom attendants DM1 and barbers and hairdressers 10%.

Sports and recreation: Tennis, water sports and, in season, skiing, are popular, and golf is catching on. Business contacts can usually arrange a golf game in the major cities, and foreign golfers are welcome but should be introduced if possible. Volunteer to pay your green fees.

Far and away the most popular spectator sport is soccer, with, at least in the east, handball and volleyball close behind.

TV and radio: TV and radio programming is in German, with a few special programs in Italian, Greek and Turkish for foreign workers.

Movies are sometimes shown in the original English version. An English-language TV news broadcast occasionally appears in the late afternoon on the regional channel. On the radio, you can easily pick up the BBC World Service, American Forces Network or the Voice of America anywhere in Germany.

What to buy: High-quality jewellery and watches as well as exquisite leather goods in all sizes and for all purposes can be found. For children, German toys are outstanding. Woodcarvings are an attractive buy, as well as books and records. Beautifully packed chocolates or small cakes make excellent gifts.

Shopping hours: 8.30am-6.30pm Monday-Friday, and 8.30am-1pm, Saturdays. In some cities shops remain open until 6pm on the first Saturday of each month.

Cities and Sights

BONN *(Telephone area code 0228)*

Airport: Köln-Bonn (28km/18 miles from Bonn), international; duty-free shop. There are bus links to Bonn, Cologne and Dusseldorf.

Tourist information office: Münsterstrasse 20; tel. 77 34 66, fax 69 03 68. For information on the Northern Rhineland, contact the Landesverkehrsverband Rheinland, Rheinallee 69, 53173 Bonn-Bad Godesberg; tel. 36 29 21.

Chamber of commerce: Bonner Talweg 17, D-53113 Bonn; tel. 228 40, fax 228 41 70.

Sightseeing: Houses of Parliament, cathedral and cloisters, Kreuzberg chapel, Schwarrheindorf church, town hall (art collections) and market square, Godesberg, Redoute, Poppelsdorf Palace and botanical gardens, university, Hofgarten, Beethoven Museum, Beethoven Hall, Pützchens Markt (September), Museum of History of the Federal Republic of Germany (from 1949).

Excursions: Siebengebirge, the Art and Brohl valleys and the Nürburgring (motor racing); Kottenforst, Venusberg, boat trips on the Rhine.

BERLIN (*Telephone area code 030*)

Airport: Tegel (8km/5 miles from city centre), international; duty-free shop. Regular bus service (No. 9) to city centre (Zoo station). Schönefeld (19km/12 miles from city centre). Regular bus to S-*Bahn* Grünau station. Half-hourly bus link between Schönefeld and Tegel, crossing the city centre.

Tourist information office: Verkehrsamt Berlin, Martin Luther-strasse 105; tel. 212 34, fax 21 23 25 20.

Chamber of commerce: Hardenbergstrasse 16-18, D-10623 Berlin; tel. 31 801, fax 31 51 00.

Sightseeing: Gedächtniskirche (memorial church), Funkturm (radio tower), Hansa quarter, Charlottenburg Castle (Egyptian museum), German Opera, Philharmonia building, Brandenburg Gate, Siegessäule (victory column), Schöneberg town hall, Grünewald (castle, museum), Pergamon museum (Egyptian and Greek archaeology), Sanssouci palace at Potsdam.

HAMBURG (*Telephone area code 040*)

Airport: Fuhlsbüttel (12km/8 miles from city centre), international; duty-free shop. Bus every 20 minutes.

Tourist information office: Tourismus-Zentrale Hamburg, Burchardstrasse 14; tel. 30 05 10, fax 30 05 12 55.

Chamber of commerce: Hamburg 11, Adolphsplatz 1, D-20457 Hamburg; tel. 36 13 80; fax 36 13 84 01.

Sightseeing: Harbour, Elbe tunnel, Church of St Michael, fish market, town hall, Jungfernstein, Alster shipping, Hagenbeck Zoo, Reeperbahn, Kunsthalle (museum).

Excursions: Blankenese, Ahrensburg, Lübeck.

MUNICH (*Telephone area code 089*)

Airport: Franz-Josef Strauss, (37km/22 miles from city centre). Duty-free shop and car hire. S-*Bahn* and direct bus connections to city centre.

Tourist information office: Fremdenverkehrsamt der Landeshauptstadt Munchen, Sendlinger Strasse 1; tel. 239 11, fax 239 13 13.

Chamber of Commerce: Marienplatz; tel. 233 64 47.

Sightseeing: National Theatre (opera house), Cuvilliés Theatre, Church of Our Lady, Nymphenburg Palace, Church of St Michael, Theatiner and Asam Churches, Königsplatz, Ludwigstrasse, Schwabing, Hofbräuhaus, Hellabrunn Zoo, Viktualienmarkt and Dult markets, Old and New Pinakothek, Residence Museum, Lenbach Gallery, Bavarian National Museum, German Museum.

Excursions: Starnberg Lake, Garmisch-Partenkirchen and Alps, Neuschwanstein Castle, Wasserburg.

COLOGNE (*Telephone area code 0221*)

Airport: Köln-Bonn (18km/12 miles from city centre), international; duty-free shop. Bus service to main railway station.

Tourist information office: Unter Fettenhennen 19 (beside the cathedral); tel. 221 33 45, fax 221 33 20.

Chamber of commerce: Köln D-50667, Unter Sachsenhausen 10-26; tel. 164 01 57.

Sightseeing: Cathedral, Roman remains (Dionysian mosaic, Praetorium, aqueducts and catacombs), Romanesque churches of St Pantaleon, St George, St Aposteln, St Gereon, St Kunibert and St Martin, Gothic churches of St Andreas, the Minoriten and Antoniter churches, medieval city wall, zoo, Rhine Park ('dancing' fountain).

Museums: Roman-Germanic Museum, Wallraf-Richartz Museum (paintings), Schnütgen Museum (medieval sacred art).

Excursions: Boat trips on the Rhine.

FRANKFURT (*Telephone area code 069*)

Airport: Frankfurt (10km/6 miles from city centre), international; duty-free shop. Inter-city connections from the airport.

Tourist information office: Verkehrsamt der Stadt Frankfurt, Kaiserstrasse 52; tel. 21 23 78 80.

Chamber of commerce: Börsenplatz 4, D-60313 Frankfurt; tel. 219 70, fax 219 74 24.

Sightseeing: Imperial Cathedral, Church of St Leonhard, Church of Our Lady, Church of St Nicholas, town hall ('Römer'), Imperial Hall, Church of St Paul, Goethe's birthplace, zoo, Palm Garden.

Museums: Städel Art Institute, Senchenberg Museum of Natural Science, National Postal Museum, Liebieg-Haus (sculptures).

Excursions: Apple-wine taverns in Sachsenhausen, Heidelberg, Wiesbaden.

DORTMUND (Telephone area code 0231)

Airport: Nearest commercial airport is Düsseldorf. Frequent rail service Dortmund-Düsseldorf.

Tourist information office: Main railway station (Hauptbahnhof); tel. 14 03 41, fax 16 35 93.

Chamber of commerce: Märekische Strasse 120, D-44141; tel. 541 71.

Sightseeing: Westphalia Park (TV tower and rose garden), Westphalia Hall.

Excursions: Sauerland, Münster.

DÜSSELDORF (Telephone area code 0211)

Airport: Lohausen (8km/5 miles from city centre), international; duty-free shop. Regular rail services from main railway station.

Tourist information office: Konrad-Adenauer-Platz; tel. 35 05 05, fax 16 10 71.

Chamber of commerce and industry: Ernst-Schneider-Platz 1, D-40212 Dusseldorf; tel. 355 70, fax 355 74 00.

Sightseeing: Königsallee ('Kö'), old town, old town hall, Church of St Lambert, Schneider-Wibbel Gasse (ornamental clock).

132 Museums: Hetjens Museum (ceramics), fine art museums.

STUTTGART *(Telephone area code 0711)*

Airport: Echterdingen (14km/9 miles from city centre), international; duty-free shop. Bus every 20-30 minutes.

Tourist-information office: Lautenschlager Strasse 3; Königstrasse 1a; tel. 222 80, fax 222 82 70.

Chamber of commerce: Jägerstrasse 30, D-70174 Stuttgart; tel. 200 50, fax 200 53 54.

Sightseeing: Old Palace, New Palace, Collegiate Church, TV tower, Killesberg Park, Wilhelma Zoo, botanical gardens, Württemberg Regional Museum, Daimler-Benz Automobile Museum.

Excursions: Ludwigsburg Palace, Black Forest, Ulm.

BREMEN *(Telephone area code 0421)*

Airport: Neuenland (3km/2 miles from city centre), international; duty-free shop. Trams to main railway station.

Tourist information office: Hillmannplatz 6, D-28195 Bremen; tel. 30 80 00, fax 308 00 30.

Chamber of commerce: Am Markt 13, Haus Schuetting D-28195; tel. 363 70, fax 363 72 99.

Sightseeing: Market and town hall, Roland Column, St Peter's Cathedral, Bleikeller with mummies, Church of Our Lady, Schütting, Böttcherstrasse, Paula Becker Modersohn House, Schnoor district.

Excursion: Weser estuary.

HANNOVER *(Telephone area code 0511)*

Airport: Langenhagen (11km/7 miles from city centre), international; duty-free shop. Frequent bus service to city centre.

Tourist information office: Ernst-August-Platz 8, Hannover D-30159; tel. 301 42 21, fax 30 14 14.

Chamber of commerce: Schiffgraben 49; tel. 310 70, fax 310 73 35. **133**

Sightseeing: Market Church, old town hall, Ballhof, zoo, Herrenhausen Palace.

Museums: Provincial Museum (art gallery, natural history, prehistory), Kestner Museum (Egyptian collection), Wilhelm Busch Museum.

Excursions: Lüneburg Heath, Hildesheim, Celle.

NUREMBERG *(Telephone area code 0911)*

Airport: Nürnberg (8km/5 miles from city centre), international; duty-free shop. Frequent bus connections to city centre.

Tourist information office: Congress und Tourismus Zentrale, Frauentorgraben 3; tel. 23 36 31, fax 23 36 66.

Chamber of commerce: Hauptmarkt 25; tel. 133 50, fax 133 55 00.

Sightseeing: Imperial castle, city walls, Dürer's house, town hall, the Schöner Brunnen fountain, Church of Our Lady (mechanical clock), Church of St Lawrence (Annunciation), Church of St Sebald, zoo (dolphin pool), Old Nuremberg (artisans' institute).

Museums: Toy Museum, Fembohaus Municipal Museum, National Germanic Museum, Transport Museum.

Excursion: Rothenburg ob der Tauber.

LEIPZIG *(Telephone area code 041)*

Airport: Leipzig-Halle (18 km/11 miles from city centre). Duty-free shop, bus transfer to city centre.

Tourist information office: Leipzig-Information, Sachsenplatz 1; tel. 34 17 95 90, fax 28 18 54.

Sightseeing: Opera House, old town hall, Church of St Thomas, technical fairgrounds ('modern struggle of the nations' exhibit), Struggle of Nations monument.

134 **Excursions**: Gohliser Schlösschen (Bach exhibit), Delitzsch, Wurzen.

Some Useful Expressions in German

good morning/afternoon	**Guten Tag**
good evening/night	**Guten Abend/Gute Nacht**
good-bye	**Auf Wiedersehen**
yes/no	**ja/nein**
please/thank you	**bitte/danke**
excuse me	**Verzeihung**
you're welcome	**bitte**
where/when/how	**wo/wann/wie**
how long/how far	**wie lange/wie weit**
yesterday/today/tomorrow	**gestern/heute/morgen**
day/week/month/year	**Tag/Woche/Monat/Jahr**
left/right	**links/rechts**
up/down	**oben/unten**
good/bad	**gut/schlecht**
big/small	**gross/klein**
cheap/expensive	**billig/teuer**
hot/cold	**heiss/kalt**
old/new	**alt/neu**
open/closed	**offen/geschlossen**
easy/difficult	**einfach/schwierig**
Does anyone here speak English/French?	**Spricht hier jemand Englisch/Französisch?**
What does this mean?	**Was bedeutet dies?**
I don't understand.	**Ich verstehe nicht.**
Do you take credit cards/traveller's cheques?	**Akzeptieren Sie Kreditkarten/Reiseschecks?**
Waiter!/waitress!	**Ober!/Fräulein!**
Where are the toilets?	**Wo sind die Toiletten?**
I'd like…	**Ich wünsche…**
How much is that?	**Wieviel kostet es?**
What time is it?	**Wie spät ist es?**
Help me please.	**Helfen Sie mir, bitte.**

Greece

Type of government:	Republic, multi-party centralized
Member of:	EU, GATT, IBRD, IDA, IFC, IMF, OECD
Population:	10.4 million
Area:	131,990sq km (50,961sq miles)
Capital:	Athens (*Athínai*, 748,000/Greater Athens with Piraeus, 3.3m)
Other major cities:	Salonica (*Thessaloníki*, 705,000) Patras (*Pátrai*, 155,000) Heraklion (*Iráklion*, 117,000) Larissa (*Lárisa*, 113,500)
Language:	Greek; English, French, German or Italian spoken in business circles.
Religion:	Predominantly Greek Orthodox, with a very small minority of Greek-rite Catholics
Time zone:	GMT+2, EST+7; DST (Apr-Sep)
Currency:	Drachma Coins: 1, 2, 5, 10, 20, 50 drachmas Notes: 50, 100, 500, 1,000, 5,000 drachmas
Electricity:	220V, 50Hz, AC

Planning your Trip

Visa requirements: For Turkish nationals. (See also p.6.)

Vaccination requirements: None. (See also p.7.)

Import allowances (see also p.7):

	Cigarettes		Cigars		Tobacco	Spirits		Wine
1)	200	or	50	or	250g	1l	and	2l
2)	(800)	or	(200)	or	(1kg)	(10l)	and	(90l)

1) Passengers from countries outside Europe; passengers arriving
   from an EU country with duty-free goods.
2) Non-duty-free goods bought within the EU.

Perfume: 1) 50g; *Toilet water*: 1) 0.25l; *Gifts*: 1) 9,000 drachmas
max. value

There are no official restrictions on goods bought non-duty-free
within the EU, provided they are for personal use only. The above
figures are guidelines to the quantities customs officials will generally find acceptable, so if you are carrying larger quantities you should
be prepared to provide proof that the goods are for your personal use.

Currency restrictions: Non-residents may import up to 100,000
drachmas and export up to 40,000 drachmas (in denominations no
larger than 5,000 drachmas). There is no restriction on the import or
export of foreign currency, but amounts in banknotes in excess of
$1,000 or equivalent must be declared upon entry, and the destination
of sums not re-exported must be proved by showing currency-
exchange receipts. Any offence is punishable by high fines. (See p.7.)

Climate: In general, the climate is Mediterranean in character, with
hot, dry summers and mild, rather rainy winters, but inland areas on
the mainland are cooler.

Clothing: From the middle of May until the end of September the
weather is hot enough for you to get along with light clothing. Winter can bring some chilly and wet weather, so your wardrobe should
be modified accordingly. Business attire remains conservative, even
in the heat of summer.

Hotels: In Athens and some other areas, hotels are classified in various categories: de luxe, A, B, C, D and sometimes E.

Hotel accommodation is scarce everywhere throughout the country in summer and also in September in Salonica during the trade fair. If you arrive without an advance reservation, hotel services at Athens airport and the tourist office in Sýntagma Square will help.

Greek tourist offices abroad: Amsterdam, Brussels, Chicago, Copenhagen, Frankfurt, Helsinki, London, Los Angeles, Madrid, Milan, Montreal, Munich, New York, Paris, Oslo, Rome, Stockholm, Sydney, Tokyo, Toronto, Vienna, Zurich.

Business Briefing

Economic Background

Main industries: Motor vehicle assembly, textiles, chemicals, food processing, tourism.

Main agricultural products: Wheat, sugar beet, maize, grapes, citrus and other fruits, tobacco, cotton.

Main imports: Practically all raw materials, luxury goods and industrial products.

Main exports: Fruit, vegetables, textile yarns and products, iron, steel, nickel, aluminium, petroleum products, tobacco.

Principal trading partners: Germany, Italy, USA, Belgium, Iraq, CIS, UK, France, Netherlands.

GNP: $54 billion; per capita: $5,340.

Inflation rate: 15.6% (1994).

Trade fairs: Main exhibitions are the International Trade Fair and the International Film Festival, both held in Salonica in September. Salonica also hosts a textile trade fair each spring and an agricultural machinery fair in February.

Selected background reading: The *Hellenews Weekly Newsletter* gives an English summary of business and economic information.

Embassy commercial departments usually issue forecasts and surveys of Greek trade and financial movements.

Greek chambers of commerce abroad: Apply to the commercial departments of Greek embassies or consulates.

On the Spot

Office hours: Generally 8am to 2 or 3pm and 5 to 7.30 or 8pm. Government offices 8am-3pm Monday-Friday (most are open to the public on certain mornings, otherwise an appointment is needed).

Public holidays

Jan 1	New Year's Day	Dec 25	Christmas Day
Jan 6	Epiphany	Dec 26	St Stephen's Day
Mar 25	Independence Day	**Movable dates**:	1st day of Lent
May 1	Labour Day		Good Friday
Aug 15	Assumption Day		Easter Monday
Oct 28	Óchi ('No') Day		Ascension

Orthodox Good Friday and Easter Monday usually fall on different days than in Catholic and Protestant countries.

Banks and currency exchange: Generally 8am-2pm, Monday to Thursday, and until 1.30pm on Fridays. Outside of normal hours currency can be changed at some banks' foreign-exchange bureaux until 7 or 8pm. In Sýntagma Square, Athens, the National Bank of Greece is open 8am-8pm Monday-Friday, 9am-4pm on Saturdays and Sundays. In Salonica, the National Bank (at Tsimiskis 11) remains open after hours.

Controls over currency transactions have been significantly relaxed with Greece's entry into the EU. Duties are no longer charged for EU cross-border transactions (except Portugal and Spain), although restrictions are in place for countries not in the EU.

Principal banks: National Bank of Greece, Commercial Bank of Greece, Ionian and Popular Bank of Greece, Credit Bank.

Credit cards and traveller's cheques: Major names of both are usually accepted by larger hotels, car-rental firms and those shops selling anything of substantial interest to the visitor. For dining out, however, you're better relying on cash.

Post and telecommunications: While all services are generally reliable, mail can be slow.

Post office hours are generally 8am-8pm Monday-Friday (smaller offices are closed in the afternoon). The post office at Sýntagma in Athens is open weekdays from 7.30 to 8.30pm, Saturdays from 7.30am to 3pm and Sundays from 9am to 2pm. Stamps are sold in machines outside post offices and at kiosks. The post office clerk is obliged to check the contents of any registered letters as well as parcels addressed to foreign destinations, so don't seal this kind of mail until it has been 'approved'.

Greece's telephone system has direct-dialling facilities to many countries around the world. Nevertheless, trunk lines are often busy and it may be advisable to place your international calls through the operator (tel. 162). At peak traffic times you may have to wait up to two hours for your connection. For assistance in telephoning call 169 for recorded information in English, French and German.

Major cities have offices of Greece's telecommunications organization (OTE), open 24 hours a day; in Athens, it's at Patissíon 85. Branch offices are open from 7am to 10 or 12pm. Public telephone booths usually carry instructions in English. In Athens, blue-painted booths are for local calls and orange ones permit long-distance and direct-dialled international calls. Telecards for cardphones can be bought at kiosks or at OTE offices.

If you want to send a fax the post office's public Intelpost service is available at all main offices. Telegrams and telexes can be sent from the O.T.E. office or from your hotel.

Some useful numbers:

Ambulance, Fire	199	Police	100
Emergency doctor	105	Telegrams (inland)	155
Operator (inland)	151	Telegrams (int.)	165
140 Operator (int.)	162	Tourist police	171

Embassies and consulates: These are listed (in English) in the blue pages of the telephone directory under *Embassies*.

Medical care and health: Emergency treatment is free but if you're insured you'll be certain of better medical care if you should be hospitalized. There are English-speaking doctors and dentists. Pharmacies (*farmakío*) can be identified by a sign with a green, blue or red cross on a white background. Pharmacies take turns in offering a 24-hour service in any main town, and the address of the pharmacy on duty is posted on all pharmacy doors. The tourist police will also be able to help you find it. Medical supplies are easily available, but it's advisable to bring any special medication with you. Certain prescription drugs, including tranquilizers and headache preparations, cannot be carried into the country without a prescription or official document. Fines, even jail sentences, have been imposed on the unwary tourist. Tap water is generally safe to drink.

Services: Translators and interpreters are listed (in English) in the blue pages of the telephone directory under *Translators – interpreters*. The commercial department of your embassy can also provide the names of reliable people. For secretarial assistance, consult the advertising columns in the *Athens News*. Photocopying facilities are widely available and listed in both the English- and the Greek-language telephone directories.

Newspapers: Principal dailies in Athens are *Akrópolis*, *Kathimerini*, *To Víma*, *Eleftherotypía*, *Eleftherios Kósmos*, *Ta Néa*, *To Éthnos*, *Y Avrianí*; *Eléftheros Lógos* and *Makedonía* are Salonica papers. Most leading European publications are sold at main news-stands. The *Athens News* and *Greek News* are published in English. *The Athenian* is an English-language monthly.

Transport
Air – international: Though Athens is the major gateway to Greece, with direct flights or same-day connections from most major cities throughout the world, Salonica, Heraklion, Rhodes and Corfu also have international airports.

Air – domestic: A total of some 30 mainland and island points are served by regular Olympic Airways flights.

Rail: Trains, with first- and second-class compartments, are not particularly comfortable or punctual and are generally avoided by business travellers. A useful fast connection to Salonica leaves from Athens' major international railway station, Stathmós Larísis. Dining service, where available, is inadequate. Advance booking is advised.

Long-distance buses: Coaches provide frequent, punctual connections to principal points on the mainland. However, taxis are often an attractive alternative over long distances where no air link is scheduled.

Waterways: A relaxing alternative to air travel if time is no object. Mainland-to-islands and inter-island boat services vary considerably, depending on route and season. (Because of these variables, travel agents outside Greece find it difficult to keep up to date and to issue valid tickets.) Local travel agents as well as the National Tourist Organization have up-to-the-minute details, and a weekly bulletin on passenger vessel movements is issued. All islands have at least one boat connection a week. Generally, three classes of accommodation (including cabins) are offered, though comfort should not be your prime consideration. The overnight crossing from Piraeus to Heraklion or Chiná (Crete) and Rhodes can be especially recommended. Larger ferries carry cars; advance reservations are absolutely essential in the summer months.

Local public transport: Athens, Salonica and other main centres have good bus services. (Athens also operates trolley-buses.) An underground (subway) line runs from Athens (Kifisiá) to Piraeus. However, walking is the most efficient way to cover short distances in Athens during rush-hours.

Taxis: Taxis are quite inexpensive in Greece. They are plentiful in towns, identifiable by a *taxi* sign in either Greek or Latin letters. Although taxi ranks exist, you are better off getting the hotel porter to hail a cab or call for one. In the capital, all cabs are metered. There's a small extra charge from the airport, the main bus terminals, ports and the railway stations. From 1am to 5am you pay double (the meter rate will be set at 2) and a surcharge applies between 5 and 7am. Drivers have cards with the rates printed. Even if the taxi isn't metered, there are established prices for certain island trips. Tip: not necessary, although you can round up the fare to the nearest 50 drachmas.

Car rental: Cars are available for rental in the larger cities and towns (although rental and fuel are expensive). Demand is high so it is best to book in advance. In Athens, several agencies are located at the Sýntagma end of Singroú Avenue as well as at the airport. Chauffeur-driven cars are also available.

Driving in Greece: An international driving permit is required for visitors bringing in their own car, except for those with EU licences. The Greek Automobile Association (ELPA) will issue an international permit upon presentation of your passport/identity card, national driving licence and one photo. The fee is approximately 1,500 drachmas. (Though car-rental companies – especially in resort areas – do, in fact, accept most national driving licences, it is as well to obtain an international document, which carries a Greek translation.) ELPA's headquarters in Athens at Leofóros Mesogíon 2 (tel. 7791 615) is open from 8.30 to 1.30pm.

Seat belts must be worn, and a red-reflector warning triangle, a fire-extinguisher and a first-aid kit are obligatory. Blood alcohol limit is 50mg/100ml. Fuel (petrol/gas) available is normal (90 octane), super (98 octane), lead-free and diesel.

Parking regulations are strictly enforced. Speed limits are 50kph (31mph) in towns, 100kph (62mph) on motorways (expressways) and 80kph (50mph) on other roads. Toll motorways are good, fast and well-surfaced, but other roads often suffer from poor grading, even in cities. In the country, watch out for wandering livestock and bumps. Right of way in practice seems to be a matter of who gets there first. Though horn-blowing is prohibited in town centres, drivers blast away merrily on winding country roads, and you should do too. Greek drivers expect immediate reactions to city traffic lights and tend to become impatient if they aren't forthcoming. Principal motorways link Athens with Salonica as well as with Corinth and Patras. **143**

Breakdown assistance is provided by ELPA, whose patrol network covers all the main highways of the mainland.

Some distances from Athens: Patras 210km (130 miles), Larissa 355km (220 miles), Salonica 510km (315 miles), Evzoni 550km (340 miles).

Social customs: Greek hospitality is sincere, generous, sometimes overwhelming. Whatever you do, don't turn your back on it. If you show respect towards your prospect's wife, a liking for his children and enthusiasm for invitations and trouble taken on your behalf, you'll be off on the right foot. If you're invited home, take flowers or a cake for the hostess.

Hints for business: Though prior appointments are not usually necessary, the courtesy of phoning ahead will be appreciated, even if the answer is 'why don't you come now?' Business discussions are often pursued over coffee and *oúzo*, the aniseed-flavoured national drink. It is advisable to avoid mention of Cyprus and other controversial aspects of international politics closely affecting Greece. The heat and the summer holidays combine to make late July-early September a period to avoid for business travel. Other unfavourable periods are Christmas to January 6, and the Greek Easter period (from about Holy Wednesday until Easter Wednesday).

Foreign chambers of commerce in Greece: American, Arab, British, German.

Crime and theft: The incidence is low by international standards, though it is only common sense to take normal precautions.

After Hours

Food and drink: Olive oil, lemon, tomatoes, onions, garlic, cheese and oregano are inevitable features of the Greek culinary landscape. Specialities include: *dzadzíki* (yoghurt, garlic and cucumber dip), *dolmádes* (grape leaves stuffed with minced meat and rice), *keftédes* (baked or deep-fried meatballs, usually of minced beef and lamb), *mousaká* (alternate layers of sliced aubergine/eggplant and minced meat baked with a white sauce and grated cheese) and a variety of spit-roasted meat dishes. In Greece, fish is generally grilled or fried, basted with oil and served with lemon sauce. Favourites are *astakós* (Mediterranean lobster or crayfish), *barboúni* (red mullet), *fagrí* (sea bream), *glóssa* (small sole), *kalamaráki* (squid) and *chtapódi* (octopus, usually cut in slices and fried or boiled). The most famous of Greek cheeses, *féta*, is widely sold.

The tangy *retsína* white wine, with its slightly turpentine-like taste, may take some getting used to, but contrasts pleasantly with local food. More familiar-tasting reds, whites and rosés are also available. Greek beer, with German origins, is excellent. Perhaps the most typical local drink is the aniseed-flavoured *oúzo*, reminiscent of French pastis. It's usually mixed with chilled water and served together with a tiny plate of olives, cheese, tomatoes or other hors d'oeuvre. Greek coffee, actually Turkish in origin, is boiled to order in a long-handled copper or aluminium pot and poured, grounds and all, into your little cup. Wait a few minutes before sipping to allow the grounds to settle.

Mealtimes: lunch 1-3pm (hotels), 2-3.30pm (restaurants); dinner 7-10pm (hotels), 9-11.30pm (restaurants). If you're invited out to dinner, don't expect to begin to eat until at least 9.30pm.

Entertainment: Nightclubs and discotheques are to be found in most resorts as well as the capital. In the Athens area, the best are along the shore road from Fáliro as far as Vouliagméni. Foreign films are usually shown in the original language. Athens has a casino.

Taxes, service charges and tipping: Hotel and restaurant bills are generally all-inclusive, but it is customary to leave the waiter a little extra – around 5%. Other tipping recommendations: porters 100 drachmas per bag, cloakroom attendants 50 drachmas, taxi drivers round off fare, barbers/hairdressers 10%.

Sports and recreation: Swimming, sailing, rowing, diving, water-skiing, deep-sea fishing, tennis, golf and riding are easily available to visitors. In winter, skiing facilities are available on Mount Parnassus. **145**

Principal spectator sports are soccer and basketball. The Athens race course is located at the bottom of Singroú Avenue, with races on Wednesdays, Saturdays and sometimes Mondays in summer.

TV and radio: The Greek National Radio (ERT) broadcasts the news and weather in English in the morning, afternoon and evening.

On short-wave bands, reception of the World Service of the BBC is extremely clear. Voice of America's English programmes are also easily picked up (there is a station on Rhodes).

Most hotels, and some bars and restaurants, have TV lounges. Many of the programmes are well-known TV series in English with Greek subtitles and satellite television is often available.

What to buy: Good buys include woollen rugs, cushion covers, blankets, sweaters, embroidery, boots, furs, woodcarvings, silver and gold jewellery, leather goods and *féta* cheese.

General shopping hours: in Athens, Monday, Wednesday, Saturday: 8am-3pm; Tuesday, Thursday, Friday: 8am-2.30pm and 5-8pm (Tourist-oriented shops stay open later.) Elsewhere, hours may vary.

Cities and Sights

ATHENS (*Telephone area code 01*)
Airports: Hellinikón (12km/7 miles from city centre), international; duty-free shop. There are two separate terminals, West and East: the West Terminal is for Olympic Airways traffic only; the East Terminal handles all foreign carriers including charters. Passengers transferring between the two airports should take a taxi: the bus service is infrequent. A bus service operates from the East Terminal to the city, and from the West Terminal to the Olympic office in town.

Double-decker express buses run from the airport to the railway and bus stations at 40-minute intervals (in winter only as far as Omónia). The A (East Terminal) and B (West) go to Kifissoú bus station – for long-distance northbound buses – and the A (East) and B (West) go to Liossíou bus station, the A stopping at the Peloponnese railway station. All four buses stop at Sýntagma/Amalías and Omónia.

Tourist information offices: The central headquarters of the National Tourist Organization (abbreviated EOT in Greek letters) is located at Amerikis 2; tel. 3223 111/9. The main information office is inside the National Bank building at Karagiórgi Servías 2, just off Sýntagma; tel. 3222 545.

Chamber of commerce and industry: Akademias 7; tel. 3604-815.

Sightseeing: Acropolis and surrounding area, especially the Agora and Theatre of Dionysos, Temple of Zeus, Pláka district at foot of Acropolis, Mount Likavittós.

Museums: National Archaeological Museum, Byzantine Museum, Benáki Museum.

Excursions: Delphi, Soúnion, Aegina (with Temple of Aphaia), Epidaurus (theatre), Mycenae.

SALONICA *(Telephone area code 031)*

Airport: Míkra (16km/10 miles from city centre), international; duty-free shop. Frequent bus service into town.

Tourist information office: Aristotélous Square 8; tel. 222 935/271 888.

Chamber of commerce and industry: Tsimiskís 29; tel. 275-341, fax 230 237.

Sightseeing: White Tower, city walls, Arch of Galerius, Byzantine churches of Ágios Geórgios, Ágios Panteleímon, Ágios Dimítrios, Agía Sofía.

Museums: Archaeological Museum, Ethnological and Folklore Museum.

Excursions: Pélla, Phílippi, Kavála, Amfípolis, Mount Áthos.

Some Useful Expressions in Greek

good morning/afternoon	kaliméra/kalispéra
good evening/night	kalispéra/kaliníkta
good-bye	chérete
yes/no	ne/óchi
please/thank you	parakaló/efcharistó
excuse me	me sinchoríte
you're welcome	típota
where/when/how	pou/póte/pos
how long/how far	póso keró/póso makriá
yesterday/today/tomorrow	chthes/símera/ávrio
day/week/month/year	iméra/evdomáda/mínas/ chrónos
left/right	aristerá/dexiá
up/down	epáno/káto
good/bad	kalós/kakós
big/small	megálos/mikrós
cheap/expensive	fthinós/akrivós
hot/cold	zestós/klistós
old/new	palio´s/kenoúrgios
open/closed	aniktós/klistós
early/late	eróns/argá
Does anyone here speak English/French/German?	Milái kanis angliká/ galliká/germaniká?
What does this mean?	Ti siméni aftó?
I don't understand.	Den katalavéno.
Do you take credit cards/ traveller's cheques?	Pérnete pistotikés kártes/traveller's cheques?
Waiter, please!	Parakaló!
Where are the toilets?	Pou íne i toualéttes?
I'd like…	Tha íthela…
How much is that?	Póso káni aftó?
Help me please.	Voithíste me parakaló.

Hungary

Type of government:	Republic, multi-party system, largely centralized
Member of:	GATT, IMF
Population:	10.3 million
Area:	93,030sq km (35,919sq miles)
Capital:	Budapest (2.1m)
Other major cities:	Debrecen (216,137) Miskolc (192,355) Szeged (177,680) Pécs (170,540) Györ (130,300)
Language:	Hungarian; the most common business language for Westerners is English, but German is also widely spoken, particularly among the older generation; Russian.
Religion:	Catholic (65%), Protestant (25%), Eastern Orthodox (3%)
Time zone:	GMT+1, EST+6; DST (Apr-Sep)
Currency:	Forint (abbr. Ft) = 100 fillérs Coins: 10, 20, 50 fillérs; Ft1, 2, 5, 10, 20 Notes: Ft50, 100, 500, 1,000
Electricity:	220V, 50Hz, AC

Planning your Trip

Visa requirements: No visa requirements for citizens of European countries and North America planning to stay for less than a month. Some Latin American citizens are exempt altogether.

Vaccination requirements: None. (See also p.7.)

Import allowances (see also p.7):

Cigarettes		Cigars		Tobacco	Spirits		Wine
200	or	50	or	250g	1l	and	2l

Gifts: Up to Ft8,000; *Perfume*: permitted in 'reasonable quantity'

Currency restrictions: Visitors may be required to report the currencies they're carrying, though there is no limit on the import of foreign funds. As for Hungarian currency, it is forbidden to import or to export more than 1,000 forints. Note that there is a restriction on the amount of forints that may be converted into hard currency when leaving the country.

Climate: Hungary has a continental climate with hot summers and cold winters. Snow can impede road traffic in winter. The rainy season is in early spring and November. Average daytime temperatures:

Spring	Summer	Autumn	Winter
15°C (59°F)	20°C (68°F)	9°C (48°F)	-2°C (28°F)

Clothing: Light clothing is sufficient in summer. In winter warm clothing should be worn, including overcoat, scarf, gloves and warm shoes. For business conservative dress is customary.

Hotels: Hotel rooms are often in short supply so reservations well in advance are advisable. Busiest periods: during international fairs, the summer holiday season and the autumn congress period. Ibusz, the state travel agency, which maintains offices abroad, is preferable for

hotel bookings. (Local travel agencies also handle hotel reservations but aren't always reliable.) A booking fee is charged. When hotels are fully booked, travel agencies can provide private accommodation.

Hungarian tourist offices abroad: Berlin, Brussels, Cologne, Frankfurt, London, Moscow, New York, Paris, Prague, Rome, Stockholm, Tokyo, Vienna, Warsaw. In most other major cities, tourist information is handled by the Hungarian state airline, MALÉV.

Business Briefing

Economic Background

Main industries: Coal, alumina and bauxite mining, machine tools, heavy commercial vehicles, polyvinylchloride and some other basic chemicals, pharmaceuticals, food and canning industries, textiles and shoe production.

Main agricultural products: Wheat, sugar beet, sweetcorn, fruit, potatoes, barley, rye, oats, wine; livestock: pigs, poultry and cattle.

Main imports: Semi-finished products, machinery, construction materials, industrial and consumer goods, oil.

Main exports: Chemicals, iron, steel, semi-finished products, machinery and instruments, agricultural and processed food products, livestock.

Principal trading partners: Germany, Austria, Italy.

GNP: $27 billion; per capita: $2,560.

Inflation rate: 23% (1994).

Trade fairs: Budapest's International Spring Fair (for machinery and heavy equipment), held in May, and the Budapest International Autumn Fair (for consumer goods), organized in September, are the two main annual expositions. For details on these and other fairs, contact Hungexpo, PO Box 44, 1441 Budapest; tel. 157 35 55, fax 127 60 31. Most exhibitions take place in Budapest.

Selected background reading: National commercial and trade statistics are issued in English annually by the country's statistical office. Other publications: *Hungarian Heavy Industries*, *Hungarian Exporters*, *Hungaropress Information Service*, *Marketing in Hungary* **151**

(available in English and German, Hungarian Chamber of Commerce). The National Bank of Hungary publishes a *Quarterly Review*.

Hungarian chambers of commerce abroad: London, Paris, New Delhi, Tokyo. Otherwise apply to the commercial departments of Hungarian embassies or consulates.

On the Spot

Office hours: 8am-4.30pm Monday-Friday, Saturday mornings 8am-1pm.

Public holidays

Jan 1	New Year's Day	Dec 25	Christmas Day
Mar 15	National Holiday	Dec 26	Boxing Day
May 1	Labour Day		
Aug 20	St Stephen's Day		
Oct 24	National Holiday	**Movable dates**:	Easter Monday

Banking and currency exchange: Banking hours are 9am-5pm Monday-Friday and 9am-11am on Saturdays. Exchange facilities exist at airports, railway stations, banks, hotels, travel agencies, some shopping centres and restaurants. Currency-exchange hours are normally 9am-10pm (closed Saturday afternoons, Sundays and public holidays). Major hotels, airports and railway stations will change money virtually round the clock.

Principal banks: Hungarian National Bank (*Magyar Nemzeti Bank*), Hungarian Foreign Trade Bank (*Magyar Külkereskedelmi Bank*), National Savings Bank (*Országos Takarékpénztár*).

Credit cards and traveller's cheques: Internationally recognized credit cards and traveller's cheques are widely accepted in tourist-oriented establishments.

Post and telecommunications: Post offices handle mail, telephone, telegraph and telex services, but not international money transfers.

The main post office in Petőfi Sándor utca in Budapest is open 7am-8pm Monday-Saturday. An international telex, telefax, telegraph and telephone office at Petőfi Sándor utca, Budapest, is also open 7am-8pm Monday-Friday, until 7pm on Saturdays, and with limited service on Sunday mornings. Major hotels also provide postal and telecommunications facilities.

Some useful numbers:

Ambulance	04	Directory inquiries in	
Fire	05	foreign languages	1172 200
Police	07		

Principal area codes: Budapest 1, Györ 96, Miskolc 46.

Embassies and consulates: Embassies and consulates are listed in the telephone directory under *Külképviseletek.*

Medical care and health: The standard of medical treatment is high. In case of emergency, health authorities will direct foreigners to specialized medical centres. In virtually every hospital some doctors speak foreign languages. Fees are very reasonable, and in emergency cases treatment is usually free. Medicine and pharmaceutical supplies are readily available at low cost; in emergency cases, they're free. A number of pharmacies are open around the clock on a rotating basis. Their addresses are posted in the windows of all pharmacies. Telephone operators and hotels have details. You can safely drink tap water.

Services: Large international hotels may be able to assist with secretarial help. Interpreters may be obtained through major tourist agencies. Translators are employed by OFFI, the state translation office, Bajza utca 52, Budapest VI; tel. 1129 610. Boy-Service/ Szolgálat (Bajcsy Zsilinszky ut 20, Budapest V) and Foto-Optika Co-operatives (Kossuth Lajos utca 17, Budapest V) handle photocopying.

Newspapers: Principal dailies: *Népszabadság, Népszava, Magyar Nemzet, Magyar Hirlap, Esti Hirlap.* All the principal foreign newspapers including *International Herald Tribune, Le Monde, Die Presse,* are available both at hotel news-stands and at kiosks throughout the capital. Local foreign-language newspapers include the bilingual English–German *Daily News/Neueste Nachrichten* (daily except Sunday and Monday). A free monthly magazine, *Programme in* **153**

Hungary, has parallel texts in German and English. The *Hungarian Observer* is an independent monthly magazine covering politics, culture and business in English. The journal *New Hungarian Quarterly* (in English) offers insights into Hungarian life, culture and politics.

Transport

Air: Budapest Ferihegy is the country's only commercial airport. There are no scheduled domestic flights.

Rail: Hungarian State Railways maintains a dense rail network, with both first- and second-class seating. For express trains, reservations are necessary, either through Ibusz or the railway station. Rail passes valid for 7 or 10 days' travel are available.

Long-distance buses: Very efficient, punctual intercity bus services are operated by Mavaut and Volán and several other companies. Buses are comfortable but business people usually prefer hired cars.

Local public transport: Buses and trams are available in major cities. The most comprehensive of all serves Budapest, where no place is more than 500 metres (1,500 feet) from a bus, tram or subway stop. Maps of all the lines, both surface and underground, are sold at major stations. Transport maps are also available in other major cities, though only Budapest has a subway (metro). Day tickets for unlimited travel can be used interchangeably on all forms of public transport.

Taxis: Taxis are available in all major towns. For destinations outside of city limits the passenger pays driver the fare for his return journey to the city boundary. You can hail a cab on the street (when the roof sign is lit), phone for one or go to a taxi rank.

Car rental: Cars can be rented from several agencies, at the airport, at railway stations and through hotels or tourist offices. Bills must be settled in hard currency.

Driving in Hungary: Roads are adequately maintained. Drive with care: the accident rate is one of the world's highest. At marked crossings, pedestrians have priority. Speed limits in towns and villages, unless otherwise indicated, are 60kph (37mph), on country roads

80kph (50mph), on two-lane motorways 100kph (60mph), and on four-lane motorways (expressways) 120kph (75mph).

Use of seat belts is obligatory, and a red-reflector warning triangle, a set of spare bulbs and a first-aid kit must be carried. The car must be fitted with rubber mudguards. Blood alcohol limit is a strictly enforced zero. Fuel (petrol/gas) available is normal (86 octane), super (92 and 98 octane), lead-free (rare) and diesel.

On the main roads yellow patrol cars of the Hungarian Automobile Association deal with breakdowns. On the Budapest–Lake Balaton motorway there's an emergency phone callbox every two kilometres. For a 24-hour breakdown service dial 252 8000 in Budapest.

Some distances of main towns from Budapest: Györ 125km (80 miles), Szeged 170km (105 miles), Pécs 190km (120 miles), Debrecen 225km (140 miles).

Social customs: Invitations to luncheons or dinners in restaurants are customary, though Hungarian hosts usually don't invite their foreign guests to their homes.

Hints for business: Appointments aren't normally made on Saturdays though most employees work mornings every other Saturday.

Due to summer holidays and year-end festivities, it's best to avoid July and August and the mid-December to mid-January period for business travel.

Foreign chambers of commerce in Hungary: Austrian, Russian.

Crime and theft: Business travellers are advised to take normal care of their belongings, valuables and business papers, though crime is not a major problem in Hungary. Beware of illegal currency transactions.

After Hours

Food and drink: Most hotels and restaurants offer a variety of local and international dishes.

Gulyásleves (goulash soup) is the Hungarian speciality: chunks of beef, potatoes, onion, tomatoes and peppers with paprika, caraway **155** seeds and garlic. (What is called goulash abroad is a Hungarian meat stew actually named *pörkölt*.) Other dishes worth trying include *ujházy tyúkleves* (chicken broth), *halászlé* (fish soup), *paprikás csirke* (chicken paprika) and *töltött káposzta* (stuffed cabbage). Be prepared for heaped servings of meat and fish with a choice of side dishes and salads – very highly flavoured, and spiced with the ubiquitous paprika.

Red wines: Egri bikavér, Villányi, Pinot Noir. White wines: Csopaki Rizling, Badacsonyi Kéknyelü, Tokaji. Aperitifs: *barack* (apricot brandy), *cseresznye* (cherry brandy). Better restaurants and bars have imported spirits, though at high prices.

Mealtimes: lunch noon-2pm, dinner 7-10pm.

Entertainment: Budapest offers many entertainment possibilities, from concerts and cinemas to discotheques. They're listed in the monthly *Programme in Hungary*, available free at hotels. The hotel staff is also able to orient foreign visitors. Most foreign films are dubbed in Hungarian.

Taxes, service charges and tipping: VAT of 25% is included in the price of most goods. A service charge is included in the bill at restaurants but 10% is generally given to the waiter. At top-class hotels 15% service charge is added to the bill. Tip taxi drivers 10%, porters Ft30 per bag, barbers/hairdressers 15%.

Sports and recreation: Hotels sometimes have swimming pools and tennis courts; hunting, horse riding and water sports in the Lake Balaton area are also favourite pursuits.

Popular spectator sports include soccer, basketball, ice hockey, volleyball, handball and water polo.

TV and radio: Local programming is mainly in Hungarian. Occasionally, on television, there are regional programmes in German. Brief news bulletins for foreigners are broadcast, in summer only, on Budapest Radio and on TV. Radio Bridge has an hourly news bulletin from Voice of America; times are listed in the weekly radio-TV guide. Around Budapest, Radio Bridge broadcasts all day in English.

What to buy: Handicrafts, woodcarvings, rugs, local wines and spirits, Herend chinaware.

Shopping hours: generally 10am-6pm Monday-Friday (until 7pm on Thursdays). Some shops are open till 2pm on Saturdays.

Cities and Sights

BUDAPEST (*Telephone area code 1*)
Airport: Ferihegy (16km/10 miles from city centre), international, is the country's only commercial airport; it has two terminals 6km (4 miles) apart, so check which one your flight is using to avoid confusion. Duty-free shop, but prices higher than in western duty-free shops. Frequent bus service.

Tourist Information offices: The Hungarian Tourinform service, situated at Sütö utca 2 in central Budapest, provides information on accommodation, entertainment and other tourist information in English, French, German, Russian and Spanish. You can also call 1179 800 in Budapest to obtain answers to your questions. If you prefer to write, contact Tourinform, PO Box 185, 1364 Budapest.

Chamber of commerce: Hungarian Chamber of Commerce, PO Box 106, 1389 Budapest; tel. 153 3333, fax 153 1285. Budapest Chamber of Commerce, Krisztina krt 99, 1016 Budapest; tel. 175 6764, fax 202 1285.

Sightseeing and excursions: Main sightseeing tours include a cruise on the Danube north of Budapest, taking in the ancient city of Esztergom with its cathedral, the church gallery, and Visegrád (the citadel); Lake Balaton and the Hungarian plain, particularly the Puszta and Bugac regions.

Some Useful Expressions in Hungarian

good morning/afternoon	**jó reggelt/jó napot**
good evening/night	**jó estét/jó éjszakát**
good-bye	**viszontlátásra**
yes/no	**igen/nem**
please/thank you	**kérem/köszönöm**
excuse me	**bocsánat**
you're welcome	**szivesen**
where/when/how	**hol/mikor/hogyan**
how long/how far	**mennyi ideig/milyen messze**
yesterday/today/tomorrow	**tegnap/ma/holnap**
day/week/month/year	**nap/hét/hónap/év**
left/right	**bal/jobb**
up/down	**fel/le**
good/bad	**jó/rossz**
big/small	**nagy/kicsi**
cheap/expensive	**olcsó/drága**
hot/cold	**meleg/hideg**
old/new	**régi/uj**
open/closed	**nyitva/zárva**
early/late	**korán/késön**
Does anyone here speak English/French/German?	**Beszél itt valaki angolul/franciául/németül?**
What does this mean?	**Ez mit jelent?**
I don't understand.	**Nem értem.**
Do you take credit cards/traveller's cheques?	**Elfogadnak hitelkártyát/utazócsekket?**
Waiter!/Waitress!	**Pincér! Pincérnö!**
Where are the toilets?	**Hol van a WC/mosdó?**
I'd like…	**Szeretnék…**
How much is that?	**Mennyibe kerül?**
Help me please.	**Legyen szives, segitsen.**

Iceland

Type of government:	Republic, multi-party centralized
Member of:	EFTA, GATT, IBRD, IFC, IMF, OECD
Population:	300,000
Area:	102,846sq km (39,709sq miles)
Capital:	Reykjavík (85,000/GUA 100,850)
Other major cities:	Kópavogur (16,500)
	Akureyri (14,000)
	Hafnarfjörur (15,500)
	Keflavík (7,500)
	Akranes (5,000)
Language:	Icelandic; English, Danish and occasionally German are spoken in business circles.
Religion:	Protestant (99%)
Time zone:	GMT, EST+5
Currency:	Icelandic króna (abbr. kr) = 100 aurar
	Coins: kr1, 5, 10, 50
	Notes: kr100, 500, 1,000, 5,000
Electricity:	220V, 50Hz, AC

Planning your Trip

Visa requirements: For nationals of Turkey and South Africa. (See also p.6.)

Vaccination requirements: None. (See also p.7.)

Import allowances (see also p.7):

Cigarettes		Cigars	Tobacco	Spirits	Wine
200	or	250g of other tobacco products		1l and	1l

Currency restrictions: Up to kr8,000 may be imported or exported. Any amount of foreign currency may be taken into the country and up to the same amount taken out of the country again. (See also p.7.)

Climate: Thanks to the moderating influence of a branch of the Gulf Stream, Iceland enjoys a cool, temperate, oceanic climate considerably less rigorous than its latitude may lead one to expect. The weather is very changeable; it is almost always windy, with gales common occurrences and hurricanes not unusual.

The wettest region is the southwest, and the driest the northeast. Snow is an occasional problem in city streets but it is usually cleared away fairly quickly. Average temperatures in Reykjavík are 0°C (32°F) in winter and 12°C (55°F) in summer, though extremes in either direction are frequent. For nearly three months in summer there is almost continuous daylight. The dark period in winter, with only 3-4 hours of daylight each day, lasts from mid-November to the end of January. The northern lights are often seen, especially in autumn and early winter.

Clothing: Warm outer clothing and good-quality shoes are needed all year round. However, light-weight suits and dresses are advisable for indoor wear as geothermal central-heating systems are seldom adjusted to less than 20°C (68°F). Casual dress is popular in Iceland, but conservative suits are considered more appropriate for business people and at almost all restaurants.

Hotels: Many hotels in the west and east of the country are open only during the summer months, while others are open all year round. They are quite expensive but well-appointed. Advance booking is essential in summer.

Icelandic tourist information abroad: The only Iceland tourist offices maintained outside the country are in Frankfurt – with branch offices in Amsterdam (Eagle Air) and Paris (Icelandair) – London, New York and Tokyo. Elsewhere information can be obtained through offices of Icelandair and Eagle Air.

Business Briefing

Economic Background

Main industries: Aluminium production, woollen textiles, knitted goods, ferrosilicon, diatomite, tourism.

Main agricultural products and fisheries: Fishing, fish processing, potatoes, turnips.

Main imports: Virtually all industrial products and many foodstuffs.

Main exports: Fish and fish products, aluminium, woollens.

Principal trading partners: USA, UK, Denmark, Germany, Norway, Sweden.

GNP: $4.3 billion; per capita: $16,473 (1992).

Inflation rate: 3.7% (1994).

Selected background reading: The most reliable survey of commercial and trade figures is contained in *Hagtölur Mánadarins* (economic bulletin) published monthly by the Central Bank in Icelandic with an English appendix. The bank also publishes the useful *Economic Statistics Quarterly*.

Other publications: *Iceland* (Central Bank), *The Economy of Iceland* (Central Bank), *Business Directory of Iceland* (Árblik), *Icelandic Firms* (Frjalst Framtak), *Handy Facts on Iceland* (Iceland Review) and *Iceland in a Nutshell* (Iceland Travel Books) provide a general picture of the country.

Icelandic chambers of commerce abroad: Apply to commercial departments of embassies or consulates.

On the Spot

Office hours: 9am-5pm Monday-Friday.

Public holidays

Jan 1	New Year's Day	**Movable dates**:
May 1	Labour Day	Maundy Thursday
June 17	National Day	Good Friday
Dec 24	Christmas Eve	Easter Monday
Dec 25	Christmas Day	1st day of summer (3rd or
Dec 26	Boxing Day	4th Thursday in April)
Dec 31	New Year's Eve	Ascension Day
	(afternoon only)	Whit Monday
		Shop and Office Workers' Holiday
		(1st Monday in August)

Banks and currency exchange: Banks are generally open 9.15am-4pm Monday-Friday (Thursday also 5-6pm). Outside these hours money can be changed at the Tourist Information Centre in Reykjavik, at hotels, restaurants and souvenir shops.

Principal banks: Bunadarbanki Islands, Landsbanki Islands, Utvegsbanki Islands. These institutions have facilities for international banking services.

Credit cards and traveller's cheques: Major credit cards and traveller's cheques are honoured at hotels, souvenir shops and restaurants.

Post and telecommunications: Inland and international postal services are essentially reliable, though bad weather inevitably causes delays, and not only in winter.

Reykjavik's central post office (Pósthusið) is open Monday-Friday 8.30am-4.30pm. The post office in the central bus station is open from noon to 7.30pm, Monday-Friday, and Saturday 9am-1pm.

The capital's telephone and telegraph office (Símstöðin) is open weekdays from 8.15am-4.30pm Monday-Friday, and from 9am to 7pm on Saturdays. In the telephone directories, subscribers are listed under their first names (see SOCIAL CUSTOMS). Most hotels and some businesses will allow guests to use their telex facilities.

Some useful numbers in the Reykjavik area:

Ambulance	11100	Pharmacy	18888
Dentist	22411	Police	11166
Doctor	696600	Telegrams (day)	06
after hours:	21230	(night)	16411
Operator	08		

Principal area codes: Akranes 92, Akureyri 96, Keflavik 92, Reykjavik 91.

Embassies and consulates: These are listed in the telephone directory in their national languages.

Medical care and health: Health care is excellent and costs are moderate. Hotels and embassies have arrangements with doctors to take care of emergencies. Virtually all medical staff speak English. For emergency medical help or in the case of an accident, call 696600, or attend the Emergency Ward at Borgarspítalin, Rejkavik. The medical health centre at Barónsstígur 47, Rejkavik, is open 5pm to 8am and 24 hours on holidays and weekends; tel. 21230.

Many remedies require a prescription in Iceland. Pharmacies (*apótek*) are open from 9am-6pm on weekdays. Additionally, there is always at least one open 24 hours in Rejkavik – look for notices in pharmacy windows. As Iceland has agreements with other countries (especially Scandinavian), health care is subsidized for some foreigners. Tap water is safe to drink.

Services: Authorized translators and interpreters can be found in the yellow pages of the telephone directory under *Skjalathýðendur og ómtúlkar*. Photocopying facilities are given under *Ljósrit*.

Newspapers: *Althyðublaðið, Dagblaðið og Vísir (DV), Morgunblaðið, Tíminn* and *Thjóðviljinn* are the nation's dailies. Many internationally known newspapers and magazines are available. *Atlantica – Icelandic Review*, issued quarterly in English, provides information of interest to visitors, as does *News from Iceland*, appearing monthly. **163**

Transport

Air – international: Iceland's gateway airport is situated 50km (30 miles) away from the capital at Keflavik. Direct flights operate to more than a dozen European and several North American cities, but same-day connections are available from many other major centres.

Air – domestic: A popular means of travel in this sparsely populated and rugged country without railways. Reykjavik and about a dozen centres throughout the country are served by regular flights. Advance booking is advised.

Long-distance buses: In summer, bus services operate throughout the country with generally one trip per day in both directions between towns round the coast. Schedules are reduced in winter.

Waterways: An infrequent coastal steamer service operates year-round. In addition, there are two principal ferry routes: Reykjavik-Akranes (four trips per day in both directions) and the south coast to the Westmann Islands (one trip daily in both directions).

Local public transport: Reykjavik has an excellent bus service which runs from 6am to 1am weekdays and 10am to midnight on weekends. All routes go via one of the two main transfer points (Laekjargata or Hlemmur). Bus stops are marked SVR, and individual tickets or booklets may be bought from the driver. A free transfer ticket can be requested if two routes are to be travelled. Few towns outside the capital have local bus services.

Taxis: Taxis are plentiful in major localities. They operate from ranks, but can also be called for. Fares are displayed. Evening and weekend rates are nearly double weekdays', and waiting charges are high.

Car rental: International and local agencies operate in Reykjavik. The choice is usually between a VW and a four-wheel-drive vehicle. While the former will be adequate for use in town and the immediate vicinity during the summer months, anybody planning to drive into the barren hinterland is strongly advised to take a four-wheel-drive jeep – with two-way radio fitted. Taxi companies can provide chauffeur-driven cars.

Driving in Iceland: The streets of Reykjavik and some main roads in the immediate vicinity are paved, and kept reasonably clear of snow in winter. Elsewhere driving has an adventurous flavour to it, with one-way bridges and rough trails prevalent and surfaced roads virtually non-existent. Service stations are rare. Fuel (petrol/gas) available is super (97-98 octane), normal (93 octane) and diesel. Special precautions (fuel supplies, extra warm clothing, food) should be taken if driving into the interior where you may not meet another vehicle for a day or two. The country is covered by a radio network for the use of drivers in distress. Seat belts are compulsory. The police strictly enforce the 50mg/100ml alcohol limit and speed limits (45kph/28mph in built-up areas and 70kph/43mph outside towns). Before undertaking a long journey, take local advice as to driving conditions, times, etc.

Social customs: One of the first things to strike a visitor is the use of first names. Icelanders are always addressed by their given names. The family name is merely an indication of whose son or daughter he or she is. (Jón Kjartansson, for instance, wouldn't be addressed as Mr Kjartansson but as Jón, the son of Kjartan.) Married women don't, in general, use their husband's name. Jón Kjartansson's wife would be, let's say, Eydis Björnsdóttir ('Björn's daughter'). She'd be known as Eydis and not Mrs Kjartansson, as she remains the daughter of Björn – not the son of Kjartan. Similarly, Icelanders find it difficult to use visitors' surnames as the honorific 'Mr' is used in Iceland only when formally addressing the nation's president or a bishop. Icelanders are reserved, although friendly, but once they've got to know you, they expect reciprocal friendship, both in the office and outside it.

Hints for business: Business people are welcome all year round but summer visits should be planned well in advance due both to the shortage of hotel rooms and also to the fact that their Icelandic counterparts often travel abroad then, combining business with pleasure. Iceland's business community is very quick to accept quality goods in the consumer field but as the market is small they may be cautious at first while they conduct a feasibility study. Appointments aren't usually necessary as a tradition prevails of 'dropping in'. However, it's advisable to telephone in advance to check that your contact is available: Icelanders take advantage of good weather by going out and enjoying it. Punctuality isn't observed in Iceland. Home hospitality is usual, and so is the return of the favour at the guest's hotel or a restaurant. At the end of a meal, or even after a coffee, the guest is expected to thank his host for the repast. The host then wishes the guest that the food 'may do you good'.

Crime and theft: The incidence is very low by world standards.

After Hours

Food and drink: Icelandic cuisine is truly international, but no visitor should ignore the country's famed fish and lamb specialities. As in the other Scandinavian countries, hotels here often put on a sumptuous cold buffet which is likely to include some unusual items – such as whale and shark. Open sandwiches are a popular snack.

There are no public bars, but cocktail lounges can be found in all major hotels and restaurants. While no strong beer is available, almost every type of spirit as well as imported wines can be found. Icelandic aquavit, *Brennivin* (locally referred to as 'the black death'), packs a punch you should be aware of in advance. Alcohol is a state monopoly and can only be purchased at special state-run shops.

Mealtimes: lunch noon-2.30pm, dinner 7-10pm.

Entertainment: A number of discotheques and dance spots – some with floor shows – highlight the nightlife scene. Cinemas show films in their original language. There are also concerts and art exhibitions.

Taxes, service charges and tipping: Tax and service charges are included in hotel and restaurant bills. Tipping is not customary – many people could be insulted if offered a tip.

Sports and recreation: Naturally heated swimming pools abound and are often crowded, even in mid-winter when it is an exquisite pleasure to swim in warm water with snow piled high round the edge of the pool. River and lake fishing is outstanding and attracts people from all round the world. Inquire about licences locally. In winter, skiing is popular. Chess is a favourite indoor game the whole year round.

The most popular spectator sports are soccer (summer) and basketball and handball (winter).

TV and radio: TV screens many foreign programmes in their original language. There is no television on Thursdays or in the month of July. Radio broadcasts are in Icelandic. News in English is broadcast daily on Radio Reykjavik between May and September. The American-manned NATO base at Keflavik puts out programmes on medium wave.

What to buy: Woollen goods are excellent, with well-stocked stores in Reykjavík and at Keflavík airport. Traditional handicrafts of high quality include silver jewellery and woodcarvings. Books are an Icelandic speciality, often in English and lavishly illustrated. The sales tax will not be refunded on goods bought for export.

Shopping hours are generally 9am-6pm Monday to Friday, 9am-noon on Saturdays (many are closed on Saturdays in summer).

Cities and Sights

REYKJAVÍK (*Telephone area code 91*)

Airports: Keflavík (50km/30 miles from city centre) is the country's only international airport; duty-free shop serves *arriving* passengers. Bus service to city centre. The Reykjavík municipal airport (close to the centre of town) serves domestic traffic only.

Tourist information centre: Laekjargafa 3; tel. 274 88, fax 62 47 49.

Chamber of commerce: Hús veslunarinnar, Kringlunni 7, Reykjavík; tel. 67 66 66, fax 68 65 64.

Rejkavík card: Allows free transport on city buses and free entry to various attractions (pools, museums) on one, two or three days.

Sightseeing: Parliament, city lake, National Museum and Art Gallery, Municipal Art Gallery, Arbær Folk Museum.

Excursions: Thingvellir (ancient parliament site), Gullfoss waterfall, Geysir (geothermal activity), Westman Islands, Akureyri, Lake Myvatn. **167**

Some Useful Expressions in Icelandic

good morning/afternoon	góan dag/gott kvöld
good evening/night	gott kvöld/góða nótt
good-bye	bless
yes/no	já/nei
please/thank you	gjöru svo vel/takk fyrir
excuse me	fyrirgefðu
you're welcome	verði þóēpu
where/when/how	hvar/hvenær/hvernig
how long/how far	hvað lengi/hve langt
yesterday/today/tomorrow	í gær/í dag/á morgun
day/week/month/year	dagur/vika/mánuður/ár
left/right	vinstri/hægri
up/down	upp/niður
good/bad	gott/slæmt
big/small	stórt/lítið
cheap/expensive	ódýrt/dýrt
old/new	gamalt/nýtt
open/closed	opið/lokað
early/late	snemma/seint
Does anyone here speak English/French/German?	Er einhver hér sem talar ensku/frönsku/þýsku?
What does this mean?	Hvað þýðir þetta?
I don't understand.	Ég skil ekki.
Do you take credit cards/traveller's cheques?	Takið þér kredit kort/ferðávísun?
Waiter!/Waitress!	Þjónn!/þjónustustúlka!
Where are the toilets?	Hvar er snyrtingin?
I'd like…	Mig myndi langa…
How much is that?	Hvað kostar þetta?
Help me please.	Viltu hjálpa mér.

Ireland

Type of government:	Republic, multi-party centralized
Member of:	EU, GATT, IBRD, IFC, IMF, OECD
Population:	3.6 million
Area:	70,282sq km (27,136sq miles)
Capital:	Dublin (*Baile Atha Cliath*, 478,000/ GUA 1m)
Other major cities:	Cork (*Corcaigh*, 282,790)
	Limerick (*Luimneach*, 109,816)
	Dun Laoghaire (55,000)
	Galway (*An Ghaillimh*, 47,000)
	Waterford (*Port Láirge*, 40,000)
Languages:	English; Gaelic, the other national language, is in limited local use mainly in certain western districts.
Religion:	Predominantly Catholic (92%)
Time zone:	GMT, EST+5; DST (Mar-Oct)
Currency:	Irish punt or pound (symbolized £) =100 pence (abbr. p)
	Coins: 1, 2, 5, 10, 20, 50p, £1
	Notes: £5, 10, 20, 50, 100
Electricity:	220V, 50Hz, AC

Planning your Trip

Visa requirements: None. *Note:* There is no passport control on traffic between the United Kingdom and the Irish Republic. Irish and United Kingdom nationals travelling without a passport are advised to carry a driving licence or other document showing place of residence and/or nationality. (See also p.6.)

Vaccination requirements: None. (See also p.7.)

Import allowances (see also p.7):

	Cigarettes		Cigars		Tobacco	Spirits		Wine
1)	200	and	50	or	250g	1l	and	2l
2)	(800)	or	(200)	or	(1kg)	(10l)	and	(90l)
1) Passengers from countries outside Europe; duty-free goods bought in EU countries by European residents.								
2) Non-duty-free goods bought within the EU.								

Perfume: 1), 2) 50g; *Toilet water*: 1), 2) 0.25l
Gifts: 1), 2) IR£34 max. value

There are no official restrictions on goods bought non-duty-free within the EU, provided they are for personal use only. The above figures are guidelines to the quantities customs officials will generally find acceptable, so if you are carrying larger quantities you should be prepared to provide proof that the goods are for your personal use.

Currency restrictions: There are no restrictions on the import of local or foreign currencies. Up to 150 Irish pounds or its equivalent in foreign money may be exported. (See also p.7.)

Climate: Ireland enjoys a mild, humid climate with few extremes. The weather is quite changeable, showers often alternating with blue sky several times a day in unsettled spells.

Some average temperatures in Dublin:

Jan	Apr	July	Oct
5°C (42°F)	8°C (46°F)	15°C (59°F)	10°C (50°F)

Clothing: Medium-weight clothing is adequate in summer, with something warmer for cool evenings. In winter a thick overcoat is needed. Rainwear or an umbrella is essential at all times of year. In business circles dress is often casual.

Hotels: During the first week of May (Spring Show) and first week of August (Horse Show), hotels soon become fully booked. Hotel bookings can be made locally through tourist offices which also have listings of hotels. Tariffs are government-controlled.

Irish tourist offices abroad: Amsterdam, Brussels, Copenhagen, Frankfurt, Helsinki, London, Madrid, Milan, New York, Oslo, Paris, Sydney, Stockholm, Toronto.

Business Briefing

Economic Background

Principal industries: Food processing, meat products, tourism, chemicals, light industry, electronics components, crystal glass, clothing, brewing, distilling, metal ores.

Main agricultural products: Beef, lamb, dairy products, sugar beet, cereals, potatoes.

Main imports: Most heavy machinery and motor vehicles, oil and petroleum by-products, consumer goods.

Main exports: Agricultural produce, livestock, textiles, metal ores.

Major trading partners: UK, USA, Germany, France, Netherlands, Japan.

GNP: $30 billion; per capita: $8,500.

Inflation rate: 2.4% (1994).

Trade fairs: Some of the principal events held annually in Dublin are the Boat Show (Jan), Coin Fair (Jan), Spring Show and Industries Fair (May), Motor Show (Feb-Mar), Futura Fashion Fair (autumn).

Selected background reading: *Economic Review* (annual) (Confederation of Irish Industry), *Irish Statistical Bulletin* (quarterly) (Government Publications), *Trade Statistics of Ireland* (monthly) (Government Publications).

Irish chambers of commerce abroad: Apply to commercial departments of Irish embassies or consulates.

On the Spot

Office hours: 9am-1pm and 2pm-5.30pm Monday-Friday.

Public holidays

Jan 1	New Year's Day	Dec 25	Christmas Day
Mar 17	St Patrick's Day	Dec 26	Boxing Day
Movable dates:			
Good Friday		1st Monday of June	
Easter Monday		1st Monday of Aug	
1st Monday of May		last Monday of Oct	

Banks and currency exchange: Banking hours are 10am-12.30pm and 1.30-3pm Monday-Friday (until 5pm Thursdays).

All major banks provide exchange facilities. Major post offices, including the GPO in Dublin, have a *Bureau de change*. Some international travel agencies also change money and traveller's cheques. In addition, the bank at Dublin Airport is open every day of the year except Christmas, 6.45am-9pm, and the O'Connell Street Tourist Information Office in Dublin and the Cork Office in Grand Parade also operate money exchange services. Most hotels will change money, but the rate is not as good as in banks or currency-exchange offices.

Principal banks are the Bank of Ireland, Ulster Bank, Allied Irish Banks and the National Irish Bank.

Credit cards and traveller's cheques: Major credit cards are accepted in larger and tourist-oriented establishments, and traveller's cheques more widely.

Post and telecommunications: Services are generally reliable. Post office hours are 9am-5.30pm Monday-Saturday. Dublin's main post office (O'Connell Street) is open until 8pm, 6.30pm on Sundays.

The national telephone network is automatic and international direct dialling facilities are available. Calls are heavily surcharged by some hotels; check before placing a call, or call from a card phone instead. Phone cards are available from many shops and newsagents.

Some useful numbers:

Emergency		Operator (general)	10
(police, fire, ambulance)	999	Operator (int. calls)	114
Inquiries	190	Telemessage	196

Principal area codes: Cork 021, Drogheda 041, Dublin 01, Galway 091, Kilkenny 056, Killarney 064, Waterford 051, Wexford 053.

Embassies and consulates: The Dublin telephone directory lists foreign embassies and consulates under *Diplomatic and Consular Missions*. Consular agencies in provincial towns are all listed in part two of the directory under the same heading.

Medical care and health: The standard of medical treatment is excellent, and fees are moderate. Pharmaceutical supplies are readily available and most major towns and cities have some late-night pharmacies. Residents of EU countries are covered by reciprocal health care in Ireland. Tap water is safe to drink.

Services: Secretarial services, translators, interpreters and photocopying services are listed in the yellow pages. Photocopying and telex services are also available at major Dublin hotels.

Newspapers: Principal dailies are the *Irish Times*, *Irish Independent*, *Irish Press* and the *Cork Examinor*. *In Dublin* contains details of what's on. Easons in O'Connell Street or Stanley Shops are the main newsagents for foreign press.

Transport

Air – international: International flights are handled by Dublin, Cork, Shannon and Knock airports.

Air – domestic: The Dublin–Cork and Dublin–Shannon routes are served. Many provincial centres are served by air taxi flights.

Rail: Trains, with first- and second-class compartments, are reasonably comfortable, punctual, and can be recommended for business travel on major routes. Dining service is available on main runs only.

The 5-day Irish Explorer card is good for unlimited rail travel, and the 8-day Irish Explorer card for rail and inter-city bus travel. Both can be purchased at railway and bus stations throughout the country.

Local public transport: Buses and suburban trains serve Irish cities. Train tickets must be purchased at stations or bus fares paid to the conductor on board. On Dublin city buses, 'An Lar' means 'town centre'.

Taxis: The most convenient way of getting around any town. Cabs may be found cruising the streets, but the majority park at designated ranks; they can also be contacted by telephone. Tip about 10% of the fare.

Car rental: International and local firms operate, some with airport agencies.

Driving in Ireland: Drive on the left. Caution is advised as there is a tendency to disregard lane demarcations. Roads are generally narrow but adequate. Speed limits: 30mph (48kph) or 40mph (64kph) in built-up areas, 60mph (97kph) elsewhere and 70mph (113kph) on expressways. Use of seat belts is obligatory. Blood alcohol limit is 80mg/100ml. Fuel (petrol/gas) available is premium leaded, unleaded, super unleaded and diesel.

In case of breakdown, call (01) 677 94 81 (Automobile Association) or (01) 677 51 41 (Royal Irish Automobile Club) in Dublin for further instructions.

Some distances from Dublin: Cork 160 miles (260km), Galway 135 miles (220km), Belfast 100 miles (160km).

Social customs: The Irish enjoy conversation, so there should be no problem in making contact. Alcohol often oils the wheels of social interaction.

Hints for business: Prior appointments are advised. If invited to an associate's home, a gift of flowers or chocolates for the hostess would be appropriate. Periods to avoid for business travel are the first week in May (unless you are going for the Spring Show), the July-August holiday period, and the Christmas-New Year stretch when many firms close down.

Foreign chambers of commerce in Ireland: American, German.

Crime and theft: The incidence of crime is not high, though normal precautions should be taken. Beware of pickpockets.

After Hours

Food and drink: Ireland's specialities include fresh and smoked salmon, Dublin Bay prawns, colcannon (mashed potatoes with leeks and cabbage) and Irish stew (lamb, potatoes and vegetables). There is a wide range of fresh seafood available. Brown soda bread (a doughy bread leavened with sodium bicarbonate) may be new to you.

Irish whiskey, usually made from malt and subject to three distillations, may be drunk as it is or in coffee topped with double cream (Irish coffee). The flavourful, rich, dark Guinness stout derives its characteristic taste from roasted barley.

Mealtimes: lunch noon-2pm, dinner 7-10pm (occasionally later).

Entertainment: Nightclubs, discotheques and casinos are found in Dublin, while a cultural programme offers concerts, plays, opera and ballet. Cinemas show films in English only. The daily newspapers give all the details.

Taxes, service charges and tipping: Hotel and restaurant bills are generally all-inclusive, though good service may merit an additional gratuity. Other tipping recommendations: taxi drivers 10%, cloakroom attendants 20p, barbers and hairdressers 10%, porters 50p per piece.

Sports and recreation: Sailing, sea fishing, swimming, surfing, game fishing, coarse fishing, boating, golf, horse riding, hunting and tennis are available in Ireland.

Favourite spectator sports include Gaelic football (in which 15 players on each side kick, punch and bounce the ball in an attempt to get it over the bar of a rugby-style goal), rugby, soccer and hurling (another team game resembling hockey).

TV and radio: Programming is largely in English, with some Gaelic broadcasts.

What to buy: Some good buys are Aran sweaters, Waterford crystal, smoked salmon, Irish whiskey, Irish tweed, mohair rugs, Irish linen.

Shopping hours: 9 or 9.30am to 5.30 or 6pm, Monday-Saturday (some close one afternoon a week). Smaller shops, particularly groceries and newsagents, often open on Sundays, many until 1pm.

Cities and Sights

DUBLIN (*Telephone area code 01*)
Airport: Dublin (9km/6 miles from city centre), international; duty-free shop, for incoming passengers too. Bus service to central bus station.

Tourist information office: 14 Upper O'Connell St, Dublin 2; tel. 284 47 68.

Chamber of commerce: 7 Clare St, Dublin 2; tel. 661 4111, fax 676 60 43.

Industrial Development Authority: Wilton Park House, Wilton Place, Dublin 2; tel. 668 66 33, fax 660 37 03.

Sightseeing: Trinity College (with *Book of Kells* in library), Phoenix Park, Guinness brewery, Bank of Ireland Building, Dublin Castle.

Museums: National Gallery, National Museum, Municipal Gallery of Modern Art.

176 **Excursions**: Trim, Howth, Wicklow, Glendalough.

Italy

Type of government:	Republic, multi-party centralized
Member of:	EU, GATT, IBRD, IDA, IFC, IMF, OECD
Population:	57.2 million
Area:	301,278sq km (116,500sq miles)
Capital:	Rome (*Roma*, 2.8m)
Other major cities:	Milan (*Milano*, 1.43m/GUA 3.8m)
	Naples (*Napoli*, 1.2m/GUA 2.7m)
	Turin (*Torino*, 992,000)
	Palermo (734,250)
	Genoa (*Genova*, 710,000)
	Bologna (411,800)
	Florence (*Firenze*, 408,400)
	Venice (*Venezia*, 355,000)
Language:	Italian, English and French are the foreign languages most widely spoken in business circles, followed by German and Spanish.
Religion:	Catholic (99%)
Time zone:	GMT+1, EST+6; DST (Apr-Sep)
Currency:	Lira (abbr. L)
	Coins: L5, 10, 20, 50, 100, 200, 500
	Notes: L1,000, 2,000, 5,000, 10,000, 20,000, 50,000, 100,000
Electricity:	Generally 220V, 50Hz, AC; in a few areas 125V outlets.

Planning your Trip

Visa requirements: For nationals of Albania, Turkey, South Africa, Baltic Republics, Czech Republic, Slovak Republic, Poland, Hungary, Romania, Yugoslavia, Bulgaria, former USSR. (See also p.6.)

Vaccination requirements: None. (See also p.7.)

Import allowances (see also p.7):

	Cigarettes		Cigars		Tobacco	Spirits		Wine
1)	200	or	100	or	250g	1l	and	2l
2)	(800)	or	(200)	or	(1kg)	(10l)	and	(90l)

1) Passengers from countries outside Europe, or duty-free goods bought in EU countries by European residents.
2) Non-duty-free goods bought within the EU.

Perfume: 1) 50; *Toilet water*: 1) 0.25l;
Gifts: 1) L594,360 max. value

There are no official restrictions on goods bought non-duty-free within the EU, provided they are for personal use only. The above figures are guidelines to the quantities customs officials will generally find acceptable, so if you are carrying larger quantities you should be prepared to provide proof that the goods are for your personal use.

Currency restrictions: As a foreign tourist, you may import up to L20,000,000 or the equivalent in foreign money. To take more than this amount in or out of the country you must fill in a V2 declaration form at the border when you arrive. All proof of exchange (bank receipts) must be kept for customs purposes. (See also p.7.)

Climate: Inland in the north, the climate tends to the continental, with hot summers and cold winters. The Ligurian coastal strip (Genoa and environs) is famed for its mild winters. Towards the south the weather becomes warmer and more Mediterranean in character. South of Rome winters are mild and summers are hot. Precipitation varies from region to region but generally rain can be expected between late-October and January and periodically in early spring.

Fog is often a hazard in Turin and Milan between November and March, and in these areas winter snow also occasionally disrupts road traffic. Some average temperatures:

	Jan	Apr	July	Oct
Milan	2°C (35°F)	13°C (56°F)	23°C (74°F)	14°C (57°F)
Rome	8°C (47°F)	14°C (57°F)	24°C (76°F)	17°C (63°F)

Clothing: Those travelling in early spring and autumn should bring light- to medium-weight clothing, and rainwear. During winter, a light topcoat is required in the south, and a normal winter overcoat for northern cities. July and August can be uncomfortably hot, and light summer clothing is recommended, with something warmer for evenings when the temperature often drops considerably. In business circles, men should wear jackets or suits and ties; women should dress smartly. Although a business meeting can be a casual affair, Italians are very elegant dressers and concerned with appearance in public.

Hotels: The government issues a list of deluxe, first- and second-class hotels for all major cities. A complete yearbook of Italian hotels can be consulted at tourist offices and travel agencies in Italy and abroad. On the spot, tourist offices are not generally responsible for reserving rooms; at most airports and train stations free hotel-information desks are available, and at Rome's Fiumicino airport free telephone connections with local hotels exist. Accommodation is difficult to obtain in most cities during the summer months as well as at Christmas and Easter. In Venice the problem is acute virtually all year round.

Italian tourist offices abroad: Amsterdam, Athens, Barcelona, Brussels, Buenos Aires, Chicago, Copenhagen, Dublin, Düsseldorf, Frankfurt, Geneva, Helsinki, Johannesburg, Lisbon, London, Los Angeles, Madrid, Montreal, Munich, New York, Nice, Paris, Stockholm, Tokyo, Vienna, Zurich.

Business Briefing

Economic Background

Main industries: Machinery, motor vehicles, chemicals, light industry, textiles, foodstuffs, iron and steel, tourism.

Main agricultural products: Maize, rice, wheat, grapes, olives, fruit and vegetables.

Main imports: Consumer goods, raw materials, steel products, machinery, petroleum, meat.

Main exports: Machinery, motor vehicles, chemicals, iron, steel, textile yarns and fabrics, clothing, fruit, wine.

Principal trading partners: EU and EFTA countries, Algeria, Latin America, Egypt, Iran, Japan.

GNP: $872 billion; per capita: $15,150.

Inflation rate: 4.2% (1994).

Trade fairs: Principal events are: Textiles and woollen goods, February, September (Florence); International Footwear and Leather Exhibition, March and May (Bologna); Agricultural and Cattle Fair, March (Verona); International Trade Fair, April and Office Equipment Exhibition, October (Milan); International Levant Samples Fair, September (Bari); International Furniture Show, April (Milan); Food and Drink Fairs, March and November (Genoa); International Motor Show, April (Turin).

Selected background reading: OECD statistics on foreign trade; business periodicals: *The Galling Report on Italy* (English monthly), *Trade Figures* (monthly); *Il Taccuino dell'Azionista* (Sasip) (annual financial, industrial and stock documentation available in Italian), *Guida alle Attività con l'Estero* (Marinelli-Buffetti), *Mondo Economico* (Italian weekly), *Studies on Italy, 1943-1975* (Lange) (selected bibliography of American and English materials in economics, political science, sociology and anthropology).

Italian chambers of commerce abroad: Athens, Bogotá, Bombay, Buenos Aires, Cairo, Caracas, Casablanca, Frankfurt, Istanbul, La Paz, Lima, Lisbon, London, Madrid, Marseilles, Mexico City, Montevideo, Munich, Paris, Porto Alegre, Rio de Janeiro, São Paulo, Santiago, Stockholm, Sydney, Tunis, Vienna, Zurich.

On the Spot

Office hours: Business: 8 or 9am to 1 or 1.30pm and 4, 4.30 or 5 to 7, 7.30 or 8pm Monday-Saturday, sometimes closed Saturday afternoon. (*Note*: some commercial offices take only an hour off for lunch, advancing their whole afternoon schedule accordingly.) Government: 8.30am-1.45pm, Monday-Friday. Meetings with senior officials can be arranged between 8am and 2pm in Rome, and from 5.30pm to 8pm elsewhere.

Public holidays

Jan 1	New Year's Day	Nov 1	All Saints' Day
Jan 6	Epiphany	Dec 8	Immaculate Conception
Apr 25	Liberation Day	Dec 25	Christmas Day
May 1	Labour Day	Dec 26	St Stephen's Day
Aug 15	Assumption	**Movable dates**: Easter Monday	

Some local public holidays are observed, though not all businesses close on these days. Examples: June 24, Florence, Genoa, Turin; June 29, Rome; Sep 19, Naples; Dec 7, Milan.

Banks and currency exchange: Banking hours are generally 8.30am-1.30pm and 3-4pm, Monday-Friday.

Currency-exchange offices (look for the sign *cambio*) in train stations and airports are usually open from 9am to 1.30pm and 2.30 to 6pm. Many are closed on Saturdays. Exchange rates are not as good as in banks. You may need your passport.

Principal banks: Banca d'Italia, Banca Commerciale Italiana, Banca Nazionale del Lavoro, Banco di Roma.

Credit cards and traveller's cheques: All major credit cards and traveller's cheques are widely accepted.

Post and telecommunications: Too many items of mail still go astray in Italy's mail system. Wherever possible, use the telex, fax, telephone or express (special-delivery) services for your communications, both inland and abroad. In Rome, the Vatican operates a more efficient post office for outgoing mail.

Stamps can also be bought after hours at tobacconists'. Some post offices which are open round the clock for telegraph services are: *Florence*: Via Pellicceria; *Genoa*: Stazione Principe; *Milan*: Via Cordusio 4; *Naples*: Stazione Centrale and Galleria Umberto; *Rome*: Piazza San Silvestro; *Turin*: Via Alfieri 10; *Venice*: Piazzale Roma.

Most subscribers in Italy are on the automatic network, and direct-dialling facilities exist to many foreign countries. Older types of public payphones require tokens (*gettoni*; available at bars, hotels, post offices, tobacconists' and from automatic dispensers); modern ones, with three separate slots, take 100-, 200- and 500-lire coins as well as *gettoni* and telephone credit cards, which are available at the above-mentioned places. It is better to make international calls from the main post office. Long-distance lines are often overloaded, so be prepared for a long wait.

Some useful numbers:

Emergency (ambulance)	113	Inquiries (Europe)	15
Police	112	Inquiries (overseas)	170
Fire	115	International telegrams	186
Inquiries (inland)	12	Time	161

An information service on 176 can help with any telephone queries.

Principal area codes: Florence 055, Genoa 010, Milan 02, Naples 081, Rome 06, Turin 011, Venice 041.

Embassies and consulates: Embassies are in Rome. Consult telephone directory listings under *Ambasciate* (embassies) and *Consolati* (consulates), respectively.

Medical care and health: The standard of medical treatment is high (as are fees) though sanitary conditions in hospitals are often inferior and nursing tends to be rather poor due to understaffing. Most doctors speak only Italian. For a list of those speaking your language, apply to your consulate or to the local tourist office. In Rome, the Salvator Mundi hospital is recommended for foreign visitors in need of emergency treatment: its staff speak English, and its standards are superior to those of other local hospitals. Other hospitals favoured by foreigners: in Turin, San Giovanni; in Genoa, l'Evangelista; in Venice, San Giovanni e Paolo.

Pharmacy hours: 8.30 or 9am to 1pm and 4 or 4.30 to 7.30 or 8pm, Monday-Friday; Saturdays until 1pm. Some pharmacies remain on duty for night and holiday services; others are open 24 hours a day. Details are published in daily newspapers or posted in the windows of other pharmacies. Note that prescriptions are mandatory for many medicines. Tap water is generally drinkable, though those with delicate stomachs may prefer to order bottled water.

Services: Translators and interpreters can be found by consulting the yellow pages under *Traduttori ed interpreti*; many of these agencies furnish secretarial services also. Photocopying facilities are offered in some bookshops and art- and office-supply shops; see also the yellow pages under *Fotocopie*.

Newspapers: Principal dailies in selected major cities are: Florence: *La Nazione;* Genoa: *Il Secolo XIX Nuovo*; Milan: *Il Corriere della Sera*, *Il Giornale Nuovo*; Naples: *Il Mattino*; Rome: *Il Messagero*; Turin: *La Stampa*; Venice: *La Gazzetta*. Leading foreign newspapers from Belgium, Britain, France, the Netherlands, Spain and Germany are regularly available, as is the Paris-based *International Herald Tribune*.

Transport

Air – international: Rome and, to a lesser extent, Milan are Italy's principal gateway cities, with a limited number of international flights operating into other provincial airports.

Air – domestic: Major centres are linked by a useful network of domestic flights often preferred for long-haul business travel.

Rail: First- and second-class compartments are available, the latter being often very crowded. Trains are comfortable but not always **183**

punctual. Dining- and sleeping-cars are available on many trains. Reservations should be made for travel during summer and around Easter and Christmas. Foreigners can buy a special 'BTLC' ticket valid for 8, 15, 21 or 30 days of unlimited travel within Italy in either first or second class. Inquire at any travel agency or railway station. for Eurailpass, see p.10.

Local public transport: All major centres have bus or tram services, except Venice, where transport is by public passenger boat *(vaporetto)* and water taxi. Rome, Milan and Naples also operate metro (underground, subway) systems. The metro is by far the fastest means of transport in these cities, but their networks are rather restricted. Payment of fare varies: tickets for most buses must be purchased at bars or news-stands. Trams sometimes have conductors at the back who sell tickets. Metro tickets are bought in a booth at the entrance to the station.

Taxis: They may be hailed on the street, picked up at a rank or obtained by telephone. Especially in Rome and Naples, make sure the meter is on and functioning. There's a supplement at night and for some airport trips. Check with your hotel for current prices. Tip the driver up to 10% of the fare.

Car rental: International car-rental agencies operate throughout the country, with airport offices. Chauffeur-driven cars are also available.

Driving in Italy: Foreigners driving their cars in Italy should carry a translation of their national driving licence, and an international licence is sometimes required for rentals. The Italian automobile association, ACI, will issue a temporary document upon presentation of your valid home driving licence. Your vehicle must also be equipped with a red-reflector warning triangle for use in case of breakdown. Seat belts are obligatory. There is no blood alcohol limit, but driving under the influence of alcohol is punishable. The speed limit is 130kph (81mph) on motorways, 110kph (68mph) on main roads outside urban areas, 90kph (56mph) on secondary or local roads and **184** 50kph (31mph) in urban areas.

Traffic on major roads has right of way over that entering from side-roads, but this, like other traffic regulations, is frequently ignored, so beware. At intersections of roads of similar importance, the car on the right theoretically has the right of way. When passing other vehicles, or remaining in the left-hand (passing) lane, keep your directional indicator flashing. The excellent network of *autostrade* (motorways, expressways) requires payment of tolls, so keep a stash of coins handy, as toll booth attendants don't like having to give change. Emergency callboxes are located every 2 kilometres on the motorway, otherwise, phone 116 for breakdown service. In Rome you should call 06 4477.

Some distances from Rome: Naples 215km (135 miles), Florence 280km (175 miles), Venice 540km (335 miles), Genoa 545km (340 miles), Milan 575km (355 miles), Palermo 990km (615 miles).

Fuel (petrol/gas) available is normal (86-88 octane), super (98-100 octane), lead-free and diesel.

Social customs: Handshakes all round are the rule in any situation, social or business. To refuse a very insistent invitation to lunch or dinner is considered ungracious, and if the occasion takes place in a private home, one should always come with wine, flowers or another suitable gift. Smoking is prohibited in public transport vehicles, taxis, cinemas and theatres.

Hints for business: Appointments should be made well in advance. With government offices one must keep in mind that all bureaucratic transactions take a long time and that patience is necessary. If speaking Italian to business associates, use the polite third-person *Lei* form of address. Write business letters in Italian if at all possible: in general, Italians will respect an attempt to communicate in their language. Best avoided for business travel: August, when many businesses close down, and other holiday seasons.

Foreign chambers of commerce in Italy: African, American, Arab, Argentinian, Australian, Austrian, Belgian, Brazilian, British, Canadian, Chinese, Czech, Dutch, EU, Egyptian, European, French, German, Irish, Israeli, Ivory Coast, Jordanian, Latin American, **185**

Norwegian, Romanian, Slovak, Somalian, South African, Russian, Spanish, Swiss, Tunisian, Turkish, Venezuelan.

Crime and theft: Pickpocketing, purse-snatching and other thefts are unfortunately common crimes in large Italian cities. Utmost precautions should be taken, especially in Rome and Naples. It's inadvisable to carry large quantities of cash, and one should be attentive on crowded buses, trams and metros.

The narrow streets of old Rome have their share of purse and bag thieves who ride in pairs on nippy motorcycles on the lookout for the unsuspecting foreigner. It's unwise to leave valuables unguarded in a hotel room; take advantage of the hotel's safety-deposit box and request a receipt.

After Hours

Food and drink: Italians take great pride in their cuisine, which varies considerably from region to region. Listed here are some specialities of the major cities:

Florence: *cacciucco* (fish soup), *bistecca alla fiorentina* (grilled T-bone steak); wine: *Chianti*.

Genoa: *pesto alla genovese* (pasta with basil sauce), *burrida* (local fish stew); *focaccia* (onion roll); wine: *Cinqueterre*.

Milan: *risotto alla milanese* (rice cooked with Parmesan cheese), *costoletta alla milanese* (breaded veal cutlet); wine: *Frecciarosa*.

Naples: *spaghetti alle vongole* (pasta with clam sauce), pizza; wine: *Gragnano*.

Rome: *spaghetti alla carbonara* (pasta with egg and bacon sauce), *abbacchio* (roast suckling lamb), *saltimbocca* (veal with Parma ham and sage), *carciofi alla giudia* (artichokes baked in olive oil); wine: *Frascati, Castelli*.

Turin: *agnolotti* (ravioli with meat and cabbage), *bagna caoda* (garlic and olive-oil dip), *finanziera* (sweetbreads, kidneys, brains in a cream sauce), *marrons glacés* (glazed chestnuts); wine: *Barolo*.

Venice: *fegato alla veneziana* (sautéed calf's liver and onions), *polenta*, squid, octopus and crayfish; wines: *Soave* and *Riesling*.

Freshly made Italian ice-cream is as excellent as its reputation, and the same goes for coffee (particularly *espresso*).

Mealtimes: lunch 12.30-3.30pm, dinner 7.30pm-midnight.

All restaurants must issue a formal receipt *(ricevutta fiscale)* indicating the sales tax or VAT (IVA). A customer may be stopped outside the premises and fined if unable to produce a receipt.

Entertainment: Rome and Milan have discotheques, nightclubs and bars listed in the yellow pages under *Locali notturni* or *Nightclub*. However, the nightlife of smaller cities, such as Venice, Florence – even Naples – centres on concerts, operas, plays and films. Many cities have special festivals, commonly during the summer months. Foreign films are seldom shown in their original language.

Taxes, service charges and tipping: Tax and service are generally included in hotel and restaurant bills, but an additional tip is usually given in bars and restaurants. Tipping recommendations: hotel porters L1,000 per bag, waiters 5-10%, taxi drivers up to 10%, cloakroom attendants L300, barbers and hairdressers up to 15%.

Sports and recreation: Public recreation in the major cities centres on gymnasiums, swimming pools, tennis courts, tracks and cycling. If within reach, Italy's beautiful beaches are an obvious attraction. Golf courses and somewhat expensive horse-riding facilities are also widely available. Skiing is a popular winter sport.

Spectator sports: soccer is by far the most popular spectator sport, and the season runs from September to May. Boxing, cycling and skiing are also popular.

TV and radio: All TV shows are in Italian apart from regular broadcasts by CNN very early in the morning (2.30am) and broadcasts of CBS news at 7.30am on the TMC station. The second radio network puts out news and tourist information in English every morning between 9 and 9.30am, between June and September. The first programme broadcasts 'Notturno d'Italia' at 10pm with light music interspersed by announcements in English, French and German.

What to buy: Hand-crafted items, for example lace, ceramics, handmade furniture, and leather goods, vary in regional style. Some beautiful hand-made musical instruments can also be found. Here is a rundown of recommended buys in various cities:

Florence: ceramics, straw and leather goods, shoes, bags, suitcases, gloves, gold filigree-work, marble, alabaster; *Genoa*: gold filigree-work; *Milan*: silks, textiles, manufactured goods, alabaster objects; *Naples*: coral, cameos; *Rome*: high fashion, antiques, pottery, woollen goods; *Venice*: lace, Murano glass, silks.

Shopping hours: generally 9 or 9.30am to noon or 12.30pm, and 3 or 3.30 to 7.30pm (generally closed on Thursday afternoons).

Cities and Sights

ROME (*Telephone area code 06*)

Airports: Fiumicino, officially called Leonardo da Vinci (28km/18 miles from city centre), international; duty-free shop. Ciampino (17km/11 miles from city centre) handles mainly charter flights. Fiumicino is linked by rail to Roma Ostiense station with services every 20 to 30 minutes through the day, and metro connections from Piramide to the city centre. Buses leave Ciampino every 20 minutes for Anagnina, connected by metro to the city centre.

Tourist information office: Via Parigi 11; tel. 488 18 51, Leonardo da Vinci airport; tel. 65 01 02 38.

Chamber of commerce: Piazza Sallustio 21; tel. 47 041.

Sightseeing: Colosseum, Forum, Palatine Hill, Pantheon, Market of Trajan, Castel Sant'Angelo, Theatre of Marcellus, Old Appian Way, catacombs, baths of Caracalla, Circus Maximus; squares: Navona, Campidoglio, di Spagna, del Popolo, Campo di Fiori, Fontana di Trevi; churches: St Peter, St Mary Major, St John Lateran, St Paul's Outside the Walls, St Peter's in Chains, Sta Maria in Trastevere, Sta Maria del Popolo; walks: Trastevere, Janiculum Hill, Via Condotti (shopping area), Porta Portese (Sunday flea market), Pincio Gardens.

Museums: Borghese Gallery, Vatican Museums, Museo Nazionale Romano and the Sistine Chapel.

Excursions: Tivoli (Villa d'Este and Hadrian's Villa), Ostia Antica, Alban Hills and Castel Gandolfo, Montecassino.

MILAN *(Telephone area code 02)*

Airports: Forlanini-Linate (8km/5 miles from city centre), international; duty-free shop. Bus service to central station.

Malpensa (47km/29 miles from city centre), international; duty-free shop. Bus service to central station.

Tourist information office: Via Marconi 1; tel. 80 96 62.

Chamber of commerce: Via Meravigli 9B, Milan; tel. 85 15 11, fax 85 15 52 27.

Sightseeing: Galleria Vittorio Emanuele II, Piazza del Duomo, Duomo, Teatro La Scala, Piazza Mercanti, Castello Sforzesco, Antico Ospedale Maggiore, Villa Reale, La Rotonda di Via Besana; churches: Sta Maria delle Grazie, Sant'Ambrogio, San Lorenzo Maggiore, Sant'Eustorgio, San Satiro, Cetosa di Garegnano.

Museums: Brera art gallery, museum of Castello Sforzesco, ambrosiana Library art gallery, Gallery of Modern Art, Poldi Pezzoli Museum, Leonardo da Vinci National Museum of Science and Technology.

Excursions: Lakes Como, Maggiore and Garda, Certosa di Pavia, Monza, Melegnano, Abbazia di Chiaravalle.

NAPLES *(Telephone area code 081)*

Airport: Capodichino (7km/4 miles from city centre), international; duty-free shop. Bus service to Piazza Garibaldi (central station).

Tourist information office: Piazza dei Martiri 58; tel. 40 53 11.

Chamber of commerce: Piazza Bovio, 80133 Napoli; tel. 20 72 22, fax 20 73 74.

Sightseeing: Palazzo Reale, Teatro San Carlo, Castello Nuovo, Piazza del Plebiscito, Santa Lucia area, Mercato Vecchio, Piazza Dante, Via dei Librai, Via del Tribunale; churches: Duomo San Gennaro, Sta Chiara, San Domenico Maggiore, San Lorenzo Maggiore, Chiesa del Gesù, Sta Maria Donna Regina.

Museums: National Archaeological Museum, National Museum of Capodimonte, Certosa San Martino.

Excursions: Campi Flegrei, Vesuvius, Pompeii, Ercolano (Herculaneum), Stabia, Capri, Ischia, Amalfi Drive (Sorrento, Amalfi, Positano, Salerno, Paestum).

TURIN (Telephone area code 011)

Airport: Caselle (17km/11 miles from city centre), international; duty-free shop. Bus service coinciding with scheduled flights.

Tourist information office: Via Roma 226; tel. 53 51 81.

Chamber of commerce: Via San Francesco da Paola 24; tel. 57 161, fax 57 164 50.

Sightseeing: Piazza San Carlo, Palazzo Carpano, Palazzo Carignano, Galleria Subalpina, Palazzo Madama, Armeria Reale, Monte dei Cappuccini, Parco and Castello del Valentino; churches: San Giovanni Cathedral, Gran Madre di Dio, San Lorenzo, Sta Cristina, San Carlo, San Filippo Neri.

Museums: Egyptian Museum, Museum of Antiquities, Galleria Sabauda, National Library, Gallery of Modern Art, Automobile Museum.

Excursions: Superga, Sauze d'Oulx, Sportinia, Colle della Maddalena.

GENOA (Telephone area code 010)

Airport: Cristoforo Colombo (7km/5 miles from city centre), international; duty-free shop. Bus service to Via Petrarca/Piazza Acquaverde.

Tourist information offices: Via Roma 11; tel. 58 14 07 and Stazione Principe.

Chamber of commerce: Via Garibaldi 4; tel. 209 41, fax 209 42 00.
190 Chamber of commerce for foreign trade: P. Banchi; tel. 208 864.

Sightseeing: Palazzo Reale, Piazza della Nunziata, Via Garibaldi, Palazzo Bianco, Palazzo Rosso, Villetta Di Negro, Via San Luca, Loggia dei Mercanti, Piazza Caricamento, Piazza San Matteo, Palazzo Ducale, Via Caneto il Lungo, Spianata Castelletto Park; churches: San Lorenzo Cathedral, San Donato, Sta Maria in Castello, San Siro, San Luca, San Carlo.

Museums: Museum of Palazzo Bianco, Spinola Gallery.

Excursions: Monte Righi, Nervi, S. Fruttuoso di Capodimonte, San Remo, Riviera di Levante.

FLORENCE (*Telephone area code 055*)

Airports: Pisa-San Giusto (83km/52 miles from city centre), international; duty-free shop. Direct rail service from the airport to Florence (60 minutes).

Peretola (5km/3 miles from city centre), for domestic flights (to Milan, Turin, Venice, Trieste) only. Bus service to Santa Maria Novella station.

Tourist information office: Via Manzoni 16; tel. 247 81 41/2/3/4/5.

Chamber of commerce: P. dei Giudici 3; tel. 279 51, fax 279 52 59.

Sightseeing: Piazza della Signoria, Palazzo Vecchio, Ponte Vecchio, Boboli Gardens, Mercato San Lorenzo, Mercato Nuovo, Piazzale Michelangelo, Forte Belvedere, Via Tornabuoni; churches: Sta Maria dei Fiori (cathedral), Sta Croce, Sta Maria Novella, San Lorenzo Orsanmichele, Sta Trinità, Sta Maria del Carmine, San Miniato al Monte.

Museums: National Gallery of the Uffizi, National Museum of the Bargello, Accademia Gallery, Museum of the Church of San Marco, Palazzo Pitti, Medici Tombs of San Lorenzo, National Archaeological Museum, Casa Buonarroti.

Excursions: Fiesole, Vinci, Siena, Pisa, Certosa di Firenze, Impruneta, Vallombrosa.

VENICE *(Telephone area code 041)*

Airport: Marco Polo (13km/8 miles from city centre), international; duty-free shop. Vaporetto (boat) service from San Marco, 'AV' or bus service from Piazzale Roma every 60 minutes; allow an hour by boat.

Tourist information offices: San Marco, Ascensione 71/c; tel. 522 87 30, Castello 4421; tel. 529 87 11, Stazione Santa Lucia; tel. 71 50 16.

Chamber of commerce: Via XXII Marzo 2032, 30124 Venice; tel. 528 95 80.

Sightseeing: San Marco Cathedral and Square, clock tower, Bridge of Sighs, Doge's Palace, Rialto Bridge; scuole (academies): San Rocco, San Giorgio degli Schiavoni; churches: San Giovanni e Paolo, Sta Maria dei Frari, San Giorgio Maggiore, Sta Maria della Salute, San Zaccaria, Sta Maria Formosa.

Museums: Accademia, Correr Museum, Guggenheim Foundation, Archaeological Museum, Naval Museum.

Excursions: Lido, Torcello, Murano, Burano, Chioggia, the Brenta Riviera, Padua.

Some Useful Expressions in Italian

good morning/afternoon	**buon giorno**
good evening/night	**buona sera/buona notte**
good-bye	**arrivederci**
yes/no	**sì/no**
please/thank you	**per piacere/grazie**
excuse me	**mi scusi**
you're welcome	**prego**
where/when/how	**dove/quando/come**
how long/how far	**quanto tempo/quanto dista**
yesterday/today/tomorrow	**ieri/oggi/domani**
day/week/month/year	**giorno/settimana/mese/anno**
left/right	**sinistra/destra**
up/down	**su/giù**
good/bad	**buono/cattivo**
big/small	**grande/piccolo**
cheap/expensive	**buon mercato/caro**
hot/cold	**caldo/freddo**
old/new	**vecchio/nuovo**
open/closed	**aperto/chiuso**
early/late	**presto/tardi**
Does anyone here speak English/French/German?	**C'é qualcuno che parla inglese/francese/tedesco?**
What does this mean?	**Cosa significa?**
I don't understand.	**Non capisco.**
Please write it down.	**Lo scriva, per favore.**
Do you take credit cards/traveller's cheques?	**Accetta carta di credito/traveller's cheques?**
Waiter!/Waitress!	**Cameriere!/Cameriera!**
Where are the toilets?	**Dove sono i gabinetti?**
I'd like…	**Vorrei…**
How much is that?	**Quant'è?**
Help me please.	**Per favore, mi aiuti.**

Liechtenstein

Type of government:	Constitutional principality with multi-party legislature
Member of:	EFTA (with Switzerland)
Population:	30,000
Area:	157sq km (61sq miles)
Capital:	Vaduz (4,887)
Language:	German; English is widely spoken in business circles.
Religion:	Catholic (87.3%), Protestant (8.3%)
Time zone:	GMT+1, EST+6; DST (Apr-Sep)
Currency:	Swiss franc (Franken, abbr. Fr) = 100 Rappen
	Coins: 5, 10, 20, 50 Rappen; Fr½, 1, 2, 5
	Notes: Fr10, 20, 50, 100, 500, 1,000
Electricity:	220V, 50Hz, AC

Liechtenstein's only embassy abroad is in Berne, Switzerland.
The principality's interests elsewhere are represented by Switzerland.

Planning your Trip

Visa requirements: For nationals of Turkey. (See also p.6.)

Vaccination requirements: None. (See also p.7.)

Import allowances (see also p.7):

	Cigarettes		Cigars		Tobacco	Spirits		Wine
European residents	200	or	50	or	250g	1l	and	2l
Residents outside Europe	400	or	100	or	500g	1l	and	2l

Gifts: (including perfume) admitted duty free up to a value of Fr100.

Currency restrictions: None. (See also p.7.)

Climate: Liechtenstein enjoys a continental climate with warm summers and cold winters. Precipitation is spread more or less evenly throughout the year, with a slight peak in March-April.

Some average temperatures:

Spring	Summer	Autumn	Winter
58-9°C	17-18°C	8-9°C	-1-0°C
(47-49°F)	(63-65°F)	(47-49°F)	(30-32°F)

Clothing: Light-weight clothing is generally adequate in summer, with something warmer for chilly evenings. Wrap up well for cold and snowy winters. In business circles, dark, conservative suits are appropriate, though subdued, colour-coordinated attire is acceptable.

Hotels: The tourist office has a booking service and a list of hotels.

Liechtenstein tourist information abroad: The principality is represented by the Swiss National Tourist Office (see SWITZERLAND).

Business Briefing

Economic Background
Industrial and agricultural activity: Wheat and fruit cultivation, light industry, ceramics, pharmaceutical supplies, furniture, precision instruments.

Some local products are exported. Virtually all industrial goods and many foodstuffs are imported.

GNP: Not calculated. See SWITZERLAND.

Inflation rate: 3.4% (1993).

Trade fairs: There are no trade fairs in Liechtenstein at present, but the principality takes part in trade fairs in Switzerland. Approximately every third year, a June fair exhibits local industrial and trade products.

Selected background reading: *Liechtenstein*, *Liechtenstein Economy* (Liechtenstein Press Office). The Liechtenstein chamber of commerce publishes an annual survey of the principality's economy.

Liechtenstein chambers of commerce abroad: The principality's interests are looked after by Swiss commercial representations.

On the Spot

Office hours: Generally 8am-noon and 2-5pm Monday-Friday.

Public holidays

Jan 1	New Year's Day	Dec 25	Christmas
Jan 6	Epiphany	Dec 26	St Stephen's Day
Feb 2	Candlemas		
Mar 19	St Joseph's Day		
Mar 25	Annunciation	**Movable dates**:	Good Friday
May 1	Labour Day		Easter Monday
Aug 15	Assumption		Ascension
Nov 1	All Saints' Day		Whit Monday
Dec 8	Immaculate Conception		Corpus Christi

Medical care and health: Health care is excellent but expensive. Many doctors speak English. If hospitalization is required, patients are sent to neighbouring Swiss hospitals such as the one in Grabs. Medicine and pharmaceutical supplies are readily available. Of the two pharmacies in Vaduz, one remains on duty after hours with a notice posted. Tap water is safe to drink.

Banks and currency exchange: Banking hours: 8am-noon and 1.30-4.30pm Monday-Friday. No after-hour currency-exchange offices exist, but larger hotels will change the more familiar foreign currencies into Swiss francs. Liechtenstein enjoys a customs and currency union with Switzerland.

Major banks: Liechtensteinische Landesbank, Bank in Liechtenstein, Verwaltungs- und Privat-Bank.

Credit cards and traveller's cheques: Both are widely accepted.

Post and telecommunications: While Liechtenstein produces its own postage stamps, the principality's postal and telecommunications systems are largely integrated with those of neighbouring Switzerland and are of an excellent standard.

Post offices are open 8am-noon and 2-6pm Monday-Friday, and 7.30-11am on Saturdays. The central post office in Vaduz is open from 8pm-6pm Monday-Friday, and from 8-11am on Saturday.

Within the principality and Switzerland, all telephone subscribers can be reached by direct dialling. The green pages in the front of the regular telephone directory give dialling codes for a large number of countries around the world.

Some useful numbers:

Operator for manual connections	114	Fire	118
		Police (emergency only)	117
Inquiries (local & Switzerland)	111	Road conditions	163
Inquiries (int.)	191	Telegrams	110
Motoring assistance	140	Time	161
News (in French)	168	Weather report	162
News (in German)	167		

Principal area code: Vaduz 075 (integrated with Swiss telephone system).

Embassies and consulates: Embassies responsible for Liechtenstein are generally located in Berne, Switzerland, and your nearest consulate is likely to be in Zurich, Switzerland (only a handful of countries maintain diplomatic representations in Vaduz). For embassies, consult the Berne telephone directory under the heading *Ambas-* **197**

sades, and for consulates the *Konsulate* or *Consulat* entries in appropriate other directories (eg Zurich or St Gall).

Services: Several firms, including offset printers and stationers', have photocopying facilities. The tourist office can provide translators and interpreters.

Newspapers: The principality's two dailies are *Liechtensteiner Volksblatt* and *Liechtensteiner Vaterland*. Leading European newspapers, the *International Herald Tribune* and some American magazines are available at larger news-stands.

Transport

Air: Liechtenstein has no commercial airport. Travellers generally choose to fly into Zurich, Switzerland, and go on from there by train and bus or hired car.

Rail: International expresses stop in Sargans or Buchs (Switzerland) where taxis and buses are available for transport to destinations within Liechtenstein.

Public transport: The principality is served by an efficient postal bus network. Tickets may be purchased at post offices or directly from the driver.

Taxis: Cabs may be hailed on the street or ordered by phone (see *Taxis* entry in phone book). Tip 10-15% of the fare.

Car rental: International and local rental agencies operate in Liechtenstein. Chauffeur-driven vehicles are also available.

Driving in Liechtenstein: Your car must be equipped with a red-reflector warning triangle for use in case of breakdown. If you normally wear glasses, you must carry a spare pair with you when driving. Seat belts must be worn. Blood alcohol limit is 80mg/100ml. Fuel (petrol/ gas) available is lead-free (91 and 95 octane), super (98 octane) and diesel.

Speed limits are well signposted and roads maintained in good **198** condition. In case of breakdown, telephone 140. Use of the horn is recommended on winding mountain roads but should be avoided elsewhere.

Social customs: Like the Swiss, Liechtensteiners are somewhat reserved, but friendly, people. Handshakes all round upon meeting and departure are the rule. Being invited to a Liechtenstein home is rare, but for the occasion don't forget flowers or chocolates for the hostess.

Hints for business: Lichtensteiners are noted for their reliability and know-how in international commercial affairs. Appointments should be made, and punctuality is essential. Never go onto a first-name basis unless your partner takes the initiative. Avoid late July and August for business travel, as this is the peak holiday period.

Crime and theft: Normal precautions are in order.

After Hours

Food and drink: Liechtenstein cooking is strongly influenced by its Swiss neighbour. Dishes are usually given their German names, though French may also be used. Some menu items you will come across are (in German): *Bündnerfleisch* (paper-thin slices of dried beef), *Egli* (perch), *Felchen* (white fish), *Forelle* (trout), *Geschnetzeltes Kalbfleisch* (sliced veal in a cream sauce), *Leberspiesschen* (skewered liver), *Rösti* (hashed-brown potatoes), and (in French): *entrecôte* (ribeye steak), *fondue* (bubbling cheese cauldron), *tournedos* (round cut of prime beef), *truite* (trout).

Local or Swiss wines and beers are well worth trying. Note that imported spirits are considerably more expensive than the popular local pre-dinner drinks such as *kir* or *blanc-cassis* (white wine with blackberry liqueur), *pastis* (aniseed liqueur) or *Campari* (a bitter tonic).

Mealtimes: lunch noon-2pm, dinner 7.30-10pm.

Entertainment: Concerts are regularly held. Foreign films are often shown in their original language. A few discos operate.

Taxes, service charges and tipping: Hotel and restaurant bills are all-inclusive. It's customary to tip porters Fr1 per bag, waiters 5% **199**

(optional), taxi drivers 10-15%, cloakroom attendants Fr1. In hair-dressing establishments, prices are normally all-inclusive.

Sports and recreation: Mountain climbing, skiing, hiking, swimming, tennis and horse riding are available to visitors.

TV and radio: While Liechtenstein has no radio or TV of its own, reception of Swiss, Austrian and German programmes is good.

What to buy: Watches, cameras, jewellery, pottery are of high quality, but compare prices. Shopping hours: 8am-noon and 1.30-6.30pm, Monday-Saturday.

Cities and Sights

VADUZ (*Telephone area code 075*)
Tourist information office: Engländerbau, Städtle 37, 9490 Vaduz; tel. 232 443.

Chamber of commerce: Josef-Rheinberger-Str. 11, 9490 Vaduz; tel. 232 2744.

Museums: Historical museum, princely art gallery, postage museum.

Excursions: Scesaplana tour (Austria), Lake Constance, Davos (Switzerland), Appenzell and St Gall (Switzerland).

For some useful expressions in German, see page 135.

Luxembourg

Type of government:	Constitutional grand duchy, multi-party centralized
Member of:	Benelux, EU, GATT, IBRD, IFC, IMF, OECD
Population:	400,000
Area:	2,586sq km (999sq miles)
Capital:	Luxembourg (75,622)
Language:	National language is 'Letzebuergisch', a local dialect of German; French and German are official languages; English widely spoken in business circles.
Religion:	Catholic (95%)
Time zone:	GMT+1, EST+6; DST (Apr-Sep)
Currency:	Luxembourg franc (abbreviated F) = 100 centimes. (The Belgian franc is also in wide circulation at parity.)
	Coins: 50 centimes (rare); F1, 5, 10, 20, 50
	Notes: F100, 500, 1,000, 5,000
Electricity:	220V, 50Hz, AC

Planning your Trip

Visa requirements: For nationals of Turkey (except permanent residents of an EU country) and South Africa. (See also p.6.)

Vaccination requirements: None. (See also p.7.)

Import allowances (see also p.7):

	Cigarettes		Cigars		Tobacco	Spirits		Wine
1), 2)	200	or	50	or	250g	1l	and	2l
3)	(800)	or	(200)	or	(1kg)	(10l)	and	(90l)

1) Passengers from countries outside Europe.
2) Duty-free goods bought in EU countries by European residents.
3) Non-duty-free goods bought within the EU.

Perfume: 1) 75g; 2) 50g; *Toilet water*: 1) 1l; 2) 0.25l;
Gifts: 1) 25,500F max. value; 2) 2,600F max. value

There are no official restrictions on goods bought non-duty-free within the EU, provided they are for personal use only. The above figures are guidelines to the quantities customs officials will generally find acceptable, so if you are carrying larger quantities you should be prepared to provide proof that the goods are for your personal use.

Currency restrictions: None. (See also p.7.)

Climate: Luxembourg enjoys a mild continental climate. Fog is common in autumn, and snowfall can be quite heavy in winter.

Some average daytime temperatures:

Spring	Summer	Autumn	Winter
8°C (46°F)	18°C (64°F)	8°C (46°F)	3°C (37°F)

Clothing: Dress should be suitable for the generally temperate climate, not too different from England's. A raincoat is advisable at all times. Conservative business attire is customary.

Hotels: Luxembourg city has only a limited number of hotels, so reservations should be made sufficiently in advance, particularly during the tourist season and for weekends. The booklet *Hotels, Auberges, Restaurants, Pensions* is available at the station, the airport and at tourist offices.

Luxembourg tourist offices abroad: Brussels, Copenhagen, Düsseldorf, Haarlem, London, New York, Oslo, Paris, Stockholm.

Business Briefing

Economic Background
Main industries and agricultural products: Iron ore mining, iron and steel industries, chemicals, wheat, grapes (wine).

Main imports: Most industrial and consumer goods, foodstuffs.

Main exports: Iron and steel, chemicals.

GNP: $10.6 billion; per capita: $28,995.

Inflation rate: 3.6% (1994).

Principal trading partners: Germany, France, Belgium, Netherlands, UK, Italy, USA.

Trade fairs: Two international fairs are held in May and October.

Luxembourg chambers of commerce abroad: Brussels, Buenos Aires, Casablanca, Cologne, The Hague, Lausanne, Montreal, New York, Paris, São Paulo, Tel Aviv, Zurich.

Selected background reading: Regular and periodic publications of the EU are the most common and objective sources of information.

On the Spot

Office hours: 8.30am-noon and 2-6pm.

Public holidays

Jan 1	New Year's Day	Nov 1	All Saints' Day
May 1	Labour Day	Nov 2	All Souls' Day
June 23	National Day	Dec 25	Christmas Day
Aug 15	Assumption	Dec 26	Boxing Day

Movable dates:	First Monday of Lent	Easter Monday
	Ascension	Whit Monday

Banks and currency exchange: Banking hours are 8.30am-noon and 2-4.30pm, Monday-Friday.

Foreign currency can also be changed at the railway station and airport virtually day and night, seven days a week, otherwise at some of the larger hotels.

All international banking transactions are quick and easy. Chief banks are Banque Générale du Luxembourg and Banque Internationale à Luxembourg. Altogether over 100 banks are represented in Luxembourg.

Credit cards and traveller's cheques: Most credit cards and traveller's cheques are widely accepted in the capital.

Post and telecommunications: All services are highly reliable.

Post office hours are 8am-noon and 2-4.30pm at city offices, and variable in country districts. The post office at the railway station is open 24 hours a day, and the one at the airport from 7am to 10pm.

Direct dialling exists within Luxembourg and to many other countries. The two main post offices have public telex facilities.

Some useful numbers:

Emergencies	012	Operator (int.)	0010
Inquiries (inland)	017	Telex inquiries	0016
Inquiries (int.)	016		

Embassies and consulates: Consult the *Ambassades* or *Consulats* entries in the telephone directory. Those countries without an embassy in Luxembourg are mostly represented in Brussels.

Medical care and health: Health services are very good but expensive. The capital has a hospital and an outpatient clinic. Many doctors in the capital speak English. Reciprocal agreements exist with a number of other European countries. One city pharmacy remains open at all times (see daily newspapers for details, or call 012). Tap water is

safe to drink.

Services: The commercial attaché of your embassy can be helpful in locating translators and interpreters. Photocopying is available at shops near the main post office. Secretarial services can be obtained through the Manpower Services Commission.

Newspapers: Main local dailies are *Républicain Lorrain* and *Luxemburger Wort* (German). Most major European newspapers, including the Paris-edited *International Herald Tribune,* are available at major news-stands.

Transport

Air – international: The grand duchy's only commercial airport, near the capital, is served by direct flights from a number of major European and North American cities and some other, rather out-of-the-way points.

Rail: Access by train is quite easy from most points. The Benelux Tourrail ticket, valid for 5 days of unlimited travel within a one-month period, in Luxembourg, Belgium and the Netherlands, can be bought at a local travel agency or railway station. For Eurailpass, see p10.

Local public transport: Both the capital and the grand duchy as a whole are served by an adequate bus network.

Taxis: Telephone numbers for various taxi services (at the airport, in the capital and in the country) are listed in the telephone directory. Taxis cannot usually be hired on the street.

Car rental: International and local agencies operate, some with desks at the airport. Chauffeur-driven cars are available in limited numbers.

Driving in Luxembourg: A red-reflector warning triangle must be carried. Seat belts must be worn. Blood alcohol limit is 80mg/100ml. Fuel (petrol/gas) available is normal (90-92 octane), lead-free (95 octane), super (98-99 octane) and diesel.

Using the horn in the capital is forbidden. Speed limits: built-up areas, 50kph (31mph); motorways (expressways), 120kph (75mph); other roads, 90kph (56mph). Local police impose on-the-spot speeding fines. Unless signposts indicate that you have priority, you **205** must give way to traffic coming from the right. Motorways to Brussels (Belgium), Trier (Germany) and Metz (France) are now open and are toll-free. In case of breakdown, call the automobile club on 45 00 45.

Social customs: Luxembourgers are friendly and like to use their foreign-language skills. They're delighted when visitors use the local dialect for phrases of greeting and thanks. Despite the large number of foreigners that reside in or transit through their country, Luxembourgers jealously guard their separate identity and should by no means be considered as vaguely French, German or Belgian.

Hints for business: Luxembourg businessmen appreciate punctuality. Handshakes all round are the rule at business meetings.

Crime and theft: Normal precautions are in order.

After Hours

Food and drink: Most restaurants offer German-style cooking, though international cuisine is available in better city establishments.

Luxembourg white wine from the Moselle valley, rarely exported, is very drinkable. Wines and spirits from all over the world are readily available in bars and restaurants. Excellent lager beer is brewed and bottled locally. Menus are usually in French and German.

Mealtimes: lunch noon-2pm, dinner 8-9.30pm.

Entertainment: A few nightclubs exist near the railway station. Discotheques and cinemas are also located in the heart of the town. Films are generally shown in their original language. Plays (in French and German), ballets and operas are occasionally staged. In summer, concerts are held daily in the Place d'Armes, and annual music festivals are organized at Wiltz and Echternach.

Taxes, service charges and tipping: Tax and service charges are generally included in hotel and restaurant bills. There are few conventions. Taxi drivers, hairdressers and waiters are often given the balance of round-figure payments. Tip porters at the airport F20-25 per bag; at functions a F20 cloakroom charge may be obligatory.

Sports and recreation: A superb 18-hole golf course is located near the airport. The River Moselle and Petite Suisse ('Little Switzerland') regions provide much in the way of open-air recreation such as hiking, camping and boating. Ice-skating is popular in winter.

Soccer, handball and basketball are the most popular spectator sports.

TV and radio: TV programming is in French. German, Belgian and French broadcasts can also be picked up. Radio broadcasts are in French or German. Radio Luxembourg puts out an English-language programme, 'Community Radio', between 2 and 5.30pm, and also broadcasts in English throughout the night.

What to buy: Good buys include porcelain and ceramics from Villeroy and Boch; Luxembourg wines (such as Rivaner, Elbling or Auxerois), and framed prints of old Luxembourg.

Shopping hours: 2-6pm on Mondays, 8am-noon and 2-6pm Tuesday-Saturday.

Cities and Sights

LUXEMBOURG (*telephone area code 352*)
Airport: Findel (7km/4 miles from city centre), international; well-stocked duty-free shop. Short- and long-term parking available. Regular bus service to and from the station (air terminal).

Tourist information office: City tourist office: Place d'Armes; tel. 40 08 08.

Chamber of commerce: 7, rue Alcide de Gasperi; tel. 43 58 53, fax 43 83 26, telex 601 74.

Sightseeing: European Parliament, casemates *(caves)*, old town, National Museum, cathedral.

Excursions: Clervaux, Echternach, Wiltz, Esch-sur-Sure, Vianden.

For some useful expressions in French, see page 116.

For some useful expressions in German, see page 135.

Malta

Type of government:	Republic, multi-party centralized
Member of:	BC, GATT, IMF
Population:	400,000
Area:	316sq km (122sq miles)
Capital:	Valletta (9,183)
Other major cities:	Sliema (20,000)
Languages:	English and Maltese; Italian fairly widely spoken in business circles.
Religion:	Catholic (98%)
Time zone:	GMT+1, EST+6; DST (Apr-Sep)
Currency:	Malta Lira (abbr. Lm) or Pound = 100 cents of 10 mils each
	Coins: 2, 3, 5 mils; 1, 5, 10, 25, 50 cents; Lm1
	Notes: Lm2, 5, 10, 20
Electricity:	240V, 50Hz, AC

Planning your Trip

Visa requirements: For South African nationals. (See also p.6.)

Vaccination requirements: None. (See also p.7.)

Import allowances (see also p.7):

Cigarettes	Cigars	Tobacco	Spirits	Wine
200	or 250g of other tobacco products		1l	and 1l

Perfume: not exceeding 10 ml.; *Toilet water* 125 ml.
Gifts: up to a value of LM50

Currency restrictions: Not more than Lm50 in local currency may be brought into the country. There are no restrictions on foreign currency, which must be declared upon entry.

Not more than Lm25 in local currency may be exported from Malta. Non-residents may take out with them the balance of unspent foreign currencies brought in by them. (See also p.7.)

Climate: The islands enjoy a temperate to warm climate. Rain falls for short periods between late October and early March. Average minimum and maximum temperatures:

Spring	Summer	Autumn	Winter
10/22°C	20/33°C	17/27°C	7/17°C
(50/72°F)	(68/91°F)	(63/81°F)	(45/63°F)

The heat is tempered by sea breezes. Average hours of sunshine are 10 per day in summer and 6 per day in winter.

Clothing: Light clothing is adequate in summer, with something warmer in winter. A subdued suit is acceptable for business meetings, and a conservative suit for official occasions.

Hotels: During the summer months advance booking is advisable.

Maltese tourist offices abroad: Canberra, Copenhagen, Brussels, Frankfurt, Geneva, London, Paris, Rome.

Business Briefing

Economic Background

Main industries: Tourism, textiles, shipbuilding, microelectronics and maintenance.

Main agricultural products: Potatoes, cereals, onions, fruit.

Main imports: Food, raw materials, manufactured goods.

Main exports: Clothing, petroleum products, ships, textiles, light industrial products and microelectronics.

GNP: $1.7 billion; per capita: $5,050.

Inflation rate: 3.1% (1994).

Principal trading partners: UK, Italy, Germany, USA, France.

Trade fairs: The International Trade Fair is held in the first half of July in Naxxar. It is visited by three-quarters of the country's population each year.

Selected background reading: *Annual Trade Directory* (Malta Chamber of Commerce), *Malta Year Book* (Giovanni Muscat), *Annual Malta Handbook* (Maltese Prime Minister's Office).

Maltese chambers of commerce abroad: Apply to commercial departments of diplomatic representations.

On the Spot

Office hours: Commercial offices: 9am-1pm and 2.30-6pm Monday-Friday (Oct 1-June 15); 8am-1pm in summer. Government offices: 7.45am-12.30pm and 1.15-5.15pm Monday-Friday (Oct 1-June 15); 7.30am-1.30pm in summer.

Public holidays

Jan 1	New Year's Day	Aug 15	Assumption Day
Feb 10	St Paul's Shipwreck	Sep 21	Independence Day
Mar 19	St Joseph's Day	Dec 8	Immaculate
Mar 31	National Day		Conception
May 1	May Day	Dec 13	Republic Day
June 7	Commemoration of June 7, 1919	Dec 25	Christmas Day
June 21	St Peter and St Paul		
Movable dates:		Easter Monday	

Banks and currency exchange: Banking hours are 8.00am-12.45pm Monday-Friday, with additional afternoon opening 2.30-4pm on Friday, and 8am-11.30am on Saturdays (June 16-Sep 30). From Oct 1-June 15 banks open at 8.30am, with afternoon opening on Tuesday and Friday, and remain open until noon on Saturday. Outside banking hours, currency exchange offices at principal centres open in the afternoon and evening. At Luqa airport, a 24-hour currency exchange service operates. On Saturdays, it is not possible to change more than the equivalent of Lm100.

Major banks: Bank of Valletta, Central Bank, Lombard Bank, APS Bank and Mid-Med Bank.

Credit cards and traveller's cheques: Both are fairly widely accepted.

Post and telecommunications: Telecommunications and postal services are generally reliable. The main post office (Auberge d'Italie, Merchants Street, Valletta) is open 7.30am-6pm Monday-Saturday (Oct 1-June 15); 7.30am-6pm Monday-Saturday (June 16-Sep 30). Malta International Airport post office is open 7am-7pm. Stamps are also available from hotels.

For telephone calls it is best to go to the main telegraph office in St George's Road, St Julian's, open 24 hours a day, the Telemalta office in South Street, Valletta, open 8am-6.30pm Monday to Saturday; or the Airport post office, open 7am-7pm daily, which also has a public telex booth. Public telephone boxes require phone cards, which can be bought from Telemalta offices or authorised dealers.

Telegrams, telex and fax messages can be sent from the main telegraph office in St George's Road, St Julian's, the branch office in South Street in Valletta or the Malta International Airport post office.

Overseas calls can be dialled direct. Telephone booths are painted red or are made of local limestone. Information in the telephone directory is in Maltese and English.

Some useful numbers:

Ambulance	196	Inquiries (Malta)	190
Fire	199	Inquiries (int.)	194
Police	191	Time	195

Embassies, high commissions and consulates: Principal diplomatic representations are listed under these three separate headings in the yellow pages. Others are found in the main directory.

Medical care and health: The Maltese medical profession is of a high standard. The government operates a modern medical program – it has reciprocal health agreements with Australia, Great Britain and a number of European countries. British nationals should inquire at their local Social Security offices about the extent of reciprocal payment agreements for medical treatment. Compared to the rest of Europe, medical fees range from low to moderate. In the case of an emergency contact St Luke's Hospital, Gwardamanġa, tel. 241 251.

Medical and pharmaceutical supplies are readily available at all dispensaries. Pharmacies open on Sundays on a roster basis. All Maltese doctors speak English and Italian. Tap water is safe for drinking.

Services: Photocopying facilities are provided by the chamber of commerce (Exchange Buildings, Republic Street, Valletta; tel. 62 72 33) and photocopying bureaus throughout the country.

Newspapers: There is one English-language daily published in Malta, *The Times*, and two main weeklies – the *Malta Independent* and *The Sunday Times*, there is also the *Financial and Business Post* and the *Malta Business Weekly*. Maltese dailies include *L'Orizzont* and *Iln-Nazzjon Taghna*. British and Italian newspapers are available, but very few other foreign publications. *What's On* (fortnightly) provides entertainment listings.

Transport

Air: There is an extensive number of scheduled flights to Malta operating chiefly from European countries and also direct flights to the Middle East including Dubai. Local scheduled helicopter flights operate between Malta and Gozo.

Local public transport: Frequent, low-cost buses run from Valletta to all towns and villages in Malta. The fare is paid to the driver.

Waterways: Car-ferry services ply between Malta and Gozo. The ferry from Pietà outside Valletta to Gozo makes two 1¼-hour daily return trips. Other ferries make several daily trips each way, leaving Malta from a point nearer to Gozo (Cirkewwa), each crossing taking half an hour; rough seas are likely to disrupt the usually punctual timetable. The Pietà-Gozo ferry operates a cafeteria service.

Taxis: Cabs are the preferred means of transport by business visitors. All taxis are white with red licence plates and have meters. Tip about 10% of the fare.

Car rental: International and local firms operate, some of which have desks at the airport. Between April and October early booking is recommended. It is advisable to examine and retain a copy of each car rental contract. Big companies are open 24 hours a day and take charge of a situation in case of accident or breakdown.

Driving in Malta: Drive on the *left*. Seat belts are not compulsory. You have to carry a red-reflector warning triangle. There is no alcohol limit, but driving under the influence of alcohol is punishable. Fuel (petrol/gas) available is super (98-100 octane), unleaded and diesel.

Country roads are often very poor, and even main roads can be in a bad state of repair. There are no toll roads. Vigilance is called for, since road discipline is often rather relaxed. Parking space in Valletta is hard to find during the day. In the case of an accident call the police immediately on 191.

Speed limits are 40kph (25mph) in built-up areas and 55kph (34mph) outside towns.

Social customs: Despite their well-deserved reputation for friendliness and a helpful disposition, the Maltese may at first be rather reserved with visitors. Don't hesitate to break the ice and make the first approach. Catholic religious sentiment is strong, and people visiting churches, especially women, are expected to be suitably clad. Most Maltese will be flattered if you learn to speak a few words of their own – very difficult – language.

Hints for business: Though business protocol is not very strict, it's better to err on the side of caution, especially with the longer-established firms. Note that punctuality is appreciated.

Crime and theft: Car thefts are on the increase. See that your car is emptied of valuables and locked.

After Hours

Food and drink: Local specialities include the larger varieties of Mediterranean fish, notably *acciola*, *dentice*, *lampuka*, swordfish and tunny (tuna), served in a variety of ways. Other favourite dishes are *bragioli* (beef olives), *soppa tal-armla* ('window's soup') and stewed or fried rabbit – all more likely to be found in rustic seaside restaurants.

A range of foreign beer, wine and spirits is available at bars and restaurants. Maltese beer, however, is excellent, and inexpensive local wines are worth sampling. Some hotel bars open only after 6pm and most close between 1 and 4 in the afternoon.

Mealtimes: lunch 12.30-2.30pm, dinner 7-10pm.

Entertainment: A good choice of nightclubs and discotheques are patronized by both tourists and local residents. The historic Manoel Theatre is the setting for opera, concerts, plays and ballet in winter. Open-air performances also take place during summer. Cinemas usually show American, British and Italian films (the latter dubbed into English). Of particular interest to the visitor are the numerous religious *festi* (folk festivals) held in most towns and villages. Colourful processions, bands and fireworks are featured. Some 30 *festi* fall in the summer months, mostly on Sundays.

Taxes, service charges and tipping: Service is included in restaurants and hotels. Recommended tips: porters (per bag) 25 cents; waiters, taxi drivers, hairdressers 10%; cloakroom attendants 25 cents; hotel maids 50 cents a week.

Sports and recreation: Sailing, water-skiing, boating and scuba diving can be enjoyed at a number of coastal areas. Temporary membership in the Royal Malta Yacht Club or the Marsa Sports Club is possible. The latter club has facilities for tennis, polo, golf and other
sports.

Top spectator sports are, in winter, soccer, played at the Empire Stadium, Gzira, and, in summer, water polo.

TV and radio: TV Malta broadcasts about six hours of programmes in Maltese and English every evening, and there are filmed programmes which come largely from America and Britain. An English newscast is a daily feature. Cable television is often available. The BBC World Service and Voice of America are easily picked up. There are several local radio stations, including the all-English station, Island Sound Radio. Italian TV reception is very good.

What to buy: Typical locally manufactured goods include gold and silver filigree articles, ornamental glassware, Malta woven lace, and stone ornaments. If you have the time, you may like to visit the Malta Crafts Village at Ta'Qali, where you can see a concentration of craft industries in operation and make your purchases from the premises.

Shopping hours: generally the same as office hours (see above), though many small shops stay open later.

Cities and Sights

VALLETTA

Airport: Malta International Airport (5km/3 miles from Valletta), international; duty-free shop, for incoming passengers too. Airport buses meet most flights.

Tourist information office: 1, City Arcades, Valletta; tel. 23 77 47. National Tourist Organisation of Malta, 280 Republic Street, Valletta; tel. 22 44 44 or 238282, fax 220401.

Chamber of commerce: Exchange Buildings, Republic Street, tel. 62 72 33.

Sightseeing: Bastions, St John's Cathedral.

Excursions: Mnajdra (Malta), Ġgantija (Gozo) (megalithic and neolithic structures), St Paul's Bay, Mdina (or Natabile).

Monaco

Type of government:	Constitutional principality with 18-member legislature (National Council)
Population:	31,008 (of which c. 20% of Monegasque nationality)
Area:	1.95sq km (0.73sq miles)
Capital:	Monaco-Ville (c. 1,200 inhabitants), which has merged with the harbour district of La Condamine, the district of Monte-Carlo and the industrial centre of Fontvieille.
Language:	French; English and Italian are widely spoken in business circles.
Religion:	Catholic (c. 90%)
Time zone:	GMT+1, EST+6; DST (Apr-Sep)
Currency:	French franc (abbr. F or FF) = 100 centimes
	Coins: 5, 10, 20, 50 centimes; 1, 2, 5, 10F
	Notes: 20, 50, 100, 200, 500F
Electricity:	220V, 50Hz, AC

Planning your Trip

Visa requirements: Same as for France. No formalities are required to cross the border between France and the principality.

Vaccination requirements: None. (See also p.7.)

Import allowances: Same as for France. (See also p.7.)

Currency restrictions: Same as for France. (See also p.7.)

Climate: Considered by many to be near-ideal, the region enjoys a mild climate in winter (minimum average temperature in January is 8°C/47°F) and warm weather in summer (maximum average temperature in July and August is 25°C/77°F). There is generally little continuous rainfall; cloudbursts lasting only an hour or two are the rule. An average of 2,583 hours of sunshine are recorded annually.

Clothing: Light clothing can be worn from spring through to autumn. Despite the generally mild winters, a topcoat is necessary for occasional cold spells. Business attire tends to be conservative: despite the often rather casual atmosphere, suits and ties are the order of the day for men and sober dresses for women.

Hotels: Some 18 hotels in the principality are classified into one-, two-, three-, four- and four-star-deluxe categories.

Book ahead during the tourist periods – Christmas-New Year, Easter and July-August.

Tourist information on Monaco: There are Monaco Tourist Offices in Frankfurt, London, Milan, New York and Paris. You can also write to Direction du Tourisme et des Congrès, 2a boulevard des Moulins, Monte-Carlo, Monaco.

Business Briefing

Economic Background: Though essentially based on tourism, economic activity also extends to light engineering, electronics, precision instrument manufacture, chemicals and clothing.

Selected background reading: In addition to providing tourist information, the Direction du Tourisme et des Congrès (2a boulevard des Moulins, Monte-Carlo, Monaco) can also furnish economic, financial, industrial and commercial data. The chamber of commerce and industry as well as the other commercial organizations listed under CITIES AND SIGHTS may also be contacted.

On the Spot

Office hours: 8.30am-noon and 2.30-6.30pm, Monday-Friday.

Public holidays

Jan 1	New Year's Day	Dec 24	Christmas Eve
Jan 27	St Dévote's Day		(afternoon)
May 1	Labour Day	Dec 25	Christmas Day
Aug 15	Assumption		
Nov 1	All Saints' Day	**Movable dates**:	Easter Monday
Nov 19	National Day		Ascension
Dec 8	Immaculate		Whit Monday
	Conception		

When a public holiday falls on a Thursday or Tuesday, some businesses close down for a four-day weekend.

Banks and currency exchange: Banking hours are 9am-noon and 2-5.30pm, Monday-Friday. Some banks also work on Saturday mornings for currency-exchange purposes. Four *bureaux de change* operate every day of the year: Banque Générale du Commerce (2 avenue des Spélugues), Compagnie Monégasque de Change (parking des Pécheurs, Monaco-Ville), Gare de Monaco (avenue Prince Pierre) and Monafinances (17 avenue des Spélugues).

Principal banks are Banque Centrale Monégasque de Crédit à Long et Moyen Terme, Banque Industrielle de Monaco, Compagnie Monégasque de Banque, Crédit Foncier de Monaco and Société de Crédit et de Banque de Monaco.

Credit cards and traveller's cheques: Main internationally accepted credit cards and traveller's cheques are recognized in most establishments.

Post and telecommunications: All services are generally reliable. Post office hours are 8am-7pm Monday-Friday, and 8am-noon on Saturdays. The main post office is on Beaumarchais square. You can telephone from the post office between 8am and 9pm seven days a week.

The principality's mail and telecommunications systems are largely integrated with those of France. Postage rates are the same as in France, but Monaco stamps must be used. The rate for calls abroad is much cheaper late in the evening, early in the morning and on Sundays.

A private company, Monte-Carlo Services, 2 rue des Iris; tel. 93 30 01 01, offers telex facilities to visitors.

Some useful numbers:

Duty doctor	141	Operator	10
Fire	18	Police	17
Hospital	93 25 99 00	Telegrams	140
Inquiries	12	Time	3699

Consulates: Some 42 consulates are maintained in the principality. Others responsible for Monaco are located in Nice (American, British and Swiss). All diplomatic representations, including those in Nice and Marseilles, are listed under *Corps consulaire étranger* in a separate section at the end of the yellow pages of the Monaco telephone directory.

Medical care and health: Medical treatment is excellent, with fees on a par with those of France. The principality's single hospital, Centre Hospitalier Princesse Grace (in avenue Pasteur; tel. 93 25 99 00) is well equipped. Pharmaceutical supplies are readily available. A notice posted on the door of a pharmacy indicates which other shops are open after hours. Some doctors speak English. Tap water is safe to drink.

Services: The yellow pages of the Monaco telephone directory list photocopying facilities (*photocopie*), secretarial services (*secrétariats*) and translators (*traducteurs*). In addition, the tourist office can be of help. Photocopies can also be made in department stores or at tobacconists'.

Newspapers: The principal daily read locally is *Nice-Matin* which has a Monaco page in the edition sold in the principality. A wide range of foreign newspapers can be found at news-stands, particularly at the Café de Paris, place du Casino.

Transport

Air – international: Monaco is served by the international airport of Nice (20km/12 miles away). Minibuses, with about ten services daily in each direction, link Nice airport with Monaco and French Riviera resorts. The bus stop in the principality is at place d'Armes, La Condamine. The run takes one hour and a quarter. A 45-minute service is also available. A helicopter service operates between the airport and several destinations in the principality, taking six to seven minutes.

Rail: The French railway network serves Monaco, with one station located in the principality. In summer, a special Métrazur service runs half-hourly between Cannes and Menton.

Local public transport: Buses link various areas of the principality. Fares are paid to the conductor on board. The ticket price is the same, regardless of destination, and reductions are available if you buy a journey card which covers 4-8 journeys.

Taxis: Taxis can be hired by telephone or directly from taxi ranks. For destinations outside Monaco booking may be required. Monaco has six taxi ranks: Casino (avenue de Monte Carlo); Fontvieille (avenue des Papalins); Larvatto (avenue Princesse Grace); Place des Moulins; Poste de Monte Carlo (avenue Henry Dunant); and at the train station (avenue Prince Pierre). Taxis are metered. For trips outside the principality, the fare goes up by about 75%. Tip the driver about 10% of the fare.

Car rental: Around a dozen agencies rent cars.

Driving in Monaco: Rules of the road are the same as in France. All drivers must possess a red-reflector warning triangle for use in case of breakdown, a fire extinguisher and a spare set of bulbs. Seat belts are recommended but not compulsory. Fuel (petrol/gas) available is normal (90 octane), super (98 octane) and diesel. The speed limit is 60kph (37mph) throughout the principality. In case of breakdown or accident, tel. 17.

Social customs: Don't forget to shake hands when meeting someone or taking your leave. Being invited to somebody's home, even after a considerable acquaintance, is rare. But for that occasion a small gift of flowers or chocolates for the hostess will be appreciated.

Hints for business: Make appointments in advance, if possible in writing. Do not go onto a first-name basis unless your interlocutor makes the first step in this direction. Business people prefer a leisurely examination of the subject under discussion, and snap decisions are rare. Avoid the Christmas-New Year, Easter and summer (July-August) periods for business travel.

Crime and theft: Normal precautions are in order. The principality is known for its low crime rate.

After Hours

Food and drink: Classic French cuisine is found on menus throughout the principality. Regional specialities include *soupe de poisson* (fish soup), *bouillabaisse* (fish stew), *pissaladière* (onion tart with anchovies and black olives) and *tourte de blette* (Swiss-chard pie).

A wide selection of French wines is available, along with imported spirits.

Mealtimes: lunch noon-2pm, dinner 7.30-10pm. Some official or society suppers run on later.

Entertainment: Plays, concerts, ballet and opera performances are presented regularly. In summer, open-air concerts are put on in the court of honour of the Prince's Palace or at the Théâtre du Fort Antoine. Gala evenings enliven the social scene at the Sporting Club, while films are screened in the club's two cinemas or (in summer) outdoors. Most films are dubbed into French, though in summer some English-language films are shown in the original version. And, naturally, the casino is a dominant hub of nightlife, supplemented by some 11 nightclubs.

Taxes, service charges and tipping: Hotel and restaurant bills are all inclusive. Tipping recommendations: taxi drivers, barbers and hairdressers 10-15%, railway porters 5F per bag.

221

Sports and recreation: Those interested in relaxing will find an imposing choice of beaches and swimming pools. Sailing, water-skiing, tennis, squash, golf and miniature golf are readily available. Several saunas and health institutes are also located in Monaco, which boasts one of Europe's biggest sports complexes (Stade Louis-II).

Top spectator attractions are the Monte-Carlo Rally and tennis championships, as well as the Grand Prix motor races.

TV and radio: Local services are in French. Radio Monte-Carlo also broadcasts religious programmes in various languages for Transworld Radio.

What to buy: The accent is on luxury at Monaco's big jewellery shops, boutiques and art galleries. Ceramics and glassware are appreciated souvenirs. For more modest budgets, Monaco postage stamps are delightful.

Shopping hours: 8 or 9am to 7pm Monday-Saturday. Most shops close for lunch between noon and 2.30 or 3pm, while souvenir shops are open on Sunday mornings.

Cities and Sights

MONACO AND ENVIRONS

Airport: The principality is served by Nice international airport (20km/12 miles away). A duty-free shop is available at the airport. Access is by bus, leaving from place d'Armes, La Condamine, about ten times daily. The trip takes one hour and a quarter. A helicopter service operates between the airport and the landing pad west of the Monaco Rock. Duration of flight: six minutes.

Tourist information offices: Direction du Tourisme et des Congrès, 2a boulevard des Moulins, Monte-Carlo, Monaco; tel. 92 16 61 16, fax 92 16 60.

Chamber of commerce and industry: 1 avenue des Costelans; tel. 92 05 20 19, fax 92 05 31 29.

Other commercial organizations:
Conseil Economique (Economic Council), 8 rue Louis Notari, La Condamine; tel. 93 30 20 82.
Département des Finances, place de la Visitation, Monaco-Ville; tel. 93 15 80 00.
Ministere d'état; tel. 93 15 88 01.

Sightseeing: Old town (ramparts, Rampe major), Prince's Palace (state apartments, changing of the guard), Exotic Garden, casino.

Museums: Palace Museum (Napoleonic mementos), Oceanographic Museum and aquarium, Waxworks Museum, Museum of Prehistoric Anthropology, National Museum of Automatons and Dolls.

Excursions: Roquebrune-Village (medieval castle), Cap Martin, La Turbie, Eze-Village, Laghet, Menton (Jean Cocteau museum), Beaulieu (Greek villa), Cap Ferrat (Ile-de-France museum), Ville-franche-sur-Mer (Cocteau's chapel), Nice-Cimiez (Marc Chagall museum), Saint-Paul de Vence (Matisse chapel), Biot (Fernand Léger museum), valleys of the Roya and the Merveilles, Vésubie and the Tinée, Loup, Cian, Daluis, Verdon gorges for hiking.

For some useful expressions in French, see page 116.

Netherlands

Type of government:	Constitutional monarchy, multi-party centralized
Member of:	Benelux, EU, GATT, IBRD, IDA, IFC, IMF, OECD
Population:	15 million
Area:	41,582sq km (15,770sq miles)
Capital:	Amsterdam (725,084/GUA 995,000)
Other major cities:	The Hague (*Den Haag* or *'s-Gravenhage*, seat of government, 445,215/GUA 675,000)
	Rotterdam (597,644/GUA 1m)
	Utrecht (234,562/GUA 500,000)
	Eindhoven (195,800/GUA 375,000)
	Groningen (170,800/GUA 210,000)
	Haarlem (150,000/GUA 220,000)
Language:	Dutch; English and German widely spoken in business circles; occasionally French.
Religion:	Catholic (38%), Protestant (31%), Jewish (4%)
Time zone:	GMT+1, EST+6; DST (Apr-Sep)
Currency:	Gulden (abbreviated *f*, fl or gld) = 100 cents
	Coins: 5, 10, 25 cents; *f*1, 2½, 5
	Notes: *f*10, 25, 50, 100, 250, 1,000
Electricity:	220V, 50Hz, AC

Planning your Trip

Visa requirements: For nationals of Turkey (except permanent residents of an EU country) and South Africa. (See also p.6.)

Vaccination requirements: None. (See also p.7.)

Import allowances (see also p.7):

	Cigarettes		Cigars		Tobacco	Spirits		Wine
1)	400	or	100	or	500g	1l	and	2l
2)	200	or	50	or	250g	1l	and	2l
3)	(800)	or	(200)	or	(1kg)	(10l)	and	(90l)

1) Passengers from countries outside Europe.
2) Duty-free goods bought in EU countries by European residents.
3) Non-duty-free goods bought within the EU.

Perfume: 1), 2) 50g; *Toilet water*: 1), 2) 0.25l;
Gifts: 1) *f*2,000 max. value; 2) *f*380 max. value

There are no official restrictions on goods bought non-duty-free within the EU, provided they are for personal use only. The above figures are guidelines to the quantities customs officials will generally find acceptable, so if you are carrying larger quantities you should be prepared to provide proof that the goods are for your personal use.

Currency restrictions: None. (See also p.7.)

Climate: The maritime temperate climate resembles that of eastern England but is slightly colder in winter. Rain falls throughout the year but in summer showers are mostly short. Pack a raincoat or umbrella with you in all seasons. It snows only occasionally in winter.

Some average temperatures:

Jan	Apr	July	Oct
4°C (39°F)	10°C (51°F)	19°C (67°F)	10°C (51°F)

Clothing: Even in high summer, evenings can be chilly, or it may cloud up suddenly during the day, so some warm clothing is necessary; don't forget to pack a raincoat or umbrella. Spring and autumn only occasionally produce balmy days, and the only sensible way to dress in the often windy winter is to bundle up warmly. Dark, conservative suits or colour-coordinated attire are both worn in business circles. In summer, light-weight suits and lighter colours are making headway.

Hotels: Advance booking is advised, especially in summer and during conference and exposition periods. Hotel-booking services at Schiphol and Zestienhoven airports as well as at larger railway stations can help if you've arrived without reserving ahead. For advance booking contact the Netherlands Reservation Centre, PO Box 404, 2260 AK Leidschendam; tel. (070) 320 2500, fax 320 2611.

Dutch tourist offices abroad: Berlin, Brussels, Chicago, Cologne, Johannesburg, London, Madrid, Mexico City, New York, Paris, San Francisco, Stockholm, Sydney, Tel Aviv, Tokyo, Toronto, Vancouver, Vienna, Zurich.

Business Briefing

Economic Background

Main industries: Petro-chemical, machinery, motor vehicles, shoes, textiles and clothing, electronics, foodstuffs, beverages, tobacco products, building materials, shipbuilding, natural gas.

Main agricultural products: Flower bulbs, dairy products, wheat, oats, rye, potatoes, sugar beet.

Main imports: Raw materials, crude oil, motor vehicles, foodstuffs.

Main exports: Chemicals, natural gas, agricultural and dairy produce, machinery, foodstuffs, lubricants, transport equipment, flower bulbs.

Principal trading partners: Germany, Belgium, France, UK, Italy, USA, CIS, Saudi Arabia.

GNP: $237.6 billion; per capita: $16,125.

Inflation rate: 1.9% (1993).

Trade fairs: Main exhibition centres in the Netherlands are Amsterdam and Utrecht, where a wide variety of trade fairs are held throughout the year, for example, the Boat Show in Amsterdam (August) and the Building Trade Fair every two years in Utrecht (February). Details can be obtained from Dutch chambers of commerce or consulates.

Selected background reading: *Statistical Yearbook* is published annually in English by the Central Bureau of Statistics. The same office issues the monthly *Industrial Statistics* in English. The AMRO Bank puts out *The Netherlands Economic Report* quarterly and *Commerce & Industry in the Netherlands* every two years – both in English.

Dutch chambers of commerce abroad: Berlin, Brussels, Buenos Aires, Caracas, Chicago, Düsseldorf, Jakarta, Lagos, London, Madrid, Manchester, Mexico, Milan, New York, Paramaribo, Paris, São Paulo, Vienna, Zurich.

On the Spot

Office hours: Generally 8.30am-5.30pm Monday-Friday.

Public holidays:

Jan 1	New Year's Day	**Movable dates**:	Good Friday
Apr 30	Queen's Birthday		Easter Monday
Dec 25	Christmas Day		Ascension
Dec 26	Boxing Day		

Banks and currency exchange: Banking hours are 9am-4pm Monday-Friday. Main branches stay open to 5pm, and on Thursday evenings, 4.30-7pm. Outside banking hours, currency can be changed at Amsterdam's main railway station (open 24 hours a day, seven days a week) and at Schiphol airport. Major hotels cash cheques. Principal banks: AMRO Bank, ABN, RABO Bank, Nederlandse Middenstands Bank.

Credit cards and traveller's cheques: Major cards and cheques are easily accepted by major businesses.

Post and telecommunications: All services are highly reliable. Post office hours are generally 9am-5pm Monday-Friday. Main post offices which are open later are, in Amsterdam: Oosterdokskade 3-5 and Singel 250; in The Hague: Prinsestraat; in Rotterdam: Coolsingel and Delftseplein. Day-and-night telegram, fax and telephone services are available in Amsterdam (at Telehouse, Raadhuisstraat 46-50, behind Dam Square) and Rotterdam (at Coolsingel post office – use Meent entrance). In Amsterdam faxes can also be sent from the Teletalk centre, Leidsestraat 101.

The Dutch telephone system is automated, and international direct dialling facilities are readily available. Public coin telephones take 25-cent, 1- and 2.50-gulden pieces.

Some useful numbers:

Inquiries (inland)	06-8008	Telegrams	06-0409
Inquiries (int.)	06 0418	Time	06-8002
Operator	06 0456	Weather	06-8003
Police/fire/ambulance	06-11		

Principal area codes: Amsterdam 020, Arnhem 085, The Hague 070, Eindhoven 040, Maastricht 043, Rotterdam 010, Utrecht 030.

Embassies and consulates: Most countries have a consulate in Amsterdam; the majority of embassies are in The Hague. Complete listings can be found in telephone directories under *Ambassade* (embassies) and *Consulaat* (consulates).

Medical care and health: Medical treatment is excellent but rather expensive. Reciprocal agreements exist with certain countries including Britain. Most doctors speak English and German, and sometimes French. Medicine and pharmaceutical supplies are readily available. Pharmacies are identified by the word *Apotheek* and the addresses of those on duty are posted in other pharmacy windows; or, in Amsterdam, you can telephone 020 694 8709 for this information (the same number will advise about emergency doctors and dentists). Emergency medical treatment is available at various hopsitals, including the Academisch Medisch Centrum in Amsterdam, Meibergdreef 9; tel. 566 91 11.

Tap water is safe to drink.

Services: Consult the yellow pages for typing and secretarial services (under *Typebureau*), translators (under *Vertaalbureau*) and interpreters (under *Tolken*). Photocopying facilities exist in some main post offices, department stores, public libraries and small printshops.

Newspapers: Principal Dutch newspapers are *NRC/Handelsblad*, *De Volkskrant*, *De Telegraaf* and *Het Parool*. Major British and Continental dailies, including the Paris-edited *International Herald Tribune*, are available at larger news-stands.

Transport

Air – international: Amsterdam's Schiphol is the major gateway to the Netherlands. The much smaller airports of Rotterdam, Eindhoven and Maastricht have some international flights to Belgium, England, France and Germany. Passengers on KLM flights can check in at the KLM desk in the Amsterdam, Rotterdam or The Hague central railway stations.

Air-domestic: Six airports serve the country's internal air network. Amsterdam's Schiphol, Rotterdam's Zestienhoven, Groningen's Eelde, Eindhoven's Welschap, Enschede's Twente and Maastricht's Beek.

Rail: Trains, with first- and second-class compartments, are punctual, comfortable but sometimes very crowded; first-class travel is advised for business purposes. On express trains a modest dining-car offers beer or other beverages and sandwiches.

The Summer Tour ticket can be obtained at any railway station in Holland, and entitles the holder to three days' unlimited train travel within 10 days. One-day and seven-day tickets are also available. For Eurailpass, see p.10; for Benelux Tourrail ticket see p.205.

Local public transport: Buses and trams serve most major cities. Amsterdam and Rotterdam have underground (subway) systems. In **229**

Amsterdam you enter buses and trams by the front door, buy your ticket from the driver and then cancel it in the yellow stamping machine. At the municipal transport board ticket office (signposted *Kaartverkoop*) outside Central Station you can buy one-, two- or three-day runabout tickets.

Taxis: Cabs do not generally cruise the streets. To get one, go to a taxi rank or call for one (see *Taxi* entry in telephone directories). Tipping: round off. A novelty is the 'Treintaxi', which operates in 80 towns (outside of the big four cities, already well-served by public transport) and takes passengers from the railway station to any place within the municipal boundaries or vice versa for *f*6. You need to buy the ticket before boarding the taxi. The Treintaxi is not for sole use and will wait for up to ten minutes for other passengers to board. They operate from 7am on weekdays and 8am on Sundays, until the arrival of the last train.

Car rental: International and local agencies operate, some with airport offices. Credit cards are preferred means of payment. Chauffeur-driven cars are also available.

Driving in the Netherlands: You must carry a red-reflector warning triangle for use in case of breakdown. Tolls must be paid at the Maastunnel, Kiltunnel, Prins William Alexanderburg and some bridges near Rotterdam. All roads are maintained in excellent condition. Motorways (expressways) connect all major cities. Speed limits: 30kph (19mph) or 50kph (31mph) in town, 100 or 120kph (62 or 75mph) on motorways and generally 80kph (50mph) on other roads. Seat belts must be worn. Blood alcohol limit is a strictly enforced 0.5 promille. Fuel (petrol/gas) available is 95 octane lead-free (*Euro loodvrij*), 98 octane lead-free (*Super Plus*), 91 octane leaded (*Super*) and diesel and LPG.

Trams and buses always have priority. Watch for cyclists, especially when turning right. Yellow emergency callboxes are located along principal motorways; otherwise in case of breakdown, call ANWB Wegenwacht (06 0888).

Some distances from Amsterdam: The Hague 50km (31 miles), Rotterdam 70km (43 miles), Groningen 200km (125 miles).

Social customs: The Dutch are very open and are quite likely to invite a visitor to their homes. A small gift of flowers to the hostess or a memento from the visitor's country is appreciated.

Hints for business: Prior appointments and punctuality are expected. For practical information, turn to the Economic Information Service (070 81 41 11 ext. 3207). A Dutch business associate will probably invite you home for drinks before continuing on to a restaurant for dinner. Avoid July-beginning of August for business travel when many people go on holiday.

Foreign chambers of commerce in the Netherlands: American, Australian, British, Canadian, French, German, Israeli, Middle Eastern, New Zealand, Russian, South American, Swiss, Turkish.

Crime and theft: Petty crime, including pickpocketing and thefts from car, is on the increase. Very late at night, avoid the *walletjes* area of Amsterdam and side-streets off main entertainment squares.

After Hours

Food and drink: A great variety of restaurants with foreign cooking exist in big cities, especially Amsterdam. Very numerous throughout the country are Indonesian restaurants. Try the Indonesian *rijsttafel* ('rice dish') which may offer over 30 items. Local specialities are: *aal* (eel), *heilbot* (halibut), *kabeljauw* (cod), *hutspot* (stew of potatoes, carrots and onions), *bruine bonen* (baked beans), *pannekoeken* (large pancakes served with bacon or apples) and *erwtensoep* (pea soup).

Bottled wine is much more expensive than open wine. Local beer is excellent. Try a *jenever* (Dutch gin) before dinner. Foreign beers and spirits are widely available.

Mealtimes: lunch noon-2pm, dinner 5.30-9.30pm.

Entertainment: Major cities have a good choice of cinemas (with films generally shown in the original language), discotheques and nightclubs. Throughout the year plays (also in English), opera, concerts and ballet are staged. Bookshops and tourist offices provide a free entertainment periodical.

Taxes, service charges and tipping: Value-added tax (in Dutch abbreviated BTW) and service are usually included in hotel and restaurant bills. Tipping recommendations: waiters, round off; hotel porters *f*2 per bag; taxi drivers, round off; cloakroom attendants *f*1; hairdresser and barbers, included; cinema and theatre ushers *f*1.

Sports and recreation: Visitors can hire a sailing-boat or yacht, swim at the North Sea beaches, ice-skate (also in summer at the Jaap Eden stadium), go cycling, fishing or horse-riding, or play tennis or golf. Soccer is the most popular spectator sport.

TV and radio: Radio and TV programming is in Dutch; German telecasts can also be received, as can BBC domestic broadcasts from England. Amsterdam also has cable TV, allowing a view of programmes from neighbouring countries.

What to buy: Good buys in the Netherlands are Dutch cigars, cheese, chocolate, *jenever* (Dutch gin), tulip bulbs, Delft blue china, diamonds, jewellery, *Haagse Hopjes* (sweets), antiques, wooden shoes, silver, Makkum pottery and pewter.

Shopping hours: most shops are open from 9am to 5.30 or 6pm Monday to Saturday, but many do not open on Mondays until 1pm.

Cities and Sights

AMSTERDAM (*Telephone area code 020*)

Airport: Schiphol (15km/9 miles from city centre), international; extensive duty-free shops. Regular rail service to Central Station with direct connections to towns throughout Holland. Also frequent train service from the airport to Amsterdam RAI (Congress Centre). KLM buses for the major hotels in Amsterdam.

Tourist information office: VVV, Stationsplein 10 (opposite the Central Station); tel. 06 340 340 66.

Chamber of commerce: De Ruyterkade 5; tel. 523 66 00, fax 523 66 77 (general) 523 67 32 (trade).

Sightseeing: Canal trip, flower market (Munttoren), Begijnhof, Dam Square (Royal Palace), Nieuwe Kerk, Oude Kerk, Westerkerk, Anne Frankhuis, Magere Brug.

Amsterdam Culture and Leisure Pass: This pass gives around 25 coupons allowing free entry, or considerable discounts at various musuems, attractions and restaurants, with discounts on water transport round the city.

Museums: Rijksmuseum, Vincent van Gogh Museum, Stedelijk Museum, Rembrandthuis, Amsterdam Historical Museum.

Excursions: Broek in Waterland, Volendam, Marken, Edam, Zaanse Schans, Haarlem, Zandvoort (beach).

ROTTERDAM *(Telephone area code 010)*

Airport: Zestienhoven (6km/4 miles from city centre), international; duty-free shop. Airport and city bus service to Central Station. Regular rail service to Schiphol airport.

Tourist information offices: Stadhuisplein 19; tel. 34 03 40 65. VVV Information Office, Coolsingel 67, 3012 AC Rotterdam; tel. 413 60 00, telex 21228.

Chamber of commerce: Beursgebouw World Trade Center, Beursplein 37; tel. 405 77 77, fax 414 57 54.

Sightseeing: Euromast (tower), Lijnbaan (main shopping street), St Laurenskerk. Delfshaven (old quarter).

Museums: Boymans-Van Beuningen Museum, Museum voor Landenen Volkenkunde (geographical and ethnographical museum), Maritiem (maritime) Museum.

Excursions: Delft, Schoonhoven, Kinderdijk, The Hague.   **233**

THE HAGUE (*Telephone area code 070*)

Airport: Access from Amsterdam or Rotterdam airports.

Tourist information office: The Hague Visitors and Convention Bureau, Nassualaan 25, 2514 JT, The Hague; tel. 361 88 88, fax 361 5459.

Chamber of commerce: Alexander Gogelweg 16; tel. 379 57 95, fax 345 76 00.

Economic information service: located at Bezuidenhoutseweg 151; tel. 81 41 11, ext. 3207.

Dutch Trade Centre: Spui 3; tel. 46 93 92; NCH, PO Box 10, 2501 CA, The Hague.

Sightseeing: Binnenhof (Ridderzaal, Buitenhof), Gevangenpoort (Prison Gate), Panorama Mesdag, Parliment Buildings, Vredespaleis (Peace Palace), Madurodam (miniature town), Omniversum.

Museums: Mauritshuis (art collection), Haagse Gemeentemuseum (municipal museum), PTT Museum.

Excursions: Leiden, Gouda, Keukenhof, Delft.

Some Useful Expressions in Dutch

good morning	**Goedemorgen/goedemiddag**
good evening/night	**Goedenavond/goednacht**
good-bye	**Dag**
yes/no	**ja/nee**
please/thank you	**alstublieft/dank u**
excuse me	**pardon**
you're welcome	**tot uw dienst**
where/when/how	**waar/wanner/hoe**
how long/how far	**hoelang/hoever**
yesterday/today/tomorrow	**gisteren/vandaag/morgen**
day/week/month/year	**dag/week/maand/jaar**
left/right	**links/rechts**
up/down	**boven/beneden**
good/bad	**goed/slecht**
big/small	**groot/klein**
cheap/expensive	**goedkoop/duur**
hot/cold	**warm/koud**
old/new	**oud/nieuw**
open/closed	**open/dicht**
early/late	**vroeg/laat**
easy/difficult	**gemakkelijk/moeilijk**
Does anyone here speak English/French/German?	**Spreekt er hier iemand Engels/Frans/Duits?**
What does this mean?	**Wat beteket dit?**
I don't understand.	**Ik begrijp het niet.**
Do you take credit cards/ traveller's cheques?	**Accepteert u credit cards/ reischeques?**
Waiter!/Waitress!	**Ober!/Juffrouw!**
Where are the toilets?	**Waar zijn de toiletten?**
I'd like…	**Ik wil graag…**
How much is that?	**Hoeveel kost het?**
Help me please.	**Help mij, alstublieft.**

Norway

Type of government:	Constitutional monarchy, multi-party centralized
Member of:	EFTA, GATT, IBRD, IDA, IFC, IMF, OECD
Population:	4.3 million
Area:	323,877sq km (125,049sq miles)
Capital:	Oslo (473,344/GUA 695,000)
Other major cities:	Bergen (218,105), Trondheim (140,718) Stavanger (95,000), Kristiansand (60,000) Drammen (50,000), Tromsø (45,000)
Language:	Norwegian (with two standard forms, bookmål and nynorsk); English and German are widely spoken in business circles.
Religion:	Protestant (94%), Catholic (4%)
Time zone:	GMT+1, EST+6; DST (Apr-Sep)
Currency:	Norwegian krone (meaning crown), (abbr. kr) = 100 øre
	Coins: 50 øre, kr1, 5, 10
	Notes: kr50, 100, 500, 1,000
Electricity:	220V, 50Hz, AC

Planning your Trip

Visa requirements: For nationals of Turkey and South Africa. (See also p.6.)

Vaccination requirements: None. (See also p.7.)

Import allowances (see also p.7):

	Cigarettes		Cigars and Tobacco	Spirits		Wine
1) European residents	200	or	250g of other tobacco products	1l	and	1l
2) non-European residents	400	or	500g of other tobacco products	1l	and	1l
*Alcoholic beverages of over 60% (120° proof) are prohibited.						

Perfume: 1) small bottle; 2) 50g; *Toilet water*: 1) small bottle; 2) 0.5l; *Gifts*: 1) kr1,200 max. value; 2) kr3,500 max. value

Currency restrictions: Any amount of foreign currency or Norwegian kroner may be imported. Foreign currency up to the amount imported and Norwegian kroner up to the amount of kr5,000 may be taken out of the country. (See also p.7.)

Climate: For its latitude, most of Norway enjoys a mild climate, thanks to prevailing southwest winds and the moderating influence of the Gulf Stream. While some rain falls in spring and autumn, most precipitation in Oslo is from winter snowfalls. Bergen is noted as a rainy city.

Some average daytime temperatures:

	Spring	Summer	Autumn	Winter
Oslo	4°C (39°F)	17°C (63°F)	5°C (41°F)	-4°C (25°F)
Bergen	5°C (41°F)	15°C (59°F)	8°C (47°F)	-1°C (30°F)

Oslo's temperature can plunge to -25°C (-13°F) in winter while in summer the thermometer can read 35°C (96°F). In summer, Oslo and Bergen enjoy 18 or more hours of daylight but in winter less than seven; the far north benefits from 24-hour daylight in summer but almost continuous darkness, or twilight, in winter. Snow affects traffic to such an extent that cars require studded tires by law from October to mid-April. **237**

Clothing: In summer, light clothes are usually adequate, but pack a raincoat and something warmer for the evenings. Heavy clothing is needed in winter, with good, waterproof, non-slip footwear. Business attire is fairly casual; sports jackets are common.

Hotels: During the Bergen Festival in the last week in May and winter sports events in Oslo (January-March), book in advance. Railway stations and airports have hotel booking facilities. If you arrive in Oslo without a reservation, try the Tourist Information Centre at Central Station (Jernbanetorget 2, N-0154 Oslo). In Bergen the Tourist Information Office at Bryggen 7 can help with accommodation. Hotel listings are found in local city brochures at airports, railway stations and ferries.

Norwegian tourist offices abroad: Amsterdam, Brussels, Copenhagen, Hamburg, London, New York, Paris, Stockholm.

Business Briefing

Economic Background

Main industries: Iron, pyrite, zinc, molybdenum ore, tungsten, antimony ore, tin, copper, aluminium production, machinery, wood and paper, electro-chemicals, food, shipping, offshore-oil drilling.

Main agricultural products and fisheries: Potatoes, barley, oats, wheat, capelin, cod, herring.

Main imports: Motor vehicles, machinery, consumer goods, food.

Main exports: Forestry products, ships, machinery, fish, crude oil and by-products, aluminium, iron, steel, petroleum and natural gas.

Principal trading partners: UK, Germany, Sweden, Denmark, USA.

GNP: $92 billion; per capita: $21,925.

Inflation rate: 2.3% (1994).

Trade fairs: Main fairs: a biennial oil conference and exhibition in Stavanger (August), a biennial building trade exhibition in Oslo and

an annual boat show in Oslo.

Selected background reading: *Mini-facts about Norway*, published annually by the Royal Ministry of Foreign Affairs, provides a survey of commercial and trade figures. *Facts about Norway* (Schibsted) published annually. Regular economic surveys and industrial reports as well as demographic statistics are issued by the Statistisk Sentralbyrå. *Norinform* provides summaries of Norwegian business news in English, French, German and Spanish.

Norwegian chambers of commerce abroad: Hamburg, London, New York, Paris, Stockholm, Toronto.

On the Spot

Office hours: 8am-3pm Monday-Friday in summer, and 9am-4pm Monday-Friday in winter. A half-hour break is usually taken for lunch.

Public holidays

Jan 1	New Year's Day	**Movable dates**:	Maundy Thursday
May 1	Labour Day		Good Friday
May 17	National Day		Easter Monday
Dec 25	Christmas Day		Ascension Day
Dec 26	Boxing Day		Whit Monday

Banks and currency exchange: Banking hours: 8.15am-3.30pm Monday-Friday in winter, till 3pm in summer (until 5pm Thursday). Currency-exchange offices at main airports, railway stations and major hotels change money after normal banking hours. Oslo Airport: 7am-8pm daily, except Saturdays, when the exchange closes at 5pm. Oslo Central Railway Station: 8am-7.30pm Monday-Saturday, 12pm-6pm on Sundays. In summer, 8am-11pm daily. Norway's leading banking institutions are Den norske Creditbank, Christiania Bank og Kreditkasse, and Bergen Bank.

Credit cards and traveller's cheques: Internationally recognized credit cards and traveller's cheques are accepted by most establishments. **239**

Post and telecommunications: Norway's postal and telecommunications systems are highly reliable.

Usual post office hours are 8 or 8.30am-4 or 5pm Monday-Friday, and 8am-1pm Saturday.

Oslo's main post office at Dronningensgate 15 is open 9am-8pm Monday-Friday, 9am-3pm Saturday. Bergen's main post office at Rådstuplass 10 is open 8am-5pm Monday, Tuesday, Wednesday and Friday; until 7pm Thursday; and 9am-1pm Saturday.

Direct-dialling facilities exist throughout Norway as well as to most other countries. Use 1, 5 or 10-krone coins in public phone booths. Telegrams can be sent from phones by dialling 138.

Telephone calls, telex messages, faxes and telegrams may also be placed from *telegrafkontor* offices, which are conveniently located in city centres. In Oslo the main telecommunications office is found at Kongensgate 21 (open 8.30am-9pm Monday-Friday, 10am to 5pm Saturdays and Sundays); in Bergen, the same services are offered at Telenor, Starvhusgt 4, by the City Park, open weekdays 8am to 4pm, closed weekends.

Some useful numbers:

Ambulance	113	Inquiries (inland and	
Fire	110	other Scandinavian)	180
Police	112	Inquiries (int.)	181
Operator (int.)	115		

For international direct dialling, use prefix 095, then country code, national trunk code and local telephone number. See section 1A of telephone directories.

	In Oslo:	*In Bergen*:
Dental services	22 67 48 46	55 32 11 20
Medical services	22 20 10 90	55 32 11 20

All area codes within Norway have now been incorporated into the telephone numbers.

Embassies and consulates: Embassies are listed in the business section of telephone directories under *Ambassader og legasjoner*; consulates under *Konsulater*.

Medical care and health: Norway's medical services are excellent though expensive (except where reciprocal agreements concerning health services exist, eg with Great Britain and other Scandinavian countries). English and/or German are spoken by doctors and many nursing staff. Most medicine is available only with a physician's prescription. Duty pharmacies *(apotek)* are listed in newspapers and posted in the windows at all other pharmacies. In Oslo, Jernbanetorvets Apotek (Jernbanetorget 4B) and, in Bergen, Apoteket Nordstjernen, Busterminal (Strømsgt. 8) are open 24 hours a day.

Tap water is drinkable – even notably good.

Services: International temporary job agencies in Oslo specialize in providing secretarial services. For translators and interpreters consult the telephone directory under *Oversettere* and *Translatører*.

Photocopying services are available at Oslo's Tourist Information Office and at some underground stations, or look under *Lysog fotokopiering* in the telephone directories. Bergen has a 'Temporary Business Bureau' at 3 Bryggen; tel. 55 31 46 05.

Newspapers: Principal dailies: *Aftenposten*, *Dagbladet*, *Verdens Gang*, *Bergens Tidende*. Those interested in shipping and oil will want to pick up a copy of *Norwegian Shipping News* and *Noroil*, both in English. Leading foreign newspapers, including the *International Herald Tribune*, are on sale. *What's on in Oslo* (English, French, German) and the monthly *Bergen This Week* give entertainment summaries. Both are distributed free at hotels. *Coming Events* (English) gives entertainment summaries.

Transport

Air – international: Oslo airport is Norway's major international airport, though Bergen and Stavanger also handle some foreign flights.

Air – domestic: Around 20 domestic airports mainly served by SAS and Braathens SAFE bring all parts of the country within easy reach of the capital. Inquire about a fare reduction on SAS on certain days and for specific flights. Air-taxi service is available, mostly in northern Norway.

Rail: Trains on the Norwegian State Railways (NSB) run on time. First and second class are offered. Seat reservations should be made, especially on express trains such as the Oslo-Bergen line. There are direct services to Sweden and the continent via Copenhagen.

Inquire at any travel agency or railway station about special weekday tickets, and for details of the Norway Rail Pass. The Nordic Tourist Ticket permits 21 days of unlimited rail travel in Norway, Denmark, Finland and Sweden. For Eurailpass, see p.10.

Waterways: Punctual, comfortable steamers link coastal towns from Bergen to the far north. Not too useful for business travel but an ideal way to enjoy Norway's impressive fjords and islands if you have the time. Frequency depends on the season. Reservations may be needed for cars in the summer.

Local public transport: Depending on the town, the traveller has the choice of bus, tram, elevated train or ferry, or, in Oslo, the underground (subway). Bus and tram fares are paid on board either to the driver or a conductor. The ticket permits one transfer during a one-hour period.

Taxis: Few people hail taxis; call for one or go to a rank (frequent all over town). Taxi drivers are not allowed to pick up passengers when less than 100 metres from taxi ranks. There's a 15% surcharge at night, starting at 8pm.

Car rental: International and local firms operate in all major towns, and are listed in the classified telephone directory under *Bilutleie*. Chauffeur-driven cars are also available.

Driving in Norway: Traffic entering from the right has priority unless otherwise indicated. Roads are generally good though narrow outside urban centres. In winter local roads are not recommended, and some are closed. Motorways (expressways) interspersed with regular highway connect Hamar-Oslo-Moss-Gothenburg (Sweden) and Oslo-Drammen. Speed limits: 30-50kph (19-31mph) in town, 80kph (50mph) on major roads and 90kph (56mph) on motorways (expressways).

Fines for drinking and driving are prohibitive. Police controls in the evening and at night are frequent and, if the slightest suspicion of drink is involved, pitiless. A breath-test is immediately asked for: with more than 50mg/100ml alcohol in the blood (c. 2 glasses of wine or ½l of beer), you face stiff fines, loss of your licence for at least six months, and possible imprisonment for 21 days. Don't count on any indulgence because of being foreign; there won't be any. The same goes for speeding. Use of seat belts is obligatory, also for backseat passengers if fixed. A red-reflector warning triangle must be carried. Dipped (low-beam) headlights must be switched on, even in broad daylight. Fuel (petrol/gas) available is normal (93 octane), lead-free (91 octane), super (98 octane) and diesel.

In case of breakdowns, several associations maintain emergency road services: in Oslo, Norges Automobil-Forbund (NAF), tel. 22 34 14 00; Falken Redningskorps Oslo, tel. 22 95 00 00; Viking Redningstjeneste, tel. 22 30 01 00. In Bergen, NAF, tel. 55 29 24 62; Falken, tel. 55 20 13 10; Viking, tel. 55 29 22 22. Viking also has a national number for all Norway:80 03 29 00.

Some distances from Oslo: Bergen 495km (300 miles), Trondheim 545km (340 miles), Stavanger 585km (365 miles).

Social customs: Norwegians shake hands upon meeting, even if introductions have already been made. If invited home, a small gift of flowers or chocolates for the hostess is appreciated. At more informal meetings a bottle of wine provides a popular gift. The ritual – and essential – 'takk for maten' (thank you for the food), addressed to the hostess at the end of a meal, expresses your appreciation of everything. Smoking during meals is common. In an informal setting it's socially acceptable to roll one's own cigarettes.

Hints for business: Norwegians are keen on punctuality, and should you be unable to keep an appointment, cancel or postpone it by phone. Most office workers take a half-hour break for lunch, and even the boss will bring a sandwich or two from home to eat at his desk. Periods best avoided for business travel are public holidays, the winter holiday (second or third week of February), Holy Week, the midsummer festival (June 23) and July-August summer holiday period. **243**

Foreign chambers of commerce in Norway: American, Belgian, Bulgarian, French, Spanish, German.

Crime and theft: The usual precautions are necessary to guard against petty theft, though crime is not a major problem in Norway.

After Hours

Food and drink: Favourite specialities are open sandwiches *(smør-brød)*, smoked lamb, reindeer, fish, pickled herring, and cured salmon and trout. Lunch is generally a light meal consisting of two or three open sandwiches. The main sustenance of the day is dinner.

The local aquavit is renowned, and packs quite a punch. Beer is high quality. Alcoholic beverages are very expensive, Spirit (liquor) is served at most major hotels and restaurants, but only between 3pm and midnight on weekdays and not at all on Sundays and holidays.

Mealtimes: lunch 11am-1pm, dinner 4-10pm.

Entertainment: For a city of its size, Oslo provides a varied night-life, with nightclubs, discotheques, bars and pubs of all sorts. Outside the capital, possibilities are few. Rich cultural opportunities exist in both Oslo and Bergen, including ballet, theatre, concerts (many outdoors in summer) and opera (in Oslo only). In June-July, English-language plays are also staged in Oslo. The latest foreign films are shown, always in their original language.

Taxes, service charges and tipping: Value-added tax (in Norwegian, *moms*) and service charges are included in hotel and restaurant bills. Tipping recommendations: hotel porters kr5 per bag; waiters, 5-10% (optional); taxi drivers, round the sum off upwards (unless extra service rendered, then 10%); cloakroom attendants, charge posted.

Sports and recreation: Visitors can go hiking, skiing, swimming, sailing, fishing, riding or camping according to the season.

Soccer matches and sailing are popular spectator sports in summer, and in winter ski-jumping, cross-country skiing, speed skating, ice hockey, bandy and curling draw crowds.

TV and radio: Virtually all programming is in Norwegian, but TV films and shows are in the original language.

What to buy: Reindeer-hide rugs and other products, pewterware, hand-painted wooden articles, sweaters, silverware, jewellery, glass and ceramics are favourite purchases.

Shopping hours vary. In Oslo, shops normally open from 9 or 10am to 5 or 7pm Monday to Friday, until 1, 2 or 3pm on Saturdays; closed on Sundays and legal holidays. Centrally situated kiosks selling newspapers, tobacco, fruit, candies, and so on, may stay open until 11pm.

Cities and Sights

OSLO (*See page 240*)

Airport: Fornebu (9km/5.5 miles from city centre), international; duty-free shop. Bus service operates every 20-30 minutes between about 8am and 10pm. Gardermoen (c. 50km/30 miles from city centre), charter flights. Bus meets flights.

Tourist information office: Vestbaneplassen 1; tel. 22 83 00 50. Tourist information offices are identified by an 'i'.

Chamber of commerce: Drammensveien 30; tel. 22 55 74 00, fax 22 55 89 53.

Oslo Card: The Oslo Card, or *Oslo-kortet*, offers visitors the chance to see the city at a fair price. Similar in appearance to a credit card, it allows the holder free entry to museums and sights, free public transport, reductions on car rental, sightseeing tours and hotel rates. Used to the full, it represents a considerable bargain. The pass is valid for one, two or three days and is available at hotels, stores and the Tourist Office.

Sightseeing: Akershus Fortress, Tryvannstårnet (tower, view of Oslo), Holmenkollen ski-jump and Ski Museum, Henie-Onstad Art Centre (on Høvikodden), Vigeland Sculpture Park, Munch Museum, Bygdøy museums (Kon-Tiki, Viking ships, etc.), boat trips in Oslo Fjord.

BERGEN (*See page 240*)

Airport: Flesland (20km/12 miles from city centre), international; duty-free shop. Bus meets flights.

Tourist information office: Brygen 7; tel. 55 32 14 80.

Chamber of commerce: Olav Kyrresgate 11; tel. 55 31 81 16.

Sightseeing: Old Bergen, fish market, funicular railway (view of Bergen), Troldhaugen (Grieg's home).

Excursions: Boat trips in surrounding fjords.

Some Useful Expressions in Norwegian

good morning/afternoon	god morgen/dag
good evening/night	god kveld/natt
good-bye	adjø
yes/no	ja/nei
please/thank you	vennligst/takk
excuse me	unnskyld
you're welcome	ingen årsak
where/when/how	hvor/naår/hvordan
how long/how far	hvor lenge/hvor langt
yesterday/today/tomorrow	i går/i dag/i morgen
day/week/month/year	dag/uke/måned/år
left/right	venstre/høyre
up/down	opp/ned
good/bad	god/dårlig
big/small	stor/liten
cheap/expensive	billig/dyr
hot/cold	varm/kald
old/new	gammel/ny
open/closed	åpen/lukket
early/late	tidlig/sent
Does anyone here speak English/French/German?	Er det noen her som snakker engelsk/fransk/tysk?
What does this mean?	Hva betyr dette?
I don't understand.	Jeg forstår ikke.
Please write it down.	Vennligst skriv det ned.
Do you take credit cards/ traveller's cheques?	Tar De imot kredittkort/ reisesjekker?
Waiter!/Waitress!	Kelner!/Frøken!
Where are the toilets?	Hvor er toalettet?
I'd like…	Jeg vil gjerne ha…
How much is that?	Hvor mye koster det?
Help me please.	Hjelp meg, er De snill.

Poland

Type of government:	Republic, multi-party system, centralized
Member of:	GATT
Population:	38.6 million
Area:	312,683sq km (120,727sq miles)
Capital:	Warsaw (Warszawa, 1.65m)
Other major cities:	Łódź (846,500)
	Cracow (Kraków, 750,600)
	Wroclaw (643,000)
	Poznań (590,000)
	Gdańsk (465,400)
Language:	Polish; English, German and French are normally spoken in business circles and hotels; Russian.
Religion:	Catholic (95%)
Time zone:	GMT+1, EST+6; DST (Apr-Sep)
Currency:	Złoty (abbr. zł) = 100 groszy
	Coins: rarely used
	Notes: 50, 100, 200, 500, 1,000, 5,000, 10,000, 20,000, 50,000, 100,000, 500,000, 1,000,000, 2,000,000zł
Electricity:	220V, 50Hz, AC

Planning your Trip

Visa requirements: Travellers from most countries within the EU, EFTA and NATO countries do not need visas to enter Poland. (See also p.6.)

Vaccination requirements: None. (See also p.7.)

Import allowances (see also p.7):

Cigarettes		Cigars		Tobacco	Spirits		Wine
250	or	50	or	250g	1l	and	1l

Gifts: Up to a value (in Poland) of 500,000zł.

Currency restrictions: No złotys may be imported or exported. Import and export (up to the amount brought in) of foreign currencies is unlimited. A currency declaration form must be completed on arrival and presented again on departure.

Climate: Poland's climate is continental, with warm summers and cold winters. Moderate rainfall is well distributed throughout the year.

Some average temperatures in Warsaw:

Jan	Apr	July	Oct
-1°C (30°F)	6°C (43°F)	19°C (67°F)	9°C (48°F)

Note that the temperature may soar to over 30°C (86°F) in summer and plunge to -30°C (-22°F) in winter.

Clothing: Light- to medium-weight clothing is adequate in summer. In winter, a heavy coat and a warm hat are advisable as well as stout shoes or boots to combat street snow and slush. Rainwear will come in handy at any time of year. On the whole, Poles don't attach much importance to dress, and casual attire is generally worn for business. **249**

Hotels: Unless your Polish host is taking care of hotel accommodation for you, hotel bookings are best made through your home travel agency. Book well ahead, especially in summer.

Polish tourist offices abroad: Amsterdam, Brussels, Chicago, Cologne, New York, Stockholm.

Business Briefing

Economic Background

Main industries: Coal, lignite, sulphur and copper mining, steel production, chemicals and fertilizers, shipbuilding, textiles, motor vehicles.

Main agricultural products: Wheat, rye, oats, barley, potatoes, sugar beet.

Main imports: Oil, gas, iron, ore, grain and fodder, machinery, chemicals.

Main exports: Coal, copper, sulphur and other chemicals, machinery, ships, textiles and shoes, foodstuffs.

Principal trading partners: CIS, UK, Germany, Czech Republic, Slovakia, USA.

GNP: $67 billion; per capita: $1,745.

Inflation rate: 23% (1993)

Trade fairs: The annual Poznań trade fair in mid-June is one of the biggest east-west market-places. But big contracts are seldom concluded at the fair unless they've been negotiated in advance. However, many western businesses consider it essential to be seen at Poznań to maintain a presence on the Polish market.

Selected background reading: The monthly *Biuletyn Statystyczny* contains trade and other economic figures, in Polish with an English **250** summary of the contents. *Poland Statistical Data* is a yearbook published in English and German. *Polish Economic Survey* is published in English, German and French.

Polish chambers of commerce abroad: Berlin, Bonn, Bratislava, Budapest, Leipzig, Moscow, New Delhi, Prague, San Francisco, Sofia, Stockholm.

On the Spot

Office hours: 8am-4pm Monday-Friday; also 8am to 1 or 2pm one Saturday a month.

Public holidays

Jan 1	New Year's Day	Nov 1	All Saints' Day
May 1	Labour Day	Nov 11	National Day
May 3	Day of 'The Third of May Constitution'	Dec 25	Christmas Day
		Dec 26	St Stephen's Day
Aug 15	Day of Mother of God's Assumption	**Movable dates**:	Easter Monday Corpus Christi

Banks and currency exchange: Banks are open 8am-5pm Monday-Friday and from 8am-2pm on Saturdays; also open one Saturday a month.

Currency can also be changed at major hotels at convenient hours, at the Orbis office (8am-4pm Monday-Friday) and at Warsaw airport.

International banking is handled by Bank Handlowy w Warszawie S.A. Other principal banks are Narodowy Bank Polski and Polska Kasa Opieki.

Credit cards and traveller's cheques: Both are accepted at major hotels, airlines, restaurants and some stores, eg Cepelia souvenir shops and Pewex hard-currency shops. American Express, Diner's Club and Master Charge (Eurocard) Access are the best-known cards.

Post and telecommunications: All services are generally reliable, though post may sometimes be delayed.

251

Post office hours are 8am-8pm Monday-Saturday, and until 9pm for telephone service. The main post office (ul Swiętokrzyska 31-33) and the branch in the central railway station are open 24 hours a day.

Long-distance telephone, telegraph and telex services are available at major hotels and large post offices. Telex and fax facilities are offered by many post offices and all hotels. Be prepared for long delays in placing calls outside Europe. The Polish telephone network is to a large extent automated.

Some useful telephone numbers:

Ambulance	999	International calls	901
Fire	998	Operator (general)	900
Directory Inquiries (int)	913	Police	997

Principal area codes: Cracow 812, Gdańsk 858, Poznań 861, Warsaw 822, Wrocław 871.

Embassies and consulates: Hotels keep listings of diplomatic representations.

Medical care and health: The standard of medical treatment is good in large towns but otherwise rather poor. Costs are moderate by western standards. Special provision is made for foreigners to receive paid medical aid at Polish health-service units. First-aid is free, as is all medical service for those visiting Poland at the invitation of Polish institutions. Visitors from some countries receive free medical treatment under inter-governmental agreements. Anyone suffering from a specific complaint requiring special drugs should bring plentiful supplies of them as often only basic medicine is available. Some doctors speak a little German or English. Every pharmacy displays addresses of duty pharmacies open after hours. Tap water is generally safe to drink in major cities and resorts, though often rather tasteless.

Services: Orbis, the Polish organization you are dealing with, or the commercial department of your embassy will be able to provide assistance. Photocopying machines are not common in Poland. Some photographers do photocopying. Look for the sign *Fotokopie* in the street. If the material is not of a confidential nature, try asking your business host.

Newspapers: The principal dailies are *Gazeta Wyborcza*, *Rzeczy-pospolita* and *Zyrcie Warszawy*. One English-language newspaper published in Poland is *The Warsaw Voice* (weekly). The daily *Nowa Europa* publishes one page of news in English.

Transport

Air – international: Warsaw is Poland's gateway airport, with good access by direct flights or connections from most parts of the world.

Air – domestic: LOT, Poland's national airline, operates frequent flights to all major cities.

Rail: Trains are often the only convenient means of business travel. Express services (not always punctual) operate to important centres. For comfort, travel first-class. Rates are moderate. Full dining service is available on some trains while others serve only snacks such as sausages or *bigos* (cabbage and pork).

Local public transport: All major cities have bus and tram networks. Tickets must be bought in advance from *ruch* stands found at most shops and elsewhere throughout the town. Punch your ticket at a machine inside the vehicle.

Taxis: Moderately priced and recommended in preference to public-service vehicles. Tip about 10%.

Car rental: To be sure of having a vehicle at your disposal, it is advisable to reserve a car when making your other travel arrangements beforehand. Chauffeur-driven cars are usually available.

Driving in Poland: An international driving licence is required. Always carry this and your passport with you as police sometimes carry out spot checks. Fuel (petrol/gas) available is normal (78 octane), super (94 octane) and diesel. Some petrol stations offer 98 octane and lead-free petrol.

Speed limits: in town, 60kph (37mph) except where otherwise indicated; outside town, 90kph (56mph) on the open road, 110kph (68mph) on the motorway (expressway). Seat belts are obligatory, and a red-reflector warning triangle must be carried. Blood alcohol **253** limit is a strictly enforced zero, and police are entitled to take you for an immediate blood test. They also levy on-the-spot fines for speeding and similar infringements.

On a roundabout (traffic circle), priority is from the right. Surfaces are adequate on arterial routes; secondary roads tend to be rather narrow. Night driving can be hazardous due to badly lit farm carts.

Call the Polski Zwiazek Motorowy (PZM) in case of breakdown; in Warsaw the number is 954, elsewhere often 981. A full list of numbers is obtainable from any PZM office.

Some distances: Warsaw-Cracow 290km (180 miles), Poznan 300km (185 miles), Gdansk 340km (210 miles).

Social customs: Consumption of hard liquor is widespread in Poland, and you may well be plied with cognac at business and other meetings. Many Poles look askance at teetotallers, but they respect the excuse that you have to drive afterwards or that your doctor forbids it. Poles also like to down a few vodkas with hors-d'oeuvre before lunch or dinner. A common toast is *na drowie* ('to your health'), although you won't normally be saying it much before 1pm – alcohol is not served or sold before this time in Poland. It's customary to observe name days rather than birthdays.

Hints for business: International trade is no longer in the hands of the state, and Poland is much more open to foreign business. Doing business is more straightforward and there are more convenient regulations which allow managers of state organizations to act independently. As a general rule, Poland is becoming more like other European countries. The Poles have a reputation for sticking to a contract – and paying on time. When meeting business associates, expect to work until mid-afternoon without a break for a meal.

Foreign chambers of commerce in Poland: Apply to commercial departments of embassies or consulates.

Crime and theft: Normal precautions are in order. Beware of pickpockets. Illegal currency transactions could be prejudicial to any future business dealings with Poland.

After Hours

Food and drink: Restaurants serve western European and typical Polish dishes. Some specialities are *kotlet schabowy* (pork chop), *golonka* (pork knuckle with horseradish sauce), *bigos* (sauerkraut with smoked pork).

The national drinks are vodka and beer. Wines are mostly Bulgarian and Hungarian such as Debroei (white) and Egri Bikaver (red), though Spanish imports are sometimes found. Foreign beer, wine and liquor are available in major hotels.

Mealtimes: lunch 3-5pm, dinner 8-10pm; traditionally Poles eat one big meal at about 4pm.

Entertainment: Theatres abound in every town. Opera houses exist in Warsaw, Poznań, Katowice, Gdańsk and Cracow. Concerts and ballets are also part of the cultural life. Quite a number of cinemas show foreign films in their original language. Folk festivals take place in various towns during the year. There are several nightclubs as well as jazz clubs or cafés and restaurants with live jazz.

Taxes, service charges and tipping: Hotel and restaurant charges are usually all-inclusive. Though tipping is officially discouraged, gratuities, given discreetly, are welcomed. Some recommendations: taxi drivers 10%; hairdressers and barbers 10%; porters 1,000-5,000zł per piece; cloakroom attendants 2,000zł.

Sports and recreation: Swimming, tennis, sailing and, in season, skiing are easily available, as is hunting (which is expensive unless it can be arranged by your host).

Favourite spectator sports are soccer in spring and autumn; cycling and athletics in summer; basketball, skiing and boxing mainly in winter; and horse-racing most of the year except winter.

TV and radio: Programming is in Polish only, but several times a day you can watch CNN's Headline News in English. Satellite TV is available in most hotels.

What to buy: Amber, jewellery, cut glass, embroidery, leather, rugs, carved wooden ornaments, silver- and metal-ware are good buys. Cepelia shops specialize in handicraft and folkloric articles; credit cards, hard currency and złotys are accepted. A chain of Desa shops sells works of art. (Antiques are usually not for export.) You can take out gifts to a value of $200 beyond this amount.

Shopping hours: 9, 10 or 11am to 7 or 8pm, Monday-Saturday. Some shops and tobacco kiosks also trade on Sundays.

Cities and Sights

WARSAW (Telephone area code 822)

Airport: Okecie Airport (10km/6 miles from city centre), international; duty-free shop. Airport and city buses.

Tourist information office: Orbis, ul Bracka 16, 00-028 Warsaw; tel. 26 02 71. Tourist information centre: Plac Zamkowy 1/13; tel. 635 18 81.

Chamber of commerce: Trębacka 4, Warsaw; tel. 26 02 21.

Sightseeing: Old town (royal castle, St John's cathedral), Krakowskie Przedmiescie (St Anne's and Holy Cross churches), Lazienki Palace and park, Wilanow Palace, Powazki and Jewish cemeteries, Palace of culture.

Museums: National Museum, Historical Museum, Ethnological Museum.

Excursions: Zelazowa Wola (Chopin's birthplace), Warka (Casimir Pulaski's birthplace), Zegrze Reservoir (recreation area), Kampinos Forest (nature reserve), Plock.

Some Useful Expressions in Polish

good morning/afternoon	**dzień dobry**
good evening/night	**dobry wieczór/dobranoc**
good-bye	**do widzenia**
yes/no	**tak/nie**
please/thank you	**proszę/dziękuję**
excuse me	**przepraszam**
you're welcome	**witam**
where/when/how	**gdzie/kiedy/jak**
how long/how far	**jak długo/jak daleko**
yesterday/today/tomorrow	**wczoraj/dzisiaj/jutro**
day/week/month	**dzień/tydzień/miesiąc**
left/right	**lewo/prawo**
up/down	**góra/dół**
good/bad	**dobry/zły**
big/small	**duzý/mały**
cheap/expensive	**tani/drogi**
hot/cold	**gorące/zimne**
old/new	**stary/nowy**
open/closed	**otwarty/zamknięty**
early/late	**wczesny/późny**
Does anyone here speak English/French/German?	**Czy ktos mówi po angielsku/ francusku/niemiecku?**
What does this mean?	**Co to znaczy?**
I don't understand.	**Nie rozumiem.**
Please write it down.	**Proszę to napisać.**
Do you take credit cards/ traveller's cheques?	**Czy przyjmujecie karty kredytowe/czeki podróźne?**
Waiter!/Waitress!	**Kelner!/Kelnerka!**
Where are the toilets?	**Gdzie są toalety?**
I'd like…	**Chciałbym…**
How much is that?	**Ile płacę?**
Help me please.	**Proszę mi pomóc.**

257

Portugal

Type of government:	Republic, multi-party centralized
Member of:	EU, GATT, IBRD, IFC, IMF, OECD
Population:	9.682 million
Area:	92,082sq km (35,550sq miles)
Capital:	Lisbon (*Lisboa*, 677,800)
Other major cities:	Oporto (*Porto*, 302,472/GUA 2m)
	Coimbra (55,000)
	Setúbal (104,040)
Language:	Portuguese; French or English widely used in business circles; Spanish is understood by virtually all Portuguese.
Religion:	Catholic (98%)
Time zone:	GMT, EST+5; DST (Apr-Sep)
Currency:	Escudo (abbr. esc, symbolized $) = 100 centavos. The $ sign normally replaces the decimal point in prices (eg 100 $00 means 100 escudos).
	Coins: 1, 2, 5, 10, 20, 50, 100, 200 esc
	Notes: 500, 1,000, 2,000, 5,000, 10,000 esc
Electricity:	220 or 110V, 50Hz, AC

Planning your Trip

Visa requirements: For nationals of South Africa and Turkey. (See also p.6.)

Vaccination requirements: None. (See also p.7.)

Import allowances (see also p.7):

(see also p.7)

	Cigarettes		Cigars		Tobacco	Spirits		Wine
1)	200	or	50	or	250g	1l	and	2l
2)	300	or	75	or	400g	1.5l	and	3l
3)	(800)	or	(200)	or	(1kg)	(10l)	and	(90l)

1) Passengers from countries outside Europe.
2) Duty-free goods bought in EU countries by European residents.
3) Non-duty-free goods bought within the EU.

Perfume: 1) 50g; 2) 75g; *Toilet water*: 1) 0.25l; 2) 0.375l;
Gifts: 1), 2) 7,500 esc max. value

There are no official restrictions on goods bought non-duty-free within the EU, provided they are for personal use only. The above figures are guidelines to the quantities customs officials will generally find acceptable, so if you are carrying larger quantities you should be prepared to provide proof that the goods are for your personal use.

Currency restrictions: Visitors can bring any amount of local or foreign currency into Portugal, but sums exceeding the equivalent of 1,000,000 escudos in foreign currency must be declared on arrival. No more than 100,000 escudos in local money may be exported per person per trip. Non-residents may take out foreign currencies up to the amount that they brought in and declared. (See also p.7.)

(See also p.7.)

Climate: Most of Portugal enjoys a temperate Atlantic climate influenced by the Mediterranean. Winter is when most rain falls. In the southern Algarve the regime is semi-tropical. Some average temperatures in Lisbon:

Jan	Apr	July	Oct
11°C (52°F)	16°C (61°F)	23°C (73°F)	19°C (66°F)

Clothing: Light clothes are sufficient in summer. In winter something warmer will be necessary, though only perhaps once or twice does the **259**

temperature dip below freezing point in the capital. As for formality, Lisbon has changed drastically over the last few years. During the hot summer months even the most conservative businessman may opt for an open-necked shirt, though you won't be out of place in more formal dress, such as a business suit and tie.

Hotels: Except for the family-run *hotéis rurais*, hotels in Potugal are graded from 2-star to 5-star deluxe. Between July and September advance bookings are essential. *Portugal: Hotels*, obtainable from Portuguese National Tourist Office branches, contains a comprehensive listing of the country's hotels.

Portuguese tourist offices abroad: Amsterdam, Barcelona, Brussels, Caracas, Chicago, Copenhagen, Frankfurt, Geneva, London, Los Angeles, Madrid, Milan, Montreal, New York, Paris, Rio de Janeiro, Stockholm, Toronto, Vienna.

Business Briefing

Economic Background

Main industries: Textiles, clothing, footwear, machine parts, cement, food processing, shipbuilding, tourism.

Main agricultural products: Wheat, maize, potatoes, grapes, cork.

Main imports: Foodstuffs, oil and petroleum products, cotton, construction materials, machinery, transport equipment.

Main exports: Textiles, wine, clothing, footwear, cork, machine parts, canned food.

Principal trading partners: Germany, USA, UK, France, Italy, Netherlands.

GNP: $44 billion; per capita: $4,261.

Inflation rate: 5.4% (1994).

Trade fairs: Major annual trade fairs are: AGRO agricultural fair in Braga (April), SIMAC building trade fair in Lisbon (May), FIL International Lisbon Fair (May), FILEME office equipment exhibition every two years (January) and Intercasa (home fittings, furniture and lighting) in Lisbon (October).

Selected background reading: The annual report and monthly statistical bulletins of the Bank of Portugal present reliable commercial and trade figures for the republic. The Department of Social Communication produces the *Foreign Investment Code*.

Portuguese chambers of commerce abroad: Algiers, Baghdad, Berlin, Brussels, Bucharest, Caracas, Casablanca, Copenhagen, Düsseldorf, Geneva, The Hague, Hamburg, Helsinki, Johannesburg, Karachi, London, Los Angeles, Luanda, Madrid, Maputo, Milan, Montreal, Moscow, New York, Oslo, Paris, Prague, São Paulo, Stockholm, Tokyo, Toronto, Vienna, Warsaw.

On the Spot

Office hours: Generally 9.30am-12.30pm and 3-7pm. Some government offices close at 5.30pm.

Public holidays

Jan 1	New Year's Day	Dec 1	Independence Day
April 25	Liberty Day	Dec 8	Immaculate
May 1	Labour Day		Conception
June 10	National Day	Dec 25	Christmas Day
Oct 5	Republic Day	**Movable dates**:	Carnival
Nov 1	All Saints' Day		Good Friday
			Corpus Christi

Banks and currency exchange: Banking hours: 8.30-3pm Monday-Friday. In large towns banks stay open on Saturday from 8.30am-1pm during the tourist season.

Outside of banking hours currency can be exchanged at Lisbon airport (24-hours), the Santa Apolónia railway station (8.30am-1pm and 2-5pm) and at two bank exchange offices in Praça dos Restauradores .

Certain foreign currencies are difficult to convert in Portugal. Check before you leave.

Principal banks are: Banco Pinto and Sotto Mayor, Banco de Portugal, Banco Nacional Ultramarino, Banco Borges & Irmão, Banco Português do Atlântico, Banco Totta & Açores, and Banco Fonsecas & Burnay. The business traveller should ensure that all documentation relating to transfers is totally in order.

Credit cards and traveller's cheques: Internationally recognized credit cards and most traveller's cheques are accepted in major establishments.

Post and telecommunications: Postal and telecommunications services are generally reliable.

Main post offices, identified by the letters CTT (*Correios, Telegrafos e Telefonos*), are open from 8.30 or 9am to 6 or 6.30pm. In Lisbon, the post office at Praça dos Restauradores 58 is open from 8.30am to 10pm Monday-Friday (until 6pm weekends). Stamps can be bought at tobacconists' as well as at post offices. Mailboxes follow the English pillar box design and are painted bright red, too.

Automatic coin phones can be found in bars and restaurants, as well as on street corners. You can dial most of the world direct or make international calls through the clerk at any post office or at your hotel. Dial 099 for the international operator for Europe, 098 for the rest of the world. For international direct dialling, use 00 followed by the country code then the area code (without the initial '0', where there is one) and subscriber's number.

Public telex booths in Lisbon are located in the Praça dos Restauradores post office, and in Oporto in that on Praça do Município.

Some useful numbers:

Emergency (police, fire, ambulance)	115
Operator (for long distance calls, inland)	090
Operator (for other countries)	098
Operator (Europe)	099
Inquiries	118
Telegrams	182, 183

Embassies and consulates: Listings of embassies and consulates are found in the telephone directories under *Embaixadas* and *Consulados*, respectively.

Medical care and health: The main cities offer a reasonable standard of medical care, but facilities in some rural areas may be inadequate. Fees are moderate by most western standards. In Lisbon, The British Hospital at Rua Saraiva de Carvalho 49, and the French Hospital at Rua Luz Soriano 182, are preferred by foreigners. Embassies can provide lists of doctors who speak their respective languages.

Farmácias (pharmacies) are open during normal business hours. At other times, one shop in each neighbourhood is always on duty round the clock. Addresses are listed in the newspapers and on the door of every other pharmacy.

Tap water is safe to drink in Lisbon. Elsewhere, those with delicate stomachs may prefer to buy bottled mineral water, of which Portugal has an excellent range.

Services: For secretarial assistance, see the yellow pages under *Dactilografia-serviços* or *Pessoal temporário*.

The National Union of Guides and Interpreters (Rua do Telhal 4, Lisbon; tel. 346 71 70, 9am-1pm and 2.30-6pm) can also provide linguistic help. Photocopying facilities, widely available, are listed in the yellow pages under *Fotocopias*.

Newspapers: Principal dailies in Lisbon are *Diário de Noticias* and *A Capital*, and in Oporto *Jornal de Noticias*. European newspapers, including the Paris-edited *International Herald Tribune*, are on sale at larger news-stands. The *Anglo-Portuguese News*, featuring information of interest to tourists, is published fortnightly. In the Algarve you will find the English-language monthly *Algarve Magazine*.

Transport

Air – international: Lisbon is far and away Portugal's major gateway, with direct and same-day connection flights from most points throughout the world. There are also some direct services into Oporto. Faro in the Algarve is served by a few weekly flights (direct **263**

or with a connection in Lisbon) from some major European – as well as North, and Central-American – cities, as are Funchal (Madeira) and Santa Maria (Azores).

Air – domestic: Daily services link Lisbon with Faro, Funchal, Oporto and Santa Maria; a few flights a week also operate to Chaves and Braganca. Advance booking is advised.

Rail: Given the relatively short distances between towns, trains are a practical means of business travel. In the major cities, first- and second-class tickets are sold at separate windows. Trains are comfortable but not always punctual. Only some intercity routes have dining-cars; others may have snack-bars. Lisbon has four principal railway stations scattered around the city. International services and trains for northern Portugal originate at Santa Apolónia station. Commuter trains for the western suburbs and Estoril and Cascais leave from Cais do Sodré. Trains for Sintra and the west depart from Rossio station. And the fourth busy station, called Sul e Sueste (South and Southeast) has ferryboats which cross the Tagus to meet the trains that go on as far as the Algarve. Several kinds of trains link Lisbon and Oporto: the *Directo* or *Regional* (slower and less reliable) and the *Alfa* and *Intercidades* (speedy and comfortable). For Eurailpass, see p.10.

Long-distance buses: Though rail travel is preferred by business travellers, comfortable, punctual coaches serving most major centres with three or four departures daily are useful alternatives. Since they leave from a number of different termini in Lisbon, visitors to the capital are advised to ask at their hotel for further information.

Waterways: Ferry services cross the Tagus river to Barreiro and Seixal (to connect with south-bound trains) and also to Cacilhas-Almada, Trafaria, Porto Brandão, Alcochete and Montijo. At Vila Real de Santo António in the south, frequent ferry services link up with the Spanish border town of Ayamonte. Sea travel to the Azores and Madeira is not generally convenient for business travellers.

Local public transport: Buses, trams or trolley-buses operate in the major cities, though they are not really suitable for business purposes.

Lisbon's *Metropolitano* underground (subway), on the other hand, is modern and fast, though it serves only about 25 stations, mainly in residential areas. On buses, the fare is normally paid to a conductor on board, and on the *metro* at the ticket window.

Taxis: Lisbon taxis are black with a green or beige roof and a sign reading *taxi*. In rural areas, similar vehicles marked 'A' (for *aluguer*, meaning for rent) perform the taxi function but without meters. Taxi ranks are scattered around the main cities. The fare is shown on the meter. Check to see it is running. There is a 20% extra charge at night, and drivers add 50% to the meter charge if you have more than 30kg (66lb) of luggage.

Car rental: International and local firms operate in major towns and tourist areas, some with airport desks. The minimum age for renting is generally 25. Credit cards are the preferred means of payment. Chauffeur-driven vehicles are often available.

Driving in Portugal: Seat belts must always be worn, and you must carry a red-reflector warning triangle. Blood alcohol limit is 50mg/100ml. Fuel (petrol/gas) available is normal (85 octane) super (96 octane) and diesel.

Speed limits are 50kph (31mph) in built-up areas, 120kph (75mph) on motorways (expressways) and 90kph (56mph) on other roads unless otherwise indicated. Parking duration is unlimited except where specified to the contrary. Road conditions vary from good motorways to poor rural lanes. A toll is charged on the Lisbon-Oporto motorway, currently under construction.

Round-the-clock breakdown service is provided by the Automóvel Clube de Portugal; tel. 942 50 95, or call 77 54 75.

Some distances from Lisbon: Setúbal 40km (25 miles), Coimbra 215km (135 miles), Oporto 330km (205 miles).

Social customs: Although manners have become rather more casual in recent years, the older generation retain a considerable amount of formality, and everyone shakes hands at every possible occasion. Foreigners may find the Portuguese custom of greeting somewhat disconcerting at first: the *abraço* (embrace) for men, an enthusiastic hugging and mutual slapping of backs, and, for women, a kiss on both cheeks. However, a simple handshake – for both men and women – is also acceptable, and it would be wiser for the foreign business visitor to stick to this. Offers of hospitality such as an invitation to a meal or drink – especially in the rural north – are virtually unrefusable.

Hints for business: It's essential to plan one's business day to avoid the hours of noon-3pm when almost everything closes down. July-August is the holiday period, when there is also a great influx of foreign tourists.

Foreign chambers of commerce in Portugal: American, Argentinian, Austrian, Belgian, Brazilian, British, French, German, Italian, Spanish.

Crime and theft: It's always wise to keep your valuables in the hotel safe. Pickpocketing and bag-snatching is prevalent in Lisbon. The government has mounted a campaign to crack down on this problem, which is particularly acute in the underground and main city squares.

After Hours

Food and drink: The only problem in Portugal is the size of the portions, but with a little practice you'll soon be coping. Lovers of seafood are in luck here. Specialities include *bacalhau* (dried codfish), *bacalhau à Gomes de Sá* (flaky, meaty chunks of cod baked with parsley, potatoes, onion and olives), *açorda de marisco* (spicy, garlic-flavoured bread-soup with seafood and raw egg), *lampreia à Minho* (lamprey on a bed of rice with a red-wine sauce), grilled tuna (*atum*) and *espadarte* (swordfish). Favourite meat dishes are *bife na frigideira* (beefsteak in a wine sauce), *cabrito assado* (baked kid served with potato and rice), *espetada mista* (chunks of beef, lamb and pork on a spit) and *feijoada* (stew of pig's feet and sausage, white beans and cabbage). The Portuguese are also fond of desserts.

The ordinary house wine in any restaurant is potable, and sometimes very good, with a wide choice of red and white. *Vinho verde* ('green wine') from the northwest is Portugal's most distinctive wine. It's actually a young white wine, semi-sparkling and delightful. Wine-producing regions include Bucelas (for a light, fresh white wine), Colares (for a light red) and Setúbal (for a mellow, sweet white wine, sometimes served as an aperitif). The two most celebrated of the country's wines, Port and Madeira, may be sipped as aperitifs. Portuguese beers, light or dark, are good. Imported spirits are easily available. *Aguardente* is the powerful local brandy.

Mealtimes: lunch noon-3pm, dinner 7.30-10pm.

Entertainment: Nightclubs, discotheques and *fado* houses (where the traditional fatalistic songs peculiar to Portugal are sung) are part of Portuguese nightlife. The São Carlos Opera House offers a full season every year, and there are several major orchestras in both Lisbon and Oporto. The National Theatre has a versatile repertory (in Portuguese). Most foreign films are shown in their original language. Casinos operate at Estoril, Espinho, Álvor, Vilamoura and Figueira da Foz.

Taxes, service charges and tipping: Hotel and restaurant bills are generally all-inclusive, though waiters are sometimes given an additional 10% if service has been very good. Other tipping recommendations: hotel porters 50-100 esc, taxi-drivers 10%, cloakroom attendants 25 esc, hairdressers and barbers 10%.

Sports and recreation: Water sports, fishing, golf, tennis and riding (near Lisbon) are available to the visitor.

Favourite spectator sports are soccer, bullfights (where the bull, Portuguese-style, is not killed), horse-racing and hockey.

TV and radio: Two government-operated channels and two private television services are broadcast; foreign feature movies are usually shown in the original version with subtitles. Higher-grade hotels have satellite TV.

The government operates four radio channels (there are numerous national and regional private radio channels). At certain times of the day you can also pick up Voice of America, the BBC World Service and Radio Canada International. Tourist information is put out in English on several radio stations.

What to buy: Favourites include capes, copperware, embroidery, filigree work, hand-knitted garments, Madeira and Port wine, pottery, shawls, hand-painted tiles and wickerwork.

Shopping hours: generally 9 or 9.30am to 1pm and 3-7pm Monday-Friday, with earlier closing on Saturday at 1 pm. New shopping complexes are often open from 10am until 10pm or even later, often on Sundays as well.

Cities and Sights

LISBON *(Telephone area code 01)*

Airport: Portela (8km/5 miles from city centre), international; duty-free shop. Frequent bus service to Santa Apolónia and Rossio railway stations.

Tourist information office: Palácio Foz, Praca dos Restauradores, 1200 Lisboa; tel. 346 36 43. Tel. 70 63 41 for information in English.

Chamber of commerce: Rua das Portas de Santo Antão 89; tel. 342 32 77, fax 342 43 04.

Sightseeing: Castelo de São Jorge, cathedral, Alfama, Bélem, statue of Christ the King (view).

Museums: Gulbenkian Museum, National Museum of Ancient Art.

Excursions: Estoril and Cascais (Costa do Estoril), Queluz palace and gardens, Sintra.

OPORTO *(Telephone area code 02)*

Airport: Pedras Rubras (18km/12 miles from city centre), international. Public transport available.

Tourist information office: Praça do Municipio; tel. 327 40.

Chamber of commerce: Palácio da Bolsa; tel. 244 97, fax 38 47 60.

Sightseeing: Igreja Santa Clara, Church of the Carmelites.

Excursions: Nossa Senhora de Serra do Pilar (Vila Nova de Gaia), Leça do Balio, Espinho, Leça da Palmeira, Miramar, Granja.

Some useful expressions in Portuguese

good morning/afternoon	**bom dia/boa tarde**
good evening/night	**boa noite**
good-bye	**adeus**
yes/no	**sim/não**
please/thank you	**faz favor/obrigado**
excuse me	**perdão**
you're welcome	**de nada**
where/when/how	**onde/quando/como**
how long/how far	**quanto tempo/a que distância**
yesterday/today/tomorrow	**ontem/hoje/amanhã**
day/week/month/year	**dia/semana/mês/ano**
left/right	**esquerdo/direito**
up/down	**em cima/em baixo**
good/bad	**bom/mau**
big/small	**grande/pequeno**
cheap/expensive	**barato/caro**
hot/cold	**quente/frio**
old/new	**velho/novo**
open/closed	**aberto/fechado**
early/late	**cedo/tarde**
easy/difficult	**fácil/difícil**
Does anyone here speak English/French/German?	**Alguém fala inglês/francês/alemão?**
What does this mean?	**Que quer dizer isto?**
I don't understand.	**Não compreendo.**
Do you take credit cards/ traveller's cheques?	**Aceita cartas de crédito/ cheques de viagem?**
Where are the toilets?	**Onde estão os toiletes?**
I'd like…	**Queria…**
How much is that?	**Quanto custa isto?**
What time is it?	**Que horas são?**
Help me please.	**Ajude-me, por favor.**

Romania

Type of government:	Democratic republic, still largely centralized after four decades of communism
Member of:	GATT, IBRD, IMF
Population:	22.7 million
Area:	237,500sq km (91,700sq miles)
Capital:	Bucharest (*Bucureşti*, 2.3m)
Other major cities:	Braşov (323,835)
	Constanţa (350,476)
	Timişoara (334,278)
	Cluj-Napoca (328,008)
	Iaşi (342,994)
	Galaţi (325,788)
	Craiova (255,000)
Language:	Romanian; English, French and German are the most widely used languages in business circles.
Religion:	Romanian Orthodox (86.8%), Roman Catholic (5%), Protestant and other minorities
Time zone:	GMT+2, EST+7; DST (Apr-Sep)
Currency:	Leu (plural: lei) = 100 bani
	Notes: 50, 100, 500, 1,000, 5,000 lei
Electricity:	220V, 50Hz, AC

Planning your Trip

Visa requirements: For all visitors except nationals of Turkey staying less than three months. (See also p.6.)

Vaccination requirements: None. (See also p.7.)

Import allowances (see also p.7):

Cigarettes	Cigars	Tobacco	Spirits	Wine
200	or 200g of other tobacco products		1l	and 4l

Perfume: A reasonable quantity for personal use
Gifts: 2,000 lei max. value

Currency restrictions: No local currency may be taken into or out of the country. Foreign banknotes and other means of payment may be imported and exported. Accommodation in most hotels must be paid for in lei, although some accept credit cards. (See also p.7.)

Climate: Romania has a generally temperate continental climate, though the Black Sea coast is milder. In winter, the average temperature falls below -3°C (26°F); in summer it rises to 22-24°C (72-76°F).
   Some average temperatures in Bucharest:

Jan	Apr	July	Oct
-3°C (26°F)	11°C (52°F)	23°C (74°F)	12°C (54°F)

Summers have moderate rainfall. In the Transylvanian Alps winters are often severe, with heavy snow.

Clothing: Light clothing is adequate in summer, with a raincoat for surprise showers. Something warmer is called for in spring and autumn, and the mid-winter cold should not be underestimated. In business circles, attire is to a certain extent variable with age: while older people stick largely to dark-blue suits, the younger generation readily wears colour-coordinated clothes.

Hotels: Accommodation should be booked well in advance, especially in summer, at Black Sea resorts and for trade fairs in Bucharest.

Hotel booking services are available at airports and main railway stations. They are also available at ONT (National Tourist Agency) offices abroad. Hotel rooms paid in advance from abroad can be cheaper than locally reserved rooms.

Romanian tourist offices abroad: Amsterdam, Berlin, Brussels, Copenhagen, Düsseldorf, Frankfurt, London, Madrid, New York, Paris, Prague, Rome, Stockholm, Tel Aviv, Vienna, Zurich.

Business Briefing

Economic Background

Main industries: Power, mining, forestry, construction materials, metal manufacturing, chemicals, machine-building, food processing, textiles, petroleum, natural gas.

Main agricultural products: Wheat, sweetcorn, seed oil, potatoes.

Main imports: Machinery, equipment, rolled steel, iron ore, coke and coking coal, cotton.

Main exports: Foodstuffs, lumber, fuel, manufactured goods.

Principal trading partners: Germany, Russia/CIS, Czech Republic, Slovakia, Bulgaria, China.

GNP: $22.8 billion; per capita: $990.

Inflation rate: 12.1% (1994).

Trade fairs: Bucharest has a large and modern exhibition centre. TIB – International Trade Fair for customer goods and chemicals – is the main annual fair (October).

Selected background reading: A regular survey of the Romanian economy, including trade figures, is offered by the *Statistical Yearbook of Romania*, issued in Romanian with English, French and German translations of the headings published in separate brochures. Other
272 works include *Romanian Foreign Trade* (a quarterly published in

English, French, German, Spanish and Russian), *Your Commercial Partners in Romania* (a booklet issued yearly in English), and *Economic and Commercial Guide to Romania* (a booklet published in English), available from Romanian diplomatic representations.

Romanian chambers of commerce abroad: Apply to commercial departments of embassies or consulates.

On the Spot

Office hours: 8am-4pm Monday-Friday.

Public holidays

Jan 1, 2	New Year	Dec 25	Christmas
May 1, 2	Labour Days	Dec 26	Boxing Day
Dec 1	National Day	**Moveable dates**:	Easter

Banks and currency exchange: Banking hours are 8.30am-1pm Monday-Friday.

Outside of banking hours, money can be changed at currency-exchange offices at airports, railway stations, large hotels and all border crossing points. The central bank, the National Bank of Romania supervises foreign exchange transactions.

Credit cards and traveller's cheques: Major international credit cards and traveller's cheques are accepted at large hotels, restaurants and shops of the Ministry of Tourism, but not otherwise.

Post and telecommunications: Telecommunications services are reliable for both domestic and international use, but international telephone lines are often hard to get.

A 24-hour telephone service operates at Bucharest central post office (37 Calea Victoriei), the North Railway Station and airports. A late-night telex facility (until 11pm) is available at the telex office located at 2 Covaci St, Bucharest. Night telegram service (8pm-7am) is provided at an office located at 10 Matei Millo St, Bucharest. Services are also available at some major hotels.

Some useful numbers:

Emergency	961	Taxi	953
Fire	981	Telegrams	957
International call	971	Time	244800
Pharmacies	965	Weather/cultural	
Police	955	events	951
Romanian automobile club (Bucharest)			927

Principal area codes: Braşov 068, Bucharest 01, Cluj-Napoca 064, Constanţa 041, Craiova 051, Iasi 032, Ploieşti 044, Timişoara 056.

Embassies and consulates: Embassies and consulates are listed under part VI of the telephone directory ('Telephone numbers of public organizations').

Medical care and health: The public health system has excellent doctors but few supplies. Fees are moderate. Many doctors speak at least one foreign language. A clinic often visited by foreigners in Bucharest is the Geriatrics Clinics – which, despite its name, provides all-round care. Pharmaceutical supplies might not be readily available, and you are advised to bring with you anything you need. For after-hours pharmacies, dial 965 in Bucharest or telephone information in the provinces. Tap water is safe to drink in most centres.

Services: Secretarial help, translators, interpreters and photocopying services can be obtained through the Terra foreign trade organization (16 Carol I Blvd; tel. 613 28 50 or 613 84 93, fax 613 84 93) and through the Argus and Publicom agencies of the chamber of commerce (in Bucharest: 22 Balcescu Blvd; tel. 15-07).

Newspapers: Principal dailies are *Adevarul, Evenimentul Zilei* and *România Libera*. Foreign newspapers (mainly British, French, German and Russian) and magazines are available in large hotels. Some foreign-language periodicals are published locally.

Transport
Air – international: Bucharest has the nation's main international airport; Arad and Constanta maintain some foreign air services.

Air – domestic: A dozen domestic airports, served by frequent Tarom flights, link Romania's main centres.

Rail: A dense railway network offers frequent *rapid* (express), *accelerat* (fast) and *personal* (local) services, all with first- and second-class compartments. Some trains are modern, heated and clean. Dining- and sleeping-cars are available on some routes.

Long-distance buses: Though not very comfortable, punctual buses provide service to most parts of the country.

Local public transport: All larger towns have bus, trolley bus or tram networks which tend to be crowded and not always punctual. Tickets are purchased at tobacconists', at stands near bus stops or from a conductor on board.

Taxis: Cabs are available in major towns (tel. 953).

Car rental: Cars can be rented from the Carpati National Tourist Office at moderate rates.

Driving in Romania: A red-reflector warning triangle is required for use in case of breakdown. Seat belts are not compulsory. The alcohol limit is a strictly enforced zero. Fuel (petrol/gas) is available in super (95-97 octane) and diesel.

Road conditions are fair on main roads but tend to be poor on secondary ones. Speed limit in towns is 60kph (37mph), and outside towns 80-100kph (50-62mph) depending on the type of car.

For emergency road assistance, telephone 927 or 618 02 73 in the Bucharest area, or 12345 in the rest of the country.

Some distances from Bucharest: Braşov 175km (110 miles), Constanţa 265km (165 miles), Timişoara 570km (355 miles).

Social customs: Any opportunity to accept or offer hospitality should be taken. If invited to a Romanian home, don't forget flowers for the hostess. You may also remember that hand-kissing is still customary when a man meets a woman.

Hints for business: Foreign trade and investment agreements may be negotiated directly with potential partners. Foreign investment is **275**

regulated by the Romanian Development Agency. For licence details, fax the RDA on 401 312 0371. The Romanian holiday month of August is best avoided for business travel.

Foreign chambers of commerce in Romania: Austrian, Italian.

Crime and theft: Normal precautions are in order.

After Hours

Food and drink: Most large hotels and restaurants offer a variety of international and local dishes. Some local specialities are: *mamaliga cu brînza* (maizemeal/cornmeal porridge with salted white cheese), *sarmale* (meatballs with sauerkraut), *mititei* (meatballs grilled with garlic, pepper and paprika), *pui cu mujdei* (roast chicken with garlic sauce).

Romania produces some very good wines, some of which are exported. Names to look out for: *Murfatlar* (red or white), *Segarcea* (red) and *Cotnari* or *Tîrnava* (white). *Tzuica* is a popular plum brandy. Western brand-name drinks are served in deluxe and first-class hotels.

Mealtimes: lunch noon-2pm, dinner 7-11pm.

Entertainment: Many cinemas show foreign films in their original language. Nightclubs, dance clubs and bars with Western music are available. Major towns stage plays and opera.

Taxes, service charges and tipping: A service charge is included in hotel and restaurant bills but small gratuities are expected (higher in the capital than in the provinces). Some tipping recommendations: waiters 5-10%; porters 50 lei per piece; taxi drivers 10% (less for short distances); cloakroom attendants 50 lei; hairdressers, barbers 10-15%.

Sports and recreation: Water sports, mountaineering, skiing and tennis. Spectator sports include soccer, handball, volleyball and tennis.

TV and radio: Radio and TV programming draws on Romanian and foreign sources. Foreign films are broadcast in their original language.

What to buy: Handicrafts, carpets, textiles, food and drink are favourite purchases. Ceramics are produced in a variety of regional styles (Maramureş, Suceava and Argeş). The Maramureş area is also noted for its woollen rugs, and the Argeş region for a particular style of embroidered blouses. In Bucharest, special 'dollar shops' offer a range of traditional products. Romanian wines, brandy and *tzuica* (plum brandy) can be obtained at bargain prices in all grocery stores. Antiques may not be exported.

Shopping hours: generally 8am-noon and 3-7pm, Monday-Saturday. Large stores stay open an hour later during the week and also work until noon on Sundays.

Cities and Sights

BUCHAREST (*Telephone area code 01*)

Airport: Otopeni (19km/12 miles from city centre), international; duty-free shop. Hourly airport bus service, urban bus service.

Baneasa (7km/4 miles from city centre), international and domestic. Urban bus and trolley-bus service.

Tourist information office: 7 Magheru Blvd; tel. 614 51 60.

Chamber of commerce and industry: 22 Balcescu Blvd; tel. 15 47 07.

Ministry of foreign trade: 17 Apolodor Street; fax 312 23 42.

Sightseeing: Old Court, Patriarchate, House of the People, University Square, Stavropoleos Church.

Museums: Village and Folk-Art Museum, National Gallery of Art, Museum of History, Theodore Aman Museum.

Excursions: Mogoşoaia Palace, Cernica, Caldăruşani and Snagov monasteries, Curtea de Argeş (old capital of Wallachia), Sinaia (mountain resort on the Prahova valley).

Some Useful Expressions in Romanian

good morning/afternoon	**buna dimineaţa/ziua**
good evening/night	**buna seara/noapte bună**
good-bye	**la revedere**
yes/no	**da/nu**
please/thank you	**vă rog/mulţumesc**
excuse me	**scuzaţi-mă**
you're welcome	**pentru puţin**
where/when/how	**unde/cînd/cum**
how long/how far	**cît durează/este departe**
yesterday/today/tomorrow	**ieri/azi/mîine**
day/week/month/year	**zi/săptămînă/lună/an**
left/right	**stînga/dreapta**
up/down	**sus/jos**
good/bad	**bun/rău**
big/small	**mare/mic**
cheap/expensive	**ieftin/scump**
hot/cold	**cald/rece**
old/new	**vechi/nou**
open/closed	**închis/deschis**
early/late	**devreme/tîrziu**
easy/difficult	**uşor/dificil**
Does anyone here speak English/French/German?	**Vorbeşte cineva aici engleza/franceza/germana?**
What does this mean?	**Ce înseamnă aceasta?**
I don't understand.	**Nu înţeleg.**
Do you take credit cards/traveller's cheques?	**Acceptaţi cărţi de credit/cecuri de voiaj?**
Waiter!/Waitress!	**Chelner!/chelneriţă!**
Where are the toilets?	**Unde este toaleta?**
I'd like…	**Aşi dori…**
How much is that?	**Cît costa?**
278 Help me please.	**Va rog să mă ajutaţi.**

Russia

Type of government:	Parliamentary democracy
Population:	147.8 million
Area:	17,075,400sq km (6,592,800sq miles)
Capital:	Moscow (*Moskva*, 8.75m)
Other major cities:	St Petersburg (4.4m)
	Novosibirsk (1.4m)
	Nizhny Novgorod (1.4m)
	Yekaterinburg (1.37m)
Language:	Predominantly Russian
Religion:	Russian Orthodox (80%) alongside Catholic, Lutheran, Baptist, Jewish, Islamic and Buddhist
Time zone (Moscow):	GMT+3, EST+8 (the CIS has 11 time zones); DST (March 31-Sep 30)
Currency:	Rouble (abbr. p) = 100 kopeks
	Coins: 1, 5, 10, 50, 100 rouble
	Bills: 100, 200, 500, 1,000, 5,000 10,000 and 50,000 roubles

Notes dated before 1993 are no longer legal tender.

Since January 1994 it has been illegal to conduct cash transactions in foreign currency. Foreign currency is however useful for exchange into roubles. US$ is the most widely accepted currency.

Electricity:	Mostly 220V, 50Hz, AC, but in older buildings sometimes 127V, 50Hz, AC. If you are using battery-operated appliances, like shavers, take spare batteries with you.

279

Planning your Trip

Visa requirements: Visas for Russia must be obtained in advance and are usually only issued if you have pre-booked accommodation or a private or business invitation. Apply for a visa from a Russian embassy at least 6-8 weeks in advance; you will probably need to provide evidence of confirmed hotel reservations for the whole trip with your application. If you are travelling as part of a tour operation the visa application will be made by the operator.

Vaccination requirements: None, although you should make sure that you have had a tetanus injection, and diptheria immunisation (at least 6 weeks before departure) is advised. Rabies is known to exist in the region and care should be taken with animals. (See also p.7.)

Import allowances: (See also p.7.)

Cigarettes		Cigars	Tobacco	Spirits		Wine
1000	or	1kg of other tobacco products		1.5l	and	2l

Perfume: A 'reasonable quantity' for personal use; *Gifts*: Up to $10,000 equivalent.

Note that the import of photographs and printed matter which might be directed against Russia (particularly anything involving military installations) is still prohibited. Any articles of value should be declared upon entry to facilitate their re-export. Loss of arrival customs declaration forms and incomplete listing of valuables can result in confiscation of the property in question.

Currency restrictions: At present there is no limit to the amount of foreign currency you can take into Russia. However, any unspent roubles remaining at the end of your trip cannot be taken out of the country, and must be reconverted to hard currency. You can only change roubles back into foreign currency if the original transaction has been recorded on your customs declaration form. (See also p.7.)

Climate: The climate of Russia shows wide variations, but in general is continental with warm to hot summers and sometimes fiercely cold winters.

Some average temperatures:

	Jan	Apr	July	Oct
Moscow	-10°C (13°F)	4°C (39°F)	18°C (65°F)	4°C (39°F)
St Petersburg	-8°C (18°F)	3°C (38°F)	18°C (65°F)	5°C (41°F)

In both Moscow and St Petersburg, temperatures may plunge to as low as -25°C (-13°F) in winter and soar to 30°C (86°F) in summer.

Clothing: In summer, medium-weight clothes are adequate, but during the rest of the year do not underestimate your needs. In winter you should wrap up well, from head to toe, in very warm clothing and sturdy overshoes. A conservative business suit is recommended.

Hotels: Russia issues visas only after hotel reservations have been confirmed. All accommodation must be paid for in advance. Make reservations through a travel agency that cooperates with Intourist (the Russian travel agency). While you are free to request the hotel of your choice, the final arrangements rest with Intourist who let you know the decision on arrival at the airport – although you can now bypass this system by dealing directly with one of the new joint-venture hotels run by major western hotel chains.

The Host Families Organisation HOFA, based in Saint Petersburg, can arrange accommodation with a Russian family, and can help with professional and business contacts; tel./fax (812) 275 1992 (or 395 1338).

Russian tourist offices abroad: Amsterdam, Athens, Belgrade, Berlin, Beirut, Brussels, Bucharest, Budapest, Cairo, Copenhagen, Frankfurt, Helsinki, Kabul, London, Luxembourg, Mexico City, Montreal, New Delhi, New York, Oslo, Paris, Prague, Rome, Sofia, Stockholm, Sydney, Tokyo, Vienna, Warsaw, Zurich.

Business Briefing

Economic Background

Main industries: Metallurgy, coal, chromite, iron ore, gold, copper, manganese and other minerals, timber, heavy industry, machinery, oil, gas.

Main agricultural products and fisheries: Wheat, rye, sweetcorn, oats, sugar beet, cattle, pigs, fish.

Main imports: Machinery, electronics and other high-technology equipment, steel products, wheat and other agricultural products, consumer goods.

Main exports: Oil and gas, raw materials, transport equipment, petroleum by-products, heavy machinery, paper products.

Principal trading partners: Germany, Italy, USA.

GNP: $157 billion; per capita: $5,592.

Trade fairs: Business fairs have become extremely important since the break-up of the Soviet Union and are growing in number all the time. The most important international fairs currently held in Moscow and St Petersburg include: consumer goods (January), medical technology (March), construction (April), machine equipment (June), automobiles (July and August), agricultural machinery (September) and textile machinery (November).

Selected background reading: *Russian Foreign Trade* (published monthly in English, French and German), *East-West Trade Newsletter* (Reuter), *East-West News Bulletin* (Business International), London's *Financial Times* has substantial east-west trade news. An indispensable publication for anyone coming to Moscow for other than a brief visit is *Information Moscow*. Issued every six months, it contains listings of all foreign residents and organizations as well as much useful data for foreigners. It can be ordered from the publisher, Leninsky Pr. 45/426, Moscow (tel. 135 11 64). Intourist publishes regular bulletins for the business traveller.

Russian chambers of commerce abroad: Many continue to be listed under *Soviet*; apply to commercial departments of Russian/Soviet embassies or consulates.

On the Spot

Office hours: 9am to noon or 1pm, and 1 or 2 to 6pm, Monday-Friday.

Public holidays

Dec 31 to Jan 2	New Year Celebrations	Mar 8	Women's Day
		May 1	Labour Day
Jan 7	Russian Orthodox Christmas	May 9	Victory Day
Jan 13	Julian Calendar New Year	June 12	Independence Day
Movable dates: Orthodox Easter Day.			

Banks and currency exchange: Banking hours are 9am-1pm Monday-Friday. The Russian banking system cannot yet provide the services taken for granted in the west. Hard currency can be changed into roubles in most hotels and international airports. You will need your passport and your customs declaration form. Cash transactions in foreign currency are now officially illegal, and credit cards are required for many purchases. Hotel and airport currency-exchange offices are often open outside normal hours.

Credit cards and traveller's cheques: Major credit cards are accepted by most Intourist shops, hotels, and major restaurants (especially joint venture establishments) but otherwise few Russian establishments recognize them and prefer cash. Travellers cheques are unpopular; dollars are more useful for exchange purposes.

Post and telecommunications: Postal and telecommunications services are moderately reliable. The post office handles postal, telegraph and telephone services. Major hotels have their own branches of the post office. In Moscow the main post office (open 8am-10pm) is situated at ul. Tverskaya 7, and in St Petersburg at 9 Pochtamtskaya ulitsa.

283

The Russian telephone system is hopelessly overburdened, and making a domestic call is often a frustrating process involving busy lines and wrong numbers. Local calls made from your hotel are usually free. Long-distance calls may be made from hotel rooms or from hotel phone booths. International calls can be now often be made from your hotel room. Many major hotels have phone booths where international calls can be made using a phone card or credit card. Charges are extremely high. It is not possible to reverse the charges for calls from Russia. Fax services are available in some of the major hotels and are becoming more common, but charges are very high.

Some useful numbers:

Ambulance	03	Fire	01
Information (Moscow)	135-1164	Police	02
Operator/directories	09	Time	100

In case of emergency you should seek help through your hotel; there is no English-speaking service on the above numbers.

Principal area codes from Moscow (Moscow code depends on where you are): Kiev 044, Minsk 07, St Petersburg 812. To call a subscriber in another city *who has a 7-digit number*, dial 8 for long-distance access (wait for a steady tone), then the area code and the subscriber's number. For example, to ring the chamber of commerce from Moscow, you would dial 8 + 812 + 273 48 96.

Notes: 1) If the subscriber's number has only six figures, add 0 to the area code (eg St Petersburg's 812 would become 8120). 2) If the subscriber's number has only five figures, add 00 to the area code (eg St Petersburg's area code would become 81200).

Embassies and consulates: These are not listed in the telephone directory. Ask Intourist or consult Information Moscow.
Some addresses:
British Embassy: Sofiyskaya nab. 14, Moscow;
tel. 230 63 33
Canadian Embassy: Starokonyushenniy pereulok 23, Moscow;
tel. 241 58 82

Irish Embassy: Grokholskiy pereulok 23, Moscow; tel. 288 41 01

US Embassy: Chaykovskogo ulitsa 19/23, Moscow; tel. 252 24 95
US Consulate: Petra Lavrova ulitsa 15, St Petersburg; tel. 274 82 35.

Medical care and health: In general, medical care in Russia suffers from a lack of sophisticated equipment and medicines. Bring along your own supply of basic medicines. Even adhesive tape and absorbent cotton can be unobtainable.

If you should fall ill, tell your Intourist guide or the hotel service desk. A doctor will visit you in your hotel, or you may be taken to a special clinic for tourists. Medicine is charged to the tourist-patient but the care is free of charge. It is advisable to ensure that you have full medical cover before arriving in Russia, including provisions for an emergency evacuation flight home. Other things you should consider bringing with you, as they are expensive or difficult to find in Russia, are spare eyeglasses or contact lenses, toiletries, razor blades, tampons, contraceptives and aspirin. If you are travelling with an infant make sure that you bring all the diapers, bottles and baby food you will need.

Pharmacies are usually open 8am to 8 or 9pm. Several pharmacies operate around the clock; Intourist can give you the addresses.

Dysentery or diarrhoea is sometimes a problem in the southern areas of the country. Diptheria has been a problem throughout Russian in recent years, and immunisation is advisable.

The water supply in Moscow and St Petersburg is contaminated with the *Giardia lamblia* organism which causes stomach cramps, nausea and diarrhoea. To avoid illness don't drink the tap water. The better hotels have filtered water systems, and their tap water is quite safe, but ask if you are not sure. Otherwise, stick to tea, coffee and mineral water.

Services: As in so many other circumstances, the Intourist linguist at your hotel desk is your best adviser if you are not with your business partners. He or she can provide an interpreter, translator or typist, given some advance notice.

Newspapers: Principal Moscow dailies are Pravda and Izvestia. Foreign newspapers can be found on city newsstands and hotels, **285**

sometimes on the same day of publication, although they can be expensive. Locally produced English language publications include the daily *Moscow Times* (free), and the bi-monthly *Moscow Magazine*, both of which provide news, features, restaurant reviews and entertainment listings. In St Petersburg you can get the bi-monthly *Neva News* and the quarterly *St Petersburg News*.

Transport

Air – international: Direct flights operate into Moscow and to a lesser extent into St Petersburg from all parts of the world.

Air – domestic: Domestic flights link Moscow with hundreds of points throughout the former Soviet Union, from major cities to Siberian settlements. Air travel can be difficult in Russia as Aeroflot has been having problems maintaining its aircraft and timetables. The Moscow Intourist office is equipped to help with problems and should be contacted before embarking on a domestic flight.

Rail: Trains are punctual and comfortable and can be recommended for business travel between major cities if time is not too much of an object. A single class of seating is available, though sleeping cars offer standard (equivalent to second-class) and soft (first-class) categories. Don't be surprised if the berth arrangements mix up the sexes among perfect strangers. Long-distance trains include dining cars.

Local public transport: Cheap tram, bus and trolleybus services are available in principal cities. Moscow and St Petersburg have extensive, efficient underground (subway) systems.

Taxis: There are city centre taxi ranks, marked by a 'T' sign. Make sure you negotiate your fare before you get into the taxi; meters are installed but they are rarely used. If you try to hail a taxi in the street you will often find that ordinary cars will stop; these are private citizens trying to make a little extra money. Never get into a private car or taxi alone if there is someone else inside apart from the driver. The safest option is to ask your hotel totelephone for a reliable private taxi, They will also be able to quote a price for your journey. Book your taxi at least an hour in advance.

The major hotels also have their own chauffered cars which are safer and less troublesome than street taxis.

Car rental: Cars may be rented through Intourist or Europcar, and reservations should preferably be made at the time you apply for your visa and make travel arrangements. Payment will probably required using a major credit card. As road and driving conditions are poor, you are recommended to hire a car with driver unless you intend exploring extensively outside the major cities.

Driving in Russia: If you intend to bring your own vehicle into Russia you must arrange your trip with Intourist at least six weeks in advance. You will have to submit a complete day-to-day itinerary, detailing routes (max. 500km/312 miles per day on authorized roads) and stopping places with all accommodation paid for in advance, before you will be issued with a visa. An international driving licence, with a Russian language insert, an insurance certificate, and all the documentation for your car (including registration documents) will also be needed.

The speed limit in all cities and towns is 60kph (38mph); 90kph (56mph) outside towns – except where signs permitting higher speeds are displayed. Use of seat belts is obligatory, and a red reflector warning triangle, a fire extinguisher and a first-aid kit must be carried. Blood alcohol limit is a strictly enforced zero. Headlamp converters must be used.

Horns may not be sounded in residential areas except to prevent an accident. In urban driving after dark, only dipped headlights should be used. A left turn or U-turn can usually only be made when specifically allowed, mostly as indicated by an arrow signal on the main traffic lights. Yield to official limousines driving in special outside lanes. Beware of undisciplined city traffic as well as poor street lighting and vehicle illumination at night. Road surfaces are often rather poor by western standards. Fuel (petrol/gas) is generally available in normal (76 or 93 octane), super (95 octane) and diesel, but high-grade and diesel fuel is sometimes difficult to find. Note that unleaded fuel is not currently available; petrol shortages are common, and service stations are few and far between, so it's advisable to fill up wherever possible. **287**

In the event of an accident or breakdown, seek help from Intourist or the traffic police. Remember that spare parts for foreign cars may have to be ordered from abroad which can take a long time. It is strongly recommended to take out emergency breakdown cover with a reputable driving association before leaving home.

Traffic in cities is controlled by armed officers of the militia (police).. You can recognize the traffic police by their grey uniform and white baton. For minor infringements, fines are sometimes levied on the spot and receipts given. Highways are patrolled by state traffic police on motorcycles and in yellow cars with broad blue stripes.

The Foreign Office in London keeps up-to-date on regional problems and can give advice on any areas that are considered unsafe for travel; tel. 0171 270 4129.

Social customs: Refer always to Russia, not the Soviet Union. Never drop anything, not even an old cinema ticket, in the street – it's both offensive to Russian tidiness and illegal. Although sensitivities are not what they were, it may be an idea to avoid discussion of politics or social conditions, for instance, your surprise at the lack of amenities. It is rare to be invited to a Russian counterpart's home, but if you are, then take flowers or alcohol.

Hints for business: First and foremost, plan a trip to Russia well in advance. A number of weeks, perhaps months, will be needed to arrange visas, contacts with Russian organizations and travel details. Appointments are absolutely essential for all government visits. Do not make spontaneous meal invitations; Russian officials need time to overcome the enduring bureaucracy and last-minute informal invitations will often embarrass. In business dealings, Russians are very price conscious, so any proposals you present must be competitive. Avoid the July-August holiday period for business travel when many officials will be unavailable. Bring a good supply of visiting cards, if possible with a Russian translation on the back.

Foreign chambers of commerce in Russia: More and more chambers are arriving in Russia. Check with embassies or consulates before departure.

Crime and theft: Be careful not to get involved with black marketeers or illegal currency dealers. Although less serious now than in the Soviet days such action could still lead to serious consequences. Normal precautions are in order to guard against petty crime such as pickpocketing. Do not tempt fate by leaving valuables lying around or wallets jutting from hip pockets in crowded places. Leave valuables in the hotel safe. Any theft or loss must be reported immediately to the police in order to comply with travel insurance. Beyond pickpocketing and burglaries, the incidence of violent crime has greatly increased. Keep all your valuables secure in inside pockets or use a money belt. Stay clear of Gorky Park at night. Another new peril: passengers' baggage stolen at Moscow's international airport. If possible, take carry-on luggage only. Otherwise, don't take expensive looking suitcases and avoid putting valuables in checked luggage.

After Hours

Food and drink: Most hotels and restaurants offer a variety of international and local dishes and have standard menus printed in four languages. Some specialities are *borsht* (beet and cabbage soup with chunks of boiled beef), *solianka* (cabbage soup), *pelmeni* (meat dumpling), *blini* (Russian pancakes with sweet, savory or caviar fillings), *okroshka* (a chilled summertime soup made of cucumber, onion and hard-boiled eggs), *kasha* (a type of porridge), *pirozhki* (small pies), *shashlik* (skewered and grilled mutton and onions served with a hot sauce), *beef Stroganov* (beef tenderloin in a sauce of sour cream, onions and mushrooms), *kotleti po-kiyevski* (chicken Kiev: boned chicken breasts filled with melted butter) and, of course, caviar.

Regional wines are well regarded but erratically distributed. Many sunny regions produce quite drinkable wines, but the biggest reputation probably belongs to Georgian reds and whites. In practice, the waiter will tell you whether there's any choice at all. Vodka is drunk straight. Russian tea can be recommended and mineral water holds an honored place on Russian tables. If you can get it, *Narzan* fizzes tastily. *Borzhomi*, more commonly available, is so good for you that its heavy mineral taste may put you off.

If you are not eating at your hotel, it is necessary to reserve a table; ask the service bureau at your hotel to do it for you.

Mealtimes: lunch 11am-3pm, dinner 6-10pm.

The latest addition to the restaurant scene is the 'Joint-Venture' (JV), a business partnership between a Russian and a western company. These places have well-trained English-speaking staff, and varied menus prepared with imported food and drink. Decor, standards of service and quality are much as you would expect at home. Many Joint-Ventures accept payment by credit cards only. For dinner at the more expensive places reservations are recommended well in advance.

Entertainment: In all the big cities there is a full programme of concerts, plays, opera, circus performances and ballet almost every night. Intourist has the monopoly on the best tickets, though at short notice you might have to settle for second or third choice. There are many movie theatres, showing mainly Russian films. Western films are usually dubbed into Russian.

Taxes, service charges and tipping: In hotels and restaurants, all charges are included. Tipping, once officially discouraged, is now accepted practice in Russia. Foreign currency is preferred. Reckon on 10% for waiters and waitresses (unless a service charge has been included in the bill), and the same for taxi drivers, unless a fare has been negotiated in advance. Tour guides and hotel maids greatly appreciate a tip, or a small gift of cigarettes, soap, toiletries or sweets.

Sports and recreation: Visitors can arrange horseback riding or tennis through Intourist. There's a bowling alley in Moscow's Gorky Park. A giant, well-heated, open-air swimming pool operates year-round close to Moscow's Kremlin. In winter, ice hockey is the most popular spectator sport, and during the rest of the year, soccer. Basketball is also a favourite as well as a variety of other sports.

TV and radio: All radio and television programming is in Russian or minority languages. Russian television transmits programmes on four channels. The language problem may prove insurmountable, except for international sporting events which are always popular. All programmes are in colour. Many hotels now offer satellite television, with CNN, MTV, and sports and movie channels. Two radio networks broadcast to the farthest reaches of Russia: Moscow Radio and the less solemn Radio Mayak. If you crave news from the outer world in a language you can comprehend, the BBC and Voice of America, among other foreign stations, may be picked up at certain times of the day.

What to buy: Good buys include caviar, vodka, amber, traditional painted wooden handicraft items, lacquered boxes with fine miniature paintings, *matryoshka* dolls, *Bukhara* and other Central Asian carpets and furs. However, there are strict regulations in force to prevent the export of Russia's few consumer goods, so it is safest to buy goods for hard currency in Beryozka (state owned) shops, and keep any receipts. Goods considered to be of cultural or historical value can be confiscated by customs to prevent their export.

Shopping hours vary considerably. Most shops are open 10am-6pm, with major stores operating longer hours (often 8am-9pm), Monday-Saturday.

Cities and Sights

MOSCOW (*Telephone area code 095, from abroad*)
Airports: Sheremetyevo (30km/18 miles from city centre), international; duty-free shop. Bus service to city terminal on St Petersburg Boulevard, but better take a taxi.

Vnukovo (30km/18 miles from city centre), domestic. Erratic bus service.

Domodedovo (40km/25 miles from city centre), domestic. Erratic bus service.

Tourist information offices: Contact the nearest Intourist office (located in hotels and at airports), or the main office at 13 Mokhovaya St, 10300 Moscow; tel. 292 44 03.

Chamber of commerce and industry: 6 Ulitsa Ilyinka (Russian Federation); tel. 923 43 23, fax 230 24 55.

Ministry of Foreign Economic Relations: Smolenskaya-Sennaya 32/34, 121200 Moscow; tel. 244 10 46. (This ministry will direct you to the appropriate state trading agency. Contact with the appropriate bilateral chamber of commerce recommended.)

Sightseeing: Kremlin, Red Square, St Basil's Cathedral, Novodovichiy Convent, Lenin's Tomb.

Museums: Tretyakov Gallery, Pushkin Fine Arts Museum.

Excursions: Zagorsk, Moskva River cruise (summer), Arkhangelskoye, Kuskovo.

ST PETERSBURG (*Telephone area code 812, from Moscow*)

Airports: Pulkovo II (17km/11 miles from city centre), international; duty-free shop. Airport bus service about every 15 minutes.

Pulkovo I, a 10-minute bus journey from terminal II, is the starting point for most domestic flights, including the shuttle service from Moscow.

Tourist information offices: Contact the nearest Intourist office (located in hotels and airports).

Chamber of commerce and industry: Naberezhnaya Krasnovo Flota 10; tel. 273 48 96.

Sightseeing: Winter Palace, Summer Palace, Peter and Paul Fortress, Nevsky Prospekt.

Museums: Hermitage, Russian Museum.

Excursions: Petrodvorets, Pushkin, Novgorod.

Some Useful Expressions in Russian

good morning/afternoon	**dobroye utro/dobriy dyen'**
good evening/night	**dobriy vyechyer/spokoynoy nochi**
good-bye	**dosvidaniya**
yes/no	**da/nyet**
please/thank you	**pozhalusta/spasibo**
excuse me	**izvinitye**
you're welcome	**pozhalusta**
where/when/how	**gdye/kogda/kak**
yesterday/today/tomorrow	**vchyera/sevodnya/zavtra**
day/week/month/year	**den/nyedyelya/myesyats/god**
left/right	**lyeviy/praviy**
up/down	**vvyerkh/vniz**
good/bad	**khoroshiy/plokhoy**
big/small	**bol'shoy/malyen'kiy**
cheap/expensive	**dyeshoviy/dorogoy**
hot/cold	**goryachiy/kholodniy**
old/new	**stariy/noviy**
open/closed	**otkritiy/zakritiy**
Does anyone here speak English/French/German?	**Zdyes' kto-nibud' govorit po-angliyski/po-frantsuzski/po-nyemyetski?**
What does this mean?	**Chto eto znachit?**
I don't understand.	**Ya nye ponimayu.**
Please write it down.	**Pozhalusta, napishitye.**
Do you take credit cards/ traveller's cheques?	**Vi byeryote Kryeditniye Kartochki/dorozhniye chyecki?**
Waiter!/Waitress!	**Ofitsiant!/Ofitsiantka!**
Where are the toilets?	**Gdye tualyety?**
I'd like…	**Ya khotyel bi….**
Help me please.	**Pomogitye mnye, pozhalusta.**

293

Spain

Type of government:	Constitutional monarchy, multi-party, largely centralized
Member of:	EU, GATT, IBRD, IDA, IFC, IMF, OECD
Population:	39.2 million
Area:	504,750sq km (194,884sq miles)
Capital:	Madrid (2.9m)
Other major cities:	Barcelona (1.6m) Valencia (752,909) Seville (*Sevilla*, 659,126) Zaragoza (590,000) Bilbao (435,000)
Languages:	Spanish; Catalan and Basque are also of regional importance in the Barcelona–Tarragona and Bilbao–Santander areas, respectively. Use of English is growing, and French is fairly widely known.
Religion:	Virtually 100% Catholic
Time zone:	GMT+1, EST+6; DST (Apr-Sep)
Currency:	Spanish peseta (abbr. pta) Coins: 1, 5, 10, 25, 50, 100, 200, 500 ptas Notes: 1,000, 2,000, 5,000, 10,000 ptas
Electricity:	Generally 220V, 50Hz, AC; 125V in some areas. Ask at your hotel.

Planning your Trip

Visa requirements: For nationals of South Africa and Turkey. (See also p.6.)

Vaccination requirements: None. (See also p.7.)

Import allowances (see also p.7):

	Cigarettes		Cigars		Tobacco	Spirits		Wine
1)	200	or	50	or	250g	1l	and	2l
2)	(800)	or	(200)	or	(1kg)	(10l)	and	(90l)
1) Passengers from countries outside Europe; Duty-free goods bought in EU countries by European residents.								
2) Non-duty-free goods bought within the EU.								

Perfume: 1) 50g; *Toilet water*: 1) 0.25l;
Gifts: 1) 6,200 pta max. value

There are no official restrictions on goods bought non-duty-free within the EU, provided they are for personal use only. The above figures are guidelines to the quantities customs officials will generally find acceptable, so if you are carrying larger quantities you should be prepared to provide proof that the goods are for your personal use.

Currency restrictions: Visitors may bring any amount of currency into Spain. On departing, you must declare any amount over the equivalent of 500,000 ptas. If you plan to carry large sums in and out again it is wise to declare your currency on arrival as well as on departure. (See also p.7.)

Climate: In the north and northwest, moderate, with well-distributed rainfall; the south and southeast coastal plains are Mediterranean – hot and dry in summer and mild and rainy in winter; most inland areas have a continental climate – hot in summer and cold in winter, with generally light rainfall.

Some average temperatures:

	Spring	Summer	Autumn	Winter
Madrid	12°C (54°F)	22°C (72°F)	15°C (59°F)	5°C (41°F)
Barcelona	15°C (59°F)	23°C (74°F)	17°C (63°F)	9°C (48°F)
Bilbao	11°C (52°F)	18°C (65°F)	15°C (59°F)	8°C (46°F)

Clothing: In spring and autumn, weather is variable: the temperature may change dramatically from day to day, and it's best for the traveller to have a sweater or a light overcoat handy. In summer a lightweight suit is practical. Spanish businessmen usually wear suits and ties but more casual wear, especially in summer, is acceptable for men and women. During winter an overcoat is usually advisable in Madrid and Bilbao, and a raincoat in Barcelona.

Hotels: Hotel rooms should always be booked as far in advance as possible. Outside Madrid, accommodation is scarce during the tourist season. Hotel space is also at a premium during major conferences or exhibitions. Local tourist offices in all main cities operate hotel booking services; they are located at airports and railway stations. A hotel guide *(Guía de Hoteles)* may be consulted at tourist offices.

Spanish tourist offices abroad: Brussels, Buenos Aires, Chicago, Copenhagen, Düsseldorf, Frankfurt, Geneva, The Hague, Helsinki, Houston, Lisbon, London, Mexico City, Milan, Munich, New York, Oslo, Paris, Rome, St Augustine (Florida), Stockholm, Tokyo, Toronto, Vienna, Zurich.

Business Briefing

Economic Background
Main industries: Automobile manufacture, engineering and steel works, coal mining, electronics, textiles, ceramics, tourism.

Main agricultural products and fisheries: Wine, fruit, vegetables, olive oil, wheat, fish, barley, sugar beet.

Main imports: Petroleum, oil products, minerals, vehicles, food-stuffs, chemical products, machinery.

Main exports: Vehicles, iron and steel products, tires, agricultural products such as wine, olives, citrus fruits and tomatoes.

Principal trading partners: USA, Germany, France, Brazil, Iran, Iraq.

GNP: $358.2 billion; per capita: $9,150.

Inflation rate: 4.3% (1993).

Trade fairs: A number of trade fairs and exhibitions held throughout the year in various parts of the country offer good opportunities for market exposure. Dates vary from year to year; details from the Spanish National Tourist Office or chamber of commerce in your country.

Selected background reading: The Ministry of Finance publishes an annual survey of commercial and trade figures, *Estadistica del Comercio Exterior de España*. Other publications: *Europa Yearbook*: a *World Survey* (Europa), *Abecor Country Report, Spain* (Barclays Bank Group), *Business in Spain* (Lloyds Bank International), *Business Study: Spain* (Touche Ross International), *Economic Report*: *Spain and Overseas Territories* (Lloyds Bank), *Foreign Economic Trends and Their Implications for the United States: Spain* (US Dept of Commerce), *Marketing in Spain* (US Dept. of Commerce), *OECD Economic Surveys: Spain* (OECD), *Spain: Economic Report* (Banco de Bilbao), *Trade and Industry* (Her Majesty's Stationery Office, London), *Ibar Anuario Comercial Iberoamericano* (trade directory of Spanish-Lusitanian and Latin American countries and the USA), *Hechos y Cifras de la Economía Española* (El Banco Exterior de España), *Anuario Estadístico de España* (Instituto Nacional de Estadistica), *Estadística de Comercio Exterior de España* (Dirección General de Aduanas), *Informe Mensual sobre el Comercio Exterior de España* (Dirección General de Aduanas).

Spanish chambers of commerce abroad: Abidjan, Algiers, Ankara, Asunción, Athens, Baghdad, Beijing, Beirut, Belgrade, Berlin, Bern, Bogotá, Bonn, Brasília, Brussels, Bucharest, Budapest, Buenos Aires,

Cairo, Caracas, Chicago, Copenhagen, Coral Gables, Dakar, Damascus, Djakarta, Douala, Guatemala City, Hamburg, Havana, Helsinki, Jeddah, Johannesburg, Lagos, Lima, Lisbon, London, Los Angeles, Malabo, Manila, Mexico City, Milan, Montevideo, Montreal, Moscow, New York, Oslo, Ottawa, Paris, Prague, Pretoria, Quito, Rabat, Rio de Janeiro, Rome, San Francisco, San Juan, Santiago de Chile, Santo Domingo, Stockholm, Sydney, Tehran, Tokyo, Toronto, Tripoli, Tunis, Vienna, Warsaw, Washington.

On the Spot

Office hours: Generally 9am-6.45pm in winter, 9am-2pm and 4.30-7pm in summer, Monday-Friday.

Public holidays

Jan 1	New Year's Day	Dec 25	Christmas Day
Jan 6	Epiphany	Dec 26	Christmas Holiday
May 1	Labour Day	**Movable dates**:	Maundy Thursday
July 25	St James' Day		Good Friday
Aug 15	Assumption		Easter Monday
Oct 12	Discovery of America		(Catalonia)
	Day (Columbus Day)		Corpus Christi
Nov 1	All Saints' Day		Immaculate
Dec 6	Constitution Day		Conception

Local holidays: In addition, each town and city in Spain has its own fiestas, for example: Madrid – May 15, Nov 9; Barcelona – May 31, June 24, Sep 11 and 24, Dec 26; Bilbao – June 19, July 31.

Banks and currency exchange: Banks are usually open from 9am to 4.30pm, Monday-Thursday and from 8.30am to 2pm on Friday. On Saturdays they are open until 1pm. From June to September, they are open from 8.30am to 2pm and closed on Saturdays. But beware – there are variations. Outside of banking hours, money can normally be changed at *cambios* at airports, railway stations, major hotels and elsewhere.

The principal banks in Spain are Banco Bilbao-Vizcaya, Banco de Santander, Banco Exterior de España, Banco Hispano-Americano, Banco de Crédito Agrícola.

Credit cards and traveller's cheques: Both are widely accepted by major businesses.

Post and telecommunications: Postal and telecommunications services are reliable for domestic and international use.

Main post offices in major centres provide facilities for sending telexes and telefaxes as well as a 24-hour telegram service. Madrid: Plaza de la Cibeles; Barcelona: Plaza Antonio López; Bilbao: 15, Calle Alameda Urquijo. Public telex booths are also available at main post offices in major cities throughout Spain. Posting documents from one of Spain's international airports saves up to two days on delivery time.

In all main towns, long-distance calls can be placed from telephone offices (usually distinct from post offices), which are usually open from 9am to midnight Monday to Saturday (from 12 noon to midnight on Sundays). Most hotels allow you to use their telephones for long-distance and international calls even if you aren't staying there. A small service charge is added to the charge ticket in such cases. The inland telephone network is almost completely automatic, and direct dialling is available to many countries.

Some useful numbers:

Ambulance (Madrid)	252 27 92	Information (inland)	009
Ambulance		International service	
(Barcelona)	30 00 422	(Europe)	008
Fire (Madrid)	23 23 232	International service	
Fire (Barcelona)	25 35 353	(outside Europe)	089
General telephone		24-hour pharmacies	098
information	003	Time	093
Operator (National)	0	Weather	094
Operator (Europe)	008	World news	095
Operator (Int.)	005		

Principal area codes: Barcelona 3, Bilbao 4, Madrid 1, Seville 54, Valencia 6, Zaragoza 76.

Embassies and consulates: Embassies and consulates are listed in the normal phone book or in the yellow pages under *Embajadas* and *Consulados*, respectively.

Medical care and health: The standard of medical treatment is generally high, and fees are moderate. Hospitals where English or other languages are spoken: British-American Hospital, 1 Calle Juan XXIII, Madrid; tel. 234 67 00, and Hospital Fra Angélico, 15-17 Calle Camelias, Barcelona; tel. 219 71 00. Many medicines and pharmaceutical supplies are readily available in pharmacies (*farmacias*). Antibiotics can be easily obtained without prescription. For minor ailments go to the local first-aid post (*ambulatorio/dispensario*). After hours, at least one pharmacy per town is open all night, called *farmacia de guardia*. The address is posted in the window of all other pharmacies and lists are published daily in local newspapers. Tap water is usually safe to drink but those with a delicate stomach may prefer to drink bottled mineral water and it is best to drink this during drought periods.

Services: All leading hotels can arrange typing and other secretarial services on request. Embassy and consular commercial departments should also be able to put visitors in contact with secretarial agencies, translators and interpreters. Many department stores, stationers' and bookshops in city centres offer photocopying services.

Newspapers: Spain's leading dailies are, in Madrid, *El País*, *ABC* and *Diario* 16; in Barcelona, *La Vanguardia* and *El Correo Catalán*; in Bilbao, *Gaceta del Norte* and *El Correo Español*. Local English-language publications include the daily *Iberian Sun*, the weekly *Guide-post* and the monthly magazine *Lookout*. Foreign newspapers and magazines, particularly from Europe, North and South America, are mostly on news-stands late on the day of publication.

Transport
Air – international: Madrid is the main gateway to Spain, though to a lesser extent travellers can also fly into Barcelona, Bilbao, Palma de Mallorca and other cities directly, without transiting via the capital.

Air – domestic: All major cities are served by frequent air services. Airtaxis are available at all airports.

Rail: Good first- and second-class service is available. Particularly recommended are the intercity *Talgo* and the *Ter*, both rapid and comfortable. An express train in Spain is called a *rápido* (*expres* trains are slower), on which clean, comfortable sleeping accommodation is available. Seat reservations are required for most Spanish trains. Some tickets include the price of a lunch or dinner. The Spanish National Railways, RENFE, offer unlimited rail travel passes for all types of trains, for Eurailpass, see p.10.

Local public transport: Major cities have excellent public transport with some priority lanes for buses and taxis. Madrid and Barcelona have *metros* (underground, subway), but they are very crowded and unmercifully hot in summer.

Taxis: They are recognized by the letters SP (for *servicio público*) and fitted with meters in major towns. Cabs are parked at ranks or can be hailed on the street when the '*libre*' sign is displayed. Additional charges are made at night and on holidays and for picking up at airports and railway stations. All taxis carry government-approved lists of charges in several languages.

Car rental: Major car-rental agencies operate throughout Spain. Chauffeur-driven cars are also available.

Driving in Spain: An international driving licence, registration papers, green card certificate of insurance and bail bond are all recommended. If you should injure anybody in an accident in Spain you could be imprisoned pending investigation, unless you have a bond to bail you out. Two red-reflector warning triangles, for use in case of breakdown, as well as fuses, a spare wheel and set of headlamp bulbs, must be part of your car's equipment. Seat belts must be worn, and children under 10 must travel in the rear. Blood alcohol limit is 80mg/100ml. Speed limits: 50kph (31mph) in built-up areas, 120kph (75mph) on motorways (expressways) and 100kph (62mph) or 90kph

(56mph) on other roads. Fuel (petrol/gas) available is leadfree super (98 octane), super (97 octane), leadfree (95 octane) and diesel.

Arterial roads are generally very good, with long stretches in the open country virtually deserted. Secondary roads can be bumpy. On certain routes, however, heavy commercial traffic often clogs inadequate two-lane highways. Spain's expanding motorway network is excellently engineered, but rather expensive tolls are charged. Motorways run from the French frontier down the Mediterranean coast to Alicante, and from Irún via Bilbao to Vigo and La Coruña. Several stretches of motorway exist in the south, particularly the one linking Cádiz and Seville. Tollroads are in construction between Bilbao and Madrid, and Barcelona and Madrid. One of the main dangers of driving in Spain is impatience, especially on busy roads. Spanish truck drivers will often wave you on (by hand signal or by flashing their right indicator). Use one of the strategically positioned emergency telephones to call for help in case of breakdowns. Otherwise phone the Guardia Civil.

Some distances from Madrid: Zaragoza 320km (200 miles), Valencia 350km (215 miles), Málaga 545km (340 miles), Barcelona 620km (385 miles).

Social customs: An invitation to a home is unusual, and if you're so honoured, a gift of flowers to the hostess the next day will be highly appreciated. Spaniards are extremely fond of children, so if you meet a Spanish family and the children are present, don't fail to devote a few minutes to them – you'll leave a favourable mark! Note that smoking is prohibited in public-transport vehicles – and in many taxis, too – as well as in cinemas and theatres.

Hints for business: Relationships tend to be casual after the initial introduction, and these days first names are much used, though letter-writing remains formal. Much business is conducted over cocktails. Spanish business people tend to entertain on quite a lavish scale. Avoid the mid-July to end-August period for business travel when most Spaniards are on holiday. Note also that when a public holiday falls on a Tuesday or a Thursday, it's common to take a long weekend.

Some government offices work mornings only throughout the year, but 'morning' can stretch into mid-afternoon in Spain.

Foreign chambers of commerce in Spain: American, Belgian, Brazilian, British, Chilean, Colombian, Dutch, French, German, Indian, Italian, Moroccan, Norwegian, Pakistani, Portuguese, Puerto Rican, Venezuelan.

Crime and theft: A rise in criminal activity over the past few years is reflected mainly in thefts from cars, pickpocketing and occasional late-night muggings.

After Hours

Food and drink: A few specialities are: roast suckling pig and lamb, seafood and *cocido* (a type of stew) in Madrid; seafood and fish in Bilbao; local sausages, steaks and seafood in Barcelona.

Local wines and beers are excellent, as are sherries and brandies. Good local wines are available throughout the country. Most restaurants carry an astonishing selection of liqueurs and fruit brandies little known outside the country, as well as more expensive imported whisky, gin and vodka.

Mealtimes: lunch 2-4pm, dinner 9-11pm.

Entertainment: In major cities, nightclubs and discotheques cater to all tastes. Foreign films are almost always dubbed into Spanish. Madrid and Barcelona are major cultural centres for the opera, concerts and the theatre. Flamenco shows are an attraction in large cities.

Taxes, service charges and tipping: Service charges are generally included in hotel and restaurant prices. Porters at airports apply a set, posted, rate per bag; at hotels, tip 200 ptas per bag. Waiters expect 10%, taxi drivers 10%, cloakroom attendants 50-100 ptas per person, barbers and hairdressers 5–10%.

Sports and recreation: Tennis and golf facilities exist near all cities, but fees tend to be rather high. The long Mediterranean and Atlantic coasts assure an abundance of water sports. Good freshwater and deep-sea fishing are available.

Spain's top spectator sport is soccer, followed by bullfighting. Except in high summer, there's usually a football match to be seen every week in most towns. The bullfight season extends through spring, summer and autumn. Other sports include horse-racing in Madrid, greyhound-racing in Madrid and Barcelona, and *jai alai*, the very fast squash-type game, in the Basque country (Bilbao area).

TV and radio: Radio and TV broadcasts are in Spanish. Both the BBC and the Voice of America can be heard on short-wave radio.

What to buy: All leather goods, ceramics, Toledo gold, lace, wine, sherry and brandies, Cuban cigars and suede products. Department stores are generally open 10am-8pm, though most shops follow the traditional Spanish hours of 9.30am-1.30pm and 4 or 5 to 8pm.

Cities and Sights

MADRID (*Telephone area code 91*)
Airport: Barajas (12km/8 miles from city centre), international; duty-free shop; Business Information Office (tel. 205 88 07). Airport bus service. Hourly shuttle flights link Madrid and Barcelona, with no advance reservations required.

Tourist information offices: Mariá de Molina 50, 28006 Madrid; tel. 411 4014, fax 411 4232. Also Chamartin railway station; Plaza Mayor 3; Duque de Medinaceli 2.

Chamber of commerce and industry: Plaza Independencia 1, 28001 Madrid; tel. 429 31 93, fax 435 55 23. Also: Huertas 13; tel. 429 31 93.

Sightseeing: Royal Palace, Retiro Park and Casa de Campo Park, Plaza Mayor.

Museums: Prado, Museo Lázaro Galdiano, Museum of Contemporary Art.

Excursions: Toledo, Segovia, El Escorial and the civil-war monument of the valley of the Fallen.

BARCELONA (*Telephone area code 93*)
Airport: Muntadas (11km/7 miles from city centre), international; duty-free shop; Business Information Office (tel. 241 03 17). Regular train service to city centre. Hourly shuttle flights link Barcelona and Madrid; no advance reservation required.

Tourist information office: Plaça de Sant Jaume (in the city hall); tel. 318 25 25. Spanish National Tourist Office, Gran Via de les Corts Catalanes 658; tel. 301 74 43.

Chamber of Commerce, industry and navigation: Av Diagonal 452, 08006 Barcelona; tel. 415 16 00, fax 237 10 28.

Sightseeing: St Eulalia Cathedral, La Rambla, fountains at Montjuïc Park, Gothic Quarter, Sagrada Familia Cathedral.

Museums: Federico Marés Museum, Picasso Museum, Museum of Art of Catalonia, Archaeological Museum.

Excursions: Montserrat, Roman ruins at Tarragona, Costa Brava resort towns, Andorra.

BILBAO (*Telephone area code 94*)
Airport: Sondica (15km/9 miles from city centre), international. Bus service.

Tourist information office: Alameda de Mazarredo; tel. 424 48 19.

Chamber of commerce, industry and navigation: Alameda Recalde 50; tel. 444 40 54, fax 443 61 71.

Sightseeing: Church of Santiago, Basilica of Begona, town hall.

Museum: Fine Arts Museum.

Excursions: Scenic coast and countryside.

Some Useful Expressions in Spanish

good morning/afternoon	**buenos días/buenas tardes**
good evening/night	**buenas tardes/buenas noches**
good-bye	**adiós**
yes/no	**si/no**
please/thank you	**por favor/gracias**
excuse me	**perdone**
you're welcome	**de nada**
where/when/how	**dónde/cuándo/cómo**
how long/how far	**cuánto tiempo/a qué distancia**
yesterday/today/tomorrow	**ayer/hoy/manana**
day/week/month/year	**dia/semana/mes/ano**
left/right	**izquierda/derecha**
up/down	**arriba/abajo**
good/bad	**bueno/malo**
big/small	**grande/pequeno**
cheap/expensive	**barato/caro**
hot/cold	**caliente/frío**
old/new	**viejo/nuevo**
open/closed	**abierto/cerrado**
early/late	**temprano/tarde**
easy/difficult	**fácil/dificil**
Does anyone here speak English/French/German?	**¿Hay alguien aquí que hable inglés/francés/alemán?**
What does this mean?	**¿Qué quiere decir esto?**
I don't understand.	**No comprendo.**
Do you take credit cards/ traveller's cheques?	**¿Acepta usted tarjetas de crédito/cheques de viaje?**
Waiter!/Waitress!	**¡Camarero!/¡Camarera!**
Where are the toilets?	**¿Doéde están los servicios?**
I'd like …	**Quisiera …**
How much is that?	**¿Cuánto cuesta esto?**
Help me please.	**Ayúdeme, por favor.**

Sweden

Type of government:	Constitutional monarchy, multi-party, centralized
Member of:	EU, GATT, IBRD, IDA, IFC, IMF, OECD
Population:	8.8 million
Area:	449,964sq km (173,800sq miles)
Capital:	Stockholm (684,576/GUA 1.5m)
Other major cities:	Gothenburg (*Göteborg*, 433,811/ GUA 700,000) Malmö (236,684/GUA 470,000) Uppsala (150,000) Norrköping (120,000) Västerås (120,000)
Languages:	Swedish is the official language; 5% of the population speaks Finnish. English and, to a lesser extent, German are widely spoken in business circles; some French and Spanish.
Religion:	Protestant (98%)
Time zone:	GMT+1, EST+6; DST (Apr-Sep)
Currency:	Swedish krona (abbr. kr) = 100 öre Coins: 50 öre; 1, 5, 10kr Notes: 20, 50, 100, 500, 1,000, 10,000kr
Electricity:	220V, 50Hz, AC

Planning your Trip

Visa requirements: For nationals of Turkey and South Africa. (See also p.6.)

Vaccination requirements: None. (See also p.7.)

Import allowances (see also p.7):

	Cigarettes		Cigars		Tobacco	Spirits		Wine
1)	200	or	50	or	250g	1l	and	2l
2)	(800)	or	(200)	or	(1kg)	(10l)	and	(90l)
1) Passengers from countries outside Europe; Duty-free goods bought in EU countries by European residents.								
2) Non-duty-free goods bought within the EU.								

Perfume: 1) 50g; *Toilet water*: 1) 0.5l;
Gifts: 1) Up to 3,500kr max. value

There are no official restrictions on goods bought non-duty-free within the EU, provided they are for personal use only. The above figures are guidelines to the quantities customs officials will generally find acceptable, so if you are carrying larger quantities you should be prepared to provide proof that the goods are for your personal use.

Currency restrictions: There are no restrictions on the amount of foreign or local currency non-residents can bring into or take out of the country (provided it is declared upon entry).

Climate: Except in the far north, Sweden enjoys a moderately continental climate. Thanks to the warm currents of the Gulf Stream, the country's west coast is mildly maritime. Rain falls mostly in March, April and July, but an umbrella is useful at any time of year.

Some average daily temperatures in Stockholm:

Jan	Apr	July	Oct
-3°C (27°F)	8°C (46°F)	17°C (63°F)	7°C (44°F)

Temperatures often plunge to frigid depths in winter and soar to heatwave level in summer.

Clothing: In spring, a warm raincoat, gloves and hat are needed. In
summer, light- to medium-weight apparel is adequate. Autumn days

are often quite warm, and summer wear will do, but cool evenings call for something extra. In winter, clothing should be warm and cover the body from tip to toe. Boots, gloves and scarves are in order.

Sweden is traditional with regard to business attire. For relaxed daytime functions, colour coordinated dress is acceptable for men, but a dark suit and white shirt are best for more formal occasions and evenings, and a smart dress or suit for women. A dinner jacket or tails can be hired, usually the same day, in all major cities. For women, black is the one colour *not* advisable on formal occasions.

Hotels: Hotels in Sweden enjoy a well-deserved reputation for cleanliness, regardless of category, and are efficiently run. It may be difficult to find accommodation, especially in Stockholm, without advance reservations. A national hotel guide in English, French and German, *Hotels in Sweden*, is available from the Swedish Tourist Board. At the same time find out about the Hotel Check system for cut-price rates at some 250 Swedish hotels. The system operates from mid-June to September and is available only outside Sweden. Hotel booking services are available at major airports and at offices called *hotellcentral* or *rumsförmedling*.

Swedish tourist offices abroad: Copenhagen, The Hague, Hamburg, Helsinki, London, New York, Oslo, Paris, Zurich.

Business Briefing

Economic Background

Main industries: Iron-ore mining, steel, pulp and paper, shipping, electronics, motor vehicles, heavy machinery, construction and engineering, medical instruments, pharmaceuticals, telecommunications equipment, glass, porcelain, timber.

Main agricultural products: Dairy products, meat, grain, potatoes.

Main imports: Oil and by-products, chemical products, semi-manufactured goods, engineering products, textile and clothing, motor vehicles, foodstuffs, fruit, vegetables and tropical products.

Main exports: Machinery, motor vehicles, paper, ships, boats, wood pulp, iron and steel, timber, chemicals.

Principal trading partners: Other EFTA countries, Germany, UK, Denmark, USA, Canada.

GNP: $184.2 billion; per capita: $21,710.

Inflation rate: 2.3% (1994).

Trade fairs: Several important trade fairs and exhibitions are held during the year, such as the International Boat Show in Gothenburg (February) and the International Technology Fair in Stockholm (October). Details can be obtained through Swedish chambers of commerce or consulates.

Selected background reading: A data profile is given in the *Annual Statistical Abstract of Sweden* and the *Monthly Digest of Swedish Statistics*, both published by the Swedish National Central Bureau of Statistics. *The Swedish Economy* is issued three times yearly in English by the National Institute of Economic Research. The Federations of Industry of Denmark, Finland, Norway and Sweden bring out *The Nordic Economic Outlook* semi-annually. The Industrial Institute for Economic and Social Research issues studies on industrial development in Sweden. Most documents contain summaries in English which are available as separate booklets. Other reading matter: *Some Data about Sweden* (Skandinaviska Enskilda Banken), *Swedish Government Administration* (Swedish Institute), *Industry in Sweden* (Federation of Swedish Industries), *Annual Report* (National Swedish Price and Cartel Office), *Current Business in Sweden* (quarterly, Svenska Handelsbanken), *Outlook on the Swedish Economy* (monthly, PKBanken), *Ekonomiskt Perspektiv* (Swedish with 1-page English summary, Skandinaviska Enskilda Banken).

Swedish chambers of commerce abroad: Buenos Aires, Düsseldorf, The Hague, London, Madrid, New York, Oslo, Paris, San Francisco, São Paulo, Sydney.

On the Spot

Office hours: 9am-5pm Monday-Friday. In spring and summer offices close at 3 or 4pm.

Public holidays

Jan 1	New Year's Day	May 1	Labour Day
Jan 6	Epiphany	Dec 25	Christmas Day
		Dec 26	Boxing Day
Movable dates:	Good Friday	Easter Monday	
	Ascension	Whit Monday	
	Midsummer Day (Saturday nearest June 21)		
	All Saints' Day (Saturday between Oct 31 and Nov 6)		

Banks and currency exchange: Banking hours are generally 9.30am-3pm Monday-Friday (some open again in the afternoon one day a week from 4 to 5.30). After hours, it's difficult to change money except at airports. The bank at Arlanda Airport operates daily 7am-10pm and the exchange bureau at the central railway station in Stockholm 8am-9pm. Foreign currency can be changed at stores and some larger hotels, but the rate is not so good.

International banking is dominated by two Stockholm-based banks: Skandinaviska Enskilda Banken and Svenska Handelsbanken. The nation's other principal banks are Götabanken and PKBanken.

Credit cards and traveller's cheques: International credit cards and most traveller's cheques are accepted almost everywhere.

Post and telecommunications: All services are highly reliable.

Post office hours are generally 9am-6pm Monday-Friday, 10am-1pm Saturdays.

The post office at Klarabergsviadukten 63 in Stockholm is open 9.30am-7pm Monday-Friday. Hours at main railway station offices vary. Postage stamps may also be bought at tobacco shops, kiosks, department stores and hotels. Post boxes are yellow.

Public phone and telegraph offices (marked 'Tele') and *Telebutiken* offer telex as well as fax, telegram and telephone services. The main office in Stockholm is located at the central railway station, Centralplan 1. You can also dictate a telegram over the phone. For addresses, consult the *Televerket* entry in the telephone directory.

Virtually all subscribers in Sweden are linked to the automatic telephone network. Direct dialling facilities exist to a large number of other countries. *The Postal Guide for Tourists*, available at all post offices gives information in major European languages.

Some useful numbers:

Emergency (all-purpose, nationwide);   90 000
for ambulance *(ambulansen)*, doctor *(jourhavande läkare)*, dentist *(jourhavande tandläkare)*, fire department *(brandkären)* or police *(polisen)*

Operator (information for all services, nationwide);   90 200
nationwide numbers for international services depend on the country to be called; see *Samtal till Utlandet* (International Calls) listing at beginning of local telephone directories (with English summary).

Tourist information in English, Stockholm;   22 18 40
(daytime only)

Principal area codes: Gothenburg 031, Jönköping 036, Lund 046, Malmö 040, Norrköping 011, Stockholm 08, Umeå 090, Uppsala 018.

Embassies and consulates: Embassies and consulates are listed in the telephone directory under the name of the country or its associated adjective.

Medical care and health: The standard of medical treatment is of the highest. Reciprocal payment agreements exist with certain other countries. English is understood by most doctors and nurses. Medical and pharmaceutical supplies are readily available. In all major cities, at least one pharmacy *(apotek)* remains on duty seven days a week. The address can be obtained from your hotel or by calling 07 975. In case of emergency dial 90 000 nationwide. The call can be placed free from any public phone booth. Tap water is safe to drink.

Services: Translators and interpreters are listed in the yellow pages (*Gula Sidorna*) under *Översättare*; or try, in Stockholm: Sveriges Exportråds Språktjänst, Artillerigatan 42, Box 5513, 114 85 Stockholm; tel. (08) 783 85 00, fax 663 93 39 and in Gothenburg: Västsvenska Handelskammaren, Mässans Gata 18, Box 5253, 40225 Göteborg; tel. (031) 83 59 00, fax 83 59 36. Secretarial services are given under *Skrivbyrå*. Secretarial agencies have photocopying services, as do most post offices.

Newspapers: The country's principal newspapers are *Svenska Dagbladet*, *Dagens Nyheter* and *Expressen* (Stockholm) and *Göteborgs Posten* (Gothenburg). Major European papers, including the Paris-edited *International Herald Tribune*, are available at news-stands one or two days after publication. *Stockholm This Week* is distributed free.

Transport

Air – international: Stockholm is Sweden's principal gateway, though international flights also operate on a smaller scale into some provincial airports, notably Gothenburg and Malmö.

Air – domestic: Most parts of the country are served by air links.

Rail: Rail travel can be highly recommended for business travel in Sweden. Trains are punctual and comfortable, with first- and second-class compartments available. Long-distance trains usually have a (no-smoking) cafeteria car. Couchettes and sleeping cars are also available. The new InterCity trains have telephones. Seat reservations are necessary on express trains (*expresståg*).

Within Sweden visitors can take advantage of various rail bargains. The Nordic Tourist Ticket allows 21 days of unlimited travel by train throughout Sweden, Denmark, Finland and Norway. For Eurailpass, see p.10.

Local public transport: All major cities have excellent public-transport networks, including, in Stockholm, a very efficient and modern underground (subway) system. In the capital, subway, commuter train and bus system makes it easy to get around the city and its suburbs from about 5am to 2am. Subway stations are indicated by a **313**

blue 'T'. Special one- and three-day tourist tickets and multi-unit cards are sold in the Pressbyrån kiosks. Buses and trams in Gothenburg have a machine inside for validating tickets beforehand. A special Conference Ticket exists in Stockholm for participants in meetings and conventions (that have been announced in advance to the authorities), valid for unlimited travel on the city's public transport, airport and other special bus lines.

Long-distance buses: Express coaches operated by Swedish Railways and private coach lines link every major centre. Although inexpensive, they are time-consuming. Frequency varies according to the day of week and season. Advance booking is possible.

Taxis: Cabs can be ordered by telephone or picked up at taxi ranks. Tip 10%. Theoretically you can flag them down anywhere in Stockholm but this rarely works. When a taxi is available the vacant sign (*Ledig*) is lit. Cabs are difficult to find during rush hours and on rainy days. It is possible to reserve one in advance.

Car rental: International and local agencies operate, and some have airport desks. You can find addresses in the business telephone directory under *Biluthyrning*. Chauffeur-driven cars are also available.

Driving in Sweden: *Sweden – A Motorist's Paradise* issued by the Swedish Tourist Board provides a wealth of information for the visiting motorist. Seat belts must be worn in the front and in the back, and you must carry a red-reflector warning triangle. Dipped headlights must be kept on, even in daytime. Routine spot checks to inspect documents and the condition of vehicles are quite common. Blood alcohol limit is a strictly enforced 20mg/100ml. Exceed this and you could end up in jail. Speed limits: in built-up areas, 50kph (31mph); on motorways (expressways), 90kph (56mph) or 110kph (63mph); and on other roads as signposted. Near schools there is a limit of 30kph (19mph).

Sweden is excellent motoring country, criss-crossed by a network of good-quality arterial roads. For car breakdowns, phone

(08) 24 10 00 (*Larmtjänst*) in the Stockholm area and (020) 91 00 40

elsewhere in Sweden. Most large service stations have a mechanic on duty during the day. Fuel (petrol/gas) available is normal (93 octane), super (96-98 octane), lead-free and diesel.

The phone number of the Stockholm headquarters of the Royal Automobile Association, Gyllenstiernsgatan 4, S-115 26 Stockholm is (08) 660 00 55; fax (08) 662 74 84.

Some distances from Stockholm: Uppsala 70km (43 miles), Norr-köping 170km (145 miles), Gothenburg 465km (290 miles), Malmö 655km (305 miles).

Social customs: If invited home, take flowers to your hostess the first time (or send them afterwards). Swedes enjoy a bit of formality at dinner. It's customary for the host to welcome his guests with a little ceremony of lifting his glass and wishing each person *skål* ('to your health') while looking him briefly in the eyes. A man usually toasts the lady on his right and the lady on his left. Don't *skål* the host or hostess, and don't put down the glass before everyone has looked at everyone else. (That goes for each time a *skål* is pronounced.) The male guest of honour is seated on the hostess' left, and at the end of the meal is expected to express the thanks on behalf of the guests. If a woman is the guest of honour (seated to the host's left and with no other women present) common sense dictates that she thank the host for the dinner. Giving thanks for the dinner afterwards is initiated by tapping a knife against a glass.

Hints for business: Swedes are formal people. Stay on a last-name basis until your Swedish business partner makes the move to more familiarity. Swedes like to plan things. Don't ask for last-minute appointments, and be thoughtful towards secretaries and aides. Letters marked 'private' stay that way. July and August – the summer holiday period – are months to avoid going to Sweden on business.

Foreign chambers of commerce in Sweden: British, Finnish, French, German, Israeli, Italian, Macao, Polish.

Crime and theft: Normal precautions are in order. Stay away from illegal gambling places.

315

After Hours

Food and drink: At a restaurant look for *dagens rätt* (day's special) if you want to get your meal fast and at a good price. Reindeer steak, *gravlax* (salmon cured with dill) and herring dishes are popular specialities. In summer Swedish cloudberries are available as a dessert. Certain fish or seafood are seasonal, such as crayfish which is served as a party speciality along with cheese. The latter is often eaten with *knäckebröd* (crispbread, hardtack). Pea soup with bacon is a favourite Thursday dish, while another is *Janssons frestelse* ('Jansson's temptation'), a casserole of potatoes, marinated sprats, cream and onions.

Beer, wine and spirits are available in bars, but drinks bought there are very expensive. A state-owned monopoly, *Systembolaget*, sells wines and hard liquor. Beer can be bought in grocery stores. Swedes usually drink only *lättöl* (light beer) for lunch. Try the Swedish after-dinner *punsch* with coffee – but be aware that it is quite powerful.

Mealtimes: lunch 11.30am-2 pm, dinner 6-10 pm.

Entertainment: Discos and dance spots are listed in tourist brochures and the daily newspapers under *Dans*. Cinemas usually show foreign films in their original version. Ballet, concerts and opera performances are frequently staged.

Taxes, service charges and tipping: Service is usually included in hotel and restaurant bills. Tipping is optional. Recommendations: porters 5kr (optional); taxi drivers 10%; cloakroom attendants 3-6kr, or charges posted; barbers and hairdressers optional.

Sports and recreation: Golf and squash are available for visitors at modest fees, but facilities must be booked in advance. The great outdoors is at the gates of every town, and winter sports – particularly cross-country skiing – are easily accessible in season.

The most popular spectator sports are soccer and ice-hockey, followed by tennis and horse-racing.

TV and radio: All broadcasting is in Swedish except for programmes geared to Finnish people and immigrant workers. Films on TV are shown in their original language, often English.

What to buy: Good buys include glassware, porcelain, silver and jewellery, Lapland souvenirs (eg items of clothing), carved objects, wooden Dala horses.

Shopping hours are generally 9.30 or 10am to 6pm, Monday-Friday, and until 1pm on Saturdays. In winter, department stores stay open later on certain days and are occasionally open on Sundays.

Cities and Sights

STOCKHOLM (*Telephone area code 08*)

Airport: Arlanda (41km/26 miles from city centre), international; duty-free shop. Bus service to town terminal, Cityterminalen, near the railway station. Limousine service.

Tourist information offices
Swedish Tourist Board: PO Box 7473, 103 92 Stockholm. Tourist Centre: Sverigehuset (Sweden House), Hamngatan 27/Kungsträd-garden; tel. 789 20 00 (789 24 90 on weekends), fax 21 35 55. (Mailing address: Box 7542, 103 93 Stockholm.)

Chamber of commerce and other business organizations
Chamber of commerce: Västra Trädgårdsgatan 9; tel. 613 18 00, fax 11 24 32.

Swedish Employers' Association: Blasieholmshamnen 4A, Stockholm (mailing address: PO Box 16120, 103 23 Stockholm); tel. 76 26 00, fax 762 62 90, telex 19923 saf s.

Federation of Swedish Industries: Storgatan 19, Stockholm (mailing address: PO Box 5501, 114 85 Stockholm); tel. 783 80 00, fax 662 35 95, telex 19990 swedind s.

Import Promotion Office for Products from Developing Countries: Nybrogatan 6, Box 5028, 102 41 Stockholm; tel. 666 11 90, fax 662 74 57.

Ministries for Foreign Affairs and Commerce, PO Box 161 21, 103 23 Stockholm; tel. 786 60 00, fax 723 11 76.

Swedish International Development Authority: Birger Jarlsgatan 61, 10525 Stockholm; tel. 728 51 00, fax 673 21 41, telex 11450. **317**

The **Stockholm Card**: *Stockholmskortet* offers visitors the chance to see the city at a fair price. Similar in appearance to a credit card, it allows the holder free entry to about 70 museums, castles and other sights, free public transport, including sightseeing buses and boats, reduced price excursion to Drottningholm Palace, etc. Used to the full, it represents a considerable bargain. The pass is valid for one adult and two children and is available for one to three days. It is available at Sweden House, Central Station and numerous other places.

Sightseeing: Kaknäs Tower, city hall (stadshuset), old town, Skeppsholmen, Djurgarden, Skansen, Wasa Warship Museum, Börsen, royal palace (kungliga slottet), Riddarhuset, parliament building (riksdagshuset).

Museums: Liljevalchs art gallery, Moderna Museet, National Museum, Nordic Museum, Strindberg Museum, Prins Eugens Waldemarsudde.

Excursions: Drottningholm, Stockholm archipelago cruise, Uppsala.

GOTHENBURG (*Telephone area code 031*)

Airport: Landvetter (24km/15 miles from city centre), international; duty-free shop. Bus service to central station.

Tourist information office: Kungsportsplatsen 2; tel. 10 07 50.

Chamber of commerce: Mässans Gata 18, Box 5233, 402 25 Gothenburg; tel. 53 59 00, fax 83 59 36.

Sightseeing: Antikhallarna, Botanical Garden, Carolus Rex, Cathedral, Elfsborg Fortress, Feskekörkan, Fish Harbour, Götaplatsen, Keillers Park, Kronhuset, Kronhusbadarna, Liseberg Amusement Park, Old Örgryte church, Queen Christina's hunting lodge, Sjömanstornet, Slottsskogen.

Museums: Museum of Art, Ship Museum, East India House.

318 **Excursions**: Tjörn Bridge, Marstrand, Kungälv, Nääs Manor.

MALMÖ (*Telephone area code 040*)

Airport: Sturup (31km/19 miles from city centre), international; duty-free shop. Bus services to central station; regular hydrofoil and bus as well as hovercraft services also operate to Copenhagen Airport in Denmark.

Tourist information office: Skeppsbron (in the main post office building); tel. 30 01 50.

Chamber of commerce: Skeppsbron 2, 211 20 Malmö; tel. 73 550, fax 11 86 09.

Sightseeing: Lilla Torg, Hedmanska Garden, Faxeska Huset, Jörgen Kocks Hus, Rosenvingeska Huset, Flensburgska Huset, Thottska Huset, Kompanihuset and Kompanigården, town hall, Residence, St Gertrude House block, St Peter's church, Sjömansgarden, Hyllie water tower, Översten restaurant (for view).

Museums: Malmö Museum, Carriage Museum, Art Gallery.

Excursions: Malmö Runt, Rundan, Torup Castle.

Some Useful Expressions in Swedish

good morning/afternoon	god morgon/dag
good evening/night	god kväll/natt
good-bye	adjö
yes/no	ja/nej
please/thank you	var så god/tack
excuse me	ursäkta mig
you're welcome	ingen orsak
where/when/how	var/när/hur
how long/how far	hur länge/hur langt
yesterday/today/tomorrow	igår/idag/i morgon
day/week/month/year	dag/vecka/manad/ar
left/right	vänster/höger
up/down	uppe/nere
good/bad	bra/dålig
big/small	stor/liten
cheap/expensive	billig/dyr
hot/cold	varm/kall
old/new	gammal/ny
open/closed	öppen/stängd
early/late	tidig/sen
easy/difficult	enkel/svår
Does anyone here speak English/French/German?	Finns det någon här som talar engelska/franska/tyska?
What does this mean?	Vad betyder det här?
I don't understand.	Jag förstår inte.
Do you take credit cards/ traveller's cheques?	Kan jag betala med kreditkort/resechecker?
Waiter!/Waitress!	Vaktmästarn!/Fröken!
Where are the toilets?	Var är toaletten?
I'd like…	Jag skulle vilja ha…
How much is that?	Hur mycket kostar det?
Help me please.	Var snäll och hjälp mig.

Switzerland

Type of government:	Federal State (Swiss confederation), multi-party, decentralized
Member of:	EFTA, GATT, OECD
Population:	7 million
Area:	41,288sq km (15,941sq miles)
Capital:	Berne (*Bern*, 136,000/GUA 285,000)
Other major cities:	Zurich (*Zürich*, 345,000/GUA 710,000)
	Basle (*Basel*, 174,000/GUA 365,000)
	Geneva (*Genève*, 170,000/GUA 335,000)
	Lausanne (125,000/GUA 225,000)
Languages:	German (64%), French (19%), Italian (7.5%) and Romansh (1%); English is widely spoken in business circles.
Religion:	Catholic (46%), Protestant (40%)
Time zone:	GMT+1, EST+6; DST (Apr-Sep)
Currency:	Swiss franc (in German: Franken, in French: franc, abbr. Fr or F) = 100 centimes (in German: Rappen, in French: centimes) Coins: 5, 10, 20, 50 centimes; Fr½, 1, 2, 5 Notes: Fr10, 20, 50, 100, 500, 1,000
Electricity:	220V, 50Hz, AC

Planning your Trip

Visa requirements: For nationals of Turkey. (See also p.6.)

Vaccination requirements: None. (See also p.7.)

Import allowances (see also p.7):

	Cigarettes		Cigars		Tobacco	Spirits		Wine
European residents	200	or	50	or	250g	1l	and	2l
Non-European residents	400	or	100	or	500g	1l	and	2l

Gifts (including perfume): Up to Fr100 max. value

Currency restrictions: None. (See also p.7.)

Climate: Switzerland has a moderately continental climate with warm summers and generally cold winters. Severity increases markedly with altitude. Limited areas in the canton of Ticino and along the Lake of Geneva enjoy milder weather. Precipitation is well distributed throughout the year. Snow is only rarely a problem in city streets, though winter tyres are advised. Several Alpine passes are closed for varying periods between November and June.

Some average temperatures in Geneva and Zurich:

	Jan	Apr	July	Oct
Zurich	-1°C (30°F)	8°C (46°F)	17°C (63°F)	8°C (46°F)
Geneva	0°C (33°F)	9°C (48°F)	18°C (64°F)	9°C (48°F)

Clothing: In summer, medium- to light-weight clothing is adequate. If a trip to the mountains is planned, a sweater is advised. In winter, a warm overcoat is necessary. A conservative suit and tie, or an equivalent outfit for women, should be worn on business occasions. Rainwear may be needed at any time.

Hotels: The *Swiss Hotel Guide*, issued each year by the Swiss Hotel Association, lists hotels in all categories.

Though a room of some category will usually be obtainable at any **322** time of year in each major city, you may have difficulty getting into your favourite hotel during conferences, festivals, fairs and both summer and winter tourist seasons, so plan ahead.

Airports and main railway stations have hotel reservation phones or accommodation offices which will assist you. Tourist offices can also help.

Swiss tourist offices abroad: Amsterdam, Berlin, Brussels, Cairo, Chicago, Düsseldorf, Frankfurt, Hamburg, Hong Kong, London, Los Angeles, Madrid, Milan, Munich, New York, Paris, Rome, Stockholm, Tel Aviv, Tokyo, Toronto, Vienna.

Business Briefing

Economic Background

Main industries: Machinery, appliances and metal products, chemicals and pharmaceuticals, watches and clocks, precision instruments, textile yarns and fabrics, chocolate, tourism.

Main agricultural products: Cheese, dairy products, livestock, wheat, barley, sugar beet, potatoes, fruit.

Main imports: Foodstuffs, agricultural and forestry products, oil, lubricants, textiles, clothing, paper, leather goods, construction materials, metal products, machinery, motor vehicles, chemicals.

Main exports: Precision instruments, watches, jewellery, machinery, electronics equipment, metal products, textiles.

Principal trading partners: Germany, France, USA, Italy, UK.

GNP: $198 billion; per capita: $30,270.

Inflation rate: 4.1% (1994).

Trade fairs: Many commercial exhibitions take place annually. Principal among them are the International Motor Show in Geneva in March, the Agriculture, Trade and Industry fair (Comptoir de Berne) in Berne each spring, the Swiss national fair (Comptoir Suisse) of the nation's agricultural and industrial products in Lausanne every September and OLMA (an agricultural fair) in St Gall in October.

Selected background reading: *Business Guide to Switzerland* (bi-monthly, GTS Publishing Ltd, Basel) *Schweizer Almanach* (Transbooks) in German and *Schweizer Brevier* (Geographischer Verlag) in English, French and German provide much useful background data. *Complete Guide to Swiss Bank Accounts* (McGraw), *Switzerland: An International Banking and Finance Center* (Dowden, Hutchinson & Ross). Leading banks publish regular statistical surveys in various languages.

Swiss chambers of commerce abroad: Argentina, Australia, Austria, Belgium, Brazil, Canada, Chile, Colombia, Czech Republic, Denmark, Finland, France, Germany, Hungary, Ireland, Italy, Japan, Mexico, Morocco, Netherlands, Peru, Poland, USA, Venezuela.

On the Spot

Office hours: Variable between 8am and 5pm Monday-Friday, with 1-2 hours lunchtime closure.

Public holidays

Jan 1	New Year's Day	**Movable dates**:	Good Friday*
May 1	Labour Day*	Easter Monday*	
Aug 1	National Day	Ascension	
Dec 25	Christmas Day	Whit Monday*	
Dec 26	St Stephen's Day*	*celebrated in most cantons	

On August 1, the Swiss National Day, some banks and shops are closed in the afternoon; in some places the whole day.

The calendar of holidays varies from one canton to another. The most important holidays observed in some cantons are January 2 and Corpus Christi.

Banks and currency exchange: Most of Switzerland's banks are open weekdays from 8.30am to 12pm and from 2 to 4.30, 5 or 5.30pm. One day a week branches keep later hours, until 6 or

6.30pm. In Zurich banks start at 8.15am, remaining open without a break till 6pm on Thursdays, and 4.30pm on the other four workdays. Currency-exchange offices at airports and the larger railway stations do business from 6.30am to 9pm (sometimes even later) every day of the week. A money-changing machine at Zurich airport takes notes in four currencies – French, German, Italian and English (£10 and £20).

Principal banks: Union Bank of Switzerland, Swiss Bank Corporation, Swiss Credit Bank and Swiss Volksbank.

Credit cards and traveller's cheques: International credit cards are widely accepted in major establishments, although smaller establishments don't like them. Payment can be made in traveller's cheques and eurocheques almost everywhere.

Post and telecommunications: Post offices display a distinctive sign bearing the letters PTT. In addition to normal postal business, they handle telephone calls, telegrams and much of the population's bill-paying. Most post offices are open from around 7.30am to 6 (small branches) or 6.30pm with a break for lunch, and on Saturday mornings from 7.30 to 11am. In bigger towns the main post office does not close at midday, and a window may be open until 10pm or even later, and at weekends, for express or special delivery mail. After hours stamps can be obtained from vending machines outside post offices and some train stations, as well as in souvenir shops and at hotel reception desks. Letter boxes are yellow.

Main post offices accept telegrams, telex and fax messages from 7.30am to 10pm. To send a telegram by telephone, call 110 from your hotel (round the clock). The charge will be added to the bill.

The Swiss telephone network is fully automated and efficient, and street-corner coin telephones are kept in good working order. Coin phones carry instructions in four languages (including English). International calls can be made from public phone booths. For overseas calls, many phones have a 5-franc slot and a slot for a credit card (*taxcard* – sold at post offices). You can also make such calls from a post office, where payment is made at the window afterwards. Charges for calls from hotels are extremely high.

Some useful numbers: (valid in most areas)

Ambulance	144	Operator (for int. calls)	114
English-speaking	157 5014	Police (emergency only)	117
information service (all areas)		Road conditions	163
Fire	118	Stock exchange bulletin	166
Inquiries (inland)	111	Telegrams	110
Inquiries (int.)	191	Time	161
Motoring assistance	140	Weather	162

Principal area codes: Baden 056, Basle 061, Berne 031, Geneva 022, Lausanne 021, St Gall 071, Winterthur 052, Zurich 01.

Embassies and consulates: Listings for embassies and consulates are found in telephone directories under *Ambassades* and *Consulats* or *Konsulate* (in German-speaking areas), and (in French-speaking areas) consulates are given under *Consulats*. In the Geneva telephone book consult the headings *Délégations* and *Missions permanentes auprès des organisations internationales* for diplomatic representations at the United Nations.

Medical care and health: The standard of medical treatment is high, and so are fees. All hospitals and clinics are accustomed to dealing with foreigners, and English is often spoken. Medicine and pharmaceutical supplies are readily available. All pharmacies display the addresses of those on duty after hours; the local press, police stations, tourist offices and most hotels also provide this information. Tap water is safe to drink.

Services: Hotels are able to provide information about secretarial services, translators or interpreters. There are various employment agencies specializing in temporary work. Look in the business phone book (*Die Gelben Seiten* in German, *Les Pages Jaunes* in French) under *Temporäre Arbeit* or *Travail temporaire*. Interpreters and translators are listed under *Dolmetscher* or *Übersetzungsbüros* in German and *Traduction, bureaux de* or *Interprètes* in French, respectively. Photocopying facilities are widely available in major post offices and stations, department **326** stores and printshops; your hotel will direct you to the nearest one.

Newspapers: In the absence of any truly national newspapers, apart from tabloids, each major city has its own, which, however, are on sale throughout the country. Leading dailies are: *Basler Zeitung* (Basle), *Der Bund* and *Berner Zeitung* (Berne), *Journal de Genève* in Geneva, *Le Nouveau Quotidien* in Lausanne and *Neue Zürcher Zeitung* and *Tages-Anzeiger* in Zurich. Newspapers from many European countries can be found at major news-stands. British dailies are widely available along with the *International Herald Tribune* (printed in Zurich), as well as magazines of all kinds.

Transport

Air – international: Zurich has a lead over Geneva as the country's major gateway. Basle also receives a number of international flights, Berne only a few.

Air – domestic: Within the country, flights operate Zurich-Geneva, Zurich-Basle, Geneva-Basle, Lugano-Zurich, Lugano-Basle, Lugano-Geneva. Except sometimes in autumn and winter when weather conditions may delay flights, they are a favoured, if expensive, means of local business travel.

Rail: Trains, with first- and second-class compartments, are comfortable, punctual, and ideal for business travel. They run at fixed intervals with hourly service between all major stations on the network. Tickets can be purchased from ticket windows or machines, as well as on the train – except those displaying an eye symbol. There are no conductors – only the occasional checker – on these services. Unlimited-travel, flat-rate passes exist for varying periods. Rail tickets can in many cases be used in conjunction with lake steamers.

Swiss Pass: An open possibility for those with the time: criss-cross the country with a Swiss Pass, valid for 4, 8, 15 days or 1 month of unlimited travel on the federal railway network (16,000km), plus scores of private railways, boat lines, 120 postal bus routes and on local buses and trams in 36 cities. Good for discounts on mountain railways, aerial cableways, etc. the card offers convenience and significant savings for travellers resident outside Switzerland. Apply **327**

for the card (show your passport) at travel agencies or Swiss tourist offices abroad, and at major railway stations in Switzerland. The Swiss Flexi Pass allows 3 days free travel (as above) within a period of 15 days. Contact a Swiss Tourist Office for details of the Family Card and Swiss Card. For Eurailpass, see p.10.

Local public transport: Bus, tram or trolley-bus services in the major cities are efficient and punctual, though usually crowded and uncomfortable during rush-hours. Tickets are purchased at automatic dispensing machines with instructions posted in four languages including English. Hold on to your ticket in case an inspector makes a spot check. In Zurich you can also get around rapidly by the modern S-Bahn system.

Taxis: Metered cabs can be hailed, taken at taxi ranks or ordered by phone. The tip is generally included in the fare.

Car rental: International and local agencies operate throughout Switzerland, some with airport offices. A credit card is the preferred means of payment. Chauffeur-driven cars are also available.

Driving in Switzerland: A red-reflector warning triangle must be carried for use in case of breakdown. If you normally wear glasses when driving, you are required to have a second pair with you. Blood alcohol limit is 80mg/100ml. Speed limits: generally 50kph (31mph) in built-up areas, 120kph (75mph) on motorways (expressways) and 80kph (50mph) on other roads. The use of seat belts is compulsory. Roads are well maintained. Before driving in mountain areas in winter, check on road conditions (tel. 163 – information given in German or French). Lane discipline is generally good. In case of breakdown, call 140 for the Touring-Club Suisse (TCS). Rapid motorways link most towns (and form part of the European network), but in the mountain areas, in spite of good ordinary roads, it can take time to get around. On mountain roads priority is given to postal buses, otherwise to the ascending vehicle. Sounding your horn is recommended on blind corners of mountain roads. Motorists who use the motorways must purchase a sticker (valid for the current year) to

be displayed on the windscreen.

Most cities have parking meters and blue zones, where parking is limited to one hour. In red zones you can park for up to 15 hours. Motorways are provided with emergency telephones at regular intervals. Fuel (petrol/gas) available is lead-free (91 and 95 octane), super (98 octane) and diesel.

Some distances from Zurich: Basle 85km (53 miles), Berne 120km (75 miles), Lugano 220km (135 miles), Geneva 275km (170 miles).

Social customs: The Swiss, though friendly, tend to be reserved. Discretion is highly valued in all circumstances. Punctuality is important for any occasion, business or social. Never go onto a first-name basis unless the Swiss takes the initiative. Being invited to a Swiss home for dinner is rare, but for the occasion don't forget flowers or chocolates for the hostess.

Hints for business: The Swiss are typically very cautious and conservative. But once they decide to buy what you're selling, they'll be clients indefinitely. High-pressure tactics on your part could elicit a quick 'no' which might never be changed. Reliability, attention to quality and respect of contractual agreements are hallmarks of the nation's business practices. Appointments are essential. It's best to avoid the August holiday period for business travel.

Foreign chambers of commerce in Switzerland: American, Arab, Argentinian, Austrian, Baltic States, Belgian/Luxembourg, Brazilian, British, Bulgarian, Czech, Danish, Dutch, Finnish, French, German, Hong Kong, Indian, Iranian, Israeli, Italian, Japanese, Latin American, Polish, Romanian, Russian, Slovakian, Spanish, Taiwanese, Thai, Turkish.

Crime and theft: Switzerland remains one of the world's safer countries, but normal precautions are in order.

After Hours

Food and drink: Swiss cuisine is heavily influenced by its French, German and Italian neighbours. Some specialities are, in German-speaking regions: *Egli* (perch), *Felchen* (white fish), *Geschnetzeltes* **329**

Kalbfleisch (veal in cream sauce), *Leberspiesschen* (skewered liver), *Bündner Fleisch* (paper-thin slices of dried beef), *Rösti* (hashed-brown potatoes); and, in French-speaking areas: *omble chevalier* (char), *truite* (trout), *perche*, (perch), *entrecôte* (rib-eye steak), *tournedos* (filet steak). Cheese fondue (a pot of bubbling cheese, white wine, kirsch and a touch of garlic) is universally available but better kept for informal occasions rather than business evenings.

Some local white wines can rival the best of France or Germany. Red wine is also produced. Most bars stock both Swiss and foreign beers and liquors. Note that exotic drinks and cocktails will be considerably higher priced in this country. Try some local pre-dinner drinks at a fraction of the price: *blanc-cassis* (white wine with blackberry liqueur), *pastis* (aniseed liqueur), *Campari* (a bitter tonic) or any of the wide range of fruit brandies.

Mealtimes: lunch noon-2pm, dinner 7-9pm.

Entertainment: Though nightclubs will hardly remind you of Paris, they are usually lively. Switzerland has a long tradition of fine symphony concerts in all major cities. Theatre is in the language of the local area. Basle and Lausanne have ballet companies of international renown, while both Geneva and Zurich have gained a good reputation in the opera world. Cinemas usually show foreign films with a German or French soundtrack, though in resort and metropolitan areas many films are shown in the original language.

Each major city produces a weekly tourist brochure featuring entertainment and attractions, available free of charge at hotels and tourist offices.

Taxes, service charges and tipping: Hotel and restaurant bills come complete with all charges and tipping has in principle been phased out, but an extra coin or two is usually appropriate for good service and will be appreciated. Service is included in hairdressing establishments, so any tip is strictly optional.

Sports and recreation: Facilities are plentiful for swimming, cycling, boating, tennis, squash and golf. The legendary Swiss countryside, never more than a few minutes away from any city, offers unparalleled hiking and climbing possibilities. Winter-sport possibilities, multiple and various, need no introduction.

Popular spectator sports are alpine ski racing, ice hockey, soccer, basketball, tennis, rowing, motorcycle and bicycle racing, and Swiss-style wrestling.

TV and radio: Radio and TV programmes in French, German and Italian can be received all over the country. Radio broadcasts are put out in English on short-wave several times a day and on channel 5 at noon, and BBC news is broadcast on channel 1 at 7pm.

What to buy: Ideal gifts to take home are watches, gold and silver jewellery, fabrics, chocolate, cheese, Swiss army knives, wooden toys, fruit brandies, stamps, clocks.

Shopping hours are 8 or 9am to 6.30pm, Monday-Friday, and until 4 or 5pm on Saturdays. Some smaller shops close at lunchtime. One evening is usually set aside for late shopping, varying according to city. Some establishments are closed Monday mornings or Wednesday or Thursday afternoons. Neighbourhood stores often close at lunchtimes.

Cities and Sights

BERNE (*Telephone area code 031*)
Airport: Belpmoos (10km/6 miles from city centre), international for flights to London Gatwick; duty-free shop. Regular bus service to Berne centre. There's also direct rail connection between Berne and Zurich-Kloten airport every 60 minutes.

Tourist information office: Central railway station; tel. 22 76 76.

Chamber of commerce: Gutenbergstrasse 1, 3001 Berne; tel. 382 17 11, fax 382 17 15.

Sightseeing: Arcaded streets, old fountains, patrician houses, bear pit, cathedral, Zytglogge (clock tower).

Museums: Berne Historical Museum, Kunstmuseum (art gallery). **331**

Excursions: Bernese Oberland (Grindelwald, Interlaken, Gstaad, Mürren), Jungfrau summit (4,158m/11,333ft), Emmental country, Aarberg, Murten.

ZURICH (*Telephone area code 01*)

Airport: Kloten (12km/8 miles from city centre), international: duty-free shop. Frequent rail service to main station, a 15-minute trip. Also direct trains from the airport to other Swiss cities.

Tourist information office: Headquarters of the Swiss National Tourist Office: Bellariastrasse 38, 8038 Zurich; tel. 288 11 11, fax 288 12 05. Tourist office: Bahnhofbruecke 1; tel. 211 40 00.

Chamber of commerce: Bleicherweg 5, 8022 Zurich; tel. 221 07 37, fax 211 76 15.

Sightseeing: Fraumünster, St Peterskirche, guild-halls, Lindenhof, Bahnhofstrasse, Niederdorf (old town), Lake Zurich.

Museums: Kunsthaus, Swiss National Museum.

Excursions: Lake and river cruise, Zug, Lucerne, Rapperswil, Appenzell, St. Gall, Schaffhausen.

BASLE (*Telephone area code 061*)

Airport: Basle/Mulhouse (12km/7 miles from city centre), international; duty-free shop. Airport bus service to railway station.

Tourist information office: Schifflaende 5, 4001, Basle; tel. 261 50 50.

Chamber of commerce: St Alban-Graben 8, 4001 Basle; tel. 272 18 88, fax 272 62 28.

Sightseeing: Old town (14th-century cathedral), terrace overlooking Rhine, 16th-century Rathaus (city hall), medieval fountains, squares.

Museum: Kunstmuseum.

Excursions: Solothurn, Augst (Roman ruins), Rhine River cruise, Black Forest (Germany), Alsace (France).

GENEVA (*Telephone area code 022*)

Airport: Cointrin (5km/3 miles from city centre), international; duty-free shop. Frequent direct train service to Geneva's main station (a 6-minute trip), to Zurich airport and to other Swiss cities.

Tourist information office: Tour de l'Ile, 1211 Geneve 11; tel. 310 50 31. Gare Cornavin (main railway station), 1201 Genève; tel. 738 52 00.

Chamber of commerce: Boulevard du Théâtre 4, 1211 Genève 11; tel. 311 53 33.

Sightseeing: Old town (St. Peter's cathedral with view from north tower, town hall, patrician houses), Reformation monument, United Nations area.

Museums: Red Cross Museum, Ariana Museum, Petit Palais, Museum of Musical Instruments.

Excursions: Boat trip on Lake of Geneva to Lausanne, Vevey, Montreux (Chillon castle), or, alternatively, a drive along the northern shore; Chamonix and Mont Blanc (France).

For some useful expressions in French, see page 116.
For some useful expressions in German, see page 135.
For some useful expressions in Italian, see page 193.

Turkey

Type of government:	Republic, multi-party, centralized
Member of:	GATT, IBRD, IDA, IFC, IMF, OECD
Population:	57 million
Area:	779,450sq km (300, 946sq m)
Capital:	Ankara (2.56m)
Other major cities:	Istanbul (6.6m)
	Izmir (1.76m)
	Adana (916,000)
Language:	Turkish is the offical language. English or German are widely spoken in business circles.
Religion:	Moslem (99%); small Christian and Jewish minorities exist, particularly in Istanbul and Izmir.
Time zone:	GMT+2, EST+7; DST (Apr-Sep)
Currency:	Turkish lira (abbr. L)
	Coins: 100, 500, 1000, 2,500, 5,000L
	Notes: 1,000, 5,000, 20,000, 50,000, 100,000, 250,000, 500,000, 1,000,000L
Electricity:	Generally 220V, 50Hz, AC; 110V may be found in Istanbul.

Planning your Trip

Visa requirements: For nationals of Portugal. Nationals of Austria, Ireland, Italy, Spain and the UK can obtain a visa with payment on arrival, though it may be advisable to check the situation before departure. (See also p.6.).

Vaccination requirements: None; however, a potential malaria risk exists from March to November, so precautions are advisable during this period. (See also p.7.)

Import allowances (see also p.7):

Cigarettes		Cigars		Tobacco	Spirits	Wine
200	or	50	or	200 g	*	*

*   5l in opened bottles, 3l of which may be whisky and 2l may be
    rakī/local drinks.

Tape recorders, transistor radios and similar items should be registered in the traveller's passport to ensure free export. The purchase and/or export of antiquities is prohibited.

Currency restrictions: Any amount of local currency may be imported. Foreign currency must be declared when entering the country so as to facilitate re-export. Local currency up to the equivalent of US $5,000, and foreign currency up to the amount imported, may be taken out of the country. (See also p.7.)

Climate: On the inland plateau, the climate is dry, with hot summers and cold winters. The western and southern coastal plains follow a Mediterranean pattern. Rainfall, mainly in winter, is much heavier in Istanbul and Izmir than in Ankara, where snow and smog are the seasonal hazards.

Some average temperatures:

	Jan	Apr	July	Oct
Ankara	0°C (32°F)	11°C (52°F)	23°C (74°F)	13°C (54°F)
Istanbul	5°C (41°F)	12°C (52°F)	23°C (74°F)	16°C (59°F)
Izmir	9°C (46°F)	16°C (59°F)	28°C (80°F)	20°C (64°F)

Clothing: In summer, tropical clothing is necessary in southern areas, and light-weight clothing inland and in the north. In spring and autumn, evenings can be chilly. Winter calls for warm clothing in most parts of the country, though a heavy overcoat is needed only in

Ankara and other inland areas. Turkish businessmen and officials tend to wear conservative business suits, though they are used to the idea that foreigners may be less formal.

Hotels: Most main towns have either first- or second-class hotels. Luxury establishments are virtually confined to Ankara, Istanbul and Izmir. Thanks to the construction of a number of new hotels in recent years, accommodation is generally no problem.

Turkish tourist offices abroad: Amsterdam, Brussels, Copenhagen, Frankfurt, Jeddah, Kuwait, London, Madrid, New York, Paris, Rome, Stockholm, Tokyo, Vienna, Zurich.

Business Briefing

Economic Background
Main industries: Iron and steel, textiles, sugar refining, cement, paper and glass manufacturing.

Main agricultural products: Cereals, tobacco, cotton, nuts, figs, grapes and other fruit, livestock.

Main imports: Machinery, raw materials, transport equipment, petroleum.

Main exports: Fruit, nuts and vegetables, textiles, clothing, glass and leather products, carpets, industrial products.

Principal trading partners: Germany, France, Iraq, USA, UK, Italy.

GNP: $74.7 billion; per capita: $1,360.

Inflation rate: 65.5% (1993).

Trade fairs: The International Trade Fair at Izmir in August/September is the country's most important, though all but a few of the visitors are ordinary members of the public. Some 50 countries participate.

Selected background reading: The Devlet Statistik Enstitüsü in Ankara publishes the *Monthly Bulletin of Statistics* in English covering manufacturing, imports, exports, construction and prices. The bulletin is summarized annually in the *Statistical Yearbook of Turkey*. The Istanbul Chamber of Commerce produces a quarterly survey, *Price Indices*, giving details of various commodities and general cost-of-living indices. *Area Handbook for the Republic of Turkey* (US Government Printing Office) is useful for a general overview. The Turkish Central Bank also publishes an annual economic report.

Turkish chambers of commerce abroad: Apply to the commercial departments of Turkish embassies or consulates.

On the Spot

Office hours: Both government departments and commercial establishments are generally open 9am-6pm Monday-Friday. Some offices are open 9am-1pm on summer afternoons.

Public holidays

Jan 1	New Year's Day	May 19	Youth and Sports Day
Apr 23	National Independence and Children's Day	Aug 30	Victory Day
		Oct 29	Republic Day

Aside from the above civic holidays, there are two important Moslem holy periods. The first of these is called *şeker bayram* (sugar holy days) and lasts three days. It follows 30 days of fasting during the Islamic month of Ramadan. Just over two months after that comes the four-day *kurban bayram* (holy days of sacrifice). Each year these holy periods, based on the lunar calendar, fall 10 or 11 days earlier compared to the standard Gregorian calendar.

Banks and currency exchange: Banking hours are 8.30am-5pm, with a lunch break from 12.30-1.30pm. After hours, money can easily be changed in major hotels. At Istanbul's Atatürk airport and Ankara airport the currency-exchange offices stay open to accommodate incoming passengers. Bank transfers to Turkey are easily made.

Chief banks are Türkiye Cumhuriyeti Ziraat Bankas, Türkiye İs Bankas, Yap ve Kred Bankas, Akbank, Pamuk Bank, Türk Ticaret Bankas, Türkiye Garanti Bankas and Osmanl Bankas (Ottoman Bank).

Credit cards and traveller's cheques: Both are generally accepted in establishments frequented by tourists.

Post and telecommunications: Post offices are identifiable by the letters PTT in black on a yellow background. Small offices are open weekdays only till 5 or 5.30pm and may close for lunch. Large hotels have post offices or will handle mail at the desk. Central post offices in bigger cities are usually open till midnight. The main Istanbul office, at Sirkeci near the western railway station, is open till 12 midnight daily, weekends inclusive, for buying stamps, sending mail, telegrams, telexes and for telephoning. Postcard and souvenir shops also sell stamps. It is advisable to send all foreign mail by air (mark it *uçak ile*).

Telegrams can be sent normal, urgent (*acele*) or lightning (*yldrm*) for Turkish destinations; normal or urgent for other countries.

The telephone system is getting better all the time. Tokens for booth telephones are sold at post offices. Many shops allow customers to use the phone. Direct dialling is available to nearly all countries. If you go through the operator for long-distance communications, there's a choice of normal, urgent or lightning service. Only some countries can be called reverse charge (collect).

Public telex booths are installed in all major cities; inquire at central post offices.

Emergency numbers for each city are listed on the first page of the telephone directory.

Embassies and consulates: Diplomatic representations are listed in the yellow pages under *Elçilikler*.

Medical care and health: Medical treatment can be equal to the best anywhere, with excellent doctors, dentists and nurses. However, out-of-the-way areas often have inadequate health services. In addition, much informal medical attention is dispensed; for instance, pharmcies will generally suggest a drug on the basis of your own description of the symptoms. Prescriptions are unnecessary even for antibiotics. In Istanbul, the Admiral Bristol Hospital is preferred by English-speaking foreigners. In other cities, English-speaking physicians can be located. Many doctors have also been trained in Germany. Some medicines, even inexpensive ones, are occasionally in short supply, so travellers are advised to bring with them anything they are likely to need during their stay. Pharmacies post a list of shops on duty after hours. Ring the doorbell and wait if the duty pharmacy seems closed.

Medical fees are generally very moderate by European standards. The commonest complaint of foreign travellers is diarrhoea. Drink only bottled spring water. Any epidemics are always given full publicity in Turkey. At such times, even bottled spring water should be boiled.

Services: Though embassies and consulates themselves are not normally able to provide secretarial, translation or interpreting facilities, they will be able to advise you on local firms and costs. Photocopies can be made at stationery and other shops bearing the sign *Fotokopi*.

Newspapers: Principal dailies are *Cumhuriyet*, *Milliyet*, *Hürriet* and *Tercüman* (all published in Istanbul). The foreign press is available at airports and large news-stands, sometimes a day or two after publication date.

Transport

Air – international: Istanbul, Izmir, Antalya and Ankara are Turkey's main gateways.

Air – domestic: Around 15 cities are linked by frequent domestic flights, making air travel a recommended means of business travel.

Rail: Fast, comfortable diesel-electrics operate on a few major routes, such as Ankara-Istanbul. Other trains are generally slow. Long-distance trains have sleeping- and dining-cars. First-class tickets are often sold out several weeks in advance.

Long-distance buses: Intercity buses are numerous, generally faster than the train, relatively safe and inexpensive. They are also apt to be uncomfortable, dusty and crowded, unless you choose a modern air-conditioned vehicle.

Waterways: Infrequent coastal passenger services with first- and second-class cabins are sold out months ahead. Car ferries operate between Istanbul and Bandirma as well as across the Gulf of Ismit.

Local public transport: All cities have bus or trolleybus services. Buy a booklet of tickets in advance, then drop your ticket into the box by the driver. However, taxis or *dolmuş* (see below) are better for foreign visitors.

Taxis: Cabs are omnipresent. Settle on the exact amount before you get in, preferably with the aid of someone who represents you and speaks Turkish. In Istanbul, taxi drivers are required to carry a printed card showing the official rates for sample destinations. Avoid getting a cab in the immediate vicinity of major hotels where you are likely to end up paying twice what you should.

Each city also has a network of shared taxis (*dolmuş*). The *dolmuş* follows a fixed route, picking up and discharging passengers who all pay the same fare.

Car rental: A limited number of agencies operate in the major cities. An international driving licence is often required. Advance bookings are advisable to ensure having the vehicle of your choice. Chauffeur-driven vehicles are available.

Driving in Turkey: Use of seat belts is compulsory, and the car must be equipped with *two* red-reflector warning triangles and a first-aid kit. The alcohol limit is a strictly enforced zero.

Driving in Turkey is marked by a certain aggressiveness which can be terrifying for a foreigner. One general rule: the driver feels no need to look behind him, but establishes his right of way by physical presence; the first one there takes precedence. Night driving is dangerous because of badly adjusted or unused headlights on oncoming vehicles. In case of accidents, foreigners may be liable for heavy damages; insurance payments are plagued with conditions and delays. Some international corporations do not allow their representatives to drive in Turkey, preferring to provide them with local chauffeurs.

Speed limits are 90kph (56mph) outside town (including motorways) and 50kph (31mph) in built-up areas. Fuel (petrol/gas) is often difficult to obtain in cities, involving long waits, but is usually available more easily outside of urban centres. Fuel available is normal (85 octane), super (95 octane) and diesel.

Roads range from sparkling new stretches of motorway (expressway) near Istanbul to narrow, beaten-earth country lanes in the depths of the countryside. The nation's two most important cities, Ankara and Istanbul, are linked by a very good highway, and the country as a whole is criss-crossed with a network of asphalted arterial roads which, however, are often overcrowded and dangerous.

Some distances from Ankara: Istanbul 440km (275 miles), Izmir 595km (370 miles), Edirne 675km (450 miles).

Social customs: Turks are hesitant to address a foreigner on a first-name basis lest they offend or seem overly friendly, but they respond enthusiastically to any overtures of friendship by the foreigner. A Turkish business associate may invite a foreigner to his home (take a bouquet of flowers or a bottle of perfume to the hostess), but is more likely to take you to a restaurant for a leisurely evening.

Hints for business: Turks enjoy doing business through friends, so it helps if you've an introduction from a mutual acquaintance. Infinite patience and gentle persistence are essential to reach a successful business conclusion. Take time for small talk. Following up one's documents in government offices is generally necessary, either personally or by someone familiar with the matter and the procedures involved.

Foreign chambers of commerce in Turkey: American, Austrian, British, Bulgarian, Czech, Dutch, French, German, Hungarian, Italian, Japanese, Polish, Romanian, Swiss.

Crime and theft: The crime rate in Turkey is low in comparison to other major cities in the world. However, take normal common-sense precautions – keep an eye on your baggage, watch out for pickpockets in crowded places, and put your wallet in an inside pocket. Leave money and valuables in your hotel safe, not in your car or hotel room, and avoid carrying large sums of money.

After Hours

Food and drink: Turkish cooking is characterized by grilled meats, savoury stuffed vegetables and pastry desserts steeped in syrup. Shishkebab (*şiş kababt*) – charcoal-grilled skewered chunks of lamb and tomatoes – is ubiquitous. One of the best kebabs is *döner kebap* (slices of lamb roasted on a vertical spit, served on a bed of rice with yoghurt). Vegetables stuffed with a mixture of chopped meat (usually lamb or mutton), rice, onion and herbs are also popular. Yoghurt is a healthy staple. Salads are excellent. In Istanbul, the fish restaurants along the shores of the Bosphorus and the Sea of Marmara are highly appreciated. Favourite dishes include *kılç şiş* (swordfish kebab), *çinarck usulü balk* (fried swordfish, seabass and prawns garnished with mushrooms and flavoured with brandy) and *lüfer frn* (seabass baked with parsley, served chilled).

Because the drinking of alcoholic beverages is restricted for Moslems, wine isn't commonly drunk in Turkey. It is generally only available in larger city restaurants. Beer, on the other hand, is quite a popular drink, as is *rakī* (aniseed liqueur). Imported spirits, except those at black-market prices, are virtually non-existent.

Turkish coffee, the only type you're likely to find in restaurants or coffee-houses, is quite strong. When it is served, leave the grounds to settle for a minute or two and then sip only half the cup. You'll have to let the waiter know in advance whether or not you want your coffee sweetened, as the sugar and coffee are brewed together. Milk or cream isn't served with coffee.

Mealtimes: lunch noon-3pm, dinner 6-9pm.

Entertainment: Nightclubs abound in major cities. Here, and in restaurants with music, it's easy to spend a small fortune. Concerts, plays and opera are staged mainly in Istanbul but also in other major centres. The Istanbul Festival of Culture and Art, from mid-June to mid-July, includes distinguished foreign musicians. Cinemas often screen foreign films in their original language.

Taxes, service charges and tipping: Hotel and restaurant bills are generally all-inclusive. Tipping recommendations: waiters, 5% for satisfactory service; airport porters, pay only the exact rate posted per article they handle; taxi drivers, round up to nearest 1,000L; hotel porters, 2,000L per bag; cloakroom attendants, posted charges; barbers and hairdressers, 15%.

Sports and recreation: Turkey's recreational assets are located chiefly along the coasts, with magnificent beaches in the south and on the Aegean coast. Skiing facilities are found at Ulu Dag near Bursa, which is a good area for hiking and camping in summer. The hot springs of Yalova, Bursa, Pamukkale and Pozanti are well-known.

The Turks are addicted to soccer. Other spectator sports include basketball and track, with some tennis matches vying for attention. Wrestling matches featuring contenders weighing in at over 200lb are held in Kirkpinar in northwestern Thrace.

TV and radio: The Voice of Turkey broadcasts in English on shortwave from 12.30 to 1pm and 8 to 9pm daily. TRT (Turkish Radio and Television) III has news and weather summaries in English, French and German on FM at intervals throughout the day.

Television is not of a high standard, but it does offer a look at Turkish life.

What to buy: Istanbul has excellent leather coats and jackets. Other leather items, silk, suede and sheepskins are of exceptional quality. The prized Turkish carpets are woven in Bünyan, İsparta, Usak, Kula, Gördes, Milas, Bergama, Hereke, Sivas and Ladik. Ornaments made of gold, silver, ceramic, alabaster, copper and brass are highly valued. Pipe smokers will want to examine the choice of meerschaums.

Shopping hours: 9am-7pm or later, daily except Sunday. Only rarely do shops close for lunch.

Cities and Sights

ANKARA (*Telephone area code 312*)
Airport: Esenboga (35km/22 miles from city centre), international; duty-free shop. Bus service to city centre.

Tourist information office: Tel. 229 2631.

Chamber of commerce: Atatürk Bul. 149, Bakanliklar, Ankara; tel. 117 77 00.

Sightseeing: Old town (ancient citadel), Kocatepe mosque, Atatürk Mausoleum, Museum of Anatolian Civilizations.

ISTANBUL *(Telephone area code 212)*
Airport: Atatürk (24km/15 miles from city centre), international; duty-free shop. Bus every 15 minutes to city centre. Some airlines operate their own coach services. *Dolmuş* (shared taxi) available.

Tourist information offices: Meşrutiyet Caddesi 57, Kat 6-7, Galatasaray; tel. 245 68 75. There is also a tourist office at the airport, and at the Hilton hotels, Karaköy, Yalova and Kocaeli.
   The Turkish Touring and Automobile Association is helpful to foreigners arriving with their own car (tel. 131 46 31).

Chamber of commerce: Gümüşpala Cad, Eminönü; tel. 511 41 50, fax 526 21 97.

Sightseeing: Haghia Sophia, the Blue Mosque, the Church of Holy Peace, the underground cistern, Topkapi, the Ottoman palace, grand bazaar, Bosphorus boat ride.

IZMIR *(Telephone area code 232)*
Airport: Adnan Menderes (15km/9 miles from city centre), international; duty-free shop. Buses and taxis to city centre, also train to Basmane station.

Tourist information office: Atatürk Caddesi 418; tel. 422 1022.

Chamber of commerce: Atatürk Caddesi 126; tel. 441 7777, fax 483 7853

Sightseeing: Ephesus, Pergamum, Pamukkale (Cotton Castle thermal springs), Bodrum (Halicarnassus).

Some Useful Expressions in Turkish

good morning/afternoon	günaydin/tünaydn
good evening/night	iyi akşamlar/iyi geceler
good-bye	Allahasmarladk*/güle güle**
yes/no	evet/hayīr
please/thank you	lütfen/tesekkür ederim
excuse me	affedersiniz
you're welcome	hoş geldiniz
where/when/how	nerede/ne zaman/nasīl
how long/how far	ne kadar/ne kadar uzak
yesterday/today/tomorrow	dün/bugün/yarin
day/week/month/year	gün/hafta/ay/sene
left/right	sol/sağ
up/down	üst/alt
good/bad	iyi/kötü
big/small	büyük/küçük
cheap/expensive	ucuz/pahalī
old/new	eski/yeni
open/closed	açik/kapal
early/late	erken/geç
Does anyone here speak English/French/German?	Burada kimse īngilizce/fransizca/almanca konuşur mĩ?
What does this mean?	Bu ne demek?
I don't understand.	Anlamīyorum.
Do you take credit cards/ traveller's cheques?	Kredi kartī/seyahat çeki aliyormusunuz?
Waiter!/Waitress!	Garson, lütfen!
Where are the toilets?	Tuvaletler nerede?
I'd like…	… istiyorum.
How much is that?	Fiat nedir?
Help me please.	Lütfen bana yardim edin.

said by the one who's leaving   **said by the one who remains**   **345**

United Kingdom

Type of government:	Constitutional monarchy, multi-party, largely centralized
Member of:	BC, EU, GATT, IBRD, IDA, IFC, IMF, OECD
Population:	58.4 million
Area:	244,100sq km (94,247sq miles)
Capital:	London (2m/GUA 6.7m)
Other major cities:	Birmingham (994,500), Glasgow (689,210)
	Leeds (706,300), Sheffield (520,300)
	Liverpool (474,600), Manchester (432,700)
	Edinburgh (418,914), Bristol (392,600)
	Belfast (360,000/GUA 550,000)
	Cardiff (275,000), Aberdeen (190,000)
Language:	English; Welsh and Gaelic of limited local importance in parts of Wales and Scotland, will not affect the non-resident.
Religion:	Protestant (Anglican) (c. 55%), Catholic (10%)
Time zone:	GMT, EST+5; DST (Mar-Oct)
Currency:	Pound sterling (symbolized £) = 100 pence (abbr. p). Coins: 1, 2, 5, 10, 20, 50p; £1 Notes: £5, 10, 20, 50
Electricity:	240V, 50Hz, AC

Planning your Trip

Visa requirements: None. (See also p.6.)

Vaccination requirements: None. (See also p.7.)

Import allowances (see also p.7):

	Cigarettes	Cigars	Tobacco	Spirits	Wine
1)	200 or	50 or	250g	1l and	2l
2)	(800) or	(200) or	(1kg)	(10l) and	(90l)

1) Passengers from countries outside Europe, or duty-free goods
   bought in EU countries by European residents.
3) Non-duty-free goods bought within the EU.

Perfume: 1) 50g; *Toilet water*: 1) 0.25l; *Gifts*: 1) £36 max. value

There are no official restrictions on goods bought non-duty-free within the EU, provided they are for personal use only. The above figures are guidelines to the quantities customs officials will generally find acceptable, so if you are carrying larger quantities you should be prepared to provide proof that the goods are for your personal use.

Currency restrictions: None. (See also p.7.)

Climate: The United Kingdom enjoys a temperate maritime climate with few prolonged periods of extreme weather. Rain can be expected at any time of the year.

Average maximum daily temperatures in London:

Jan	Apr	July	Oct
7°C (45°F)	13°C (56°F)	22°C (72°F)	15°C (59°F)

Though snow can lie for considerable periods in Scottish areas, it rarely affects city streets for more than a few hours. In the south, snowfall is generally lighter. Fog can be a driving hazard in winter. **347**

Clothing: Medium-weight clothes are generally adequate in summer, with something warmer for cool spells. A warm overcoat and hat would be advisable in winter. An umbrella and rainwear will always come in useful.

Hotels: Difficulties in booking accommodation, particularly at the cheaper end of the market, may be experienced in the summer season. Prime tourist centres such as London and Edinburgh are likely to be the worst affected. Advance booking is therefore advisable. Special telephones for booking hotels are often provided at airports and railway stations.

British tourist offices abroad: Amsterdam, Atlanta, Brussels, Buenos Aires, Chicago, Copenhagen, Dallas, Dublin, Frankfurt, Hong Kong, Johannesburg, Los Angeles, Madrid, Mexico City, New York, Oslo, Paris, Rome, São Paulo, Singapore, Stockholm, Sydney, Tokyo, Toronto, Zurich.

Business Briefing

Economic Background
Principal industries: Manufacturing (iron and steel, machinery, motor vehicles, textiles, chemicals, food products, consumer goods), mining (coal, limestone, tin, natural gas), oil drilling, construction.

Main agricultural products: Dairy farming, livestock, fishing.

Main imports: Petroleum products, foodstuffs, machinery and transport equipment, manufactured goods, raw materials.

Main exports: Manufactured goods, petroleum products, machinery and transport equipment, vehicles, chemicals, electrical equipment.

Principal trading partners: USA, Germany, Australia, Canada, Irish Republic, France, Denmark.

GNP: $842.3 billion; per capita: $14,676.

Inflation rate: 2% (1993).

Trade fairs: Many facilities are available in the UK for staging conferences, exhibitions and trade fairs. A wealth of trade events in various fields of commerce are held throughout the year, such as Interbuild in Birmingham (November, alternate years) and the International Food and Drink Exhibition in London (April, alternate years). Calendars of such functions for the current year may be obtained from: Exhibition Industries Federation, 115 Hartington Road, London SW8 2HB; tel. (0171) 498 3306, fax (0717) 627 8287.

Selected background reading: *Guide to the British Economy* (Penguin), *The Social Structure of Modern Britain* (Pergamon), *Britain in the Common Market* (Longman). *Britain 199-,* an official handbook published yearly, provides a reliable guide to all aspects of the UK economy. Sold by Her Majesty's Stationery Office.

British chambers of commerce abroad: Abidjan, Amsterdam, Athens, Bangkok, Barcelona, Bilbao, Bogota, Brussels, Buenos Aires, Casablanca, Cologne, The Hague, Istanbul, Jakarta, Lisbon, Madrid, Mexico City, Milan, Montevideo, New York, Oporto, Paris, Rio de Janeiro, Santiago, São Paulo, Seoul, Stockholm, Tel Aviv, Tokyo, Vienna, Zurich.

On the Spot

Office hours: 9 or 9.30am to 5 or 5.30pm Monday-Friday. Offices are often open over lunch as employees take short, staggered breaks. Government offices open at 8 or 8.30am, closing at 4 or 4.30pm.

Public holidays

	England and Wales	Scotland
New Year's Day	Jan 1	Jan 1 and 2
St David's Day	Mar 1 (Wales only)	
May Day	1st Monday in May	1st Monday in May
Spring Bank Holiday	last Monday in May	last Monday in May

	England and Wales	**Scotland**
Summer Bank Holiday	last Monday in Aug	1st Monday in Aug
Christmas Day	Dec 25	Dec 25
Boxing Day	Dec 26	Dec 26
Movable dates:	Good Friday, Easter Monday	

Northern Ireland observes the same public holidays as England, with the addition of St Patrick's Day (March 17) and Battle of the Boyne Day (July 12).

Banks and currency exchange: Banking hours are 9.30am-3.30pm (or in some cases 4.30pm), Monday-Friday. Major banks are open on Saturday mornings.

Several currency-exchange offices (called *bureaux de change)* are located in central London. A list of approved establishments open after banking hours may be obtained from the National Tourist Information Centre at Victoria Station. In the provinces out-of-hours exchange facilities are rare. Beware of hefty commissions – rates should in all cases be displayed.

All major banks are experienced in international transactions including bank transfers. Principal banks are Barclays Bank, Lloyd's Bank, Midland Bank, National Westminster Bank; in Scotland you are more likely to find Royal Bank of Scotland, Bank of Scotland, National Westminster, Trustee Savings Bank.

Credit cards and traveller's cheques: Major credit cards as well as traveller's cheques are readily accepted in larger shops, hotels and restaurants.

Post and telecommunications: Services are generally reliable, though mail deliveries are sometimes delayed.

Larger post offices are open from 9am to 5.30 or 6pm Monday-Friday, 9am-12.30pm Saturdays. Smaller branches work shorter hours. In London, the office at 24-28 William IV Street, near Trafal-**350** gar Square, is open until 8pm Monday to Saturday. A two-tier mail system is in operation for domestic destinations. Send letters first class to ensure speedy distribution.

Telemessages have replaced inland telegrams. Overseas telegrams and Telemessages may be sent from any telephone; ask the operator for details.

Except for very remote areas subscribers in the British Isles are connected to the automatic telephone network, and direct dialling exists to most countries. International calls can be dialled direct from most UK telephones and from many call boxes. Dial 155 for international operator assistance in English. You may be able to place calls via the operator in your home country if this country is part of the Home Country Direct scheme. The number is given with the codes for the country in the International pages of any local telephone book.

Digital-display pay phones. These are either coin-operated or accept pre-paid cards only:

1. Coin-operated payphones. These take 10p, 20p, 50p and £1 coins. Calls may be dialled direct to anywhere in the UK and to all the countries to which International Direct Dialling is available. Wholly unused coins will be returned at the end of the call. To make a second call using unexpired credit, do not hang up, but press the continuation button on the handset hook to regain dial tone.

2. Phonecard phones. To use these phones, you must first buy one of the special cards, which are on sale in post offices and shops displaying the green sign 'Phonecards sold here'. You may then make any number of calls up to the value of the card (it comes in units of 20, 40, 100 and 200), without the need for cash.

'Pay-on-answer' payphones. These are the older type of payphone, usually to be found in red phone booths – but they are now found increasingly rarely, mainly only in the countryside. They take 10p coins only: push the money into the slot when your party answers.

Cheap-rate calls. Most international direct-dialled calls, all inland long-distance calls, and local calls from private telephones, are cheaper in the evening from Monday to Friday and all day Saturday and Sunday. For calls within the UK, the cheap-rate period is from 6pm to 8am, for international calls from 8pm to 8am.

Hotel telephone surcharges. Most hotels allow guests to make calls from bedroom or reception telephones. But beware! With very few exceptions, you will be charged at a much higher rate than the official price for the call. It is not unusual to be charged two or three times the official rate. A few hotels subscribe to the 'Teleplan' scheme and guarantee somewhat more limited surcharges. The best way to avoid excessive surcharges is to use public payphones.

BTI bureaux. In London, international calls can be made from BTI (British Telecom International) bureaux at Heathrow Airport and in Victoria Street (near the Westminster underground station).

Information on many topics from weather to the correct time is available by telephone. The numbers to ring are shown with the local dialling instructions. For operator assistance, dial 100.

Some useful numbers:

Emergency (ambulance, fire, police – nationwide)	999
Time	123
National Weather	0891 500 400

Principal area codes: Aberdeen 01224, Belfast 01232, Birmingham 0121, Bristol 0117, Cardiff 01222, Edinburgh 0131, Glasgow 0141, Leeds 0113, Liverpool 0151, London (Central) 0171, (Greater) 0181, Manchester 0161, Sheffield 0114.

Embassies and consulates: These are listed alphabetically in the telephone directory under the name of the country or its derivative. eg *French Embassy*, *United States of America*.

Medical care and health: The standard of medical treatment is generally high. The National Health Service is free for anyone in need of urgent attention: foreigners not from EU countries have to pay for non-emergency treatment. Except in cases of emergency, patients should consult a doctor (listed in the yellow pages under *Doctors*) for an introduction to a suitable hospital. Medical and pharmaceutical supplies are readily available from any pharmacy (called a 'chemist's') with a doctor's prescription when required. In London,

Bliss, at 50 Willesden Lane, London NW6, is open 9am to midnight. Tap water is generally safe to drink.

Services: The yellow pages list *Secretarial Services*, *Translators and Interpreters* and *Copying and Duplicating Services* under those headings. Photocopying machines can also be found at railway stations and in some public libraries.

Newspapers: Principal 'quality' British dailies are *The Times*, *The Financial Times*, *The Guardian*, *The Independent* and *The Scotsman*. *The Observer* appears on Sundays only, alongside special Sunday editions of the main dailies. *The Guardian* has a special Saturday edition. Numerous other large-circulation and local newspapers exist. Papers from western European countries, including the Paris-edited *International Herald Tribune,* are easy to find in city centres.

Transport

Air – international: Though London is the country's main gateway, altogether more than 20 British airports serve destinations abroad. If you have business in the provinces, look into direct flights to bypass a London stopover.

Air – domestic: Nearly 60 airports connect all points of the British Isles.

Rail: The train is generally recommended for intercity trips within the UK, except for journeys to Scotland or Northern Ireland, where air travel is a more convenient alternative. Trains are comfortable and reasonably punctual, with first- and standard-class compartments; standard-class can become very crowded when travelling at peak times from London. The InterCity 125 (125mph/200kph) and 225 (140mph/225kph), operate mainly from London and have greatly reduced journey times. Dining-car services are available on some routes, with sleepers on overnight services to Scotland. Apart from normal day-return reductions and a bewildering array of special offers and passes, the Britrail Pass offers savings for those travelling frequently by train. This ticket must be bought outside Britain.

Local public transport: An extensive underground (subway) system is available in London, Liverpool, Newcastle and Glasgow. Trams have made a comeback in Manchester. Bus services are available in all centres. Until you have oriented yourself in a town, you would be well advised to make use of taxis since buses can be difficult to use without local knowledge. In London the underground is reasonably safe and can be recommended. Maps are displayed in station booking halls, showing the locality of the station. Underground fares are paid at automatic ticket machines or to the booking-office clerk before travelling. Bus fares are paid either to the driver on entry or inside the bus to a conductor. Have small change ready. The Visitor Travelcard, valid for unlimited travel on both the underground and all London Transport buses and British Rail trains in Greater London, is sold for periods of one, three, four or seven days and is available through pre-purchase from travel agents and tour operators in Britain and abroad.

Taxis: Though city streets often seem full of taxis, it can be hard to find a free one at rush-hours. A more modern vehicle, the Metrocab, is taking to the streets. Even roomier than its predecessor (though still black), it carries up to five passengers. Generally, all you do in London is hail a cab on the street when its yellow 'For Hire' sign is lit. In London, unlicensed taxis, known as minicabs, can be hired by telephone and are listed under *Minicabs* in the yellow pages. Fares should be negotiated individually when using minicabs.

Car rental: There are many car-rental firms listed in the yellow pages under *Car Hire*. It's well worth shopping around for the most favourable rates. Car-rental agencies often have offices at ports, airports and stations. Chauffeur-driven vehicles are generally available.

Driving in the United Kingdom: The driver and all passengers must use seat belts if they are available; fines for not attaching them are very high. Cars are driven on the *left* in the United Kingdom. Those unused to this system should pay special attention at crossroads and round-abouts (traffic circles). A private car is, generally speaking, of little use in central London because of severe parking problems. Road conditions are generally good but congested in many urban areas. Speed **354** limits are 30mph (48kph) (unless otherwise marked) or 40mph (64kph) in towns, 70mph (112kph) on motorways (expressways), and 60mph (96kph) on other roads. Blood alcohol limit is a strictly enforced 80mg/100ml. Fuel (petrol/gas) available is 4-star super (98 octane), lead-free (95 octane) and diesel, sold in both litres and Imperial gallons (about 10% more than the US gallon). The price for both is shown.

Pedestrians have absolute priority at striped ('zebra') crossings. An extensive, toll-free motorway network covers most main routes. Emergency phones are provided at regular intervals along motorways; follow arrows marked on posts at the side of the road.

Some distances from London: Birmingham 110 miles (175km), Manchester 200 miles (320km), Edinburgh 400 miles (640km).

Social customs: Toasts at formal dinners are often the occasion for a short speech. In such a case, the one being toasted should prepare a few words in reply.

Hints for business: British business people almost never return home to eat at lunch time. Business entertaining is normally done over lunch or (more rarely) dinner. It is unlikely that an initial invitation will be to eat at your host's home. Office attire can be worn to almost all restaurants and is also suitable for home visits. Contrary to myth, the English are not particularly reserved or formal in their business and social life. First-name relationships are likely to come fairly easily. The British normally take their holidays in June, July or August so it is wise to avoid a visit during those months.

Foreign chambers of commerce in the United Kingdom: American, Anglo-Zaïre, British-American, Arab-British, Australian-British, Belgo-Luxembourg, Brazilian, Canada-UK, UK-Caribbean, Chinese, Egyptian-British, French, German, Hungarian, Indian, British-Israeli, Italian, Japanese, Mauritius, Netherland-British, New Zealand-UK, Nigerian-British, Norwegian, UK-Pakistan, Portuguese, Spanish, Swedish, British-Soviet, Turkish-British.

Crime and theft: Guard against pickpockets and petty thieves. Wherever crowds gather, close watch should be kept on wallets and purses. Cars should always be locked when parked, and all visible objects removed. Lock up valuables in the hotel safe.

After Hours

Food and drink: The raw materials of British cooking are generally of excellent quality, and cooks have shown increasing imagination in their preparations over recent years. Some specialities: steak and kidney pie, or steak and kidney pudding, roast beef and Yorkshire pudding, shepherd's pie, game (especially grouse after August 12), haggis (a traditional Scottish dish consisting of minced meat and oatmeal cooked in a sheep's stomach), fish and chips. The English breakfast (eggs, bacon, sausages, kidneys, or perhaps kippers, followed by toast and marmalade) always gives a good start to the day. The nation produces a wide selection of fine cheeses, notably Stilton, Cheddar and Cheshire (but avoid the mass-produced versions), with an increasing number of farm-produced local cheeses available.

Imported wines and other beverages are readily available. Don't neglect to try some of the best Scotch malt whiskies or the distinctive range of beers. Try the local brands of dark beer (or 'bitter'), rather than the imported fizzy 'lagers' or light beers. Bitter tends to be served at room temperature rather than chilled, and varies widely from pub to pub. The English pub is a unique institution, often serving good food as well as drinks, at reasonable prices.

Alcoholic drinks may be served on licensed premises only. With the liberalization of licensing hours, many pubs remain open all day, from 11am to 11pm. Sunday hours are shorter, from noon to 3pm and from 7 to 10.30pm, and no alcohol may be bought outside these hours on a Sunday, even in supermarkets or specialized shops.

Mealtimes: lunch noon-2pm, dinner 6-10pm. In larger towns restaurants often stay open later, but pubs tend to stop serving meals around 2 and 9pm.

Entertainment: London is the nation's undisputed entertainment capital, with something to suit every taste. There is an unrivalled variety of nightclubs, discos and restaurants. *Time Out* gives a comprehensive weekly guide to events in the capital.

Notable events include the Sir Henry Wood promenade concerts at London's Royal Albert Hall, from July to September, and the Edinburgh festival in August. The Royal Opera House in Covent

Garden, the Barbican Centre for Arts and Conferences and the South Bank complex provide fine performances. Foreign films are likely to be dubbed unless shown in small, art-film cinemas. All provincial cities offer something in the way of nightlife as well as – in some cases – excellent cultural activities.

Taxes, service charges and tipping: Hotel and restaurant bills generally include VAT and service, but it's advisable to ask. If service is not included, leave waiters 10-15%. Tipping recommendations: hotel porters, minimum 50p per bag, taxi drivers 10-15%, cloakroom attendants 20p, barbers 10%, hairdressers 15% plus 5% to the assistant.

Sports and recreation: Most cities have extensive parks, and London is particularly fortunate in this respect. Jogging in London's parks is now fairly common. Public swimming pools are available all over the country. Golf clubs often allow non-members to play during the week; you may hire clubs. Many municipal courses are open to all, and in Scotland some of the best and most famous golf courses in the world, including those at St Andrews near Edinburgh, are public. Many cities operate squash and tennis courts as well as athletics facilities for all to use. Details can be obtained from local tourist offices.

Top spectator sports are: soccer (Aug-May), rugby (winter), cricket (summer), tennis (Wimbledon championships are held in London at the beginning of July), horse-races (Derby, Royal Ascot in May/June) and motor racing. *Time Out* also lists sporting events in London.

TV and radio: Virtually all programming is in English. Broadcasts from the Continent can be picked up on longwave radio.

Two BBC television channels and several commercial independent television networks are on the air, some around the clock. There is an expanding satellite network, plus cable. On radio, five BBC stations provide news, music and feature shows for virtually all tastes: Radio 1 pop and rock music; Radio 2 light entertainment and easy listening; Radio 3 mostly classical music; Radio 4 current affairs, arts and drama; Radio 5 sports commentary, education and comedy. The BBC World Service provides excellent international coverage. BBC local and commercial stations are useful for local news and events.

What to buy: Good buys include cashmere and lambswool knitwear, suits and fabrics for tailor-made apparel, tablecloths and teatowels in Irish linen, English cheeses, sweets (perhaps treacle toffee, humbugs or fudge), marmalade, chutneys, fine malt whiskies, tea. Craft workshops where skilled craftsmen use traditional materials and techniques are widespread throughout the UK.

Shopping hours are generally 9am to 5.30 or 6pm, Monday-Saturday, with late-night shopping in central London on Thursday until 8pm, and on a specified evening in many other centres. Many large supermarkets now open on Sundays. Some shops may close Saturday afternoons and one afternoon per week, often Wednesday.

Cities and Sights

LONDON (Telephone area code 0171 or 0181)

Airports: Heathrow (24km/15 miles from city centre), international; duty-free shop; Business Centre. Airport and urban bus service. Underground to city centre (Piccadilly line, approx. 45 minutes).

Gatwick (43km/27 miles from city centre), international; duty-free shop. Airport and urban bus service. Express train to city centre (Victoria station – approx. 30 minutes).

London City Airport (10km/6 miles east of the City in the Docklands); scheduled flights to UK and European destinations.

Tourist information centres: The London Tourist Board and Convention Bureau provides information and leaflets to personal callers at their Victoria Station Forecourt branch in Victoria Station, London. Recorded information is available by telephoning (0839) 123456 (from within the UK only – calls are charged at 39p per minute cheap rate and 49p per minute at all other times). The London Tourist board also operates a Telephone Accommodation Booking Service, tel. (0171) 824 8844 (credit cards only).

Information offices available at Heathrow underground station, in the Tower (April-October), in Selfridges and Harrods stores, and (for events within the City of London) in St Paul's Churchyard, London EC4; tel. (0171) 332 1456.

Chamber of commerce and industry: 33 Queen Street, London EC4R 1AP; tel. (0171) 248 4444, fax 489 0391.

Sightseeing: Westminster Abbey, St Paul's Cathedral, Buckingham Palace, Queen's Gallery, Tower of London, London Zoo (Regent's Park), Covent Garden, Camden Lock, Portobello Road.

Museums: British Museum, National Gallery, Tate Gallery, South Bank Centre.

Excursions: Windsor Castle, Hampton Court Palace, Greenwich (Royal Naval College, 'Cutty Sark', Observatory), Thames Barrier (via Thames river boat), Kew (Botanical Gardens), Hampstead Heath (Kenwood House), Hertford (Hatfield House), Brighton (Royal Pavilion), Oxford, Cambridge.

BIRMINGHAM (*Telephone area code 0121*)
Airport: Elmdon (13km/8 miles from city centre), international; duty-free shop. Airport bus and train services to city centre.

Tourist information centre: The Piazza, National Exhibition Centre; tel. 780 4321; and at 2 City Arcade and the airport.

Chamber of commerce and industry: PO Box 360, 75 Harborne Road; tel. 454 6171, fax 455 8670.

Museums: Art Gallery, Central Library (Shakespeare Collection), Aston Hall.

Excursions: Stratford-upon-Avon, Malvern Hills, Vale of Evesham, Cotswolds, Coventry, Kenilworth Castle.

GLASGOW (*Telephone area code 0141*)
Airport: Abbotsinch (14km/9 miles from city centre), international; duty-free shop, car rental. Regular airport bus connections to city centre.

Tourist information centre: 35-39 St Vincent Place; tel. 204 4400.

Chamber of commerce: 30 George Square; tel. 204 2121, fax 221 2336.

Sightseeing: Bothwell Zoo, Glasgow School of Art, summer boat trips on the Firth of Clyde.

Museums: Glasgow Art Gallery, Burrell Collection, University collections.

Excursions: Provan Hall, Loch Lomond, Scottish Highlands, Trossachs, Fort William.

MANCHESTER (*Telephone area code 0161*)

Airport: Ringway (20km/12 miles from city centre), international; duty-free shop. Airport bus service and trains to city centre.

Tourist information centre: Town Hall Extension, Lloyd Street; tel. 234 3157; and at the airport.

Chamber of commerce and industry: 56 Oxford Street, Manchester M60 7HJ; tel. 236 3210, fax 236 4160.

Sightseeing: Town hall, cathedral, Manchester ship canal, Royal Exchange Theatre, John Rylands Library, much Victorian Gothic architecture.

Museums: City Art Gallery, Whitworth Art Gallery.

Excursions: Heaton Hall, Platt Hall, Wythenshawe Hall, Peak District National Park, Lake District, Chester.

EDINBURGH (*Telephone area code 0131*)

Airport: Turnhouse (11km/7 miles from city centre), international; duty-free shop. Airport bus service to city centre; car rental, special coach service to Dundee.

Tourist information centre: Waverley Market, Princes Street; tel. 557 1700; and at the airport.

Chamber of commerce and manufactures: 3 Randolph Crescent; tel. 225 5851, fax 220 1508.

Sightseeing: Castle, Holyrood Palace, Royal Mile, St Giles' Cathedral, New Town (18th century).

360 **Museums**: National Gallery of Scotland.

Excursions: North Berwick, Pentland Hills, East Neuk of Fife, Forth road and rail bridges, golf courses of Fife.

BRISTOL (*Telephone area code 0117*)
Airport: Lulsgate (11km/7 miles from centre). Bus service to centre.

Tourist information centre: Colston House, Colston Street; tel. 926 0767.

Chamber of commerce: 16 Clifton Park; tel. 973 7373, fax 974 5365.

Sightseeing: Quay area (taverns), Theatre Royal, Little Theatre, Clifton Suspension Bridge, SS 'Great Britain', City Art Gallery.

Excursions: Bath (Roman baths), Blaise castle woods, Clevedon Court, Wye Valley (Tintern Abbey), Chepstow Castle, Cheddar Gorge.

BELFAST (*Telephone area code 01232*)
Airport: Aldergrove (22km/14 miles from city centre); international. Bus service to city centre.

Tourist information centre: 53 Castle Street; tel. 22 7888.

Chamber of commerce and industry: Chamber of Commerce House, 7th floor, 22 Great Victoria Street; tel. 24 4113, fax 24 7024.

Sightseeing: City hall, Stormont Castle, Cone Hill.

Excursions: Carrickfergus Castle, Antrim, Mount Stewart Gardens.

CARDIFF (*Telephone area code 01222*)
Airport: Rhoose (19km/12 miles from city centre), international; duty-free shop. Urban bus service to city centre.

Tourist information centre: Welsh Tourist Office, 3 Castle Street; tel. 227281.

Chamber of commerce: Corys Building, 57 Bute Street; tel. 481648, fax 489785.

Sightseeing: Castle, civic centre, bay.

Museums: National Museum of Wales (Impressionist paintings).

Excursions: St Fagan's Castle (Welsh Folk Museum), Llandaff Cathedral, Old Beupre Castle, Castell Coch.

ABERDEEN *(Telephone area code 01224)*
Airport: Dyce (10km/6 miles from city centre) international; duty-free shop. Half-hourly airport bus to city centre.

Tourist information centre: St Nicholas House, Broad Street; tel. 632727.

Chamber of commerce: 10 Albyn Grove; tel. 212626, fax 213221.

Sightseeing: Harbour (fish market), King's College, cathedral.

Excursions: Muchalls Castle, Drum Castle, Pitmedden Gardens, Crathes Castle, Dunnottar Castle, the Highlands.

Former Yugoslavia

Although there are areas within the region which are safe to visit, notably Slovenia, Macedonia, the Federal Republic and some of the coastal resorts of Croatia, most of the geographical area of Former Yugoslavia is prone to outbreaks of hostilities and is also the subject of a massive United Nations peacekeeping effort. In the period leading up to publication, the region has been the subject of blanket economic sanctions against the warring factions, in an escalating involvement of thousands of UN troops engaged in humanitarian and policing projects.

The wars have deprived Europe of some of its most important towns and cities. Dubrovnik on the shores of the Adriatic has been scarred by a massive artillery bombardment since the siege of 1992, while Sarajevo, the Bosnian capital which staged the 1984 Winter Olympic Games, is now a site of starvation and destruction that has shocked the world.

Global diplomatic efforts are being focused on finding a solution to the masive economic and political problems of the region and, although the long-term goal is the peaceful dissolution of Former Yugoslavia to a state of peaceful cohabitation, such a conclusion seems far-off. This guide cannot, at present, recommend the Federal Republic of Yugoslavia, Bosnia or Croatia as business destinations although Slovenia, with its lack of ethnic divisions, is safe and will welcome business visitors. With this in mind we have provided full coverage of Slovenia and included some of the most vital and relevant details for the other countries. Information refers to Slovenia except where otherwise stated.

FEDERAL REPUBLIC OF YUGOSLAVIA

Population:	11 million (Serbs 65%, Albanians 17%, Montenegrins 5%, Hungarians 4%, Slavic Muslims 3%)
Area:	102,173sq km (39,449sq miles)
Language:	Serbian; the Cyrillic alphabet is used. Other languages include Albanian.
Religion:	Eastern Orthodox (70%), Catholic (7%), Muslim (17%)
Time zone:	GMT+1, EST+6; DST (Apr-Sep)
Currency:	Dinar (abbr. din) = 100 paras Coins: 10, 20, 50 paras; 1, 2, 5din Notes: 50, 100, 200, 500din

Note: the Republic's economic system is in chaos, so these figures – and those for Croatia and Bosnia – should only be considered as loose guidelines only.

Electricity:	220V, 50Hz, AC

CROATIA

Population:	5 million (Croats 78%, Serbs 12%)
Area:	56,538sq km (21,829sq miles)
Capital:	Zagreb (930,000)
Language:	Croatian; the Latin alphabet is used.
Religion:	Catholic (78%), Eastern Orthodox (12%)
Time zone:	GMT+1, EST+6; DST (Apr-Sep)
Currency:	Croatian Dinar (abbr. HRD) = 100 paras Coins: 10, 20, 50 paras; 1, 2, 5din Notes: 50, 100, 200, 500din
Electricity:	220V, 50Hz, AC

BOSNIA

Population:	5 million (49% Muslim Slavs, 32% Orthodox Serbs, 19% Catholic Croats)
Area:	51,129sq km (19,740sq miles)
Capital:	Sarajevo (no reliable population information)
Language:	Serbo-Croatian; both Latin and Cyrillic alphabets are used.
Religion:	Eastern Orthodox (42%), Catholic (32%), Muslim (10%)
Time zone:	GMT+1, EST+6; DST (Apr-Sep)
Currency:	Yugoslavian Dinar (abbr. din) = 100 paras Coins: 10, 20, 50 paras; 1, 2, 5din Notes: 50, 100, 200, 500din
Electricity:	220V, 50Hz, AC

SLOVENIA

Type of government:	Democratic republic with multi-party democracy, formerly part of Yugoslavia
Population:	2 million (Slovenes 90%, Italian 3%, Hungarian 2%)
Area:	20,256sq km (7,820sq miles)
Capital:	Ljubljana (340,000)
Other major cities:	Maribor (108,000)
Language:	Slovene
Religion:	Catholic (82%), Protestant (7%)
Time zone:	GMT+1, EST+6; DST (Apr-Sep)
Currency:	Tolar (abbr. SIT), Coins: 1, 2, 5 tolar Note: 1, 2, 3, 4, 5, 10, 20, 50 tolar

Note: At the time of publication the Slovenian currency was relatively stable. The best exchange rate is usually given for the German Mark.

Electricity:	220V, 50Hz, AC

Planning your Trip

Visa requirements: Visitors arriving in any of the states may be asked for proof of visible means of support to cover a stay in the country. Departure must be guaranteed by holding all documents needed for the destination, and either return or onward tickets or sufficient hard currency to buy return or onward tickets. Most nationalities require only a passport for entry to Slovenia (See also p.6.)

Vaccination requirements: None. (See also p.7.)

Import allowances (see also p.7): At present the borders are in a state of flux; the customs allowances listed are for Slovenia but also apply at present to The Federal Republic and Croatia.

Cigarettes		Cigars		Tobacco	Spirits		Wine
200	or	50	or	250g	1l	and	2l

Perfume: 50g; *Toilet water*: ¼l

Currency restrictions: While you may bring unlimited sums of foreign currency into any of the states, it is often difficult to change local currency back into foreign currency and there are tight restrictions on how much of the local currency you can export. It is advised that you do not exchange foreign currency into any more local currency than you will need. (See also p.7.)

Climate: The states of Former Yugoslavia have climate ranges which vary from Mediterranean on the Adriatic coast through moderate temperate in most inland areas to alpine in the mountains of Slovenia. The rainiest months are April and November.

Clothing: Warm clothing is necessary for winter, with light clothing adequate for summer. Business attire can be casual, particularly in summer when a jacket and open-neck shirt are common for men. Dark, conservative suits are rare.

Hotels: Most travel agents can supply a hotel list showing facilities and rates. Hotels in Slovenia tend to be relatively expensive, and advance reservations are not usually necessary. Breakfast is usually included in the price. Daily rates are normally lower for long stays and can be considerably reduced off-season. Motels are situated along the main highways or on the edge of town. Most offer facilities similar to a B-class hotel. Car-repair services and fuel (petrol/gas) may be available. Boarding houses (pansion) are comfortable but with fewer facilities than a hotel. These establishments are graded in three categories, I to III.

Slovenian tourist offices abroad: Budapest, London, Lucerne, Middleburg (Netherlands), New York, Oberursel (Germany), Prague, Vienna.

Business Briefing

Main industries: Iron, machinery, electrical equipment, chemicals, wood and timber products, textiles and leather.

Main agricultural products: Potatoes, corn, wheat, hops, apples, grapes, wine, meat, milk.

Main imports: Agricultural equipment, petroleum products, electronic equipment, machinery.

Main exports: Furniture, automobiles, transport equipment, agricultural products, steel products, nonferrous metals, chemicals, clothing and footwear, wine.

Principal trading partners: Germany, Italy, Croatia, France, USA, Austria, Russia, UK.

GNP: $12.1 billion; per capita: $6,050.

Trade fairs: Check with consulates abroad for information on new trade fairs starting after independence.

Selected background reading: *Discover Slovenia* (available in English), published by Cankarjeva Zalozba, available from consular offices abroad.

Chambers of commerce abroad: Business enquiries can be made through consular offices abroad.

On the Spot

Office hours: 8am-8pm Monday-Friday, 8am-1pm on Saturdays.

Public holidays:

Jan 1, 2	New Year	Nov 1	Remembrance Day
Feb 8	Preseren Day	Dec 25	Christmas Day
April 27	Day of Uprising	Dec 26	Independence Day
May 1, 2	Bank Holiday		
June 25	National Day	**Moveable dates:**	Easter Sunday
Aug 15	Assumption		and Monday
Oct 31	Reformation Day		Whit Sunday

Banks and currency exchange: Banking hours are generally 8am to 6pm Monday-Friday and 8am to noon on Saturday. Outside these hours hotels and some currency-exchange offices can change money. Try to assess how much cash in the local currency you will need, and remember to keep currency-exchange receipts if you intend to reconvert money. Money transfers can be a time-consuming process and exchange rates can vary considerably from place to place.

Credit cards and traveller's cheques: Internationally recognized credit cards are accepted in most hotels and large stores, as are most traveller's cheques, although there are usually better exchange rates for cash.

Post and telecommunications: Services are generally reliable. Most post offices are open 7am-8pm without a break, though some operate on a reduced schedule. The main post office in Slovenia is in Ljubljana: Cigaletova 15.

Mail boxes in Slovenia, square and painted yellow, are normally **368** affixed to walls. Post offices are marked by yellow PTT signs.

Most public places have coin- or token (žuetoni)-operated telephones for local calls. An increasing number of payphones can be used for long distance, too. Tokens (žuetone) are available from post offices and tobacconists'. For calls abroad it's best to go to the local post office. From most localities in Slovenia you can dial direct to western Europe.

Some useful numbers:

Ambulance	94	Inquiries	988
Fire	93	Police	92
General information	98 12	Telegrams	96

Area codes: Ljubljana: 061.

Consulates: Consulates are listed in the telephone book under *Konzulai*.

Medical care and health: Charges for medical services in Slovenia are very reasonable, and standards are satisfactory. Citizens of the following western countries are entitled to virtually free medical care: Austria, Belgium, Luxemburg, Netherlands, UK, Germany, the Czech Republic and Croatia. Medicine and pharmaceutical supplies are readily available, though not necessarily the same brands you're used to. The addresses of pharmacies on duty after hours are published in the daily newspapers. Tap water is safe to drink.

An *apoteka* supplies over-the-counter non-prescription remedies as well as medicines made up according to a prescription. A *drogerija* sells a great range of toiletries, cosmetics, and sometimes films.

Services: Contact the Chamber of Commerce in Ljubljana; tel. (061) 125 01 22, fax (061) 21 82 42 for information on local secretarial help, personnel, translators and interpreters. Travel agencies may also be able to assist.

Newspapers: The principal daily is *Delo*. Newspapers from France, the UK, Italy, the USA and Germany are on sale in Ljubljana. *Slovenija* is a tourist magazine published monthly in English.

Transport

Air: International flights operate to the Slovenian international airport in Ljubljana. There are a couple of small airports within Slovenia which cater for small charter flights, the most popular being in the resort town of Portorz.

Rail: It is easy to enter Slovenia by rail, particularly from Austria, Italy and Germany, with regular services from Vienna, Salzburg, Trieste and Munich. Services from neighbouring Balkan countries have been disrupted by the war. Inside Slovenia all the major towns are linked by rail, and both normal and express trains operate on these routes.

Local public transport: Slovenia has an extensive bus network and it is the only form of public transportation to serve the tourist attractions of Bled and Bohinj.

Taxis: Taxis are available at stands in all towns. City taxis have meters; in smaller towns, agree on a price in advance. Tipping is optional (round off the fare).

Car rental: A number of firms operate, some with airport offices.

Driving in Slovenia: Speed limits are 60kph (38mph) in towns, 120kph (75mph) on expressways, 100kph (62mph) on other main roads and 80kph (50mph) on secondary roads. Seat belts must be worn. Motorists are required to have in their vehicle a spare set of bulbs, a first-aid kit and a red reflector warning triangle for use in case of breakdown. The blood alcohol limit is 50mg/100ml. Major highways connect Ljubljana with Kranj and Postojna, and Maribor with Celje. In the event of a breakdown dial 61 987. Fuel (petrol/gas) available is normal (86 octane), super (98 octane), lead-free (in major towns) and diesel. In the event of breakdown, dial 987.

Social customs: Handshaking, seemingly at every opportunity, is a must when greeting almost anybody. If a Slovene offers you a drink it's virtually obligatory to accept. If you're not in the mood for brandy, say yes to coffee. You aren't expected to stand the next round; the hospitality can be returned at a later date.

Hints for business: Patience is the keynote to business negotiations. Be sure to confirm all appointments before arrival. Consulars are usually good sources of advice. Avoid the July-August holiday period for business travel.

Foreign chambers of commerce in Slovenia: Apply to commercial departments of consulates.

Crime and theft: Violent crime is rare, but pickpockets and sneak thieves know no bounds, so it is probably wise to store valuables in the safe in your hotel. Otherwise, normal precautions are in order.

After Hours

Food and drink: National dishes are heavily influenced by Slovenia's German and Austrian neighbours. You will find a wide variety of dishes throughout Slovenia, with each region producing its own style of cuisine. Always ask for typical regional dishes in restaurants as you travel around the country. All of the regions produce a wide variety of meat dishes, vegetable dishes and pastries. Pizzas, hot-dogs and hamburgers are also available everywhere. *Restavracija* means restaurant; a *gostilna* is a village inn. A *kavarna* is a pastry-and-snack shop. *samopo-strežna restavracija* indicates an inexpensive self-service restaurant and a *bife* is a snack bar.

Slovenia produces some excellent wines and spirits. The best region for dry and sweet white wine is Štajerska (producing *Maribor* and *Ptuj*) while the best dry white and red wines are produced in Primorska (including *Koper* and *Nova Gorica*). *Viljamovka* is a Slovenian speciality worth sampling; a spirit made from the Slovenian pear. Imported alcoholic beverages are also readily available.

Mealtimes: lunch noon-3pm, dinner 7-10pm.

Entertainment: Ljubljana boasts a wide range of entertainment from theatres and opera to cinemas, nightclubs and discos.

Taxes, service charges and tipping: Hotel bills are all-inclusive. Though restaurant bills feature a 10% service charge, it is usual to tip the waiter 5-10%. Other tipping recommendations: hotel porters **371**

about 0.50US$ per bag; barbers and hairdressers 10%; cloakroom attendant $0.25; for taxi drivers, round off the fare.

Sports and recreation: This is mountainous country and offers excellent facilities for skiiers and hikers and many water sports.

TV and radio: Programmes are broadcast in Slovene. Foreign films are not dubbed. Satellite programs are available almost everywhere. If you have a short-wave set you can tune in to the BBC and Voice of America.

What to buy: Good buys include leather goods, woodcarvings, furniture, textiles, outdoor clothes and equipment, woollens and alcoholic drinks. Shopping hours: 8am-6pm Monday-Friday; Saturdays until noon. Some food shops in the larger towns open until 9pm Monday-Saturday, and 9am-noon on Sunday.

Cities and Sights

LJUBLJANA (*Telephone area code 061*)
Airport: Brnik (35km/22 miles from city centre), international; duty-free shop. Regular bus service keyed to arrivals and departures.

Tourist information centre: Slovenska 35, 61000, Ljubljana; tel. 21 57 333, fax 21 55 16.

Chamber of Economy of Slovenia: Slovenska 41, 61000, Ljubljana; tel. 125 01 22, fax 21 82 42.

Sightseeing: Old town, Franciscan, St Nicholas', St James' and Ursuline churches, Castle and St George's chapel, Modern Gallery, Tivoli Hall, National Museum.

Excursions: Bled and Bohinj lakes, Predvor and Kranjska Gora.

Some Useful Expressions in Slovene

good day	**dober dan**
good-bye	**nasvidenje**
yes/no	**da/ne/ja**
please/thank you	**prosim/hvala**
excuse me	**dovolite mi**
you're welcome	**dobrodošli**
where/when/how	**kje/kdaj/kako**
how long/how far	**kako dolgo/kako dalec**
yesterday/today/tomorrow	**včeraj/danes/jutri**
day/week/month/year	**dan/teden/mesec/leto**
left/right	**levo/desno**
up/down	**gor/dol**
good/bad	**dobro/slabo**
big/small	**veliko/malo**
cheap/expensive	**poceni/drago**
hot/cold	**vroče/mrzlo**
old/new	**staro/novo**
open/closed	**odprto/zaprto**
early/late	**zgodaj/pozno**
easy/difficult	**lahko/težko**
Does anyone here speak English/Italian/French?	**Ali kdo govori Angleško/ Italijansko/Francosko?**
What does this mean?	**Kaj to pomeni?**
I don't understand.	**Ne razumem.**
Please write it down.	**Prosim, napišite mi to.**
Do you take credit cards/ traveller's cheques?	**Sprejmete kreditne kartice/ potovalne čeke?**
Where are the toilets?	**Kje je stranišče?**
I'd like …	**Rad bi …**
How much is that?	**Koliko stane?**
Help me please.	**Pomagajte mi, prosim.**
My name is...	**Jaz sem...**

373

Reference Section

All countries of continental Europe employ the metric system. While the English-speaking world is increasingly changing over to this mode of measurement, traditional weights and measures continue to be used to varying degrees. The charts on the following pages provide a quick means of converting from one system to the other for everyday purposes.

In these charts, the figure in the centre column refers to both metric and Anglo-American measurements. For example, in the chart below, 1 centimetre = 0.40 inches, and 1 inch = 2.54 centimetres.

Metric Conversion Tables

Length		
centimetres (cm)		inches (in)
2.54	1	0.40
5.08	2	0.80
7.62	3	1.20
10.16	4	1.60
12.70	5	2.00
15.24	6	2.40
17.78	7	2.80
20.32	8	3.20
22.86	9	3.50
25.40	10	3.90
38.10	15	6.00
50.80	20	7.90
63.50	25	10.00
254.00	100	39.40

Length (continued)

metres (m)		feet (ft)
0.30	1	3.28
0.61	2	6.56
0.91	3	9.84
1.22	4	13.12
1.52	5	16.40
1.83	6	19.69
2.13	7	22.97
2.44	8	26.25
2.74	9	29.53
3.05	10	32.81
4.57	15	49.21
6.10	20	65.62
7.62	25	82.02
30.48	100	328.08

kilometres (km)		miles
1.61	1	0.62
3.22	2	1.24
4.83	3	1.86
6.44	4	2.49
8.05	5	3.11
9.65	6	3.73
11.26	7	4.35
12.88	8	4.97
14.48	9	5.59
16.09	10	6.21
24.14	15	9.32
32.18	20	12.43
40.23	25	15.54
160.90	100	62.14

Weight

grammes (g)		ounces (oz)
28.35	1	0.035
56.70	2	0.070
85.05	3	0.105
113.40	4	0.140
141.75	5	0.175
170.10	6	0.210
198.45	7	0.245
226.80	8	0.280
255.15	9	0.315
283.50	10	0.350
425.25	15	0.525
567.00	20	0.700
708.75	25	0.875
2,835.00	100	3.500

kilograms (kg)		avoirdupois pounds (lb)
0.45	1	2.205
0.91	2	4.409
1.36	3	6.614
1.81	4	8.818
2.27	5	11.023
2.72	6	13.227
3.17	7	15.432
3.62	8	17.636
4.08	9	19.841
4.53	10	22.045
6.80	15	33.068
9.06	20	44.090
11.33	25	55.113
45.30	100	220.450

Area

square centimetres (sq cm)		square inches (sq in)
6.45	1	0.15
12.90	2	0.31
19.36	3	0.46
25.81	4	0.62
32.26	5	0.77
38.71	6	0.93
45.16	7	1.08
51.62	8	1.24
58.07	9	1.39
64.52	10	1.55
96.78	15	2.32
129.04	20	3.10
161.30	25	3.87
645.20	100	15.49

square metres (sq m)		square feet (sq ft)
0.093	1	10.764
0.186	2	21.528
0.279	3	32.292
0.372	4	43.056
0.465	5	53.820
0.557	6	64.584
0.650	7	75.348
0.743	8	86.112
0.836	9	96.876
0.929	10	107.640
1.394	15	161.460
1.858	20	215.280
2.323	25	269.100
9.290	100	1,076.400

Area (continued)

square kilometres (sq km)		square miles (sq miles)
2.59	1	0.39
5.18	2	0.77
7.77	3	1.16
10.36	4	1.54
12.95	5	1.93
15.54	6	2.32
18.13	7	2.70
20.72	8	3.09
23.31	9	3.47
25.90	10	3.86
38.85	15	5.79
51.80	20	7.72
64.75	25	9.65
259.00	100	38.61

hectares (ha)		acres
0.41	1	2.47
0.81	2	4.94
1.21	3	7.41
1.62	4	9.88
2.02	5	12.36
2.43	6	14.83
2.83	7	17.30
3.24	8	19.77
3.64	9	22.24
4.05	10	24.71
6.07	15	37.07
8.09	20	49.42
10.12	25	61.78
40.47	100	247.1

Temperature

To convert centigrade into Fahrenheit, multiply centigrade by 1.8 and add 32.

To convert Fahrenheit into centigrade, subtract 32 from Fahrenheit and divide by 1.8.

Temperature

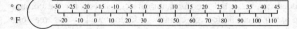

° C   -30   -25   -20   -15   -10   -5   0   5   10   15   20   25   30   35   40   45

° F   -20   -10   0   10   20   30   40   50   60   70   80   90   100   110

Fluid Measures

litres	imp gal	US gal	litres	imp gal	US gal
5	1.1	1.3	30	6.6	7.9
10	2.2	2.6	35	7.7	9.2
15	3.3	4.0	40	8.8	10.6
20	4.4	5.3	45	9.9	11.9
25	5.5	6.6	50	11.0	13.2

Tire Pressure

lb/sq in	kg/sq cm	lb/sq in	kg/sq cm
10	0.7	26	1.8
12	0.8	27	1.9
15	1.1	28	2.0
18	1.3	30	2.1
20	1.4	33	2.3
21	1.5	36	2.5
23	1.6	38	2.7
24	1.7	40	2.8

International Direct Dialling (telephone)

Most European countries and dozens of others throughout the world are now linked to the international direct dialling (IDD) system. Unless you need to go through the operator for special services, it is in most cases easier, quicker and cheaper to dial direct.

Procedure: First dial the international access code for the country you are in, then the foreign-country code, followed by the area code and the subscriber's number.

Example: if you are in Great Britain and wish to call Geneva (Switzerland) 712 34 56, dial 00+41+22+712 34 56.

International Telephone Access Codes

Austria	*	Luxembourg	00
Belgium	00	Monaco	19
Bosnia	99	Netherlands	09
Bulgaria	00	Norway	095
Croatia	99	Poland	80
Czech Republic	00	Portugal	*
Denmark	009	Romania	None†
Estonia	10	Russia	8
Finland	990	Slovakia	00
France	19	Slovenia	00
Germany	00	Spain	07
Greece	00	Sweden	009
Hungary	00	Switzerland	00
Ireland	00	Turkey	99
Italy	00	United Kingdom	00
Latvia	10	Yugoslav Federal	
Lithuania	10	Republic	99

* *Varies according to where you are and which country you are calling*

380 † *At time of writing international calls can only be made through the operator*

Principal Telephone Country Codes

Algeria	213	Liechtenstein[1]	4175
Argentina	54	Lithuania	370
Australia	61	Luxembourg	352
Austria	43	Malta	356
Belgium	32	Mexico	52
Brazil	55	Monaco[2]	33
Bulgaria	359	Morocco	212
Canada	1	Netherlands	31
Chile	56	New Zealand	64
Colombia	57	Norway	47
Croatia	38	Poland	48
Czech Republic	42	Portugal	351
Denmark	45	Romania	40
Estonia	372	Russia	7
Finland	358	Saudi Arabia	966
France	33	Singapore	65
Germany	49	Slovakia	42
Gibraltar	350	Slovenia	386
Greece	30	South Africa	27
Hong Kong	852	Spain	34
Hungary	36	Sri Lanka	94
Iceland	354	Sweden	46
India	91	Switzerland	41
Iran	98	Taiwan	886
Iraq	964	Thailand	66
Ireland	353	Tunisia	216
Israel	972	Turkey	90
Italy	39	United Kingdom	44
Japan	81	USA	1
Latvia	371	Venezuela	58
Lebanon	961	Yugoslav Federal Republic	38

1) *integrated with Swiss national telephone network*
2) *integrated with French national telephone network*

Average commercial flying times between certain Major Cities (in hours)

	Athens	Copenhagen	Frankfurt	London	Madrid	Moscow	New York	Paris	Rome
Athens	–	4	3	3¾	4	4	12	3	1
C'hagen	4	–	1	1	3	3	8	1	3
Frankfurt	3	1	–	1	2	3	9	1	1
London	3	1	1	–	2	3	7	1	2
Madrid	4	3	2	2	–	5	8	1	2
Moscow	5	3	3	3	5	–	12	4	4
New York	10	8	8	6	7	10	–	7	8
Paris	3	1	1	1	1	4	8	–	1
Rome	1	3	1	2	2	4	10	1	–

Baggage codes for principal European airports

ABZ   Aberdeen
AMS   Amsterdam
ANK   Ankara
ANR   Antwerp
ARN   Stockholm
          Arlanda
BCN   Barcelona
BEG   Belgrade
BFS   Belfast
BGO   Bergen
BHX   Birmingham
BOD   Bordeaux
BRE   Bremen
BRN   Berne

BRQ   Brno
BRS   Bristol
BRU   Brussels
BSL   Basle
BTS   Bratislava
BUD   Budapest
BUH   Bucharest
CDG   Paris Charles de
          Gaulle
CGN   Cologne
CPH   Copenhagen
CWL   Cardiff
DUB   Dublin
DUS   Düsseldorf

EDI   Edinburgh
FCO   Rome Leonardo
          da Vinci
FRA   Frankfurt
GLA   Glasgow
GOA   Genoa
GOT   Gothenburg
GVA   Geneva
HAJ   Hanover
HAM   Hamburg
HEL   Helsinki
IST   Istanbul
IZM   Izmir
KBP   Kiev

KEF	Keflavík	MLA	Valletta	SNN	Shannon
LBG	Paris Le Bourget	MMA	Malmö	SOF	Sofia
		MRS	Marseilles	STR	Stuttgart
LCY	London City	MUC	Munich	SVO	Moscow Sheremetyevo
LED	St Petersburg	MXP	Milan Malpensa		
LEJ	Leipzig	NAP	Naples	SXB	Strasbourg
LGW	London Gatwick	NCE	Nice	SXF	Berlin Schönefeld
LHR	London Heathrow	NUE	Nuremberg		
		OPO	Oporto	TIA	Tirana
LIL	Lille	ORY	Paris Orly	TLS	Toulouse
LIS	Lisbon	OSL	Oslo	TRN	Turin
LJU	Ljubljana	PMO	Palermo	TXL	Berlin Tegel
LUX	Luxembourg	PSA	Pisa/Florence	VCE	Venice
LYS	Lyons	PRG	Prague	VIE	Vienna
MAD	Madrid	RTM	Rotterdam	WAW	Warsaw
MAN	Manchester	SKG	Salonica	ZRH	Zurich

International motor vehicle codes in Europe

A	Austria	GR	Greece
AL	Albania	H	Hungary
AND	Andorra	HR	Croatia
B	Belgium	I	Italy
BG	Bulgaria	IRL	Republic of Ireland
CC	Consular Corps	IS	Iceland
CD	Diplomatic Corps	L	Luxembourg
CS	Czech Republic	M	Malta
CH	Switzerland	MC	Monaco
D	Germany	N	Norway
DK	Denmark	NL	Netherlands
E	Spain	P	Portugal
EW	Estonia	PL	Poland
F	France	RO	Romania
FIN	Finland	RUS	Russian Federation
FL	Liechtenstein	S	Sweden
GB	Great Britain	SK	Slovakia
GBZ	Gibraltar	TR	Turkey

Berlitz – pack the world in your pocket!

Africa
Algeria
Kenya
Morocco
South Africa
Tunisia

Asia, Middle East
China
Egypt
Hong Kong
India
Indonesia
Japan
Jerusalem
Malaysia
Singapore
Sri Lanka
Taiwan
Thailand

Australasia
Australia
New Zealand
Sydney

Austria, Switzerland
Austrian Tyrol
Switzerland
Vienna

Belgium, The Netherlands
Amsterdam
Brussels

British Isles
Channel Islands
Dublin
Ireland
London
Scotland

Caribbean, Latin America
Bahamas
Bermuda
Cancún and Cozumel
Caribbean
French West Indies
Jamaica
Mexico
Mexico City/Acapulco

Puerto Rico
Rio de Janeiro
Southern Caribbean
Virgin Islands

Central and Eastern Europe
Budapest
Hungary
Moscow and St Petersburg
Prague

France
Brittany
Châteaux of the Loire
Côte d'Azur
Dordogne
Euro Disney Resort
France
Normandy
Paris
Provence

Germany
Berlin
Munich
Rhine Valley

Greece, Cyprus and Turkey
Athens
Corfu
Crete
Cyprus
Greek Islands
Istanbul
Rhodes
Turkey

Italy and Malta
Florence
Italy
Malta
Milan and the Lakes
Naples
Rome
Sicily
Venice

North America
Alaska Cruise Guide
Boston

California
Canada
Disneyland and the Theme Parks of Southern California
Florida
Greater Miami
Hawaii
Los Angeles
Montreal
New Orleans
New York
San Francisco
Toronto
USA
Walt Disney World and Orlando
Washington

Portugal
Algarve
Lisbon
Madeira

Scandinavia
Copenhagen
Helsinki
Oslo and Bergen
Stockholm
Sweden

Spain
Barcelona
Canary Islands
Costa Blanca
Costa Brava
Costa del Sol
Costa Dorada and Tarragona
Ibiza and Formentera
Madrid
Mallorca and Menorca
Seville

IN PREPARATION
Bali and Lombok
Bruges and Ghent
Cuba
Edinburgh
Israel
Portugal
Spain

029/504 LUD